A CULTURE OF CORRUPTION?

A CULTURE OF CORRUPTION?

*Coping with Government
in Post-Communist Europe*

WILLIAM L. MILLER,
ÅSE B. GRØDELAND
and
TATYANA Y. KOSHECHKINA

CEU PRESS

Central European University Press

Published by

Central European University Press

Nádor utca 15.
H-1051 Budapest
Hungary

400 West 59th Street
New York, NY 10019
USA

Distributed in the United Kingdom and Western Europe by
Plymbridge Distributors Ltd., Estover Road, Plymouth PL6 7PZ
United Kingdom

ISBN 963 9116 98 X Cloth
ISBN 963 9116 99 8 PB

Library of Congress Cataloging in Publication Data
A CIP catalog record for this book is available upon request

Printed in Hungary by Akaprint

CONTENTS

LIST OF TABLES

LIST OF FIGURES

xvi

PREFACE AND ACKNOWLEDGEMENTS

THIS is a book about how ordinary citizens cope with government in four parts of post-communist Europe: Ukraine, Bulgaria, Slovakia and the Czech Republic. In particular, it is about how citizens in these countries cope as individuals in their day-to-day dealings with low-level officials and state employees. It is about what have been termed 'bureaucratic encounters' with 'street-level bureaucrats'. It focuses on how citizens and officials interact, on how they feel about those interactions, on how they interpret them, and on how they would reform them. It becomes a study of corruption only insofar as citizens' interactions with street-level officials involve corrupt behaviour. That, however, is a common experience, and an even more common perception, in post-communist Europe.

At a more systemic level, our focus is on the quality of democracy, on the gap between democratic ideals and performance. In a 'fully consolidated' or 'complete' democracy, citizens should expect not only 'free and fair' elections, but also 'fair and equitable treatment' by state officials—and without the need to use contacts, presents and bribes in order to get it. Respect for the *electorate-as-a-whole* should be balanced by respect for *electors-as-individuals*. And the democratic criteria of freedom, fairness and political equality should apply to the *outputs* of government as well as to the *inputs*.

Our research was funded by the DFID (Department for International Development) under grant R6445 to Miller and Koshechkina, and by the ESRC (Economic and Social Research Council) under grant R222474 to Miller and Grødeland, with additional funds from the University of Glasgow. Fieldwork was carried out by OPW of Prague under the direction of Ladislav Köppl, by MVK of Bratislava under the direction of Pavel Haulik, by CSD Sofia under the direction of Alexander Stoyanov, and by GfK-USM of Kyiv under the direction of Tatyana Koshechkina. Focus-group discussions were led by highly experienced professional focus-group moderators: by Alexander Fedorishin (in Ukraine), by Andrej Nonchev and Elena Lazarova (in Bulgaria), by Patrik Minar in Slovakia, and by Ladislav Köppl in the Czech Republic. Marichka Padalko in Ukraine, Mitra Myanova in Bulgaria, Zuzana Vrastiakova in Slovakia, and Klara Flemrová in the Czech Republic provided simultaneous translation as we observed the focus-group discussions. All questionnaires were translated by OPW, CSD, MVK or Gfk-USM, but we must also thank the East European ex-pats residing in Glasgow who double-checked and helped to revise these translations for us.

We received a great deal of helpful advice, comment and encouragement from colleagues at Glasgow University and elsewhere, especially those we met through NISPAcee (the Network of Institutes and Schools of Public Administration in Central and Eastern Europe). Some of their ideas we have adopted, others we have contested, and they bear no responsibility for what we have eventually written, but we are deeply grateful for their generosity. We should thank especially:

János Bertók	Bohdan Krawchenko	Jeremy Pope
Christopher Berry	Alena Ledeneva	Vadim Radaev
Joanne Caddy	Richard Masters	Susan Rose-Ackerman
Leonid Fituni	Mary McIntosh	Dina Smeltz
Juliet Gole	George Moody-Stewart	Pawel Starosta
Paul Heywood	Massimo Nardo	Ivar Tallo
Michal Illner	Paddy O'Donnell	Federico Varese
Jak Jabes	Barry O'Toole	Tony Verheijen
Weiwei Jin	Sarah Oates	Viera Wallnerová
Emilia Kandeva	Inna Pidluska	Stephen White
James Kellas		

As the project developed we presented partial and interim findings at conferences of NISPAcee, BASEES (British Association for Slavonic and East European Studies) and IPSA (International Political Science Association), and in the pages of *Public Administration and Development* (1997), *Political Studies* (1997, 2001), *Crime, Law and Social Change* (1998), *Europe-Asia Studies* (1998), the *Journal of Communist and Transition Studies* (1998), the *International Review of Administrative Sciences* (1999), *Nations and Nationalism* (2000), the *Journal of Medical Ethics* (2000) and elsewhere. However, this is the first full exposition of our theory, argument and findings.

Glasgow 2000

William L. Miller
Åse B. Grødeland
Tatyana Y. Koshechkina

CHAPTER 1

COPING WITH GOVERNMENT: DEMOCRATIC IDEALS AND STREET-LEVEL BUREAUCRATS

This is a book about how ordinary citizens in post-communist Europe cope with government. Specifically it covers four countries: Ukraine, Bulgaria, Slovakia and the Czech Republic. In particular, it is about how citizens in these countries cope as individuals in their day-to-day dealings with low-level officials and state employees—about what have been termed 'bureaucratic encounters'[1] with 'street-level bureaucrats'.[2] These low-level officials are not important people, but they can have a critically important impact on the daily lives of ordinary citizens.[3]

It is about what happens in these 'bureaucratic encounters' between citizens and officials. But it is not only about what happens. It is also about why it happens. More important still, it is about the nature and the interpretation of these encounters—primarily the interpretation put upon them by the citizens and officials involved, and by the wider community within which they live or work. And it is about support for reform, about what citizens and street-level officials in post-communist Europe think could and should be done to improve the relationship between them.

At a more systemic level, it is about the quality of democracy, about the gap between democratic ideals and performance in post-communist Europe. In a 'fully consolidated' or 'complete' democracy, citizens should expect not only 'free and fair' elections, but also fair and equitable treatment by state officials. Respect for the electorate-as-whole should be balanced by respect for electors-as-individuals. The democratic criteria of freedom, fairness and political equality should apply to the outputs of government as well as to the inputs. The opportunity to play a small role in the democratic input to law-making is a sham and a fraud if the laws are ignored by the state and its officials, whether they be heads of ministries concerned with high-level policy decisions, or street-level bureaucrats interacting with individual clients.

It would be disingenuous to pretend that we had no interest in citizens' use of contacts, presents and bribes to influence officials. But in principle this is not a study of corruption. In principle, it focuses simply on how citizens and officials interact, on how they feel about those interactions, on how they interpret them, and on how they would reform them. It becomes a study of corruption only insofar as citizens' interactions with street-level officials involve behaviour that is commonly regarded as corrupt. Corruption may then be an answer to our research question about the relationship between citizens and officials, but it is not our fundamental question.

For those whose principal concern is corruption itself, our theoretical approach has the disadvantage of ruling out much consideration of high-level corruption. But our principal concern is the relationship between state and citizen. That largely excludes high-level corruption, but at the same time it includes more than low-level corruption. Corruption is only one aspect of the relationship between citizens and officials even in post-communist Europe. Despite the fascination of corrupt behaviour and the relative tediousness of other aspects of bureaucratic encounters it is important to keep that bigger picture in mind. Building a study around 'bureaucratic encounters' has a number of advantages over the narrower perspective of 'low-level corruption'. It allows us:

- to avoid the problem of imposing our own definition of corruption from the outside, and giving too much weight to it in our analysis.

The interminable debate about definition goes on. Agnieszka Klich complains that the legal definition enshrined in the *US Foreign Corrupt Practices Act* 'fails to capture the essence of transition', and that alternative definitions 'that come from the field of political science', including classic definitions proposed by Samuel Huntington or by Joseph Nye, 'do not provide reliable criteria to apply to countries in economic transition'.[4] But there is now a debate about the debate. Michael Johnston argues critically that 'no issue is more enduring in the corruption debate, and none has so frequently pre-empted promising discussions, as that of definitions'.[5] Vito Tanzi claims that the question of definition used to absorb an unprofitably large proportion of the time at conferences, but, 'like an elephant', corruption is 'difficult to describe [but] not difficult to recognise'.[6] András Sajó suggests that the definition de-

bate is a waste of time: 'Experts will never agree on any single definition.' Worse, he goes on to argue that the definition debate can actually
be pernicious: 'The problem of contemporary corruption is that its
definition almost always reflects the moral opprobrium of outsiders.'[7]

Clearly that is a debate best avoided. Building a study around citizen
encounters with street-level bureaucrats allows us:

- to focus instead on concrete actions, such as the use of contacts,
  small presents, or large gifts to influence officials—clearly sepa-
  rating non-judgmental description from moral or other interpretations;
- then to investigate how citizens and officials themselves interpret
  the use of contacts and gifts;
- to set the use of contacts and gifts in the context of other strategies which are used by citizens to influence officials—strategies
  which are both more democratically legitimate and sometimes
  more frequently employed;
- to set the acceptance or even the extortion of gifts by officials in
  the context of other things that officials do which cause frustration and resentment amongst citizens. 'Were it not for the drum-
  beat of external criticism, corruption would not be construed as an
  acute social problem, at least not in East Central Europe', according to Sajó.[8] Our own findings, which extend beyond East Central
  Europe into the former Soviet Union and the Balkans, give some
  support to Sajó's view. They show that corruption is neither the
  most frequently annoying nor the most intensely annoying aspect
  of encounters with street-level bureaucrats in any of the countries
  that we study—though it is nonetheless a very significant source
  of annoyance in some of them;
- to set proposals for anti-corruption reforms in the context of other
  reforms designed to solve other problems in the relationship between citizens and officials. Even an incorruptible bureaucracy
  may still be inefficient, insensitive, unresponsive, arbitrary, capricious or unfair;
- above all, to retain a sense of proportion, fully recognising the
  problems caused by the use of contacts and gifts without over-
  dramatising their significance—that is to say, to take a cool and
  holistic view of the problems involved in the relationship between
  citizens and officials, and a correspondingly holistic view of proposals for reform.

THE DEMOCRATIC IDEAL: A 'COMPLETE DEMOCRACY'

Linz and Stepan structure their *Problems of Democratic Transition and Consolidation* around the concepts of a 'completed democratic transition' to a 'consolidated democracy'.[9] By a 'consolidated democracy' they mean a political situation in which democracy has become 'the only game in town', and politics is 'no longer dominated by the problem of how to avoid democratic breakdown'.[10]

Rose, Mishler and Haerpfer, on the other hand, separate the concepts of 'consolidated' and 'complete'. They argue that, by the mid-1990s, democracy in Central and Eastern Europe was 'consolidated' but not 'complete'.[11] It was *consolidated* in the sense that there was little support for any coherent alternative such as communism or fascism, military, monarchical or technocratic rule. But it was *not complete* in that it lacked the full character of a 'complete democracy', of what others might call a 'liberal democracy', the ideal if not quite the reality of modern Western democracy. In this view, West and East have a common goal, a common ideal of democracy, but Central and Eastern Europe are still further away from it than the West. A more nuanced, more quantitative and less crudely categorical approach is to focus on the 'quality of democracy' rather than on whether or not democracy has got sufficiently close to perfection to be classified as 'complete'. There may be no perfectly complete democracies anywhere in the world, but that does not exclude the possibility that some are a lot better than others.

Linz and Stepan are quick to dismiss the 'electoralist fallacy', as they call it that free elections are 'a sufficient condition' for democracy. In their view, free elections are a necessary but insufficient condition for democracy.[12] They are the core institution of a democratic system and the ultimate safeguard against an unpopular government remaining in office against the will of the people. But by themselves free elections are far too blunt an instrument to guarantee truly responsive and inclusive government with a deep concern for individual citizens.

Elections do affect the general political culture. They set the tone of democratic government and although they can sometimes lead to the tyranny of the majority, which was the great fear of the liberal critics of democracy, they tend on the whole to legitimate voters individually as well as collectively. They tend to encourage government to respect individual citizens as well as the collective decision of the whole electorate.[13] They tend to transform officials and bureaucrats from servants of the state into servants of society, even into servants of their clients. But these tendencies are no more than contingent, and it is as much these contingent correlates of free elections—freedom, respect and consideration for citizens—as the guaranteed promise that competitive elections will provide some slight influence over public policy that makes democracy so attractive. It is not simply conceptual incompetence that confuses liberalism with democracy. It is the considered conclusion that democracy without liberalism, respect for the electorate without respect for individual electors, is not just a different kind of democracy but an inferior or an 'incomplete' version.

Linz and Stepan are concerned about a range of other conditions for a complete democracy: that the elected government should not be subordinate to some continuing military junta or to a board of religious guardians; that opposition should be tolerated; that government should operate 'within the law'; that censorship should be restrained; and that civil organisations should be encouraged. But in our view even that is not sufficient. This menu is focused too much on the inputs to government and too much on collective and corporate bodies—too much, that is to say, on organised civil society rather than on individual citizens. Linz and Stepan interpret even the 'rule of law' in terms of constitutionalism rather than the honest and considerate application of the law by street-level officials in their dealings with clients.[14]

By contrast, Rose, Mishler and Haerpfer argue that 'corruption has replaced repression as the main threat to the rule of law' in postcommunist Europe.[15] But even the 'rule of law' can be as much part of the problem as part of the solution if it is not applied with consideration. Its strict application can be the instrument of petty oppression even when its content ensures that it is not the instrument of grand oppression. 'The rule of law is the third great aspiration, after markets and democracy, of post-communist states' according to Stephen Holmes. But he continues: 'What do law and legality mean for the average citizen in the region today? How do individuals encounter the law when conducting their daily affairs?' In Holmes' view 'the rule of law sometimes degenerates into the rule of petty bureaucrats'.[16]

In *The Civic Culture*, their classic study of the 'culture of democracy', Almond and Verba gave equal weight to high and low politics, to the inputs and outputs of government, to the citizen as part of a mass electorate and the citizen as individual. They drew attention to the importance of what they called 'citizen competence' and 'subject competence'.[17] In terms of perceptions, Almond and Verba measured 'citizen competence' by the percentage of the public who said they could do something about an unjust law at both the national and local level, and they measured 'subject competence' by the percentage of the public who expected serious consideration in their dealings with a government office or with the police. In Almond and Verba's view, both 'citizen competence' and 'subject competence' were required for a truly democratic culture.

In a previous study of the political culture in five post-communist countries we measured 'subject competence' using a single question derived from those set out by Almond and Verba in *The Civic Culture*. We asked:

> Suppose there were some problems you had to take to a government office—for example, a problem about tax or housing. Do you think you would be treated fairly by the officials in that office?

Almond and Verba asked their respondents whether they thought they would get 'equal treatment—I mean, would you be treated as well as anyone else', though in the text they used the words 'fair' and 'equal' interchangeably.[18] In post-communist Europe we judged it useful to avoid any potential ambiguity between 'fair' and 'equal'. Equally unfair treatment by officials who routinely refused to provide services to which citizens were legally entitled might merit the perverse description of 'equal treatment' but it would not be the kind of equal treatment that citizens should expect in a 'complete democracy'. So we replaced 'equal treatment' by 'fair treatment' in our question. In another innovation, our interviewers were instructed to note any replies that indicated respondents would expect to get fair treatment 'only by using connections or bribes', though they were also instructed never to offer that alternative if it did not emerge spontaneously.

In Russia and Ukraine two-thirds of the public replied that they did *not* expect fair treatment in their day-to-day dealings with government officials (Fig. 1.1). By contrast, in the former Czechoslovakia the corresponding figure was only one-third (and, if we take Almond and Verba's figures as comparable, less than one-sixth in Britain or the USA). Perhaps even more significantly, more than half the minority of the public who thought that they could get fair treatment in Russia or Ukraine spontaneously volunteered the opinion that they would have to use connections or bribes to get it.[19]

Expectations of fair treatment in post-communist Europe correlated quite strongly with trust in 'the government' ($r = 0.24$) and only slightly less with trust in 'the police' ($r = 0.21$). But they did not reflect a general lack of trust: they correlated hardly at all with trust in 'most ordinary people that you meet in everyday life' (r = 0.07). Interestingly, the classic American study *Bureaucratic Encounters* found that clients' ratings of their actual experience of interactions with officials (which did not include bribery or extortion but nonetheless varied in other respects that were important to the clients) correlated fairly strongly with their general evaluations of the government (r = 0.25) and the bureaucracy (r = 0.29) but hardly at all with interpersonal trust (r = 0.09).[20]

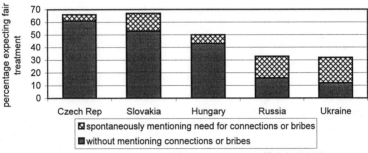

Fig. 1.1. Low expectations of fair treatment by officials (1993)

There is clearly a close connection between expectations of bureaucratic encounters and trust in government within post-communist Europe. But it is overlaid by cross-national differences. Those who 'completely distrusted' their Czech or Slovak governments expected fairer treatment from officials than those who 'completely trusted' their governments in Russia or Ukraine. Similarly, those who described themselves as 'opponents' of the government in Slovakia or the Czech Republic were much more likely to expect fair treatment from officials than those who described themselves as 'supporters' of the government in Russia or Ukraine. Expectations of fair treatment by officials therefore reflected something more than general political satisfaction or dissatisfaction. These sharp cross-national differences seemed to indicate that citizens' expectations of fair treatment were grounded in real differences of treatment by different bureaucracies rather than merely in different levels of general political trust in governments. At the same time the correlation with trust in government *within* countries perhaps indicates that actual or expected ill-treatment by street-level bureaucrats erodes trust in government generally.

To investigate this interaction between street-level officials and citizens across post-communist Europe in more depth we chose the two countries in our post-communist values survey that had differed most in terms of public expectations of fair treatment: Ukraine and the Czech Republic. We added Slovakia and Bulgaria, which were historically and culturally close to the Czech Republic and Ukraine respectively, without being quite the same in either case. Geographically, Bulgaria is a long way from the Czech Republic and separated from Ukraine only by a hundred-mile strip of Romanian coast, but much of its trade and its ambitions for the future are oriented towards Central and Western Europe. Slovakia stretches from the borders of the Czech Republic to the borders of Ukraine. Indeed, post-1944 Ukraine includes some former Slovak territory. But Slovakia's capital city is on its far western border, close to Austria and the Czech Republic. So Bratislava looks towards Vienna and Prague, not towards Kyiv.

In fact, our findings do suggest that Slovakia and Bulgaria may be regarded as 'intermediate cases' between the extremes of the Czech Republic and Ukraine. But there is no fixed spectrum. In many respects our findings put Slovakia rather than Bulgaria closer to the Czech Republic. But in some important respects it is Bulgaria, not Slovakia that comes closer to the Czech Republic. This ambiguity within our own study reflects the findings of a variety of other, more limited, studies, some of which put Slovakia closer to the Czech Republic while others put Bulgaria closer. It serves as a warning against over-simplistic attempts to locate countries on a single spectrum of 'Eastern versus Western' or 'Catholic versus Orthodox' culture and civilisation.[21]

SHOULD PUBLIC-SECTOR CORRUPTION BE CONDEMNED?

Those whom András Sajó calls 'moral crusaders and lawyers with do-gooder inclinations'[22] may simply condemn the use of contacts, presents and bribes as intrinsically immoral or illegal—a 'sin' or a 'crime'. Legal scholar Agnieszka Klich asserts that arguments about 'the positive or negative aspects' of corruption in relation to the economy, social peace, or even 'the public interest' are 'immaterial' because they 'fail to recognise that corruption is widely perceived as immoral'.[23] John T. Noonan, a distinguished moralist who also happens to be a judge in the US Court of Appeals, goes further and asserts that bribery is not merely 'widely' but 'universally shameful'.[24] Of course, others have argued that the shame is less than universal and that 'corruption is an accepted practice among developing countries',[25] but Klich and Noonan would simply disagree.

Legalists, who are not always professional lawyers, might seek to define corruption in legal terms, and then condemn the use of contacts, presents and bribes as illegal.[26] Anyone familiar with the English 'common law' tradition (as contrasted with the continental 'statute law' tradition) would immediately note the circularity of basing law upon customary morality and then basing moralistic condemnation upon the law. But legalists might reasonably take an amoral position, and focus on illegality as central to their concerns irrespective of whether the law was moral or not. They might also dismiss empirically based claims that the law is often 'a poor guide to what the public finds right or wrong'[27] as irrelevant.

But economists and political scientists are neither such strict moralists nor such strict legalists. Economists give priority to economic efficiency and political scientists to legitimate and effective government— to 'economies that work' and 'governments that work'. Provided corruption has a positive effect on economic efficiency and political stability, economists and political scientists may not rush to condemn it. Samuel Huntington, along with others such as Nathaniel Leff, once argued that by improving both the economic efficiency and the human rights record of a repressive and inflexible dictatorship, public-sector corruption could help to maintain an autocratic regime: 'corruption may thus be functional to the maintenance of a political system in the same way that reform is...and both corruption and reform may be substitutes for revolution'.[28] In Eastern Europe corruption may have helped to lubricate the creaky old machinery of communism. Many observers of the Soviet Union took the view, expressed by Robert Service, that 'the system was found unworkable unless fraud and deception were allowed on a vast scale'.[29] Tony Verheijen and Antoaneta Dimitrova claim that 'some forms of corruption in the communist past even helped to humanise relations between street-level bureaucrats and their clientele'.[30] In a similar vein, Richard Paddock argues that 'bribery is an indispensable part of Russian life. It softens the edges of an authoritarian society and enables citizens to circumvent a ponderous state bureaucracy'[31]— though the sad irony is that the 'authoritarian society' to which Paddock refers in that quotation is not the communist Soviet Union but post-communist Russia.

But even if Huntington and Service were right about corruption ameliorating and sustaining an autocratic regime, to argue that the inflexibility and brutality of an autocratic regime may be softened by corruption is like arguing that paying tribute to a conquering army is preferable to being enslaved by it. At best it is the lesser of two evils. Corruption is 'at most a second-best response to a government failure'.[32] The argument in favour of corruption simply should not apply to free-market democracies that are neither economically inflexible nor administratively brutal.

Carolyn Hotchkiss now claims that 'the new conceptualisation of the corruption battle frames the issue in economic rather than moral terms' which 'enables a less judgmental approach to some of the fundamental causes of corruption' and has 'allowed new strategies [for combating corruption] to emerge'.[33] But what is new about this conceptualisation is not the moral neutrality of an economic or political science perspective, as she claims. That has been around for long enough: 'In the 1960s it was fashionable to follow Samuel Huntington and Nathaniel Leff's view that in the early stages of a country's modernisation, corruption is economically efficient...[and] furthermore, in developing democracies, corruption is democratic [because] it offers opportunities to those who would otherwise be excluded.'[34] What is new is the revisionist judgement that after all, corruption is neither good for economic growth nor for political stability—new empirical findings, not a new moral neutrality.

Rose-Ackerman claims that 'cross-country empirical work has confirmed the negative impact of corruption on growth and productivity' and that 'even when corruption and economic growth coexist, payoffs introduce costs and distortions'.[35] Schleifer and Vishny argue that the distortion is worse than the cost as such, and that corruption therefore damages economic development 'more than its sister activity, taxation'.[36] Corruption is not only a tax but 'an arbitrary tax'.[37] Leslie Holmes even disputes the old argument that corruption sustained authoritarian communism. He claims that corruption has proved 'more destructive in communist countries than elsewhere' and that liberal democracies are more able to survive bouts of official corruption 'because of their higher level of legitimacy'.[38] The legitimacy of liberal democratic regimes depends less exclusively on performance and more on procedural values.

Even so, there is some evidence that corruption may also destabilise democratic regimes. Public-sector corruption degrades rather than enhances both the economic efficiency[39] and the civil rights record of a free-market democracy. It increases public disaffection and it contributes to instability. Almond and Verba's view is that unless the 'output performance' (by which they meant fair treatment of citizens rather than economic performance) of a democratic regime 'can match the aspirations of its citizens' it is 'living off its capital of system affect'.[40] Linz's work *The Breakdown of Democratic Regimes* quotes West European evidence of 'a significant correlation between the image of politicians as dishonest and the readiness to turn to violent means' to overthrow them.[41] Economists Schleifer and Vishny argue that corruption not only distorts the economy but weakens central government.[42] Paolo Mauro, in a celebrated and influential article, finds strongly negative correlations not only between corruption and economic growth,[43] but also between corruption and political stability.[44] At best 'the economic advantages of corruption are only in the short run, while its destabilising effects on the political regime are undeniable'.[45]

Pervasive public-sector corruption in a democratic regime can lead to demands for a 'strong hand' to solve the problem: 'Better an honest dictatorship than a corrupt democracy', as one Venezuelan commander-in-chief declared.[46] That view is not restricted to military commanders, nor to Latin America. In our previous study of political culture in post-communist Europe we found relatively little public support for the proposition that 'it would be acceptable for the government to suspend the usual rights of citizens and take emergency powers' in order to deal with a 'campaign of slander against the government' or an 'obstructive parliament': around 40 per cent in the former Soviet Union and 28 per cent in East Central Europe agreed with the use of emergency powers to deal with such problems. But twice as many (around 80 per cent in the former Soviet Union and 62 per cent in East Central Europe) would accept the use of emergency powers to deal with 'widespread public disorder', or 'widespread corruption and mafia crime'.[47] Across nine countries in post-communist Europe, Rose, Mishler and Haerpfer found a negative cross-national correlation of 0.23 between the *Central European Economic Review*'s index of corruption[48] and their own survey findings on support for the new post-communist regime and rejection of various 'undemocratic alternatives'. Indeed, their multiple regression analysis suggests that the level of corruption is a more important determinant of attitudes towards these 'undemocratic alternatives' than the country's democratic tradition, its current level of freedom or its current economic performance.[49]

Economists and political scientists tend to view the connection between democracy and corruption in very different ways. When they consider the relationship between corruption and democracy, economists ask whether democracy encourages or discourages corruption and thereby affects economic performance.[50] When political scientists consider the relationship between corruption and democracy, they put the question the other way round: they ask whether corruption degrades the quality of political democracy and thereby affects political legitimacy. Political stability is not the only concern of political scientists. The quality of democratic governance is also important. Thus public administration specialists with a moral bent might agree with Noonan that: 'Bribery is a betrayal of trust...the notion of fidelity in office, as old as Cicero, is inextricably bound to the concept of public interest distinct from private advantage. It is beyond debate that officials of the government are relied upon to act for the public interest not their own enrichment. When they take bribes they divide their loyalty' and become traitors to the people.[51] The OECD has recently adopted a set of 12 principles to promote 'ethical conduct in the public service', on the grounds that it would contribute to 'the *quality of democratic governance* and economic and social progress' as well as addressing 'increased public concern with confidence in government' which has implications for political stability.[52]

DOES STREET-LEVEL CORRUPTION MATTER?

Our focus in this book is on the interaction between ordinary citizens and street-level officials. That excludes high-level corruption from our inquiry, except insofar is it impinges upon the imagination of ordinary citizens. But low-level corruption is not divorced from high-level corruption. A corrupt example at the top is likely to encourage corruption at the bottom. Conversely, it is unlikely that a junior official trained by experience in bribery and extortion will suddenly give it all up when he or she gets promoted. Wider horizons simply present new opportunities. So-called zero-tolerance policing is now fashionable in Britain and America.[53] It is based upon the assumption that a permissive attitude to low-level crime not only degrades the living environment and lifestyle of ordinary citizens but also encourages street-level criminals to graduate to higher-level crime. The analogy with public-sector corruption is close.

At a systemic level, pervasive low-level corruption itself becomes a high-level problem. General Yuri Kravchenko, Ukrainian minister of the interior was reported as feeling 'proud of the militia' and 'surprised to learn' that 'the militia, especially the traffic police, is the most corrupt in Ukraine'.[54] But other reports suggest that the growing 'appetites of customs officers, road police and other inspectors'—typical 'street-level bureaucrats'—doubled the cost of transporting a container from Odessa to Moscow. Such 'bureaucratic extortion' cost Ukrainian ports at least 20 million US dollars as cargoes were diverted to avoid transhipment across Ukraine.[55] Similarly, in Bulgaria, under the newspaper headline 'Parents are Prone to Corrupt Practices during the Campaign for Admission to Universities', the deputy minister of education Anna-Maria Totomanova recently complained that bribes lead to a significant distortion in university intakes. Worse, they lead students who get entry by bribes to 'believe that they will only be able to go ahead by making further payments'.[56] Ultimately this devalues the qualifications awarded by Bulgarian universities. Low-level corruption adds up.

From a democratic perspective, however, low-level corruption is principally important for its own sake, not because of its high-level consequences. It distorts and corrupts the relationship between citizens and the state, and between one citizen and another. Democracy is founded on the principle of political equality, and public-sector corruption is founded on the principle that the state will treat its citizens arbitrarily and unequally. In a free-market democracy, political equality operates to offset the accepted inequalities of wealth and power.[57] But public-sector corruption reinforces those very same inequalities. One participant in the focus-group discussion we held in Sofia put it very well: 'Corruption causes a distinction; in reality there should exist no difference, every citizen is equal before any administrative official and should be treated equally, that is what equality should mean.'(So-A 6)

Inequalities of wealth provide the means to pay bribes, while inequalities of power provide the means to extort them. Far from softening the hard edges of society, 'a state with endemic corruption can be especially brutal to the very poor who have no resources to compete with those willing to pay bribes'.[58] 'Bribery is a sell-out to the rich.'[59] That is why Michael Johnston asserts that 'serious corruption makes political systems less democratic'.[60] That is why Almond and Verba defined a well-functioning democracy not only in terms of citizen influence over high policy, but also in terms of fair and equal treatment by junior state officials.

On one thing moral crusaders, economists and political scientists can agree: 'The level of bribes is not the critical variable', it is 'what was purchased by the payoff'.[61] According to Noonan, one of the most frequent arguments against the condemnation of bribery is that its 'material effect' is 'either trivial or undemonstrated'—a small gift to a street-level bureaucrat or a small percentage 'commission' to a more senior official is trivial, whether it is legal or illegal, moral or immoral.[62] But to Noonan it is a 'betrayal of ideals' and those who dismiss it as quantitatively trivial 'ignore the massive popular discontent that can be ignited by corruption'.[63] In politics, as in economics, the inequities and distortions are often out of all proportion to the scale of the bribes that are paid. At elite levels in post-communist Europe, 'bribery and extortion are rampant because the price of bureaucrats is still extraordinarily low' according to Agnieszka Klich.[64] But irrespective of the price, at high levels and low, time and resources are wasted on negotiating the bribery; officials have an incentive to create unnecessary problems for their clients in order to create or maintain the conditions for bribery; state contracts for unnecessary projects are awarded to inefficient and uncompetitive companies; and state benefits and services go to citizens who are not most entitled to them. The state is cheated out of revenue by those who bribe tax and customs officials or traffic police.[65] So it has to impose greater (and eventually unbearable) tax burdens on those that cannot or will not avoid payment by bribing officials. Or it must watch helplessly as public services collapse through lack of funds. Either way the state loses public respect and political legitimacy.

To democratic theorists, low-level corruption is important because, in itself, it constitutes unfair treatment of citizens and because it also encourages officials to be unfair in other ways in order to sustain the conditions in which corruption can flourish—often manufacturing artificial and unnecessary problems for their clients in order to reap a reward for solving them.

From the perspective of the bribe giver it may be important to distinguish between bribes given to obtain favours and bribes given to obtain something which the bribe giver is legally entitled to get for free. The bribe giver is likely to feel more aggrieved if they have to give bribes to get their legal rights, and less aggrieved if they pay to get a favour—though the distinction is often less clear in practice than in principle,[66] and bribe givers are often unsure about whether they are purchasing a favour or not. But from the perspective of the economist or the political scientist both kinds of corruption produce inequities and distortions. A favour to a bribe giver may satisfy the bribe giver but it necessarily means unfair and unequal treatment for those who do not give bribes. The economist laments the economic inefficiency—the 'economic distortions and high costs of public projects'.[67] The political scientist or democratic theorist laments the inequity, the unfairness, and the consequent alienation from—and delegitimation of—the political regime.

But it matters whether citizens themselves are sensitive to these inequities. If all citizens felt they were fairly treated by state officials then democratic theorists would be a lot less concerned about whether officials took bribes from their clients. If citizens were as happy to tip an official with ten per cent of the bill as they are to tip a waiter in a restaurant by the same amount then democratic theorists would also be a lot less concerned about whether officials took bribes from their clients. Conversely, even if officials never took bribes from their clients, democratic theorists would remain concerned about whether citizens were treated fairly or unfairly. Fairness and equity are fundamental, corruption is merely one mechanism of inequity and unfairness. That is why we have paid so much attention in our focus-group discussions and interview surveys to the way citizens feel about their interactions with officials—whether they feel officials treat them fairly, whether they feel officials treat them with respect 'as equals', whether they offer officials gifts 'out of gratitude', or whether they do so with fear and resentment.

The views of those who participate in low-level corruption have important implications for the possibility of reform. We might distinguish two contrasting ideal-type models of low-level corruption:

- the '*culture of corruption*' model—a culture of mutual favours in which citizens are happy to give bribes and officials are happy to accept them. Both sides justify the practice, perhaps even morally justify it, and neither feels that they are acting under duress;
- the '*victims of circumstances*' model—or what might be called a '*corruption despite culture*' model—in which neither citizens nor officials justify the practice, in which neither feels happy, in which both feel ashamed, but in which neither feels able to avoid the practice.

It is not only citizens who can feel themselves to be 'victims of circumstances'. Citizens may feel that they are the victims of extortion by officials. But officials may feel that they are the victims of governments that fail to pay them, or victims of clients who tempt them beyond their powers of resistance. They may even feel they are the victims of clients who threaten violence or other retribution (perhaps exposure of previous bribe taking) if they do not submit, accept the 'gift', and provide the requested favour. One senior tax officer in Ukraine complained to the press about the pressures on tax officials: 'Where bribery does not work threats and often violence are used.'[68] In our own research we came across anecdotal evidence of university staff (not in Ukraine) who had been in one case ostracised by their colleagues, and in another savagely beaten up, for refusing to join the system of taking bribes to award unearned grades.

Commenting on the communist regime's statement that 'the people had forfeited the government's confidence' by taking part in the 17 June 1953 Berlin uprising, Bertolt Brecht famously suggested: 'Wouldn't it be simpler in that case if the government dissolved the people and elected another?'[69] Given that the people were not convinced communists, the only long-term option for the survival of the system was to 'reform the people'—not impossible perhaps but very difficult and ultimately unsuccessful. In a similar way, if corruption is based upon a 'culture of corruption' and has the full support of the people then it can only be changed significantly by 'reforming the people'.

But there is no reason to believe, without investigation, that even the most pervasive corruption reflects a genuine 'culture of corruption'. If pervasive corruption is not based on a 'culture of corruption', if the participants are merely 'victims of circumstance', then it is sufficient to reform the institutions and the environment. There is no need to reform the people. Reform 'goes with the grain' of public opinion. The people need only to be liberated from the oppression of corruption rather than reformed. Reforming institutions and procedures may be difficult, but not nearly so difficult as reforming the people.

Of course, the two models of a 'culture of corruption' and 'victims of circumstances' are ideal-types. The real world no doubt consists of a bit of both. Or a structured mix of the two—such as a 'culture of corruption' model for the behaviour of officials and a 'victims of circumstances' model for the behaviour of citizens. Or, more generally, a 'culture of corruption' model for 'them' and a 'victims of circumstances' model for 'us'. But the distinction between the two ideal models is important nonetheless. That is why we paid so much attention in our focus-group discussions and interviews to feelings about the use of contacts, presents and bribes, and to what are called 'values and norms', the condemnations, justifications and interpretations placed on these activities by both citizens and officials. It is also why we paid so much attention to personal experience of extortion by officials and to officials' reports about the frequency of tempting offers from their clients—both of which may affect behaviour despite contrary values and norms.

DO HISTORY AND CULTURE EXCLUDE
THE POSSIBILITY OF REFORM?

Our four countries—Ukraine, Bulgaria, Slovakia and the Czech Republic—all shared the experience of at least half a century of communist rule. All were ruled by autocratic empires until late in the nineteenth century. There were of course historic differences as well as similarities. Ukraine had a longer experience of communist rule and suffered more from its excesses. The Czechs and Slovaks had a longer and more successful experience of democracy between the wars than the Bulgarians, though only the Czechs (and not the Slovaks) now look back on the inter-war Masaryk period with affection.[70] The pre-communist autocracies of the Romanovs, Habsburgs and Ottomans differed somewhat in character, though all three regarded the Ukrainians, Bulgarians, Czechs and Slovaks as, to a greater or lesser extent, 'subject peoples'. Despite all the differences, all four countries have a history of governance that has been more autocratic, alien and corrupt than democratic, legitimate, accountable and honest.

Communist regimes were traditionally depicted as bureaucratic, in Laski's sense of that word rather than Weber's: 'A system of government…so completely in the hands of officials that their power jeopardises the liberties of ordinary citizens.'[71] Citizens could expect neither serious consideration nor fair treatment without some means of 'interesting' the official in their case. Dependence upon the use of bribes and contacts was notorious. Like its tsarist predecessor, parodied so well by Gogol in *The Government Inspector*, the Soviet regime even at its best could reasonably be described as an autocracy increasingly tempered by corruption.

Towards the end of the communist regime, a majority of respondents in DiFranceisco and Gitelman's survey of Soviet émigrés suggested that bribery or connections could be used to change an unwelcome work assignment or to get a dull child into a good university department.[72] Surveys of those still living in the USSR tended to corroborate these findings. Sogomonov and Tolstykh's surveys put 'the widespread use of pull' in third place on the list of the 'most pressing problems facing our country today'. It rose to first place when combined with 'dependence on officials in solving housing questions'—which probably reflected the use of bribes or influence to get better state flats.[73]

But the key question for our study is not whether previous regimes were corrupt. Rather, it is whether this history determines the nature of relationships between citizens and officials in post-communist Europe. There are several models of historical influence:

- the '*dead hand of history*' model—a deterministic model ensuring the continuity of traditional ways of thinking;
- the '*irrelevance of history*' model—the opposite of the 'dead hand' model, this model suggests that current behaviour patterns reflect only current conditions;
- the '*fading legacy*' model—a half-way house between the 'dead hand' and 'irrelevance' models, this model suggests evolutionary change as new experiences overlay historical experience and gradually change thinking and behaviour, allowing the possibility that old ways will be subject to progressive reform. It would be inconsistent to suggest that the conditions of the past could mould minds and behaviour while denying that the conditions of the present may do so too;
- the '*escape from domination*' model—unlike the 'fading legacy' model, this model predicts an immediate and dramatic change in behaviour, though not in thinking, as people suddenly escape from the constraints of a historic domination. (We use the Bulgarian term 'domination', but it applies to life under any authoritarian regime.) Later change may not be progressive, and may often reverse or attenuate the initial change. Reform is possible, but it must address the problems of the present, often problems created by the excesses of the 'escape', rather than the legacy of the past.

These models have very different implications for the possibility of reform. If history determines culture and culture determines contemporary relationships, as the 'dead hand' model suggests, then there is no escape from the past and no realistic possibility of reform in the foreseeable future. But if that 'dead hand' model really applied necessarily rather than contingently, it would be difficult to explain why Sweden is now so free of corruption when 'corruption flourished' there 'in the second half of the 18th century and early 19th century'.[74] It would also be difficult to explain similar trends since the eighteenth century in Britain. No doubt Peter the Great's Russia was corrupt, but since his time lots of other countries have been through the mire of corruption and come out the other side. In more recent years Singapore, Hong Kong and Portugal have all 'reduced the incidence of corruption significantly'.[75]

Conversely, under the 'irrelevance of history' model, history is only an interesting and entertaining narrative with no implications for the present. Current behaviour reflects current conditions and will quickly change as those conditions change. Reform is possible and changes in economic and institutional conditions will have immediate effects on behaviour. Human behaviour is always affected by circumstance as well as by personal factors. But objective circumstances have a particularly powerful impact on behaviour even when they do not affect culture and motivations to the same extent. People do 'what they have to do' in the circumstances in which they find themselves, without necessarily internalising the moral implications of their behaviour patterns. The same person pays bribes routinely in one country but not in another. The same person is honest within the circle of family and friends, but totally dishonest in their dealings with authority, especially authority that they regard as illegitimate. The same person becomes honest or dishonest as conditions dictate. Kevin Rafferty quotes an international lawyer based in Hong Kong as the date of the communist take-over approached: 'People who have been perfectly honest for years are seizing opportunities for making fast bucks to buy their way into Australia or Canada.' Abuses got so serious, so rapidly, that some Hong Kong companies were taking out 'fidelity insurance' to guard against being cheated by their workers desperate 'to make enough money to emigrate'.[76] Similarly, when Robert Service describes the Soviet system as 'unworkable' without corruption, or when Paddock describes corruption as 'an indispensable part of Russian life', the implicit model is one in which behaviour is determined by current conditions, not by history and tradition.

The 'fading legacy' model argues that people enter the present with all the baggage of their past. They may adjust to current conditions, but that takes time. Reforms have a gradual effect. It will take time for the old corrupt ways of communism to be replaced by those of free-market democracy, but change and reform are possible, even natural. Old ways and old thinking may linger on but if the conditions that created and sustained them no longer exist, then they will fade. Bohdan Krawchenko claims that communist and pre-communist autocracies may have left a situation in which 'citizens, be they private individuals or businesses, are considered dependants pleading for benefits rather than consumers of services paid for by the taxpayer'.[77] The anonymous director of an NGO in post-communist Europe finds it necessary to assert that 'a civil society is one where citizens have rights and not just obligations'[78]— neatly inverting the rhetoric of contemporary advocates of 'the middle way' in Western Europe, such as Antony Giddens, who offer 'a prime motto for the new politics: No rights without responsibilities'.[79] Clearly Eastern and Western Europe are coming from a different past, but that does nor exclude the possibility of a common future.

But insofar as communism had a restraining rather than a motivating influence, insofar as it held citizens back against their will, then we might expect to find evidence of an 'inverse legacy' of communism— not the product of continuing communist domination of 'hearts and minds', not even the product of a 'fading legacy' of communism, so much as the product of a sudden end to communist restraint on behaviour.

The 'dead hand of history' model clearly does not work in terms of political values, nor in terms of the free choices that voters are able to make in post-communist elections. Indeed, their first electoral choice was decisively to reject the past—more in line with the 'escape from domination' model than any other. There is increasing evidence that history does not constrain political values. Pippa Norris sums up the conclusions of a distinguished team who analysed the 1995–97 *World Values Survey* thus: 'By the mid-1990s most citizens world-wide shared widespread aspirations to the ideals and principles of democratic government', although they evaluated 'the practice of democracy' very differently in different countries.[80] More specifically, in our own previous study over half of the public in Ukraine said they had once believed in communist values, but only one-sixth still did so in the early 1990s, while a large majority in East Central Europe said they had never believed in communist ideals.[81]

It is especially unlikely that history can exercise a determining influence over political values or behaviour when history does not represent a political or cultural tradition. It is important to distinguish between a voluntary tradition and an imposed domination of the kind that constituted so much of the history of our four countries. The first may be carried forward by the people, and with some enthusiasm. The second is nothing but a set of chains to be cast off at the first opportunity. Communism was seen as an alien domination in central Europe, like Ottoman rule in Bulgaria, like Habsburg rule in the Czech Republic, and like both Habsburg and (to a lesser extent) Czech rule in Slovakia. Once the people escaped from the physical constraints of communism they voted to reject it, and they voted to reject it most decisively as soon as the domination ended. It was later that they developed more nostalgia for it.

Might the same be expected of citizens' relationship to street-level officials? If the legacy of history so clearly failed to determine political values and political behaviour with respect to the input side of governance (elections), why should it have any more influence over the output side (bureaucratic encounters)? If the 'dead hand of history' model applied, we should expect no change in the relationship between citizens and officials, for good or ill. If the 'fading legacy' model applied, we should expect to see a gradual transition from the historic pattern of relationships that reflected autocracy to a new one, more reflective of the new democratic system. If the 'escape from domination' model applied we should expect to see a sharp rise in the assertiveness of citizens, a greater willingness to hold officials to account, and less willingness to accept unfair treatment.

Perversely, of course, in the peculiarly chaotic conditions of transition, citizens might feel less constrained in their use of corrupt as well as legitimate methods of influencing officials. Freedom might be interpreted as lack of any constraint, internal or external, and in the same chaotic conditions street-level officials might feel less constrained in their behaviour also. If so, then the 'escape from domination' model would imply an explosion in corrupt practices that was not due to the dead hand of history but to its opposite, the removal of constraint. As Umit Berkman notes, 'there seems to exist a relationship between the rate of change of a social system and corruption...norms become blurred, tolerance limits for deviance widen'.[82]

It is easy to interpret corruption in post-communist Europe as simply an extension of the corruption that existed under communism. Nonetheless, there is a critically important difference between rampant corruption that results from a long-term and immutable historical-cultural tradition and rampant corruption that results from the chaos of transition. The first is a 'climate of corruption' which, almost by definition, excludes the possibility of reform in the foreseeable future. The second is a mere 'season of corruption' which, at best, may come to a natural end as the transition is completed, and at worst does not exclude the possibility of reform. Paradoxically, if there has been an explosion of corruption in post-communist Europe then that is itself proof that the corruption is not culturally and historically predetermined, and it is a sign that reform is at least possible, though it is by no means certain. In the perspective of the 'escape from domination' model, the problems of post-communist Europe in the 1990s are not centuries old, despite the fact that similar problems existed in the past.

Because these four models have such different implications for the possibility of reform, we pay attention to the impact of current conditions, the communist legacy, and longer-run culture on the interactions between citizens and officials. That is why we look for evidence of significant generational effects. It is also why we distinguish between will and circumstance, that is to say between personal motivation and submission to circumstance. The aim is to decide whether, in terms of their relationships with officials, the citizens of post-communist Europe are likely to be lifelong prisoners of their communist past; whether they are making progress towards a better future; or whether they are prisoners of a post-communist present, but with perhaps some hope of eventual release.

WHY SURVEYS?

There are a number of disadvantages to studying bureaucratic encounters and/or corruption, as we do, by survey research methods. Juliet Gole provides a particularly comprehensive and convincing list of the disadvantages.[83] Some, though not all, of the disadvantages attributed to survey research methods can be overcome. Gole argues that 'corruption surveys may skew the results merely by asking the questions—if a person hardly thinks about corruption on a daily basis but is suddenly presented with dozens of questions on this topic' their answers may overstate the importance of corruption in their lives, or even in their dealings with officials. We have not been able to avoid asking 'dozens of questions on this topic', but by wording them carefully and embedding them in a wider discussion about other aspects of bureaucratic encounters we have tried to assess the true importance of corruption relative to other bureaucratic problems. As we have already noted, our findings suggest that although corruption amongst street-level officials is a problem in some (but not all) of our four countries, it is never the most frequent nor the most annoying problem in bureaucratic encounters in any of our four countries.

Gole also argues that survey methods are not the best way to study high-level corruption or what is termed 'grand corruption' at ministerial level—though it may be the best way to study public perceptions of 'grand corruption' and public reactions to it. That criticism seems unanswerable. Our methodological approach (survey research and associated methods) does indeed rule out a study of grand corruption. But then our theoretical approach (focused on the democratic right of citizens to fair treatment in their day-to-day encounters with street-level officials) also rules out a study of grand corruption. So our methodological approach imposes no additional restriction on our own study beyond that already imposed by our theoretical approach, though we would certainly recommend a very different and more investigative approach for a study of 'grand corruption'.

But in any case, there are advantages and disadvantages with most methodologies and a survey research approach can solve some of the problems that other methods cannot. A variety of other methods have been used to study bureaucratic encounters and/or corruption under communist and post-communist regimes, including:

- an author's personal impressions and anecdotes—some personal, some drawn non-systematically from press stories;
- direct observation—using ethnographic or investigative reporting techniques;
- systematic analysis of press cuttings;
- official statistics;
- cross-national correlations or similar statistical analyses of country-level statistics.

Of these, an author's use of personal impressions and anecdotes is the least systematic. It can be highly entertaining and it can convey a strong sense of insight, especially if the author has lived for many years under the regime in question.[84] But it is still the very personal view of a single individual and it lacks any real sense of quantity, extent or variance. For that reason we have made almost no use of personal anecdotes although we have our own treasured store. Almost by definition, authors are not typical individuals and there is no reason to believe that their experience is typical. Even if the author is typical, we get no sense of whether most citizens are typical or whether there are great variations in experience within the same society. Greater reliance on the press makes the approach less personal but still not systematic.[85] Ethnographic and investigative studies are more outward looking, but they are still very personal accounts and often very local. They suffer from much the same restricted vision as anecdotal accounts, though not to quite the same degree.

Systematic analysis of press cuttings may be used in an attempt to broaden the vision, to depersonalise and quantify the findings.[86] We have used several electronic sources of press reports, including the UCIPR's (Ukrainian Center for Independent Political Research, Kyiv) monthly *Corruption Watch* which trawls the Ukrainian press for corruption stories, and CSD/Coalition 2000's *Weekly Review of Bulgarian Press Coverage of Corruption*, supplemented by RFE/RL's *Newsline* for more general coverage of events in the region. But we have used these sources mainly for illustrative purposes. Even if the press is sampled systematically, its content is determined by the restrictions and enthusiasms of editors and censors or by the post-communist 'oligarchs' who now control much of the media. So a rash of press stories about corruption may reflect an official anti-corruption 'campaign' rather than a surge in corruption, while a dearth of press coverage may simply reflect an official cover-up.

Official statistics suffer even more directly from the fact that they are controlled by the authorities. Even some Western economic statistics appear to have been manipulated for political ends.[87] In addition, crime statistics are notoriously unreliable. Victims under-report crime because they have little confidence in the police, and the police under-record reported crime to make their record look better. Official corruption statistics are even less reliable than other crime statistics because, as Richard Lotspeich notes, 'no party to the transaction has much incentive to report it'[88] and, he might have added, the police are often involved in it themselves.

Moreover, there is a general problem of content that afflicts all studies based on anecdotal, media, or official data about bureaucratic encounters. Published anecdotes and published statistics inevitably focus on dissatisfaction rather than satisfaction, and on illegal rather than legal methods of obtaining satisfaction. Anecdotes about bribing an official are more entertaining, and therefore more likely to be published, than anecdotes about arguing with an official or behaving in an ingratiating manner towards an official. Bias is therefore built in to studies based on these types of data.

There are also particular problems when country-level data is used in a cross-national statistical analysis. The most important of these is what statisticians call the 'ecological effect' or the 'ecological fallacy'.[89] Briefly stated, the 'ecological fallacy theorem' proves that a correlation between two variables at one level need not exist at another level, or may even have a different sign at another level. Thus, for example, a cross-national correlation between (country-level indices of) low-paid officials and corruption does *not* prove that, within countries, low pay encourages officials to take bribes. Paradoxically, it is often the highest-paid officials in the poorest countries who are the most corrupt.

In principle this 'ecological effect' can take many forms but it usually manifests itself as a 'super-additivity effect' which leads to greater differences between areas than might be predicted from the composition of their populations. In electoral studies this super-additivity effect is familiar and powerful: the party-political polarisation between richer and poorer areas can be twice as great as their class composition would predict because people tend to adopt some of the attitudes and behaviours of the social milieu in which they live.[90] From our analysis it seems that this super-additivity effect is also operating cross-nationally with respect to bureaucratic encounters in post-communist Europe. Unfairly treated clients are more likely to live in Ukraine than in the Czech Republic. Unfair treatment tends to affect attitudes towards reform, but all clients in Ukraine tend to adopt the attitudes of an unfairly treated client even if their own treatment was not so bad. Conversely, all clients in the Czech Republic tend to adopt the attitudes of a fairly treated client even if their own treatment was unfair. When treatment seems 'exceptional' within a particular context it can arouse strong personal feelings, but these may not translate completely into more general attitudes towards the bureaucracy. Such tendencies can never be discovered and investigated simply by correlating country-level data. Individual-level survey data is essential.

A second problem is that cross-national statistical studies of corruption are often hybrid in nature, correlating official statistics on the economy or bureaucratic structure with survey-based indices of corruption perceptions—such as those published by *Transparency International* or the *European Bank for Reconstruction and Development*, or commercially available from *Business International* or *World Competitiveness Report*.[91] All of these corruption indices are based on surveys of perceptions and impressions—some on the perceptions of the general public, some on the perceptions of 'experts' or 'correspondents', but none on a quantitative measure of actual corrupt practices. Thus, even cross-national analyses are usually based, at least in part, on limited use of survey data.

But the survey method is a particularly flexible tool. Interview surveys and associated methods can provide much more information than that typically used in cross-national statistical studies. It can provide not only information on the country-wide level of corruption but information on: (i) variations in corruption within each country; (ii) motivations for corruption; (iii) the evaluation and interpretation of corrupt practices; and (iv) the relative frequency and significance of corruption as compared to other ways of influencing officials.

WHAT SURVEYS?

Our own findings are mainly based on a combination of interview and discussion methods, including:

- focus-group discussions
- in-depth interviews
- large-scale structured-interview surveys.

We began with free-ranging *focus-group discussions*, typically involving between 6 and 12 participants and lasting for between one and two hours. Although these were loosely guided by a pre-prepared schedule of topics, these discussions allowed participants to express their own ideas about the relationship between citizens and officials. The *in-depth interviews* followed a similar pattern, guided by the same schedule, except that each participant was interviewed in private instead of contributing to a round-table discussion. The disadvantages of these methods are that: (i) the relatively free format of the discussion or interview means that different participants may choose to express themselves at greater or shorter length on different topics; and (ii) the numbers of participants are relatively small. Consequently they should not be used to make quantitative inferences about the public as a whole. But the advantage of these methods is that they encourage participants to express their own views with a minimum of guidance or prompting from the investigators (though participants in discussions stimulate and challenge each other), and without any restriction on their answers. In fact, our focus-group discussions and in-depth interviews included a total of over three hundred participants spread widely across the regions of Ukraine, Bulgaria, Slovakia and the Czech Republic. (The locations of these focus-group discussions and in-depth interviews are given in the appendix to this chapter.) So although they do not provide a firm basis for quantifying different views exactly, it is likely that they 'cover the range' of views, opinions and experiences.

These focus-group discussions and in-depth interviews informed the content (the questions and the answer categories) of the more structured questionnaires used for our large-scale surveys. We commissioned three types of large-scale survey:

- *representative nation-wide samples* of the public;
- additional 'booster' samples of the public in *ethnic minority areas* (including both members of the ethnic minority and members of the 'titular nationality' living within the ethnic minority area);
- *nation-wide quota samples of street-level officials* in health, education, social services, the police, and legal services.

These samples are large enough and representative enough to provide a firm basis for quantifying both the frequency and the variance of views, opinions and experiences amongst the general public, amongst significant ethnic minorities (and their neighbours from the titular nationality), and amongst street-level officials. Where possible we have checked our findings against USIA surveys. They tend to corroborate each other, though the degree of overlap between USIA surveys and our own is relatively small except in Bulgaria, where Coalition 2000 used our survey as the basis for a later series of tracking surveys, funded by USIA.

Altogether we commissioned 26 focus-group discussions (with 187 participants) and 136 semi-structured in-depth interviews towards the end of 1996. These were followed in the winter of 1997–98 by 4,778 fully structured interviews with representative samples of the public, supplemented by another 1,272 interviews with additional samples in regions where an ethnic minority was concentrated. Finally, in the summer of 1998 we sought the views of 1,307 junior officials, using a fully structured questionnaire that contained many of the same questions previously used in interviews with the public. Other questions were rephrased to cover a topic from the different perspective of an official instead of a client.

Vito Tanzi suggests that 'questionnaire-based surveys' measure only 'perceptions of corruption rather than corruption per se'.[92] Indeed, a recurrent criticism of survey-based studies of corruption is that they focus on general perceptions of the incidence of corruption rather than personal experience—because the investigators fear that their respondents will be unwilling to incriminate themselves.[93] That fear may be exaggerated. In all our focus-group discussions, in-depth interviews and large-scale surveys, we asked about:

- perceptions and gossip
- actual experience.

Our findings clearly indicate a large but variable gulf between gossip and general perceptions on the one hand, and actual personal experience on the other. If our findings are correct they cast doubt upon studies based on anecdotes, and even on more systematic studies based on perceptions. They show that Vito Tanzi is right to emphasise the distinction between perceptions and experience of corruption, even if he is wrong to suggest that surveys only ask about perceptions. They also give some support to András Sajó's complaint that 'Western experts rely on anec-dotes...Exaggerating the problem...fosters a spiralling delegitimation of the new democracies'.[94] In darker mood, General Yuri Kravchenko, Ukrainian minister of the interior, was reported as claiming that reports of corruption in Ukraine were 'multiplied' by the media and, in his view, 'the world community, probably not without evil intent, was fed the obvious lie in order to humiliate Ukraine'.[95] But our own findings suggest that it is not just 'Western experts' or those 'with evil intent' but also the ordinary citizens who live in post-communist societies themselves who 'exaggerate the problem' when they 'rely on anecdotes'. They tell a different and less dramatic story when they rely on their own personal experience.

Moreover, our findings indicate that the gulf between perceptions and experience varies systematically with the level of corruption. Thus the differences between countries in terms of corruption experiences is actually greater than in terms of corruption perceptions: in places where there is rumoured to be less corruption than elsewhere, there is actually *very* much less. The trouble with over-reliance on the 'anecdotes and perceptions' approach is not just that it is insufficiently quantitative, and not just that it exaggerates the extent and importance of low-level cor-ruption, but that it fails to discriminate sufficiently. At worst it can lead to the vague and misleading over-generalisation that 'there is corruption everywhere' and then to the enervating conclusion that 'nothing can be done to eliminate it'. A focus on actual experience leads to the rather different conclusion that street-level corruption is 'very variable', that it is 'very low indeed in some countries', and that even where it is higher 'something can be done to reduce (if not eliminate) it'.

PLAN OF THE BOOK

Chapter 2 reviews public perspectives on the transition from commu-nism—the perceived gains and losses, the perceived winners and losers. According to the public the principal beneficiaries of the transition to a market economy have been 'politicians and officials' followed by 'the mafia'. Only a negligible 2 per cent think 'ordinary citizens' have been the main beneficiaries so far, and only a few more think ordinary citizens will be the main beneficiaries even in the long run.

Chapter 3 looks at public perceptions of politicians and officials—their lack of trustworthiness, their declining standards of behaviour, and their willingness to take presents and bribes. But it also records the public's actual experience of favourable, fair or unfair treatment by officials, including their experience of extortion. Only a minority of the public report that they have 'usually' been treated fairly. The public sees corruption as a problem and a growing problem, but a problem that is neither the most frequent nor the most annoying feature of their day-to-day interactions with officials. They have many other complaints.

Chapter 4 reviews the range of strategies that the public reports they have actually used in their dealings with post-communist officials in recent years. Large numbers confess that they have used contacts, presents and bribes recently. But they also report that they have used other strategies even more frequently—strategies such as appeals to higher officials, argument, persistence, unusually pleasant behaviour or even passive submission. Attempted extortion by officials clearly stimulates the public's use of contacts, presents and bribes but it stimulates argument and persistence almost as much. When faced by incompetent or lazy officials the public responds more with increased use of argument and persistence than with increased use of bribes.

Chapter 5 focuses on the public's use of presents and bribes in more detail. The use of money, presents, favours or contacts to influence officials is not seen as a legacy of communism so much as a product of the transition. It is almost universally condemned but widely practised. The public's actual use of bribery is influenced more by extortion on the part of officials than by the public's own 'values and norms'. Nonetheless, both extortion and values have an independent impact. Condemnation stiffens resistance to extortion, even if many of those who condemn it still submit to it. But the ability of personal values to stiffen resistance to extortion varies, and it is exceptionally ineffective in Ukraine.

Chapter 6 looks at the treatment and behaviour of ethnic minorities. These are particularly sensitive issues in central Europe and the Balkans. There is a very widespread perception that officials treat clients of their own 'nationality' or ethnic group better than other clients. In their own experience, most ethnic minorities report even lower levels of fair treatment than the titular nationality, though the actual difference in experience is less than that implied by perceptions and suspicions. The response of ethnic minorities in general is to 'try harder'. By their own account, minorities make more use of any and every strategy for influencing officials—they argue more than the titular nationality and they also use contacts, presents and bribes more frequently. The one clear exception to this rule is Gypsies, who seem to have 'given up'. They, and they alone, use any and every strategy far less than the titular nationality. This combination of findings points to a 'curvilinear model' of ethnic response to stress under which moderate levels of discrimination prompt a 'try harder' response, while greater levels prompt a 'give up' response.

Chapter 7 looks at the view 'from behind the desk'—at the perspectives of street-level officials or similar public employees who deal with the public. They feel caught between state and citizen—and undervalued by both. Street-level officials complain about their own inadequate pay and about the lack of resources to meet their clients' needs. But they also complain about the behaviour of their clients as well as their employers. What upsets officials most, however, is not their clients' use of contacts, presents or bribes but their clients' use of other strategies such as appeals, argument or persistence—and, above all, their clients' threats of violence.

Officials' experience of clients, and their attitudes towards clients, vary according to the institution in which they work. Those employed in education put the highest priority on freedom and discretion to organise their work, the police put the highest priority on strict application of rules and regulations, and those in health care put the highest priority on helping their clients as much as possible. However, it is those in health care who are also the most willing to justify charging their clients 'informal payments' for extra or faster service. They have an institutional culture of gift taking as well as an institutional culture of caring.

Chapter 8 focuses on the gift-taking behaviour of officials. A majority of officials confessed that they had recently accepted a small present from a client. Up to a quarter in some countries said they are willing to accept 'money or an expensive present' from a client, though far fewer had actually done so recently. We look at the influence of institutional cultures, economic pressures and temptations or opportunities on the gift-taking behaviour of officials.

Our analysis suggests that the strongest chain of influence or causation runs from the bargaining power of certain types of official in relation to their clients, through frequent offers from these clients, then through uninhibited willingness to accept, and eventually to actual acceptance. A second, but very much weaker, chain of influence runs from national economic conditions, through inadequate salaries for officials, then through a reluctant willingness to accept only because the official 'cannot afford to refuse', and finally to actual acceptance.

The significant impact of offers from clients on the behaviour of officials balances our earlier finding (in Chapter 5) about the significant impact of extortion by officials on the behaviour of the public. Offers from clients or demands from officials have a powerful effect upon the behaviour of the other side, even though personal values moderate the impact of offers and demands.

Chapter 9 focuses on reform. We probed attitudes towards a wide variety of proposals for reform. Though some key questions did specify fair treatment 'without having to give money or presents' in order to obtain it, we focused attention on reforms 'to ensure fair treatment for citizens' rather than on reforms to reduce corruption as such.

As we found earlier, citizens can get unfair treatment from lazy, incompetent, authoritarian and capricious officials as well as from corrupt ones. Not surprisingly, both the public and street-level officials give considerable support to proposals for better training and less bureaucracy—especially in the Czech and Slovak Republics. Fewer official forms, fewer documents, certificates and permissions might help reduce the opportunities for extortion, but they would be welcomed even in societies with zero levels of corruption. Similarly, higher salaries for officials might reduce the motivation for corruption but even the most incorruptible officials would welcome higher salaries. These are not just anti-corruption reforms.

Nonetheless, some reform proposals included in our questionnaires— such as punishing bribe givers equally with bribe takers—are specifically aimed at reducing corruption. That particular reform wins significantly more support from officials than from the public, though the greatest differences between officials and the public are in the priorities that they give to stricter controls and penalties on the one hand, versus higher salaries on the other. More significant, however, is the fact that both citizens and street-level officials very wisely back multi-track packages of proposed reforms rather than single 'magic bullet' solutions. They are willing to make some tough choices, too. There is, for example, surprisingly strong public support in poverty-stricken Bulgaria and Ukraine for a combination of higher salaries for health-care employees linked to official user-charges for health-care clients, if only to regularise the unofficial and illegal payments they already have to make for health care.

Our own analytic findings highlight the corruptibility of both citizens and street-level officials in the face of extortion or temptation. That leads us to put more weight than do either the public or officials themselves on opening up the interactions between officials and their clients. Rather than prioritising stricter controls and penalties (as do the public) or higher salaries (as do officials), our analytic findings point to the importance of providing clients with alternative access points, to better appeal procedures, to a more public setting for client—official interactions, to more clearly and publicly set-out rights for clients on the one hand, and to more clearly and publicly set-out user-charges on the other—all designed to stiffen clients' resistance to extortion and to reduce their incentive to offer gifts. Large numbers of the public and street-level officials describe such measures as 'very effective', but relatively few pick them as their top priority.

In a context where so many reforms win public approval it is worth drawing attention to those which are described as 'unnecessary or harmful' by significant numbers of the public or street-level officials. Significant numbers of the public oppose 'higher salaries for officials' and 'stricter penalties for bribe-giving clients'. Significant numbers of street-level officials oppose a wider range of reforms including, in descending order, 'encouraging whistle-blowers', 'mandatory codes of conduct for officials', 'requiring officials to explain their actions to citizens and the press', 'displaying the rights of citizens in offices' and, perhaps more surprisingly, 'stricter penalties for bribe-giving clients'.

More important than all this detail, however, is that both the public and street-level officials believe that reform is possible. An overwhelming majority of the public think it would be possible to cut corruption in their country if their government made 'a strong and sincere effort' to do so. Both the public and street-level officials reject the notion of a permanent and immutable 'culture of corruption' in their country. In their view, the transition from communism has proved to be a more recent and hopefully more transient 'season of corruption'. They claim that corruption has increased since the fall of communism and that it could and should be reduced.

Unfortunately, neither the public nor street-level officials think that their government is sincerely committed to reducing corruption. One consequence of that is widespread public support for international pressure to be exerted on their own country in order to reduce corruption. Corruption is not, in their view, an 'internal affair'.

APPENDIX: THE STUDY DESIGN

The study involved three main phases: (i) focus-group discussions (FGs) and one-to-one in-depth interviews (IDIs); (ii) large-scale surveys of public opinion; and (iii) interviews with junior officials themselves.

Table 1.A1. Focus-Group Discussions and In-Depth Interviews

| | Former Czechoslovakia | | Bulgaria | Ukraine | |
	Czech Rep	Slovakia		East	West
Capital city (higher educ)	*Prague*-B	**Bratislava*-A	**Sofia*-A	*Kyiv*-A	
Capital city (lower educ)	*Prague*-A	**Bratislava*-B	**Sofia*-B	*Kyiv*-B	
Medium town	**Hradec Králové*	*Zvolen*	**Yambol*	**Khartsysk*	**Striy*
Small town	**Kutná Hora*	*Prešov*	**Straldja*	*Volnovakha Maryinka* (IDI)	**Horodok*
Village	**Olesnice Castolovice* (IDI)	*Dolný Kubín*	**Tenevo*	*Nikolayevka Rybinskoye* (IDI)	**Sholomia*
Ethnic minority areas	–	**Nové Zámky* (Hungarians)	**Kurdjali* (Turks)	*Sevastopol* (Tatars)	
FG participants	38	49	45	55	
IDIs	30	30	30	46	

Notes on FGs and IDIs:

1 FGs and IDIs were carried out during the second half of 1996.

2 FGs and IDIs were organised by USM (Ukrainian Surveys and Market Research) of Kyiv, CSD (Center for the Study of Democracy) of Sofia, and OPW (Opinion Window Market Research and Analysis) of Prague, which was responsible for FGs and IDIs in both the Czech and Slovak Republics.

3 All 26 FG discussions were video taped. Computer readable vernacular and English-language transcripts were made from these tapes. In addition, simultaneous translation was provided by Marichka Padalko in Ukraine, Mitra Myanova in Bulgaria, Zuzana Vrastiakova in Slovakia, and Klara Flemrová in the Czech Republic during the 16 FGs marked with an asterisk, which were all attended in person by the authors. Koshechkina also attended the Kyiv FGs without the need for translation facilities.

4 FGs in eastern Ukraine were located in the Donetsk region, those in western Ukraine in the Lviv region, all chaired by Alexander Fedorishin using the language chosen by the participants— Russian in Kyiv, Sevastopol and eastern Ukraine, Ukrainian in western Ukraine. FGs in Bulgaria were chaired by Andrej Nonchev (except for the one in Straldja which was chaired by Elena

Lazarova), all in Bulgarian. FGs in Slovakia were chaired by Patrik Minar in Slovak (except for the one in Nové Zámky, which was chaired by Ladislav Köppl speaking in Czech while participants responded in Slovak). FGs in the Czech Republic were chaired by Ladislav Köppl using Czech.

5 Usually five IDIs were held in the same place as each FG. Where the associated IDIs were held in a nearby place rather than the same small town or village this is indicated by (IDI).

6 Italics indicates the short form of town names used to identify respondents in the text. Thus, for example, (Ky-B 1) in the text indicates a quotation from the first participant in the focus-group Kyiv-B. For the relatively few quotations from IDIs we have indicated that explicitly, for example (Te-IDI 4). Otherwise, quotations are from FGs.

7 To provide an accurate description of what people actually said in the FGs we avoid choosing a few lengthy extracts that may be interesting but perhaps atypical. Instead we use sufficient short quotations to be representative of the views expressed. Where appropriate we occasionally quantify them. The QSR:NUD●IST package provided a convenient method of selecting those quotations as well as quantifying them.[96] There is a popular misconception that qualitative data should not be subjected to quantitative analysis. In fact, quantitative analysis is entirely valid and appropriate provided it is used to construct a precise description of the discussions as they actually occurred. It is the assertion that these discussions are necessarily representative of the country as a whole that is invalid—and that assertion is equally invalid irrespective of whether the description of the discussions is expressed in words or numbers.

8 Most quotations in this book come from the FGs rather than the IDIs. The reason for that is simple. We have complete transcripts of the FGs and indeed attended a majority of them in person (assisted by simultaneous translators where necessary). The IDIs, on the other hand, were carried out in private by professional interviewers who wrote summary reports. These reports included some verbatim quotations, but not complete transcripts. So while the IDIs provided valuable insights that have guided our analysis[97] the FGs provide a richer source of verbatim quotations for illustrative purposes.

Table 1.A2. Large-Scale Surveys of the Public and Officials

	Czech Republic	Slovakia	Bulgaria	Ukraine
Nation-wide representative surveys:				
total respondents	1,003	1,056	1,519	1,200
Additional samples in ethnic minority areas:				
additional respondents	none	325	347	600
locations		'Hungarian areas'	'Turkish areas'	Crimea Zakarpatia
Surveys of street-level officials:				
total respondents	309	386	312	300

Notes on large-scale surveys:

1 Surveys of the public were carried out during the winter of 1997–98. Surveys of street-level officials were carried out in summer 1998.

2 Surveys were carried out by OPW of Prague under the direction of Ladislav Köppl, by MVK of Bratislava under the direction of Pavel Haulík, by CSD Sofia under the direction of Alexander Stoyanov, and by GfK-USM under the direction of Tatyana Koshechkina.

3 Ethnic minority area samples were not restricted to the ethnic minority itself since we were also interested in the reactions of people from the 'titular' state nationality when they lived in an area where an ethnic minority was concentrated.

4 In Slovakia the additional ethnic minority area sample was drawn from randomly selected representative samples in areas where, according to the 1991 census, ethnic Hungarians were in the majority—the '*okres*' of Dunajská Streda and Komárno; or where the population was divided about equally between Hungarians and Slovaks—Galanta, Nové Zámky, Levice, Rimavská Sobota, and Trebišov.

5 In Bulgaria the additional ethnic minority area sample was drawn from randomly selected representative samples around Kurdjali (Kurdzhali) where the 1992 census indicated 65 per cent were Turks, Razgrad (48 per cent Turks), Turgovishte (34 per cent Turks), Slistra (33 per cent Turks), and Shoumen (29 per cent Turks).

6 In Ukraine the minority area sample consisted of quota samples with 100 ethnic Ukrainians, 100 Russians and 100 Tatars in Crimea; and with 100 Ukrainians, 100 Rusyns (Ruthenians)and 100 Hungarians in Zakarpatia (also known as 'Transcarpathia' or 'Transcarpathian Ukraine').

7 To ensure cross-national comparability we specified that the quota samples of street-level officials in each country should consist of at least 60 interviews with officials in each of five categories of public service: health services, education, welfare services, the police, and a mixed bag of legal services (court, passport and customs officials). Within each category we further specified that the 60 interviews should comprise 20 interviews with each of three more tightly specified occupations. Insofar as appropriate (not every kind of official is located everywhere), we requested that these quotas be spread widely across each country, in small towns and rural areas as well as large towns and the capital, and also spread across ages and genders.

NOTES

1 Katz, Gutek, Kahn and Barton, *Bureaucratic Encounters*.

2 Lipsky, *Street-Level Bureaucracy*.

3 Lipsky, *Street-Level Bureaucracy*, 8.

4 Klich, 'Bribery in Economies in Transition', 126–30.

5 Johnston, 'Fighting Systematic Corruption', 89.

6 Tanzi, 'Corruption Around the World', 564.

7 Sajó, 'Corruption, Clientelism and the Future of the Constitutional State in Eastern Europe', 38.

8 Sajó, 'Corruption, Clientelism and the Future of the Constitutional State in Eastern Europe', 37.

9 Linz and Stepan, *Problems of Democratic Transition and Consolidation*, 3.

10 Linz and Stepan, *Problems of Democratic Transition and Consolidation*, 5.

11 Rose, Mishler and Haerpfer, *Democracy and Its Alternatives*, especially Chapter 10: 'Completing Democracy?'

12 Linz and Stepan, *Problems of Democratic Transition and Consolidation*, 4.

13 Harrop and Miller, *Elections and Voters*, Chapter 9.

14 Linz and Stepan, *Problems of Democratic Transition and Consolidation*, 248.

15 Rose, Mishler and Haerpfer, *Democracy and Its Alternatives*, 219.

16 Stephen Holmes, 'Citizen and Law after Communism', 70

17 Almond and Verba, *The Civic Culture*, especially Chapter 7: 'Citizen Competence and Subject Competence'.

18 Almond and Verba, *The Civic Culture*, 69–70.

19 Miller, White and Heywood, *Values and Political Change in Post-Communist Europe*, 105.

20 Katz, Gutek, Kahn and Barton, *Bureaucratic Encounters*, 172.

21 Huntington, 'The Clash of Civilisations'; Huntington, 'The West v the Rest'.

22 Sajó, 'Corruption, Clientelism, and the Future of the Constitutional State in Eastern Europe', 37.

23 Klich, 'Bribery in Economies in Transition', 129.

24 Noonan, *Bribes*, 702.

25 Eigen, 'Combating Corruption Around the World', 160.

26 Scott, *Comparative Political Corruption*, 4.

27 Jackson and Smith, 'Inside Moves and Outside Views', 25.

28 Huntington, 'Modernization and Corruption', 495; see also Leff 'Economic Development Through Bureaucratic Corruption'.

29 Service, 'Russia's Putrefying Corpse'.

30 Verheijen and Dimitrova, 'Corruption and Unethical Behaviour of Civil and Public Servants', 226.

31 Paddock, 'Greasy Palms are Rampant in Russia'.

32 UNDP, *Corruption and Good Governance*, vii.

33 Hotchkiss, 'The Sleeping Dog Stirs', 111.

34 Sajó, 'Corruption, Clientalism and the Future of the Constitutional State in Eastern Europe', 39.

35 Rose-Ackerman, *Corruption and Government*, 3.

36 Schleifer and Vishny, 'Corruption', 599.

37 Tanzi, 'Corruption Around the World', 583.

38 Holmes, *The End of Communist Power*, 273.

39 Della Porta and Vannucci, 'The Perverse Effects of Political Corruption'.

40 Almond and Verba, *The Civic Culture*, 364.

41 Linz, *The Breakdown of Democratic Regimes*, 31.

42 Schleifer and Vishny, 'Corruption', 615.

43 Mauro, 'Corruption and Growth', 701.

44 Mauro, 'Corruption and Growth', 687.

45 Sajó, 'Corruption, Clientelism, and the Future of the Constitutional State in Eastern Europe', 39.

46 Girling, *Corruption, Capitalism and Democracy*, 15.

47 Miller, White and Heywood, *Values and Political Change in Post-Communist Europe*, 156.

48 Reed, 'The Great Growth Race'.

49 Rose, Mishler, and Haerpfer, *Democracy and its Alternatives*, 188–90.

50 Rose-Ackerman, *Corruption and Government*, Chapter 8: 'Democracy and Corruption'.

51 Noonan, *Bribes*, 704.

52 OECD, *Improving Ethical Conduct*.

53 Mallon, Bratton, Pollard, Orr, Griffiths and Dennis, *Zero Tolerance*.

54 *Corruption Watch* 1, no. 18 (11 November 1998).

55 *Corruption Watch* 2, no. 11 (32) (26 May 1999).

56 *Weekly Review of Bulgarian Press Coverage of Corruption* (31 July–6 August 1999): 7.

57 Verba, Nie and Kim, *Participation and Political Equality*.

58 UNDP, *Corruption and Good Governance*, viii, 45–47.

59 Noonan, *Bribes*, 703.

60 Johnston, 'Public Officials, Private Interests, and Sustainable Democracy', 74.

61 Rose-Ackerman, *Corruption and Government*, 4.

62 Noonan, *Bribes*, 691.

63 Noonan, *Bribes*, 700.

64 Klich, 'Bribery in Economies in Transition', 132.

65 Tanzi, 'Corruption Around the World', 586.

66 Ayres, 'Judicial Corruption', quoted in Rose-Ackerman, *Corruption and Government*, 53.

67 Rose-Ackerman, *Corruption and Government*, 123.

68 *Zhyzn* (4 July 1998), quoted in *Corruption Watch* 1, no. 9 (8 July 1998).

69 Bertolt Brecht 'The Solution', in Bold, *The Penguin Book of Socialist Verse*, 240.

70 Miller, White and Heywood, *Values and Political Change in Post-Communist Europe*, 90.

71 Heady, 'Bureaucracies', 305.

72 DiFranceisco and Gitelman, 'Soviet Political Culture', 613.

73 Sogomonov and Tolstykh, 'Our Most Pressing Problems', 75.

74 Lindbeck, 'Swedish Lessons', 3, quoted in Tanzi, 'Corruption Around the World', 586.

75 Tanzi, 'Corruption Around the World', 586.

76 Rafferty, *City on the Rocks*, 211.

77 Krawchenko, *Administrative Reform in Ukraine*, 13.

78 Osborne and Kaposvári, *Non-governmental Organisations*, 11.

79 Giddens, *The Third Way*, 65.

80 Norris, *Critical Citizens*.

81 Miller, White and Heywood, *Values and Political Change in Post-communist Europe*, 85.

82 Berkman, 'Bureaucracy and Bribery', 1359–60.

83 Gole, 'Public Opinion Polls as an Anti-corruption Technique'.

84 Simis, *USSR: Secrets of a Corrupt Society*, 146–174.

85 Shlapentokh, *The Public and Private Life of the Soviet People*, especially Chapter 9: 'Illegal Life Inside the State'.

86 Holmes, *The End of Communist Power*, especially Chapter 3: 'Patterns of Corruption and Its Reporting in the USSR and the PRC'.

87 Levitas, 'Fiddling While Britain Burns'.

88 Lotspeich, 'Crime in the Transition Economies', 577.

89 Miller, 'Quantitative Methods', 155.

90 Miller, 'Social Class and Party Choice'.

91 EBRD, *Ten Years of Transition*, 125; Mauro, 'Corruption and Growth', 684; Ades and Di Tella, 'The New Economics of Corruption', 499.

92 Tanzi, 'Corruption Around the World', 577.

93 Lancaster and Montinola, 'Towards a Methodology for the Comparative Study of Political Corruption', 193–4.

94 Sajó, 'Corruption, Clientelism, and the Future of the Constitutional State in Eastern Europe', 37.

95 *Corruption Watch* 1, no. 18 (11 November 1998).

96 Weitzman, *Computer Programs for Qualitative Data Analysis*.

97 Grødeland, Koshechkina and Miller, 'Foolish to Give'; Grødeland, Koshechkina and Miller, 'In Theory Correct'.

CHAPTER 2

CONTEXT:
AN UNFINISHED TRANSITION

An uneven mix of reform and chaos followed the collapse of communism, and it is this mix of reform and chaos that provides the context for our study of bureaucratic encounters in post-communist Europe. Throughout the 1990s, the countries of Central and Eastern Europe were in the midst of a transition. The transition involved much more than the introduction of competitive elections at the national level. Other changes, much closer to the daily lives of ordinary citizens, included local government reform, privatisation and restitution, moves towards a market economy and, in many countries, economic collapse. It was more clearly a *transition from* communism than a *transition to* a functioning market economy and a fully consolidated and complete democracy. Even its most ardent supporters would admit that the transition to democracy in Central and Eastern Europe was at best 'unfinished business'. At worst it came close to chaos. The reforms should have helped to improve the relationship between street-level officials and their clients. The chaos did not.

Although the situation is still evolving, the most important period for the purposes of our study is that up to about 1997–8. Our study is based essentially on citizens' experience of the mid-1990s as reflected in their memories, feelings and reactions during the late 1990s. Although we asked about contemporary attitudes and perceptions, in our 1996–8 surveys we asked respondents about their recent experience of economic trends and dealing with street-level officials 'over the last five years'. No doubt respondents gave greater weight to their more recent experiences even within this 'five year' time frame but it remains true that late-1990s interpretations of the transition reflected the recent past as well as the immediate present.

THE DEMOCRATISATION OF LOCAL
GOVERNMENT

Local government has an immediate impact on the lives of ordinary citizens. Access to housing, house repairs and local services have a more visible and immediate impact than foreign or defence policy—and they bring ordinary citizens into personal contact with officials much more frequently. It is only local government that can really 'bring government close to the people' and give them a real sense of empowerment.

Although there were important differences of structure and timing between different countries, it was generally true that there was a rapid change in the principles of local governance. It has been described as a move 'from democratic centralism to local democracy'.[1] Under the communist regime local governance (like so much else) was an openly top-down process. Local governments did not themselves own property, they had little or no discretion, they were not elected in any meaningful sense, and they did not represent their locality except as petitioners seeking favours from an all-powerful central authority. Local-government bodies acted primarily to implement centrally set policies.[2] Moreover, the local-government structure was paralleled by that of the Communist Party. The Party, not the people, was in control.

With the collapse of the old regime, local government was given more responsibility for tasks previously undertaken by central government. In addition to their responsibilities for local development and services such as sewage, drainage and local law and order, local authorities were now given responsibility for housing, which had been controlled by industrial and commercial state enterprises under communism.[3] Local authorities could raise money through service charges and privatisation proceeds as well as through taxation.

In principle, the move to democracy meant that local government was now to have an independent existence based upon a democratic mandate from below rather than on instructions from above. Insofar as this had any effect at all on the relationship between street-level officials and their clients, it should have helped to change the status of ordinary people from mere subjects into citizens, from servants into masters. In turn, that should have encouraged fairer treatment by officials and more attention to the complaints of citizens.

In a reaction against the discredited centralism of communism there was also a rapid fragmentation of local governance, particularly in the Czech and Slovak Republics where it produced almost 9,000 elected local governments for a population that totalled only 15 million, emphasising localism and democracy even at the expense of operational efficiency. Since these local authorities were far too small to carry out local government tasks for themselves, they were forced to use (but also able to choose between) external agencies, some public, others private, which could provide services under contract. Again that element of choice, albeit indirect, should have changed the balance of status and power in favour of those who consumed public services and against those who provided them. There should have been less need for citizens to put up with arbitrary decisions.

Deconcentration of central government agencies, the opening of many more local offices and the acceptance of some degree of 'oversight' by local authorities in recognition of their new electoral legitimacy should also have encouraged even (central) ministry officials to behave more like public servants and less as mere agents of high authority.

At the same time, there were some apparently contradictory changes, notably the imposition of 'presidential representatives' (whose powers sometimes appeared to conflict with those of local authorities) on the regions and districts of Ukraine. Though that was usually presented as a move to strengthen the reform process rather than as a move towards centralism, fears for the integrity of the state combined with a power conflict between the parliament and the president to leave local and regional governments 'with important responsibilities for communal and municipal services and infrastructural support to industry and agriculture' but 'little authority or control of revenues'.[4]

Overall, however, we might have expected that the democratisation of local government would curb the excesses of officials and improve the status of their clients. That was certainly the intention. But Elander argues that local government was slow to acquire democratic legitimacy, that citizens focused their hopes on national leaders, and that the tide soon 'turned in favour of more centralist hopes and policies'.[5] By the mid-1990s, the extreme fragmentation of local governments in parts of post-communist Europe had come to be regarded as an 'obstacle to democratic reform',[6] and even in the Czech Republic 'decentralisation was halted half way without its potential being fully exploited'.[7]

PRIVATISATION AND RESTITUTION

The transition from communism was aimed as much at a transition to a market economy as to democracy. That meant privatisation and competition to improve economic efficiency. But privatisation was also designed to right old wrongs, often at the expense of economic efficiency. It is common to distinguish between three types of privatisation:

(i)   large-scale privatisation—of larger scale state enterprises;
(ii) small-scale privatisation—of shops, restaurants, wine bars and beer houses, for example;
(iii) restitution—the return of property seized by the communists to its former owners or their descendants.[8]

In principle, both the economic and the moral aims were laudable enough. But in practice privatisation provided enormous opportunities for officials at all levels to enrich themselves. In a 12–month period one Czech study identified '33 cases of personal gain in the areas of privatisation' totalling 25 billion Czech crowns but only resulting in two prosecutions.[9]

Even if they did not act purely in their own interests, officials were likely to take decisions that were bound to leave many citizens with deeply felt grievances. Restitution especially was fraught with problems. In Slovakia, for example, it was described as 'a lengthy and tedious bureaucratic process, complete with audits and appraisals that generate legal quagmires…alternative housing must be found by new owners before tenants can be evicted…[and so] the Restitution Act has had only a minor impact on housing privatisation'.[10] Attempts at restitution, whether ultimately successful or not, were likely to leave either the claimants or the sitting tenants dissatisfied with officials.

At the same time, restitution combined with reductions in public housing construction to produce a large unsatisfied demand for public housing in the Czech and Slovak Republics.[11] Due to a lack of funds, local authorities also found it hard to renovate or even maintain the remaining communal property. People were encouraged to buy the houses and flats they lived in from the local councils but often they could not afford the cost.[12] All of this caused additional problems between citizens and housing officials.

The privatisation scheme introduced in the Czech Republic for state enterprises, shops and restaurants was perhaps fair in principle, but it was complicated. Badly drafted legislation left loopholes for bribery and corruption.[13] It was 'often only a substantial bribe or an offer to share the property that could speed up the procedure. The exclusive administrative monopoly of the district council was the main source of their power. Complaints filed regarding their bureaucracy, intentional procrastination, unfounded objections or professional incompetence seldom meet with a positive response and applicants generally avoid raising them for fear of the council's retribution.' The local council could 'refuse approval...order financial audits or controls of hygiene, or simply harass the entrepreneur on endless, often fictitious, charges'.[14]

In agricultural restitution the 'key factor of advantage' was the 'social capital of personal contacts...that provided access to capital and machinery'.[15] A survey of Ukrainians and Russians found that those wishing to become private farmers tended to be young, educated and ideologically committed to the free-market system. Actual involvement in small-scale farming had no effect on the desire to buy or lease land for private farming.[16] There were difficulties with getting access to equipment, fertilisers and supplies which were still controlled by public officials. It was 'a climate dominated by clientalism and distrust for public institutions' and by 'the dependence of the private sector on selected individuals in the collective and state farm system'.[17]

Considerable scepticism towards privatisation was also revealed in a study of ethnic Hungarian villages within Slovakia, although, in contrast to Ukraine, much of the land in these villages had only been seized by the state as recently as 1951.[18] Many people working in farming collectives had already lost their 'peasant soul'. Others, though not against privatisation in principle, were unhappy at decisions about village life being made over their heads. 'Once again somebody decides about the peasant and nobody asks him. First we were forced into the cooperatives, today they disperse us...forceful collectivisation was not right, but it is equally unjust when somebody from the top, who is not familiar with it, then wants to remove the idea of common farming.' Leaders of co-operatives put numerous obstacles in the way of farmers wishing to go private. Older people applying for their share of co-operative land to sell it to private owners were told that they would lose their pensions.[19]

In Bulgaria people were issued with shares according to their previous property or, if they had none, according to the time they had been working for the state. The task of dividing these assets was assigned to specially appointed liquidation committees often appointed on political, rather than professional grounds. Reclaiming or buying land proved too expensive for most people since it cost more to obtain a legal title than they would earn from one or two years of farming the land. Consequently, only 10 per cent of Bulgarian farmers owned their land by 1995.[20]

On balance it seems probable that while a few did well out of privatisation and restitution it did not help to improve the relationship between citizens and officials. Indeed, the envious and the disappointed were probably in the majority.

ECONOMIC AND MORAL CHAOS

Of the countries in our study only the former Czechoslovakia implemented a far-reaching purge of officials from the old regime.[21] The Czechoslovak 'lustration' law, banning former communists from senior state and business positions for five years, was continued by the Czech Republic (though not the Slovak Republic)[22] and later extended to run to the end of the year 2000. Elsewhere, post-communist officials were mainly the same officials operating in a new environment. There was even a high level of continuity amongst elected officials: after the first post-communist local elections, 44 per cent of mayors in the Czech Republic and 65 per cent in Slovakia proved to have had experience as local officials under communism.[23] If anything was to be 'new', it was a question of 'new thinking', a new operating environment and new relationships, more than 'new people'.

But the economic and moral chaos of the new environment was likely to affect the relationship between citizens and officials adversely. New thinking might not necessarily be better thinking. Indeed, times of transition are likely to be times of corruption: historically speaking, high political ideals and low standards of personal behaviour go together at such times. According to Philippe Schmitter, 'the problem in fledgling democracies is that regime transition is often accompanied by the simultaneous need to make major transformations in other socio-economic domains...Even where the thrust of change is toward unleashing market forces, the process of accomplishing this offers very attractive opportunities for illicit enrichment on the part of the politicians who set the norms, sell off the enterprises, and award the contracts. Ironically...the short-term effect is to increase the potential payoffs to be had from the exploitation of public authority.'[24]

A surge of high-level corruption in post-communist Europe would simply fit the usual pattern in times of transition. A recent EBRD survey of over 3,000 firms in 20 transition countries suggests that over a third of firms in Slovakia and Ukraine and a quarter in Bulgaria and the Czech Republic 'frequently' pay bribes to officials.[25] Transparency International's *Corruption Perception Index* (Transparency International, 1999) now ranks the Czech Republic 39th out of 99 countries for corruption, Slovakia 53rd, Bulgaria 65th, and Ukraine 77th. (The most corrupt, Cameroon, is ranked 99th.)[26] Meanwhile, at lower levels, the end of communism brought unemployment, poverty, a sharp decline in health and welfare services, a rise in nationalist tensions and a general climate of aggressive and often desperate individualism and communalism. Economic dislocation made many entrepreneurs and senior officials conspicuously rich, and by no means legitimately so. At the same time it put the incomes of street-level officials under severe pressure. The moral of a reputedly corrupt privatisation and restitution process may not have been lost even on those officials who could not participate in it to any significant degree. If so, it would encourage them to take what they could in other ways.

Paradoxically, communist regimes had so many means of control, through enterprise management and through the internal security services for example, that they did not need a well-developed civil service on Western lines. Since society and the state were fused together, there was neither space for a civil society independent of the state nor for a public service independent of society. There were complaints that Ukrainian officials were remarkably few in number and not well qualified for their tasks.[27] Even if that did not lead to corruption it was likely to lead to bureaucratic confusion. Czech and Slovak civil servants were 'not very experienced, not properly educated and in some instances also not very motivated'.[28] As opportunities developed in the private sector, there was also a loss of competent officials to better-paid positions outside public administration. At the same time, what was often unclear and complicated legislation allowed great scope for discretion in dealings with clients. So although the old communist system with its peculiar scope for corruption was replaced, the new post-communist system provided its own new incentives and opportunities.

Of course, while a lack of motivation, unclear responsibilities, low wages and poor monitoring all provide conditions for officials to become corrupt, they neither dictate nor excuse it. New values such as support for post-communist reform, empathy with citizens suffering hardship, or the perception that taking bribes or bowing to influence is wrong, could prevent officials making use of these abundant new opportunities for corruption. On the other side, a new self-confidence amongst citizens might make them less willing to submit to ill-treatment or extortion. But there was no guarantee that new values in post-communist

Europe would be an improvement on old values, either amongst officials
or amongst their clients. During the transition from communist order
through disruption and chaos towards the distant goal of a functioning
market economy, new values might be more individualistic, more acquisitive, and more market oriented whether the market in question was
legitimate or not.

In fact, the transition was accompanied not only by a collapse of the
old communist economic system but also by a collapse of belief in the old
communist value system. In our previous study of post-communist values,
31 per cent in East Central Europe and 56 per cent in the former Soviet
Union told us that they had once 'believed in communist ideals', though
only 20 per cent in East Central Europe and a mere 18 per cent in the former Soviet Union did so 'now'.[29] Michal Illner points to the combination
of 'the anomie following the fall of the communist regime and the breakdown of the legitimacy of its normative system', as well as to the interpretation of individual freedom as the reckless pursuit of individual interests
and 'the extraordinary opportunities which privatisation and other forms
of redistributing state property opened to criminal behaviour' even in the
Czech Republic.[30] Verheijen and Dimitrova point to 'the general deterioration of values' and to the 'moral wasteland' in post-communist countries
as a prime cause of increasing corruption amongst post-communist officials.[31] They quote Huntington's argument that 'democratisation can bring
corruption in the short term by temporarily weakening the state and loos-
ening social inhibitions...By bringing into question authority in general,
democratisation can bring confusion about standards of morality in general and promote anti-social behaviour.'[32]

We might expand this argument of Huntington's by adding that the
transition towards a market economy—quite separately and independ-
ently from any transition towards a democratic system—may also bring
about an increase in specifically monetary corruption. The communist
system of corruption based on non-monetary privileges might be replaced by a more market oriented system in which everything has its
price. Alena Ledeneva suggests that the transition had two effects upon
the use of contacts and bribery. The predominant use of '*blat*' (contacts
and influence) shifted from the everyday life of ordinary citizens up to
the networks of former nomenklatura who were now turning themselves
into quasi-criminal businessmen. At the same time, in the everyday life
of citizens crude monetary bribes increasingly supplemented or even
replaced the more subtle, and occasionally civilising, use of contacts.[33]
Similarly, Daniel Bell suggests that 'in totalitarian societies corruption

is the arbitrary use of power' while 'in a democracy, on the other hand, corruption is money'.[34] Daniel Kaufmann and Paul Siegelbaum suggest that the transition in post-communist Europe was a 'transition from the exploitation of power and access to goods and special perks, to the unchecked appropriation of wealth for private use'.[35] Under communism the 'most blatant forms of corruption were somewhat held in check by the discipline of the Communist Party, draconian anti-bribery laws and the rigidity of the overall system itself'.[36] There were 'limited opportunities for cash bribes…mid-level bureaucrats had to be content to vie for preferred access to scarce low-quality consumer goods and perks…and patronage for jobs…rather than large bribes or kick-backs.' But 'the breakdown of the socialist system created an ideal medium for the growth of monetary corruption'.[37]

John Girling takes an even more critical view. He attributes corruption simply to the market economy itself and not just to the transition from communism. He builds on Yves Meny's argument that the spread of corruption in France originated in the 'enfeeblement of public values under the assault of neo-liberal economic policies and the penetration of market values' into the political sphere.[38] A typical American view is that the political equality of democracy is a necessary—and perhaps a sufficient—counterweight to the economic inequalities of a market economy. But Girling sees both a contradiction in principle, and also a dangerous tension in practice, between democracy and a market economy. 'In the age of capitalism the values of the market place (= everything can be bought and sold) permeate formerly autonomous political and social spheres.'[39] 'Corruption is the excessive or shocking aspect of normal practice: *the unacceptable face of capitalism*…it stems from the incompatibility in important respects of the economic and political systems' of capitalist democracy.[40] The ethos of a market economy encourages the rich to vote with their wealth as well as with their persons, buying favours from officials.

In Girling's view, the market economy alters the culture of officials as well as the culture of their clients. 'The raison d'être of officials' in a democratic system, he claims, is 'to serve the common interest as defined by the electoral majority and its political leadership', but 'the raison d'être of the capitalist system, to the contrary, is private profit'.[41] Thus the capitalist ethic tends to legitimise officials selling their services as well as clients buying them.

In the short term, Girling's view is simply an unusually pessimistic perspective on the universally acknowledged mix of political equality and economic inequality that constitutes a liberal democracy. But in the longer term, it implies that corruption is not merely the temporary product of the transition from communism but a permanent part of a liberal democratic culture. In this perspective, public-sector corruption is neither a problem of the (communist) past nor of the (transitional) present but a problem for the (capitalist democratic) future.

Despite the contrary perspective of John Girling, however, we might guess that democratisation and a move to a market economy should, in themselves, encourage street-level officials to behave better. But the general climate of economic and moral chaos that accompanied this transition may have encouraged both officials and clients to behave worse.

THE POLITICAL CONTEXT

Many aspects of public perceptions and opinions depend upon whether the public thinks their elected government and parliament are 'part of the solution' or 'part of the problem'. So political developments, especially elections and changes of government, constitute a very significant element of the context for our study. In order to view our findings in their political context it is important to relate the timing of our focus-group discussions (late 1996), in-depth interviews (also late 1996), large-scale surveys of public opinion (winter 1997–98) and interviews with street-level officials (summer 1998) to the timing of key political events. For the proper interpretation of our findings, the most significant of these political events occurred in Bulgaria.

Early in 1997 a series of rallies, protests and riots forced the Bulgarian Socialist Party government to concede early elections. They took place in April. The Socialist Party government which had ruled since 1994 was defeated and replaced by the main opposition grouping, the United Democratic Forces (ODS) headed by Ivan Kostov, the leader of the Union of Democratic Forces (SDS) which was the largest party in the ODS. When sworn in as prime minister, Kostov declared that 'years of false reform' and 'officially sanctioned theft' had come to an end. He declared an 'all-out war on crime and corruption'.[42] Such dramatic events came close to a revolutionary and illegal, even if popular, change of government, though constitution forms were formally observed. They probably conveyed the sense of a new beginning and a new determination to fight corruption. That perception emerged, of course, *after* our

1996 focus-group discussions in Bulgaria but *before* our large-scale surveys. It lasted through to our interviews with the public towards the end of the year, and perhaps to our interviews with officials in the following summer—though by October 1999 Bulgarian president Petar Stoyanov, in a statement reprinted in all the national daily papers, was accusing the new government of itself containing too many 'corrupt, incompetent, and self-satisfied officials'.[43]

The quasi-revolutionary Bulgarian experience of early 1997 contrasted with the lack of a similarly dramatic break between the administrations of Prime Ministers Václav Klaus and Miloš Zeman in the Czech Republic. Klaus resigned at the end of 1997 but there was no immediate election. The former governor of the National Bank, Josef Tosovsky, formed an interim government and prepared for elections in June 1998. After those elections no party or coalition gained a majority. Instead, the Czech Social Democrats (ČSSD) under Miloš Zeman signed an 'opposition agreement' with Václav Klaus's former governing Civic Democrats (ODS). Zeman became prime minister, while Klaus became chairman of the Chamber of Deputies. Both parties denied this was a coalition agreement but they nonetheless operated 'as a kind of parliamentary coalition, albeit unusual and covert...The oxymoronic label of "opposition agreement" itself became a butt of criticism and ridicule'.[44]

The dramatic events in Bulgaria contrasted still more sharply with the continuity of government—and the continuity of corruption—under President Leonid Kuchma in Ukraine and Prime Minister Vladimir Mečiar in Slovakia. Mečiar was defeated and lost office late in 1998, but that was after all of our interviews had been completed. Later still, Mečiar's successor as Slovak prime minister, Mikuláš Dzurinda, launched an anti-corruption drive in February 2000 with the claim that two-thirds of Slovaks had 'encountered corruption', though he criticised the people themselves for 'not hesitating to bribe doctors and teachers'.[45]

Thus, when commenting on high officials or on their governments' efforts to combat corruption, for example, our respondents were passing judgement:

- on the long-established governments under Kuchma in Ukraine and Mečiar in Slovakia;
- on the continuing 'cloakroom politics...explicitly based on insider bargaining'[46] of Klaus and Zeman in the Czech Republic;
- on the completely new, and as yet untainted, government under Kostov in Bulgaria (in our surveys—though not in our earlier fo-

cus-group discussions which took place in the closing months of
the unpopular Socialist government).

On balance, in our surveys a majority of the public in Bulgaria declared their 'support' for 'the present government and its policies'. In
every other country a majority said they were 'opposed' to their government and its policies. In other respects also, but especially in those
related to corruption, we should expect our surveys to reflect the post-
election 'honeymoon period' for the new, untainted and reforming
Kostov government in Bulgaria.

PUBLIC PERSPECTIVES ON THE UNFINISHED TRANSITION

Public perspectives on the transition itself form the essential background
to our study of the interactions between clients and officials during this
period.

ECONOMIC PESSIMISM

According to EBRD (European Bank for Reconstruction and Development) figures there was a clear spectrum of economic deprivation that
ran from the relatively prosperous Czech Republic through Slovakia and
then Bulgaria to relatively impoverished Ukraine.[47] In addition, according to EBRD figures, while the first decade of the transition from communism left real GDP in both the Czech and Slovak Republics roughly
where it had been back in 1989, it cut Bulgaria's by one-third and
Ukraine's by two-thirds.[48]

We found that economic perceptions within our four countries paralleled the conclusions of the EBRD's economists, though public perceptions were even more pessimistic. A majority of the public in every
country felt that both their country's economy and their own family income had declined over the previous five years. The Bank's figures
would not support quite that degree of pessimism. According to the
Bank's figures the Bulgarian and Ukrainian economies had declined
over the previous five years but the Czech and Slovak economies had
recovered after a decline in the early 1990s.

The cross-national pattern of public pessimism did reflect the Bank's
figures, however (Table 2.1). On average, half the public thought their
country's economy had got 'much worse', though that ranged from only

30 per cent in the Czech Republic through 41 per cent in Slovakia and 50 per cent in Bulgaria to 78 per cent in Ukraine. '[It was] better under Todor Zhivkov...you could walk along the streets without any fear, there were no scavengers in front of the garbage-bins.'(So-A 6) ('So-A 6' indicates a quotation from participant number 6 at focus-group discussion A in Sofia. See Appendix I to Chapter 1 for details.)

Table 2.1. Economic pessimism—past and present

	Average	Czech Republic	Slovakia	Bulgaria	Ukraine
	%	%	%	%	%
Over the last five years has (the country's) economy generally got...					
much better?	1	2	2	1	1
a little better?	17	23	24	18	4
a little worse?	32	44	34	32	17
much worse?	50	30	41	50	78
Over the last five years has your family's standard of living got...					
much better?	4	6	6	2	1
a little better?	27	40	40	21	6
a little worse?	33	40	36	35	23
much worse?	36	14	19	42	70
Family income now is...					
not really enough to survive on	31	11	14	45	53
only just enough to survive on	43	43	48	43	40
enough for a 'fair' or 'good' standard of living	26	46	38	12	7

Notes: 'Don't know', 'mixed/depends', etc. answers were recorded if given spontaneously, but never prompted; they have been excluded from the calculation of percentages.

'(The country's)' was replaced by the name of the country in which the interview took place.

Public perceptions of the decline in their *own family's income* were less pessimistic, especially in the Czech and Slovak Republics—though in Bulgaria and Ukraine people were almost as pessimistic about their family's declining standard of living as about their country's declining economy.

On average, 31 per cent told us their family income was now 'not really enough to survive on', though that ranged from only 11 per cent in the Czech Republic through 14 per cent in Slovakia and 45 per cent in

Bulgaria to 53 per cent in Ukraine. Conversely, 26 per cent said their income was enough for a 'good' or at least a 'fair standard of living', mainly the latter, but that ranged down from 46 per cent in the Czech Republic through 38 per cent in Slovakia and 12 per cent in Bulgaria to a mere 7 per cent in Ukraine. (When we asked the same question in a 1995 survey of the British public,[49] 70 per cent told us their family income was enough for a 'good' or at least a 'fair standard of living'.)

As for the future, a majority in the Czech Republic and in Ukraine thought decline would continue, from very different starting points of course. A majority in Slovakia and Bulgaria hoped the worst was now over and that things might now get 'a little' (but only 'a little') better. Even that was not a pleasant prospect, however: 'No wonder all young people flee to the West. I, for instance, were it possible, would have run away, since there is no future for me here.'(Ku 4)

What emotions were triggered by these perceptions? How did people feel about economic conditions in their country? We asked whether they were 'happy, angry, worried or ashamed' about economic conditions in their country. Naturally enough, very few were happy. On average, 60 per cent were 'worried', about a fifth were 'angry', and rather less were 'ashamed'—except in Ukraine where 33 per cent actually felt 'ashamed'. Ukrainians had thought themselves more advanced, more capable, and, at least in relative terms, more successful in the past. Economic chaos in post-communist Ukraine had gone beyond worry and anger to hit self-esteem (Table 2.2).

Under communism, citizens had been encouraged by the authorities to show a degree of public concern and involvement even if it was largely formal. In fact, the private sphere had always been more important to communist citizens than it appeared on the surface. But during the transition the political pressure to participate in public affairs was replaced for most citizens by increased economic pressures to survive (and for a few by increased economic opportunities). Over 90 per cent in every country told us that people in their country were now 'completely focused on their own private problems and opportunities' rather than giving sufficient priority to 'building a new future' for their country. In the economic chaos of post-communism, concern, focus and attention had been 'privatised' as people retreated from public concerns to focus more on personal economic survival or, if they belonged to the fortunate minority, on new opportunities for personal economic success.

Table 2.2. Emotional reactions to economic decline

	Average %	Czech Republic %	Slovakia %	Bulgaria %	Ukraine %
Which one of these words best describes how you feel about economic conditions in (your country)?					
worried	60	61	63	70	45
angry	21	26	19	16	21
ashamed	15	6	10	11	33
happy	4	7	8	3	0

Notes: 'Don't know', 'mixed/depends', etc. answers were recorded if given spontaneously, but never prompted; they have been excluded from the calculation of percentages.

'(Your country)' was replaced by the name of the country in which the interview took place.

THE MARKET ECONOMY

Throughout all the countries in our study, ordinary people felt that they were the victims rather than the beneficiaries of the transition to a market economy. That is not to say that they opposed the changes in principle, for they did not. 'The path we have taken is correct...we should go the way all Europe is going. Despite the present difficulties that is the only path for the country.'(Te-IDI 4) 'The transition to the market economy is necessary since the whole world lives like that.'(Ho 1) 'The whole world lives, and it lives better than we do, in market conditions. I think that it was necessary to move.'(Sh 5) 'Something had to be changed.'(Kh 6) 'The market approach...a very correct decision.'(Se 4)

But while a large majority in every country except Ukraine said the move to a market economy had been 'right in principle', a large majority in every country felt it had been 'fairly badly' or even 'very badly' handled (Table 2.3). 'It is a good thing but I think it should not be the way it has started in this country.'(Ky-B 1) 'They broke everything apart and have not built anything.'(Se 1) 'Democracy is something very nice, but we misinterpreted it...instead of achieving...we kept destroying.'(Te 4) 'A country this beautiful and nice...it has all been ruined.'(Stral 1)

Jacek Szymanderski argues that the 'fundamental principle' of a market economy is that 'fair profits may only be obtained by means of

the market [and] this excludes conquest, theft or extortion'.[50] By that
standard, several participants in focus groups or in-depth interviews,
especially in Ukraine, quite rightly denied that there had in fact been a
transition to a market economy at all. 'We still have not built a market.'(Se 3)

Table 2.3. The market economy in principle and in practice

	Average	Czech Republic	Slovakia	Bulgaria	Ukraine
	%	%	%	%	%
Do you feel that the move to a market economy in (your country) was right or wrong in principle, whatever the problems about the way it was done?					
right in principle	63	64	63	81	44
Do you think the move to a market economy was handled...					
very well?	1	1	1	1	1
fairly well?	22	30	25	27	8
fairly badly?	45	53	52	42	31
very badly?	32	16	22	30	60

Notes: 'Don't know', 'mixed/depends', etc. answers were recorded if given spontaneously, but
never prompted; they have been excluded from the calculation of percentages.
  '(Your country)' was replaced by the name of the country in which the interview took place.

Ordinary people had a strong sense of being pushed aside or cheated
by powerful groups and individuals in the privatisation process: 'A
small group of people will live well thanks to privatisation of state property. Privatisation is a big swindle.'(Ky-IDI 3) 'As far as plants and
factories are concerned, it seems to be more likely not *privatizatsia*
[privatisation] but *prikhvatisatsia* [grabbing].' (Ryb-IDI 5) Similarly, a
very large majority (75 per cent) in every country except Ukraine approved the process of restitution 'in principle', but around 86 per cent
said their family had not benefited personally from the process. In
Ukraine most could not decide whether restitution was right or wrong in
principle but they were overwhelmingly certain (91 per cent) that they
had not benefited from it personally.

INCREASING BUREAUCRACY

Public criticism of the transition was not limited to its economic aspects but was extended to criticism of administrative and political changes as well. All too often the laudable aims of privatisation, restitution and more generally the attempt to construct a legal state on the ruins of a bureaucratic state, simply created more official forms, documents, permissions and certificates. Everywhere, a majority complained that they needed more official papers and documents now than they had under communism. Bureaucracy, in the quantitative sense, had got worse. These complaints were particularly strong in the Czech and Slovak Republics where over 90 per cent complained about increased bureaucracy compared to only 60 to 65 per cent elsewhere.

THE FAILURE OF COMPETITIVE ELECTIONS
TO EMPOWER CITIZENS

The public was also critical of the transition towards electoral democracy as well as the transition towards a market economy. Again, the high hopes of 1989 had been dashed by bitter experience. On average, a majority said they did not think that having competitive elections gave ordinary people much influence over politicians. Nor did they think that having competitive elections had much effect on how bureaucrats and

Table 2.4. The failure of competitive elections

	Average	Czech Republic	Slovakia	Bulgaria	Ukraine
	%	%	%	%	%
Competitive elections...					
do *not* give ordinary people much influence over politicians?	56	67	63	38	55
do *not* have much effect on how officials treat ordinary citizens?	58	65	63	50	55

Note: 'Don't know', 'mixed/depends', etc. answers were recorded if given spontaneously, but never prompted; they have been excluded from the calculation of percentages.

officials treated ordinary citizens (Table 2.4). The exception was Bulgaria where, in the immediate aftermath of the street protests and electoral defeat of the Socialists in early 1997, the public was significantly and more impressed by the effectiveness of elections—especially as a means of influencing politicians, though less as a means of affecting the behaviour of street-level officials.

CUI BONO? (WHO BENEFITS?)

Trend analyses based on USIA surveys suggest that in the initial stages of the transition the public in Ukraine (and Russia) was optimistic about the transition eventually benefiting ordinary people, but that this optimism steadily declined and had turned to pessimism by 1993.[51]

Table 2.5. Cui bono? (Who benefits?)

	Average	Czech Republic	Slovakia	Bulgaria	Ukraine
	%	%	%	%	%
Who do you think has benefited most from the move to a market economy?					
politicians and officials	42	49	56	30	35
the mafia	31	20	19	41	44
the former communist nomenklatura	19	23	21	19	13
foreigners	6	6	3	6	7
ordinary citizens	2	3	1	4	1
Looking ahead, who do you think will eventually benefit most from the move to a market economy?					
politicians and officials	43	47	61	31	35
the mafia	29	20	22	34	40
foreigners	10	14	5	10	9
the former communist nomenklatura	9	11	9	8	9
ordinary citizens	9	8	3	17	7

Note: 'Don't know', 'mixed/depends', etc. answers were recorded if given spontaneously, but never prompted; they have been excluded from the calculation of percentages.

By the late 1990s, our surveys suggest that very few in any country thought that 'ordinary citizens' had been—or ever would be—the chief beneficiaries of the transition. On average, 42 per cent of the public thought the chief beneficiaries so far had been 'politicians and officials'. About a third named the vaguely defined 'mafia', which in the public mind simply meant 'criminal elements' rather than a specific criminal organisation. About one-fifth named 'the former communist nomenklatura'. But only 6 per cent named 'foreigners' and a mere 2 per cent 'ordinary citizens' (Table 2.5, Fig.2.1).

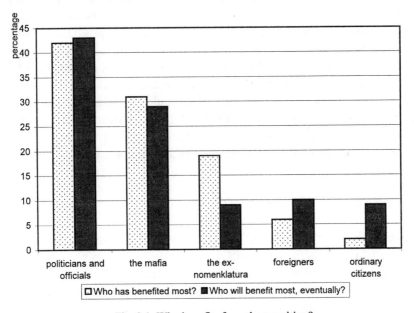

Fig. 2.1. Who benefits from the transition?

Looking to the future, the public thought that foreigners and ordinary citizens might do rather better and the former nomenklatura rather less well. But even so, only 9 per cent named ordinary citizens as the principal beneficiaries in the long run. Politicians and officials together with criminal elements still came top.

However, there was a sharp difference between Bulgaria and Ukraine where the public put the mafia ahead of 'politicians and officials', and the Czech and Slovak Republics where they put 'politicians and officials' a long way ahead of the mafia. Ironically, that may have reflected a clearer tendency amongst Czechs and Slovaks to see their politicians primarily as politicians (albeit politicians 'on the make') rather than merely as criminals-in-parliament. The head of the Ukrainian tax administration, Mykola Azarov, recently alleged that 'parliamentary deputies and their enterprises control 25 per cent of imports and 10 per cent of exports in Ukraine...failing to pay over 4 billion hryvni in taxes' in the process.[52] It was not so easy to distinguish between politicians and criminal elements (or 'mafia') there.

In Ukraine there was a public perception that the transition itself was the final criminal act of the communist regime and its officials. 'What's going on now is a lie of the first order.'(Ky-B 4) 'It is clear that [the transition] is being effected with the old Soviet methods—the same special shares, special distributions and special privileges every- where.'(Se 4) 'The former managers are now directors of banks, private commercial ones.'(Sh 4) 'Those in power are the same, but [our] life has become 100 times worse.'(Vo 1) 'Old managers remain in new struc- tures...they knew that the Soviet Union would be collapsing [and took] a combine harvester or any other machine.'(Sh 2) Meanwhile, 'we have got nothing to cultivate the land with, there is neither tractor nor com- bine.'(Sh 3) 'They have given out plots of land that are useless.'(Sh 4)

CONCLUSION: VICTIMS OF A NECESSARY TRANSITION

In summary, by the late 1990s the public was highly sceptical about the course of the transition. Citizens were extremely pessimistic about eco- nomic trends. They supported the move to a market economy in princi- ple but felt it had been handled with a mixture of incompetence and cor- ruption. They pictured themselves as the victims rather than the benefi- ciaries of the transition. Interestingly, the public did not blame the West for their problems. In the public's view the chief beneficiaries had not been foreigners but their own politicians and officials, rivalled only by their own criminal mafiosi—insofar as the public could distinguish the one from the other.

NOTES

1 Coulson, 'From Democratic Centralism to Local Democracy'. See also: Coulson, *Local Government in Eastern Europe*; Davey, 'The Czech and Slovak Republics'; Jepson, McDonnell and Mollov, 'Local Government in Bulgaria'; Campbell, 'Regional and Local Government in Ukraine'; Elander and Gustafsson, 'The Re- emergence of Local Self-Government in Central Europe'; Bennett, *Local Govern- ment in the New Europe*; Boukhalov and Ivannikov, 'Ukrainian Local Politics after Independence'; Friedgut and Hahn, *Local Power and Post-Soviet Politics*; Council

of Europe, *Structure and Operation of Local and Regional Democracy in Bulgaria, Slovakia and the Czech Republic.*

2 Baldersheim, Illner, Ofterdal, Rose and Swianiewicz, *Local Democracy and the Processes of Transformation,* 11; Elander and Gustafsson, 'The Re-emergence of Local Self-Government in Central Europe', 300.

3 Turner, Hegedűs and Tosics, *The Reform of Housing in Eastern Europe*; Soulsby and Clark 'Privatisation and the Restructuring of Enterprise, Social and Welfare Assets in the Czech Republic'.

4 Hague, Rose and Bojcun, 'Rebuilding Ukraine's Hollow State', 419.

5 Elander, 'Between Centralism and Localism', 143.

6 Illner, 'Territorial Decentralisation'.

7 Illner 'Local Democratisation', 76.

8 Grime and Duke, 'A Czech on Privatisation'.

9 Reed, 'Transition, Dysfunctionality and Change', 326.

10 Faltan and Dodder, 'Privatising the Housing Sector', 394.

11 Benacek and Zemplinerova, 'Problems and Environment of Small Businesses', 447–48; Faltan and Dodder, 'Privatising the Housing Sector', 394.

12 Khakhulina and Tuchek, 'Living Conditions in the Former Soviet Union', 34.

13 Shafik, 'Making a Market', 1149.

14 Benacek and Zemplinerova, 'Problems and Environment of Small Businesses', 442.

15 Swain, 'Agricultural Restitution', 1208.

16 Bonanno, Kuznetsov, Geletta and Hendrickson, 'To Farm or Not to Farm'.

17 Bonanno, Kuznetsov, Geletta and Hendrickson, 'To Farm or Not to Farm', 419.

18 Danglova, 'Rural Community in the Process of Socio-economic Changes'.

19 Danglova, 'Rural Community in the Process of Socio-economic Changes', 141–42.

20 Levine, 'Excuse Me…I've No Machinery', 99.

21 Grime and Duke, 'A Czech on Privatisation', 754; Siklova 'Lustration'.

22 Reed, 'Transition, Dysfunctionality and Change', 334.

23 Baldersheim, Illner, Ofterdal, Rose and Swianiewicz, *Local Democracy and the Processes of Transformation,* 116.

24 Schmitter, 'Dangers and Dilemmas of Democracy', 89.

25 EBRD, *Ten Years of Transition,* 125.

26 Transparency International, *Corruption Perception Index 1999.*

27 Hague, Rose and Bojcun, 'Rebuilding Ukraine's Hollow State', 422.

28 Potucek, 'Current Social Policy Developments', 223.

29 Miller, White and Heywood, *Values and Political Change in Post-communist Europe,* 85.

30 Illner, 'The Changing Quality of Life', 162.

31 Verheijen and Dimitrova, 'Private Interests and Public Administration', 212.

32 Verheijen and Dimitrova, 'Corruption and Unethical Behaviour', 228—quoting Huntington, 'Democracy for the Long Haul', 7.

33 Ledeneva, *An Economy of Favours,* Chapter 6.

34 Bell, 'After Ideology, Corruption', 18.

35 Kaufmann and Siegelbaum, 'Privatisation and Corruption', 424.

36 Kaufmann and Siegelbaum, 'Privatisation and Corruption', 423.

37 Kaufmann and Siegelbaum, 'Privatisation and Corruption', 422–3.

38 Meny, *The Corruption of the Republic,* 218.

39 Girling, *Corruption, Capitalism and Democracy*, 167.
40 Girling, *Corruption, Capitalism and Democracy*, viii-ix.
41 Girling, *Corruption, Capitalism and Democracy*, 4.
42 Crampton, 'The Bulgarian Elections', 562–3.
43 *Weekly Review of Bulgarian Press Coverage of Corruption*, (23–29 October 1999).
44 Marada, 'The 1998 Czech Elections', 56.
45 *RFE/RL Newsline* 4, no. 42, part 2 (29 February 2000).
46 Marada, 'The 1998 Czech Elections', 58.
47 EBRD, *Ten Years of Transition*, 213, 265, 205, 281.
48 EBRD, *Ten Years of Transition*, 73.
49 Miller, Dickson and Stoker, *Models of Local Governance*.
50 Szymanderski, 'Moral Order and Corruption', 249.
51 *USIA Opinion Analysis*, (18 February 1998) 2–3.
52 *RFE/RL Newsline* 4, no. 80, part 2 (21 April 2000).

CHAPTER 3

PUBLIC PERCEPTIONS AND PUBLIC EXPERIENCE OF OFFICIALS

We know that the public regards politicians and officials as the chief beneficiaries of the transition. But that does not tell us directly about public perceptions of how officials behave. In particular it does not tell us directly about public perceptions of how officials treat ordinary citizens, still less about citizens' personal experience of their own treatment by street-level officials.

In this chapter we explore public perspectives on the relations between officials and clients. First we consider general public perceptions of officials. We look at *public perceptions* of the 'typical behaviour' of officials in each country and at public perceptions of the trends in that behaviour since communist times. We also look at public perceptions of officials in comparison to workers in the private sector and in comparison to officials in other European countries. Secondly, we look at citizens' reports of their actual *personal experience* of dealing with officials, mainly street-level officials. We look at whether citizens felt they were treated with respect; whether they were treated fairly or unfairly; whether officials asked them for bribes; and whether, on the whole, they were satisfied with their experience of dealing with these officials.

Experience differed dramatically from perceptions. In all four countries there was a great deal of general grumbling about politicians and officials. In political debate, in the press and in gossip amongst ordinary citizens, there were widespread allegations of corruption amongst both top politicians and street-level officials. But such allegations were much less frequent in specific recollections of the personal experiences of ordinary citizens than in vague and unspecific gossip. We do find a great deal of evidence of negative experiences. But negative experiences were nowhere near as universal as negative perceptions. Moreover, the gap between the perception and experience of corruption varied cross-nationally—as did the gap we found in the previous chapter between perceptions of the national economy and trends in family income.

PUBLIC PERCEPTIONS OF POLITICIANS AND TOP GOVERNMENT OFFICIALS

The public has least direct experience of senior politicians and its criticism of them was the most severe. We asked the public whether they generally 'trusted' or 'distrusted' the press, a variety of elected and appointed officials, and the 'ordinary people you meet in everyday life'.

Members of parliament topped the list for levels of distrust in every country: on average, four-fifths distrusted their elected members of parliament. Second and third on the list of those most distrusted were elected members of local councils and (appointed) officials in state and local government offices—over three-fifths of the public distrusted both. Over half distrusted the police. Over half also distrusted 'newspapers in general' but only a third distrusted television or 'the newspaper they read most often'. Less than one-fifth distrusted 'ordinary people they met in everyday life'.

Interpersonal trust was high, but trust in elected or appointed officials was low, and trust in elected members of parliament the lowest of all.

But the distrust of politicians varied so little across our four countries that we must view it with some scepticism. Contrary to the proverb, there seems some evidence that familiarity bred trust rather than contempt. Conversely, distance and lack of direct experience seemed to inflate distrust. Hence people trusted those they met and the papers they read, while they did not trust politicians and officials whom they did not meet or papers that they did not read. Indeed the gap between trust in 'ordinary people' and politicians was much the same in post-communist Europe as it was in Britain (though trust levels are generally higher in Britain).[1] Such patterns of trust hint at actual experience being generally better than distant perceptions.

Nonetheless, perceptions of politicians were extremely negative. An overwhelming majority of the public in every country said that most of their politicians were 'mainly interested in gaining special privileges for themselves and their friends' rather than 'trying to do what they thought was best for the country (Table 3.1). 'A good half of them…look more after their own interests.'(Ho 1) 'Every one is for themselves.'(Vo 3) 'Power is necessary for money.'(Ky-B 6) 'Here politicians strive to get into the cabinet in order to gain financially.'(Zv 7) 'We have got nothing to buy a piece of bread with, and yet the comrades travel to Atlanta [for the Olympic Games]. They can afford cruises.'(Kh 3) 'They are stuffing their wallets.'(Ni 3)

Table 3.1. Perceptions of politicians

	Average	Czech Republic	Slovakia	Bulgaria	Ukraine
	%	%	%	%	%
Even though they often quarrel and make mistakes, do you feel most politicians try to do what they think is best for (your country) or are they mainly interested in gaining special privileges for themselves and their friends?					
mainly interested in gaining special privileges	80	80	84	68	87

Notes: 'Don't know', 'mixed/depends', etc. answers were recorded if given spontaneously, but never prompted; they have been excluded from the calculation of percentages.

'(Your country)' was replaced by the actual name of the country—'Ukraine', 'Bulgaria', 'Slovakia', 'the Czech Republic', as appropriate.

In Ukraine, focus-group participants raised the issue of deputies' immunity: 'Shielding yourself with the help of deputies' immunity is necessary when your pocket is full.'(Vo 1) Outside experts agree that 'granting immunity to parliamentary members has compounded the criminalisation of the Ukrainian legislature'.[2] The Ukrainian parliament had abolished immunity for elected members of local councils but resisted the abolition of immunity for its own members[3]—although it did lift the immunity of former Prime Minister Pavlo Lazarenko (by then living in the USA) in February 1999.[4] President Kuchma included the abolition of parliamentary deputies' immunity in his plans for a referendum in mid-April 2000.[5] Significantly, he argued in favour of abolishing deputies' immunity on the grounds of the 'equality' of all citizens enshrined in Article 24 of the Ukrainian constitution[6]—the very grounds on which, as we argued in Chapter 1, corruption itself should be condemned by democratic theorists. In the event, when the referendum took place on 16 April 2000, the turnout was 79 per cent, and 89 per cent of voters agreed that deputies' immunity from criminal prosecution should be abolished.[7] Just a week later, the Bulgarian Prime Minister, Ivan Kostov, pledged to introduce measures to remove the immunity of parliamentary deputies except only 'for statements made in parliament'.[8]

Table 3.2. Perceptions of declining standards in the behaviour of politicians

	Average	Czech Republic	Slovakia	Bulgaria	Ukraine
	%	%	%	%	%
Do you think that most politicians now behave better or worse than they did (under communism)?					
better now	25	27	15	46	11
worse now	56	50	65	31	77
no difference	20	23	20	24	12
better – worse	–31	–23	–50	+15	–66

Notes: 'Don't know' answers were recorded if given spontaneously, but never prompted; they have been excluded from the calculation of percentages.

The phrase '(under communism)' was replaced by 'during the Soviet period' in Ukraine; and by 'before 1989' elsewhere.

On average, two out of three citizens with a view said that 'most' politicians in their country now behaved worse than they did 'under communism'. (Table 3.2) Perceptions of declining standards were particularly high in Slovakia and Ukraine. Only the Bulgarians detected a net improvement—once again perhaps reflecting the early hopes that Bulgarians placed in the new Kostov government after public rallies, protests and riots had forced the former Socialist (BSP) government out of office. That interpretation is reinforced by USIA surveys in the fall of 1997, which also show that a plurality of Bulgarians claimed that 'political corruption' was 'no worse now than under communism' while a plurality of Czechs and Slovaks took the opposite view.[9]

An overwhelming majority in every country (averaging 85 per cent) said that their press, radio and television gave too little rather than too much coverage to corruption of every kind, whether corruption amongst their businessmen, top government officials or street-level officials. But corruption at the top provoked the greatest public anger. In every country a large majority (64 per cent on average) said corruption amongst 'top government officials' annoyed them most. Corruption amongst 'top businessmen' annoyed them least (average 13 per cent). Except in the Czech Republic, corruption amongst street-level bureaucrats was significantly more annoying (overall average 23 per cent) than amongst businessmen but significantly less annoying than amongst top politicians.

Public anger at corruption in the public sector reflects the fact that officials are public servants while businessmen are not. Officials also have more monopoly power over the lives of individual citizens than private businessmen competing with each other in the marketplace. Thus Wing Lo found wide public support for repressive measures against corruption amongst street-level civil servants in Hong Kong, but much less for similar action against corrupt millionaire businessmen. 'The public do not always feel as threatened by corrupt businessmen as they do by corrupt public servants...public-sector corruption is often related to extortion and solicitation of bribes by civil servants...[which is] far more annoying and disturbing to the daily lives of the people.'[10]

From Wing Lo's perspective it is perhaps more surprising that the public claimed to be angered more by corruption amongst top officials than by corruption amongst street-level officials. The public had relatively few direct dealings with top officials. The corruption directly experienced by most ordinary citizens most of the time was corruption amongst the street-level officials 'who deal with ordinary people', not amongst 'top government officials'. High-level public-sector corruption was something citizens heard about through the media, through hearsay, gossip or rumour, but not something from their own experience. In principle a small band of top officials could accumulate vast personal wealth without much affecting the national income, the rate of taxation, or the level of public services—provided it was limited to the very few at the very top. They might, at the same time, retain public support by enforcing honest administration at lower levels. This is after all the principle on which Europe's various monarchies—some of them still quite popular—were traditionally based, nor is it so very different from the principle on which the much admired and popular regime in Singapore is based (though it claims to be open about its very high, self-determined 'salaries'). But the problem is to prevent the corruption (or the notion of high, self-determined 'salaries') cascading downwards from the top. The view amongst the public in post-communist Europe seems to be expressed in the popular East European proverb articulated by one of our focus-group participants: 'The fish rots from the head down.'(Striy 3) In this view, even corruption at lower levels could be blamed on top officials.

The public was sufficiently annoyed by corruption at the top to claim that it would affect their votes in elections. Paradoxically, in Ukraine, where public-sector corruption angered citizens most, it seemed likely to have the least effect upon their voting choice. The numbers who said corruption would affect their vote 'not at all' rose from a mere 8 per cent in the Czech Republic, through 10 per cent in Slovakia and 15 per cent in Bulgaria, to 35 per cent in Ukraine. The relatively unstructured nature of politics in Ukraine, with very weak party identification and high levels of apathy, seems to indicate that voters in Ukraine were so disgusted with the available parties and politicians that they had switched away from voting altogether. If most or all of the available politicians are perceived to be corrupt, how can corruption affect voting choice—except insofar as it affects the choice not to vote at all?

PUBLIC PERCEPTIONS OF STREET-LEVEL OFFICIALS

In focus-group discussions attitudes towards even street-level officials were more negative than positive. For a systematic, quantitative analysis we divided each focus-group discussion into 'text units', where each 'text unit' was defined as the contribution to the discussion made by one participant before another participant intervened. Typically such 'text units' consisted of about two or three lines of text on the transcript, though they could be shorter or longer than that. We indexed all text units that mentioned officials according to whether they revealed positive or negative attitudes. Although many comments were neutral, or non-evaluative, or combined praise and criticism, there were more negative than positive comments about street-level officials. Even in the Czech Republic the balance was negative by 38 per cent to 11 per cent.

Indexing text units by whether they suggested the behaviour of officials under the post-communist regime had improved or got worse since the end of communism indicated some improvement in the Czech Republic, but only by the narrow margin of 8 per cent: 31 per cent indicated an improvement against 23 per cent who indicated a decline. Everywhere else the balance of focus-group comments indicated a turn for the worse—by margins of 20 per cent in Slovakia, 32 per cent in Bulgaria and 37 per cent in Ukraine.

In our Czech focus groups almost half the relevant text units indicated no change in the behaviour of street-level officials. 'They have not changed, have they?'(KH 7) 'Where new officials have taken over, they are often not experts, so nothing has changed.'(KH 4) 'Old structures survive...in relation to officials, those who accepted [bribes] before accept them today as well, and the newcomers have learned very quickly.'(KH 5) But other participants associated bribery more with the lack of consumer goods and services under communism than with street-level officials in the post-communist period. The main criticisms in the Czech Republic concerned inefficiency, incompetence, unhelpfulness and increasing bureaucracy rather than corruption. 'Paperwork has increased substantially.'(KH 9) 'Bureaucracy has grown and one comes into contact with officials more often now than in the past.'(Pra-A 3) 'There is more paperwork today as compared with the past...you need so many documents...we need more of these papers than in the past.'(Pra-B 7)

In Ukraine, at the other extreme, complaints about street-level officials went far beyond allegations of bureaucratic inefficiency. Certainly they included inefficiency, laziness, unhelpfulness and arrogance. 'Low-level officials exploit their authority.'(Ky-A 3) 'Nobody gives comprehensive information.'(Ky-A 5) Officials 'choose who they are going to receive...a simple problem always turns into a complicated one.'(Striy 3) 'You come and there is a chairman but no secretary, or there is a secretary but no chairman.'(Sh 4) 'You have to wait for half a day until he will look into it there.'(Sh 1) 'You sit in front of a door for two or three hours.'(Vo 1) 'He does not want to bother with it.'(Ni 2) But complaints about street-level officials in Ukraine also included extortion. 'There are decent people [amongst officials]...and it is great to deal with them...but the system lets them take bribes...encourages bribes.'(Ky-A 2) 'Bureaucrats are unjust, unless you offer a bribe.'(Sh-IDI 5) 'If it is urgent you should go with a present, and then your problem will be solved more simply, you will be treated with respect, the problem will be solved quickly, competently.'(Ky-B 2) 'Now...you may be told at every turn which sum of money, whom to give.'(Ho 1) 'If you want to solve [a problem], you have to take something along.'(Kh 3)

Moreover, citizens' explanations for the decline in standards of conduct amongst street-level officials had a quite different flavour in Ukraine from that in the Czech Republic. A few text units in Ukraine mentioned the confusion caused by rapid changes in the law. 'There is one law today, another tomorrow, a third the day after tomorrow.'(Vo 2) Some partially excused officials because their salaries or perks had declined. 'Now the economic situation is poor and the state officials are really badly paid which takes its effect on their relations with citizens.'(Ky-IDI 10) 'They had good salaries [in the past].'(Ky-B 4) 'Any street-level official [under the communist regime] could get lots of so-

cial benefits for himself.'(Ky-B 5) 'The militia [now] get a pit-
tance.'(Striy 5) 'You come to a doctor…who does not have a salary.'(Striy 4) But the most frequent explanation for declining standards
of official behaviour in Ukraine was that officials were no longer so
'afraid' as they had been under communism.

Officials had been *afraid of losing their jobs*. 'They were afraid of
losing their place.'(Ho 3) 'They were afraid of losing their position.'
(Ho 1) They had been *afraid of the Party*. 'They were punished…there
was discipline. They were afraid of the Party organisation.'(Striy 3)
'There was a Party…they were afraid of it.' (Ho 4) 'Now in comparison
with the communist regime people get worse help because at that time
control was more rigid…The Party controlled the subordinated more.
Now everybody interprets the law in the way he or she wants. Nobody is
afraid anymore.'(Ho-IDI 3) 'There was a kind of Party discipline.'(Sh 2)
Or officials had *simply been afraid* in some unspecified way. 'They were
afraid, they were just afraid.'(Sh 6) 'Maybe then they were afraid.'(Vo 1)
'Fear was at work.'(Ky-B 5) 'It was stricter before.'(Vo 5)

Table 3.3. Perceptions of trends in the behaviour of street-level officials

Now some questions about officials who deal with ordinary people and their problems in (your country). I mean officials like those you might meet in tax, housing or social security offices; in the health and education services; in passport offices, customs, the police, courts or the army; and other similar officials.	Average	Czech Republic	Slovakia	Bulgaria	Ukraine
	%	%	%	%	%
Do you feel that most of these officials treat people better or worse now than they did (under communism)?					
better	27	38	25	38	9
worse	47	34	49	31	75
no difference	25	28	26	31	16
better – worse	–20	+4	–24	+7	–66

Notes: 'Don't know', 'mixed/depends', etc. answers were recorded if given spontaneously, but never prompted; they have been excluded from the calculation of percentages.

The phrase '(your country)' was replaced by the name of the country in which the interview took place.

The phrase '(under communism)' was replaced by 'during the Soviet period' in Ukraine; and by 'before 1989' elsewhere.

Now, street-level officials were *no longer afraid.* 'They are not afraid and they do not respect the law [now].'(Ho 3) 'During the communist regime [we got] better assistance. There was more order...[officials] were afraid of something.'(Sh-IDI 2) 'There was more order in the administration, even in the use of connections. Everything was more orderly.'(Ky-IDI 10) 'They are afraid of nothing, of no one [now]. That is why there is no hope for the better.'(Kh 3) There were no more than very occasional and very weak echoes of such explanations in the Czech Republic: 'There is more of it [bribery]...the former strict conditions ruled this out, it was just a flower or a token, but now it has shifted to a financial level.' (Pra-A 5)

Our large-scale surveys also indicated public perceptions of a decline in the standards of conduct of street-level officials. (Table 3.3) By a margin of 20 per cent, on average, the public felt that the behaviour of street-level officials had deteriorated since the end of communism. The large-scale surveys also revealed perceptions of a slight improvement in the Czech Republic, a sharp decline in Slovakia and a precipitous decline in Ukraine. But they indicated more positive feelings than the focus-group discussions about the changing behaviour of officials in Bulgaria. Our Bulgarian focus-group discussions in late 1996 occurred during the unrest that preceded the change of government in Bulgaria, while our large-scale surveys in the winter of 1997–98 occurred in the more hopeful atmosphere of the post-election euphoria. Whether or not the behaviour of street-level officials in Bulgaria actually changed in that time, some of the post-election euphoria probably influenced attitudes to governance at all levels even though, rationally, it should perhaps have been restricted to evaluations of the elected government rather than extending to appointed officials.

More disturbingly, a majority of citizens in every country including Bulgaria (though less in Bulgaria than elsewhere) claimed it was now more difficult than it had been under communism to find the right official to deal with their problems, more difficult to get an official to do a favour for them and, worst of all, more difficult to get fair treatment. Once again, perceptions of change were most negative in Ukraine.

On average, however, the public was less critical of declining standards of conduct amongst street-level officials than amongst politicians. Differences between public perceptions of politicians and street-level officials are illustrated in Figure 3.1. In Ukraine, the public was very critical of both. In Bulgaria, following the recent change of government, the public was more positive about their politicians than about street-level officials. But in both the Czech and Slovak Republics the public was significantly more critical of politicians than street-level officials.

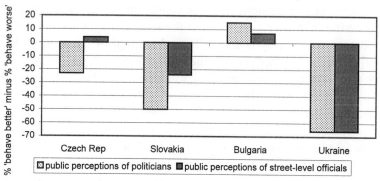

Fig. 3.1. Public perceptions of politicians and street-level officials

PUBLIC PERCEPTIONS OF COMPARATIVE CORRUPTION

On average, the public in our four post-communist countries thought their officials no better and no worse than in most other East European countries, but significantly less corrupt than in Russia. Conversely, by an average margin of 30 per cent or more, the public thought their officials were more corrupt than 'officials in Germany' and also more corrupt than 'people who worked in private businesses' within their own country. (Table 3.4)

What is striking about each public's perception of comparative corruption amongst its own country's officials is how well that fits with cross-national analyses of non-comparative corruption perceptions. During 1998–99, USIA surveys asked the public in various East and West European countries to evaluate corruption amongst their own officials. In Bulgaria, Slovakia and the Czech Republic (along with France and Italy) over two-thirds thought 'most officials' in their country took bribes, but only one-third in Germany and Britain.[11] The levels of allegations in these USIA surveys reinforce our suspicion that perceptions of corruption in Eastern Europe, as elsewhere, are grossly inflated, but they do suggest significantly lower perceptions of corruption in Germany than in Eastern Europe at the time of our surveys. Whether German officials would now be regarded, either inside or outside Germany, as quite such a benchmark of probity after the scandals surrounding Helmut Kohl's CDU (Christian Democratic Union) is another matter.

Within Eastern Europe we found sharp cross-national variations in perceptions of comparative corruption. By a large margin the Czech public thought their officials less corrupt than in most of Eastern Europe and, by a huge margin, less corrupt than in Russia. By somewhat smaller margins the Slovak public took a similar view about their officials. In Bulgaria the public felt their officials were more corrupt than in the rest of Eastern Europe but less corrupt than in Russia. Albeit by only a small margin, the public in Ukraine felt that their officials were actually more corrupt even than officials in Russia!

Table 3.4. Perceptions of comparative corruption

	Average	Czech Republic	Slovakia	Bulgaria	Ukraine
		'more – less corrupt than' comparison			
	%	%	%	%	%
Do you feel that officials in government offices in (your country) are more or less corrupt…					
than people who work in private businesses?	+35	+28	+32	+35	+45
than officials in Germany?	+30	+30	+25	+26	+37
than officials in most other East European countries?	0	–27	–15	+15	+29
than officials in Russia?	–22	–52	–36	–11	+13

Note: Since there were unusually large numbers of 'don't know' answers to these questions, they have not been excluded from the calculation of percentages. The figures show the difference between the percentages that said 'more' or 'less'.

The phrase '(your country)' was replaced by the name of the country in which the interview took place.

Once again these perceptions of comparative corruption are broadly consistent with cross-national variations in non-comparative perceptions of corruption. Although USIA surveys indicate fairly similar perceptions in Ukraine and Russia about the level of corruption in their own police, courts, parliament, government and universities, they also indicate that perceptions of corruption were generally a little higher in Ukraine.[12] Outside experts also conclude that the 'level of corruption in Ukraine surpasses that of Russia'.[13] So there seems some external corroboration for the Ukrainian public's pessimism about the comparative level of corruption in their country.

PUBLIC PERCEPTIONS OF THE NEED TO USE CONTACTS AND BRIBES

In our large-scale surveys people in all countries were inclined to suggest that even when a person 'asks an official for something to which he/she is *entitled by law*' they would probably have to approach the official 'through a contact', or 'offer something' in order 'to get a successful outcome'. Perhaps in this casual, unanchored gossip, they exaggerated the need to use contacts, presents and bribes. As we shall see later, they tended to report rather less need to use presents and bribes in their own personal experience. Nonetheless, the figures are very high and even if they are mistaken, distorted or exaggerated, such perceptions are a psychological fact. They are an important element of public opinion whether or not they accurately reflect the reality of corruption.

Table 3.5. Perceptions of the need to use contacts, presents or bribes
to obtain legal rights

	Average	Czech Republic	Slovakia	Bulgaria	Ukraine
	%	%	%	%	%
Suppose a person asks an official for something to which he/she is entitled by law. To get a successful outcome, is it likely (rather than *not likely*) that he/she would...					
approach official through a contact?	85	76	87	86	90
offer a small present?	79	62	80	84	91
offer money or an expensive present?	65	44	62	72	81

Note: 'Don't know', 'mixed/depends', etc. answers were recorded if given spontaneously, but never prompted; they have been excluded from the calculation of percentages.

Between 76 and 90 per cent in different countries said it was more 'likely' than not that a person seeking no more than their legal entitlements would nonetheless have to approach an official 'through a contact'. Between 62 and 91 per cent said it was likely that a 'small present' would be necessary; and between 44 and 81 per cent said it was likely that 'money or an expensive present' would be necessary. (Table 3.5) Contacts, presents and bribes were all considered most necessary in Ukraine and least necessary in the Czech Republic. The difference was most striking on the question of bribes: the difference between perceptions in Ukraine and the Czech Republic grew from 14 per cent on contacts, through 29 per cent on small presents, to 37 per cent on the need to give 'money or an expensive present'.

Expectations varied across different kinds of state official. (Table 3.6) At the top of the list, an average of 81 per cent in our surveys said it was more likely than not that clients 'seeking something to which they were entitled by law' would 'have to offer money, a present or a favour' to 'officials in state ministries'. 'They would expect something at the tax office.'(Do 6) 'Yes, definitely at the tax office.'(Do 7)

Table 3.6. Perceptions of the need to offer gifts to obtain legal rights
from different officials

	Average	Czech Republic	Slovakia	Bulgaria	Ukraine
	%	%	%	%	%
Now think of a person seeking something to which he/she is *entitled by law*. Is it likely (rather than *not likely*) that such a person would have to offer money, a present or a favour to get help from each of the following—I mean offer more than the official charge?					
officials in state ministries	81	70	85	82	87
hospital doctors	81	47	89	93	94
customs officials	76	53	71	92	86
court officials	72	44	75	80	87
members of parliament	71	54	74	74	80
university staff	69	34	78	73	89
officials in local government offices	68	49	58	79	87
the police	67	42	64	72	89
elected officials on local councils	61	44	52	69	80
people working in the private sector	55	42	55	63	61
schoolteachers	40	10	36	45	68
Average	67	44	67	75	83

Note: 'Don't know', 'mixed/depends', etc. answers were recorded if given spontaneously, but never prompted; they have been excluded from the calculation of percentages.

Rows arranged in descending order of average likelihood.

The need to bribe hospital staff tied for top place. Respondents in USIA surveys across six post-communist countries in Central Europe also rated hospitals as the most corrupt of 13 institutions, well ahead of privatisation agencies, the police, the government, courts, parliament, local government or universities.[14] '[If you do not pay] they say "wait, die if you wish" and there is nobody to look at you.'(Ku 7) 'They look at your hands when you enter [a hospital]...Once you had to bang the door with your leg because your hands were full. And now what you have to carry is a small envelope with some money enclosed in it.'(So-A 5) 'I think that doctors will take from old ladies. Even an egg is accept- able, everything. A jar of something. Antiques.'(Ol 4) 'Though they have [by law] to do it for free, they do everything for money.'(Se 1) 'People say that to get treatment for free is to get treatment in vain. We pay for it twice. The first time the money is subtracted from our wages as a tax and the second time you need to pay at the hospital.'(Sh 5) 'It is not enough to pay the person who performs the operation. You pay the head nurse who does the instruments. You pay the anaesthesiologist— this is absolutely necessary so that she does not put you to sleep finally and fully.'(Kh 1)

In our survey, customs officials, court officials, members of parlia- ment, university staff, local government officials and the police (in that order) followed hospital doctors. An average of 69 per cent in our sur- veys said it was more likely than not that clients would have to offer money, a present or a favour to university staff. 'There are those who have bought their university degrees.'(Ku 3) 'You must know the fee of the lecturers when you go to university. Most lecturers have fixed their fees. If you don't know how much their fee is, at least you must offer some money.'(So-B 1) 'Everybody knows that to get into university he has to give something.'(Ho 6) 'She knew someone there who knew the dean. Money was even involved.'(NZ 8) On average, 67 per cent said it would be necessary to bribe the police. 'Even the police accept bribes.'(Ho 1) 'In general, I would say that the state police is a clear ex- ample of the extent of corruption.'(Br-B 3) Traffic police were specially prominent in focus-group discussions. 'Professional drivers know how much money they should give to traffic policemen.'(Ya 4) 'If you do not want them to draw up a statement against you, you must pay.'(Ya 3) 'As soon as the traffic police receive their licence...they stand in the roads and collect money.'(Sh 2)

Schoolteachers came at the bottom of the list. They were the only public employees to come lower than private-sector workers. On aver- age, only 40 per cent of the public thought some offer of a gift to schoolteachers would be necessary, though that ranged from just 10 per cent in the Czech Republic up to 68 per cent in Ukraine.

Taking all these officials together, perceptions varied sharply across different countries. In the Czech Republic, at one extreme, less than half thought such offers were likely to be necessary, but in Slovakia two-thirds, in Bulgaria three-quarters and in Ukraine five-sixths.

PUBLIC PERCEPTIONS OF OFFICIALS' MOTIVES AND FEELINGS

We asked what was 'the main reason why officials take money or presents'. Was it because 'officials are greedy' or because 'the government does not pay officials properly'? Or was it perhaps because their clients were 'desperate to buy favours' from them? One focus-group participant in Ukraine answered: 'We ourselves are guilty.'(Kh 3) That focus-group participant was not typical, however. In our large-scale surveys people in Ukraine most frequently blamed *greedy officials*. (A survey of 323 directors of Russian enterprises reached the same conclusion.[15]) But in Bulgaria, the public most frequently blamed *the government*, and in Slovakia and the Czech Republic the public most frequently blamed bribery on *clients trying to buy favours*. (Table 3.7) Even in the Czech Republic, however, only half the public absolved the state by blaming the people. Half the people in the Czech and Slovak Republics, and far more in Bulgaria and Ukraine, blamed either the state or its street-level officials.

Table 3.7. Perceptions of the main cause of bribery

	Average	Czech Republic	Slovakia	Bulgaria	Ukraine
	%	%	%	%	%
Which comes closest to your view? The main reason why officials take money or presents is…					
the officials are greedy?	39	37	30	39	48
the government does not pay officials properly?	25	12	19	47	23
the people are desperate to buy favours?	36	51	50	14	30

Note: 'Don't know', 'mixed/depends', etc. answers were recorded if given spontaneously, but never prompted; they have been excluded from the calculation of percentages.

Why might officials be more willing to accept presents and bribes than under communism? Remarkably few of the public responded to this question by volunteering the comment that officials were *not* more willing to accept gifts now than they had been under communism. The most popular explanation was that their clients no longer knew where to complain (47 per cent). In the past, as they told us in focus-group discussions, they could complain about officials to the Communist Party. The Party had played the role of ombudsman. Indeed, another 25 per cent of the public attributed officials' increased willingness to accept gifts specifically to the fact that they were no longer controlled by the Communist Party. (Table 3.8) Inadequate salaries came a clear third on the public's list of likely explanations (18 per cent). The same pattern of explanation recurred, with slight differences of emphasis, in every country—except in Bulgaria where there was an unusual level of sympathy for badly paid officials.

Table 3.8. Why the public thinks officials are more willing to take gifts now

	Average	Czech Republic	Slovakia	Bulgaria	Ukraine
	%	%	%	%	%
Here are some reasons why officials might be more willing to accept money or presents now than (under communism). Which do you feel is the most important?					
people no longer know where to make a complaint	49	52	61	45	39
officials are no longer controlled by the Communist Party	25	31	25	13	33
officials are so badly paid now	18	11	10	37	15
officials are *not* more willing to accept money now	8	7	5	6	13

Notes: 'Don't know', 'mixed/depends', etc. answers were recorded if given spontaneously, but never prompted; they have been excluded from the calculation of percentages.

The phrase '(under communism)' was replaced by 'during the Soviet period' in Ukraine; and by 'before 1989' elsewhere.

Why might officials be less willing to accept gifts now than under communism? This time, four times as many respondents (32 per cent instead of 8 per cent) rejected the premise on which our question was based. (Table 3.9) Only the Czech public seemed at all comfortable with the implication that officials were less willing to take gifts than they had been under the communist regime. The most popular explanation of why officials might be less willing to accept gifts was that their clients were no longer afraid to complain (39 per cent). Only half as many attributed it to the replacement of old officials with 'new blood', and only a miserable 7 per cent attributed any possible improvement in the behaviour of street-level officials to the control exercised by democratically elected politicians.

Table 3.9. Why the public thinks officials are less willing to take gifts now

	Average	Czech Republic	Slovakia	Bulgaria	Ukraine
	%	%	%	%	%
Here are some reasons why officials might be less willing to accept money or presents now than (under communism). Which do you feel is the most important?					
people are no longer afraid to complain about officials	39	56	37	29	34
officials are *not* less willing to accept money now	32	14	29	53	31
many officials have been replaced by new officials	22	24	27	15	23
officials are now controlled by elected politicians	7	6	7	3	12

Notes: 'Don't know', 'mixed/depends', etc. answers were recorded if given spontaneously, but never prompted; they have been excluded from the calculation of percentages.

The phrase '(under communism)' was replaced by 'during the Soviet period' in Ukraine; and by 'before 1989' elsewhere.

Table 3.10. Public perceptions of officials' feelings about taking bribes

	Average		Czech Republic		Slovakia		Bulgaria		Ukraine	
	%	%	%	%	%	%	%	%	%	%
A: Suppose an official accepted money or a present, would that official be most likely to feel…										
B: But if that official thought very few other officials accepted these things, would that official then be most likely to feel…										
	A	(B)	A	(B)	A	(B)	A	(B)	A	(B)
happy?	65	(31)	48	(17)	59	(21)	81	(54)	72	(32)
worried?	21	(41)	35	(49)	22	(43)	9	(17)	17	(56)
ashamed?	12	(24)	14	(31)	15	(29)	10	(26)	9	(8)
angry?	2	(4)	3	(3)	4	(7)	1	(2)	2	(4)

Note: 'Don't know', 'mixed/depends', etc. answers were recorded if given spontaneously, but never prompted; they have been excluded from the calculation of percentages.

A large majority of the public (65 per cent) thought those officials who 'accepted money or a present' would be most likely to feel 'happy' about it. (Table 3.10) Only a fifth thought such officials would feel 'worried' and only one in eight that they would feel 'ashamed'.

Less than a third of the public thought that bribe-taking officials would still feel 'happy' if they felt their behaviour was unusual (i.e. that 'very few other officials accepted these things'). Fully 41 per cent of the public thought bribe takers in that situation would feel 'worried', and 24 per cent that they would feel 'ashamed'. However, public perceptions of the chances that officials would feel ashamed, even in these circumstances, ranged down from a maximum of 31 per cent in the Czech Republic to a mere 8 per cent in Ukraine. The Ukrainian public felt that if bribe-taking officials were convinced that their colleagues did not take bribes, they would feel very much more 'worried' than they do now, but scarcely any more 'ashamed'. In this respect, as in others, fear rather than shame characterised Ukrainians' views about their street-level officials.

PUBLIC EXPERIENCE OF DEALING WITH OFFICIALS

One of our recurrent findings was the difference between perceptions and experience. Questions about experience have to be asked with care. Questions about experience are far more specific and therefore somewhat more sensitive than questions about perceptions. They involve confessions as well as allegations. They are inevitably intrusive. So in our interviews we turned to questions of personal experience only after a long introduction of over a hundred other questions had established a degree of rapport between respondents and interviewers.

Philip Coulter alleges that studies of bureaucratic encounters have often been invalidated by 'Type I' or 'false negative' errors, in which respondents fail to recall the fact that they have been in contact with an official. (Claims that respondents contacted an official when they did not, 'Type II' errors, are less frequent and less important according to Coulter.)

'Misinterpretation of the term "local public official" or its equivalent can induce such faulty recall.'[16] To avoid this problem we aided recall and effectively defined the term 'official' in the context of this study by taking respondents through a check-list. Our battery of questions went as follows:

We have talked about officials in general. But now I want you to think about your own or your family's personal experiences of dealing with officials in the last few years—let's say approximately the last four or five years.

In the last few years, which of the following did these personal experiences involve: health problems; education; tax; official contracts; pensions or other benefits; unemployment; privatisation or restitution; customs; services such as electricity, gas or water; passports (internal or external); housing problems; the police; court officials; other officials?

In terms of the frequency with which the public reported such dealings, health care and public utilities (gas, water, electricity etc.) topped the list. Pensions, tax and official certificates came next. They were followed by problems with passports and identity documents, unemployment, education and housing, and finally by privatisation, the police, courts and customs. But our ulterior motive was not really to quantify these different kinds of experience. Rather, it was simply to remind people, in a natural but effective way, of the many contacts they were likely to have had with officials of one kind or another, and thus to provide an adequate 'frame' for subsequent questions about the nature of those contacts.

After this long list of reminders we put a summary question: 'How often have you or your family had to deal with officials in the last few years—frequently, occasionally, rarely or never?' Very few said they or their families had never dealt with officials in recent years—except in Ukraine where the figure rose to 12 per cent and may indicate some deliberate avoidance of contact with officials. (Outside Ukraine the figure averaged 3 per cent) Nonetheless, even in Ukraine the vast majority said they had dealt with officials and were therefore in a position to tell us about their personal experiences if they chose to do so.

EXPERIENCE OF BEING TREATED WITH RESPECT

One measure of the respect accorded to citizens is whether they felt that the officials they dealt with had treated them 'as equals'—that is, as the equals of the officials, not merely as equal to other clients (a very important distinction in authoritarian and post-authoritarian countries). On average, just under a third said the officials they met 'rarely or never' treated them as equals. The figure rose from 22 per cent in the Czech Republic to 47 per cent in Ukraine, with Slovakia and Bulgaria in the middle—though Slovaks complained more than Bulgarians. (Table 3.11)

Table 3.11. Experience of being treated with respect

	Average	Czech Republic	Slovakia	Bulgaria	Ukraine
	%	%	%	%	%
How often did these officials treat you or your family as equals?					
usually	37	52	32	40	23
sometimes	32	27	37	36	30
rarely or never	31	22	31	24	47

Note: 'Don't know', 'mixed/depends', etc. answers were recorded if given spontaneously, but never prompted; they have been excluded from the calculation of percentages.

EXPERIENCE OF FAVOURABLE TREATMENT

Favours often consisted of getting something done faster than could reasonably be expected. To achieve this, citizens often paid (or had to pay) what public administration experts call 'speed money'. 'If I pay some extra money they have it ready for me in an instant…an example, I need an extract from the land register and I know they have fixed terms but I need it today.' (HK 4) 'He has a big pile of work accumulated and I need something done faster.'(Ni 3) 'Just to make the bureaucratic machine work faster.'(Striy 4) 'Some [medical] examinations could be speeded up.'(HK 4) 'Just after closing time there was this other guy and he says, "Look miss, I will pay you for half an hour of work."'(Ol 2) 'In the passport department they say, "Do you want to get this document faster?"'(Ho 1)

Some favours involved avoiding legal costs in various ways. 'I forgot to hand in my tax return by May 3rd, and they, as friends, wrote April 29th.'(Ol 4) 'For a speed of 165 km/h they first threatened legal proceedings, then it went down to a 2,000 crown fine on the spot and finally it changed to 500 crowns which I gave them very quickly.'(KH 8) Similarly, 'I paid 200 crowns knowing that it could have been 800.'(Pra-B 3) 'I go for a preventative examination twice a year and since at my age I am only allowed to go once, I always bring them coffee and the dentist turns a blind eye to it and does not charge me anything.'(Pra-A 6) 'If you go through the chief then there would be an official sum of money, and if you talk it over with the secretary, well…'(Ky-B 1) 'The customs officers saw that we had alcohol…we said, "Did no one tell you about us?"'(Ho 4)

Other favours involved something more than that. A tradesman told us: 'When I tender for a job...I need a friend [in the office] who can hold jobs for me.'(Ol 2) 'Everybody knows that to get into university he has to give something.'(Ho 6) 'Money...to guarantee [university] admission.'(Sh 6) 'Is your son getting bad [school] grades?...well if you bring something...'(Kh 3) 'That girl got an "excellent" because...'(Ky-B 5) 'You can even get your foreign passport in a week...without changing this old [internal] passport for the [new] Ukrainian one...there is a law...until you change your [internal] passport to the [new] Ukrainian one, it is impossible to get your foreign passport without a bottle of cognac and a box of sweets.'(Ky-B 1)

All citizens in a democratic state have a right to fair and equal treatment by officials—reflecting their equality of status as citizens. But it is more difficult on grounds of democratic equality to justify 'favourable' treatment. Difficult, but not impossible. Specially favourable treatment for those with special needs (the poor, people with a specially urgent problem etc.) can be justified on grounds of equity. But specially favourable treatment for those with special wants, special greed or special avarice cannot.

Table 3.12. Experience of 'favourable' treatment

	Average	Czech Republic	Slovakia	Bulgaria	Ukraine
	%	%	%	%	%
How often did these officials give you or your family favourable treatment?					
usually or sometimes	28	35	37	14	26
rarely	30	37	36	26	22
never	42	28	27	60	52

Note: 'Don't know', 'mixed/depends', etc. answers were recorded if given spontaneously, but never prompted; they have been excluded from the calculation of percentages.

Significantly, within every country our large-scale surveys reveal that those who reported their income as 'fair' or 'good' said they got 'specially favourable' treatment more often than those who reported their income as 'not enough to survive on' or 'only just enough'. 'Specially favourable' treatment was not in fact directed towards those with 'special needs' but to those with better incomes. So perhaps it is reassuring that only a minority anywhere said they 'usually' or even 'sometimes' got 'specially favourable' treatment. (Table 3.12) Indeed, the fact that 35 per cent in the Czech Republic 'usually or sometimes' got 'specially favourable' treatment is too high for good governance! (Within the Czech Republic the figure rose steadily from only 24 per cent amongst those with incomes 'not enough to survive on', up to 40 per cent amongst those with an income sufficient for a 'good standard of living'.)

EXPERIENCE OF FAIR (OR UNFAIR) TREATMENT

Although the stories about favours catch our attention, most of our focus-group discussions did not revolve around obtaining favours. Indexing text units according to whether the citizen appeared to be seeking an entitlement (fair treatment) or a favour showed that Czech discussions focused more on ways to get favourable rather than merely fair treatment—by a margin of 11 per cent. But by margins of between 25 and 31 per cent everywhere else, focus-group discussions focused more on the minimum objective of obtaining fair rather than favourable treatment.

On average, less than half the respondents in our large-scale surveys said they had 'usually' been treated fairly—ranging from two-thirds in the Czech Republic, through half in Slovakia and just over a third in Bulgaria, down to a fifth in Ukraine. Conversely, the numbers that said they had 'rarely or never' been treated 'fairly' rose from a mere 8 per cent in the Czech Republic to 39 per cent in Ukraine. (Table 3.13, Fig. 3.2)

Table 3.13. Experience of 'fair' treatment

	Average	Czech Republic	Slovakia	Bulgaria	Ukraine
	%	%	%	%	%
How often did these officials give you or your family fair treatment?					
usually	44	66	51	38	20
sometimes	37	26	37	44	42
rarely or never	19	8	12	18	39

Note: 'Don't know', 'mixed/depends', etc. answers were recorded if given spontaneously, but never prompted; they have been excluded from the calculation of percentages.

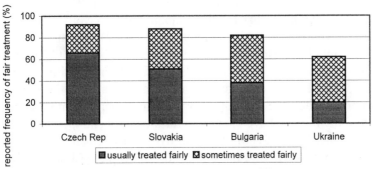

Fig. 3.2. The public's actual experience of fair treatment

EXPERIENCE OF EXTORTION

Direct personal experience of extortion by corrupt officials was extensive even if not always frequent. 'Sometimes it happens that an official who you visit can tell you approximately in what form he prefers to receive.'(Sh 2) That was particularly true in hospitals and surgeries. 'They tell you right away that you will need that much for that, and that much for that, and that much for surgery.'(Ky-A 1) 'Nowadays doctors in hospitals openly name the amount of payment for each procedure, for delivery and so on.'(Sh 5) 'The doctor asked why you did not bring anything, no milk, no sour cream, nothing.'(Ni 5) 'Our mother was going to have surgery and the surgeon said that she had to give so much to the surgeon, so much to the neuropathologist, so much to the anaesthesiologist, and so much to the assistant. He directly said how much.'(Ho 4) 'They told me straight out.'(Kh 5) 'There they say loud and clear, how much for what.'(Kh 3) 'The doctor said they should settle the delivery with the midwife. The fee of the midwife was 15,000 levs, whereas the fee of the doctor was 30,000 levs. That was last year, this is what is taking place in our hospital.'(Ya 6) 'They say what is the price of each thing.'(Se 1) 'I needed an operation…it would, they said, cost fifty dollars…but when I went in she looked at me, all very pleasantly, and then said "It'll cost a hundred dollars"…It's already gone up!'(Ky-A 2)

But participants in our focus-group discussions also reported direct requests from other officials, outside the health service. 'I faced it myself in the notary's office…if you haven't brought anything you will probably sit there for three days minimum if not three weeks…I have been there five or six days. Until you buy something and bring it there, you are given no attention and no service.'(Vo 5) 'The official said: "Give me 500,000 so that I make a labour card for you"—and I never heard that you must pay for a labour card!'(Vo 2) 'The housing office said we could have had a flat but only if we had given 30,000 crowns— that is 30,000 crowns to the officials there...My husband had started a business.'(Zv 1) 'My daughter was raped a year ago, at the age of 17. Three months ago she was taken away again. When I went to the police they told me I had to have 2,000 levs for the petrol and then we could go search for her.'(Stral 5) 'My husband lives in Belarus now...I have not lived with him for five years. I went to the People's Court to fight for something and they told me: "Let's start looking for him—but you have to pay for it."'(Vo 3) 'In accordance with the Law of Restitution, friends of mine...are entitled to the property [but the municipality would not hand it over]...So they decided to contact their MP. The MP found the guts and told them how much it would cost them for the favour...10 per cent of the cost of the property.'(Ya 4)

More subtly—and more safely for them—officials could convey their expectations or demands by hints, by complaints about their workload, or by comments about the special efforts they are making. 'My dentist told me: "If you insist on being treated here, I want to tell you that we are short of materials. But I can fix up your tooth...Just opposite the polyclinic is my private dental surgery"—So I decided to spend some of my money on my tooth and have it better treated.'(Ya 6) 'Officials did not say anything directly, but they were making hints.'(Striy-IDI 5) 'In the case involving the militia it was their hints that made me do it.'(Ho-IDI 4) 'One police officer...not very explicitly, but clearly enough, named a price.'(So-IDI 4) 'I think every governmental official from top to bottom is likely to expect a present.'(So-B 2)

In our large-scale surveys we asked: 'Did an official ever ask you or your family directly for money or a present, or not ask directly but seem to expect something?' Less than half said it had never happened to them. Only 6 per cent said they had been asked directly but another 51 per cent had been given the clear impression that the official wanted something, without being 'asked directly'. Overt demands were most frequent in Bulgaria and Ukraine, while hints and impressions seemed most frequent in Slovakia.

Hints and expectations could mean more than mere 'body-language'. 'Bureaucrats propose to do it unofficially, mentioning the difficulties of solving the problem.'(Ky-IDI 9) 'I got refusals because I could not afford to pay.'(Stral-IDI 2) 'For each paper you have to pay illegally, then they find the right forms, and no more refusals. Bureaucrats treat us like puppets. Extort a lot.'(Kh-IDI 5) Over half the public in our surveys reported that, in their personal experience, officials had 'made unnecessary problems in order to get money or a present for solving them' (Table 3.14), while 29 per cent reported that this had happened to them 'more than rarely'. That figure rose from 19 per cent in the Czech Republic to 42 per cent in Ukraine.

Table 3.14. Experience of extortion

	Average	Czech Republic	Slovakia	Bulgaria	Ukraine
	%	%	%	%	%
In these last few years, did an official ever ask you or your family directly for money or a present, or not ask directly but seem to expect something?					
asked directly	6	2	4	7	11
seemed to expect	51	44	64	39	56
neither	43	54	32	54	33
How often did these officials make unnecessary problems for you or your family in order to get money or a present for solving them?					
usually or sometimes	29	19	30	24	42
rarely	25	25	27	25	25
never	46	56	44	52	33

Note: 'Don't know', 'mixed/depends', etc. answers were recorded if given spontaneously, but never prompted; they have been excluded from the calculation of percentages.

On both indicators extortion seemed least frequent in the Czech Republic and most frequent in Ukraine. More surprisingly, for those like Huntington who believe there is a single cultural fault-line dividing Catholic from Orthodox and Muslim Europe, extortion seemed more prevalent in Slovakia than in Bulgaria (on both indicators).

THE MOST FREQUENT OR MOST ANNOYING PROBLEMS WHEN DEALING WITH STREET-LEVEL OFFICIALS

While the public may have regarded corrupt officials as a problem and a disgrace, it was not necessarily the most important problem they faced in their personal dealings with officials. Ill-treatment by officials need not involve corruption, if we define 'corruption' narrowly as the giving and taking of presents, bribes and 'unofficial' payments. Officials could ill-treat and annoy citizens by being rude, lazy, incompetent, capricious, unhelpful, uncommunicative, inaccessible (because of restricted office hours, for example) or under-resourced—and no doubt much else be-sides—as well as by being corrupt. Unsatisfactory, and even unfair, treatment does not, by itself, imply corrupt officials. Conversely, we shall leave until later chapters the question of whether corruption, by itself, implies unsatisfactory treatment.

We asked explicitly which of four problems with officials had been the 'most frequent' and the 'most annoying' in the personal experience of our respondents over the last few years. Was it officials who 'wanted money or presents', or officials who were 'incapable' or 'lazy', or who 'did not provide enough information'? All of these criticisms had emerged from our focus-group discussions.

Uninformative officials had caused the most frequent problems (45 per cent) and the greatest annoyance (38 per cent). In focus-group dis-cussions participants with lower levels of education in particular had complained that they did not receive sufficient information from offi-cials. 'Officials are unable to explain the new legislation and they them-selves do not know what to do.'(Pra-A 3) 'When you know your rights, you know how to use them. We should know our rights but who is go-ing to tell us?'(Te 4) Incompetent officials came next both in terms of causing frequent problems (31 per cent) and in terms of the public an-noyance that they caused (35 per cent). In focus-group discussions par-ticipants with a higher level of education had complained especially about incompetence. 'Every organisation is headed by somebody not qualified enough to run it...they got on the job just like that, without any preparation for the activities they are supposed to perform.'(Ku 5) 'Most officials are not competent for the positions they occupy.'(So-A 1) 'They are not sufficiently qualified.'(Br-A 7) 'I think that the people there have absolutely no knowledge of how they should work. They are simply there and that is all.'(Zv 2) 'The problem is due to the turnover of staff...an entirely new situation occurred here after the revolu-tion.'(Pra-B 2)

Lazy officials came further down the list and officials who wanted money or presents came last. (Table 3.15, Fig. 3.3)

Corruption, therefore, was one problem but it was not the only prob-lem. Very few cited it as either the most frequent or the most annoying problem in the Czech or Slovak Republics, just 10 per cent in Bulgaria, and only 22 per cent in Ukraine. Even in Ukraine, more of the public cited uninformative or incompetent officials than corrupt officials as the cause of their most frequent and most annoying problems. Corrupt officials were clearly a significantly annoying problem in day-to-day dealings with officials in Ukraine, but, even there, they were not the only annoying problem and not even the most annoying.

Table 3.15. The most annoying problems in the public's experience

	Average	Czech Republic	Slovakia	Bulgaria	Ukraine
	%	%	%	%	%
In your actual experience and that of your family in the last few years, which of these made you most angry? Officials who…					
did not provide enough information	38	48	45	35	23
were incapable	35	33	35	35	37
were lazy	18	16	14	20	20
wanted money or presents	10	4	6	10	21

Note: 'Don't know', 'mixed/depends', etc. answers were recorded if given spontaneously, but never prompted; they have been excluded from the calculation of percentages. An average of 15 per cent reported no problems. They have also been excluded.

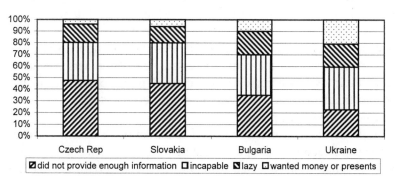

Fig. 3.3. The most annoying problems in actual dealings with officials

At the other extreme, in the Czech Republic our evidence suggests that despite public perceptions about corruption in general, corrupt officials had very little impact on actual day-to-day interactions between citizens and officials. Czechs were annoyed with street-level officials, but they were annoyed far more frequently by other aspects of these officials' behaviour than by corruption.

PUBLIC SATISFACTION WITH STREET-LEVEL OFFICIALS

Surprisingly, perhaps, in the light of many of our other survey findings, twice as many were satisfied as dissatisfied with their personal treatment at the hands of officials. (Table 3.16) However, an unusually large number of mixed, neutral or conditional responses were volunteered to this question even though such answers were not invited—18 per cent on average, rising to 28 per cent in Ukraine. This seems a reasonable response to a single question about many personal experiences of interactions with officials. On average, just over half the public found their experiences with officials broadly satisfactory, just over a quarter found them broadly unsatisfactory, and the remainder looked back on their experiences with mixed feelings. We should stress that it was the number of unprompted 'mixed/depends' answers that was unusually large, not the number of unprompted 'don't know' answers, which was in fact no higher than usual. The public was neither unable nor unwilling to answer the question. Many simply insisted on reporting mixed feelings, based no doubt upon mixed experiences.

As might be expected from answers to the detailed questions about the behaviour of street-level officials, the public in Ukraine was much less satisfied than elsewhere. Almost equal numbers were satisfied (39 per cent) as dissatisfied (33 per cent). Perhaps the surprise is that the Czech public was not markedly more satisfied than others. By any criterion, their own reports clearly indicated much better treatment by Czech officials. But perhaps that simply raised the standard of expectation among the Czech public.

However, there was a strong and remarkably consistent correlation between satisfaction and type of treatment. Within each country varying levels of satisfaction reflected variations in the quality of treatment and not simply variations in willingness to tolerate ill-treatment. Satisfaction correlated very strongly and consistently with experience of 'fair treatment' ($r = 0.50$ on average) and only a little less strongly with being treated with respect 'as equals' ($r = 0.43$ on average). But it correlated very much less strongly with experience of 'specially favourable' treatment ($r = 0.22$ on average)—as indeed it should in a democratic culture! (Table 3.17)

Conversely, dissatisfaction correlated with explicit or implicit attempts to solicit bribes, especially if the official made 'unnecessary problems' in order to get them (r = 0.36 on average). These correlations were less strong than the correlation between satisfaction and fair treatment, however. Of course, as we have argued repeatedly, extortion was not the only form of unfair treatment. Moreover, correlations with attempted extortion, unlike those with fair treatment, varied quite sharply across the four countries in our survey. They were significantly less strong in Ukraine than in the Czech Republic. Thus Czech sensitivities to extortion were clearly much more acute than in Ukraine—even though Ukrainian sensitivities to what they judged to be 'unfair' treatment were almost as acute as in the Czech Republic.

Table 3.16. Satisfaction with experience of dealing with officials

	Average	Czech Republic	Slovakia	Bulgaria	Ukraine
	%	%	%	%	%
On the whole, were your personal experiences of dealing with officials in the last few years satisfactory or unsatisfactory?					
satisfactory	55	61	61	58	39
neither/depends	18	16	15	15	28
unsatisfactory	27	24	25	27	33
net balance: satisfactory – unsatisfactory	+28	+37	+36	+31	+6

Note: 'Don't know' answers were recorded if given spontaneously, but never prompted; they have been excluded from the calculation of percentages. Usually we have also excluded spontaneously given 'mixed/depends' answers from percentage calculations but there were an unusually large number of them in answers to this question.

Simple patterns of percentages illustrate this point. On average, the rate of satisfaction varied from 90 per cent amongst those who felt they had 'usually' been treated fairly, down to just 23 per cent amongst those who felt they had 'rarely or never' been treated fairly—a difference of 67 per cent. The impact of unfair treatment was only a little higher than that in the Czech Republic and only a little lower elsewhere. In every country, the impact of unfair treatment was at least 62 per cent. (Table 3.18)

Table 3.17. Correlation between public satisfaction and experience

	Average	Czech Republic	Slovakia	Bulgaria	Ukraine
	r x 100	r x 100	r x 100	r x 100	r x 100
Correlation between 'satisfaction'…					
and 'fair 'treatment	50	54	49	47	51
and treated 'with respect as equals'	43	46	41	44	41
and 'specially favourable' treatment	22	28	24	13	23
and 'official made unnecessary problems'	−36	−45	−46	−28	−23
and 'official asked for, or expected, a bribe'	−21	−33	−19	−19	−13

Note: r x 100 is (Pearson) correlation coefficient times 100.

Table 3.18. Public satisfaction—by frequency of fair treatment and extortion

	Average	Czech Republic	Slovakia	Bulgaria	Ukraine
	% satisfied	% satisfied	% satisfied	% satisfied	% satisfied
By how often respondent had received fair treatment…					
if 'rarely or never'	23	11	30	25	26
if 'sometimes'	58	46	53	68	64
if 'usually'	90	88	92	89	89
impact of *unfair* treatment on satisfaction	−67	−77	−62	−64	−63
By how often officials made unnecessary problems in order to get money or a present for solving them…					
if 'sometimes' or 'usually'	40	31	41	46	43
if 'rarely'	70	71	73	70	67
if 'never'	80	86	89	79	64
impact of extortion on satisfaction	−40	−55	−48	−33	−21

Note: 'Don't know', 'mixed/depends', etc. answers were recorded if given spontaneously, but never prompted; they have been excluded from the calculation of percentages. An unusually large number gave 'mixed/depends' answers to the satisfaction question.

But a similar calculation shows that the impact of attempted extortion averaged only 40 per cent and also that its impact varied cross-nationally—from a maximum of 55 per cent in the Czech Republic down to a minimum of only 21 per cent in Ukraine.

CONCLUSION: EXTREMELY NEGATIVE PERCEPTIONS, MODERATELY NEGATIVE EXPERIENCES

Public perceptions of officials were extremely negative. On average, two-thirds of the public thought it more likely than not that a citizen seeking no more than their legal entitlements would have to offer a favour or bribe to an official. Over four-fifths thought it more likely than not that the citizen would have to bribe an official in a state ministry or a doctor in a hospital. Overwhelmingly, the public thought their officials more corrupt than officials in Germany and more corrupt than people who worked in the private sector within their own country. In the public's view, the behaviour of officials had deteriorated since the end of communism.

But although citizens' actual experience of dealing with street-level officials was also negative, it was far less negative than their perceptions. Not far short of half had 'usually' been treated fairly (ranging from 66 per cent in the Czech Republic down to 20 per cent in Ukraine, however) and only a fifth had 'rarely or never' received fair treatment. Extortion was neither the most frequent nor the most annoying cause of actual problems in dealing with street-level officials.

Over half (ranging from 61 per cent in the Czech Republic down to 39 per cent in Ukraine, however) were positively satisfied with their personal experience of dealing with street-level officials in recent years.

NOTES

1 Miller, *Alternatives to Freedom*, 39.
2 Shelley, 'Organised Crime and Corruption in Ukraine', 658.
3 *Corruption Watch* 1, no. 17 (28 October 1998).
4 *Corruption Watch* 2, no. 5(26) (3 March 1999).
5 *RFE/RL Newsline* 4, no. 18, part 2 (26 January 2000).
6 *Vinnychyna* (18 December 1998), quoted in *Corruption Watch* 1, no. 1(22) (6 January 1999).
7 *RFE/RL Newsline* 4, no. 76, part 2 (17 April 2000).
8 *RFE/RL Newsline* 4, no. 81, part 2 (25 April 2000).
9 USIA, *The People Have Spoken: Global Views of Democracy*, Vol. I, 9.
10 Wing Lo, *Corruption and Politics in Hong Kong and China*, 148–9.
11 Smeltz and Sweeney, *On the Take*, 2.
12 USIA, *The People Have Spoken: Global Views of Democracy*, Vol. II, 25–6.
13 Shelley, 'Organised Crime and Corruption in Ukraine', 649.
14 USIA, *The People Have Spoken: Global Views of Democracy*, Vol. II, 37.
15 Radaev, *Corruption and Violence in Russian Businesses*.
16 Coulter, 'There Is a Madness in the Method', 302.

CHAPTER 4

CITIZEN STRATEGIES FOR DEALING WITH OFFICIALS

How could citizens deal with officials? What coping strategies could they use when faced with unfair or unacceptable treatment? A range of strategies emerged in our focus-group discussions and in-depth interviews. Citizens could passively accept whatever the official said or did. But they could also use a number of more active strategies. Even if officials have excessive power, 'this does not mean that clients are helpless in the relationship...clients have a stock of resources and thus can impose a variety of low-level costs...[even] order in a prison is a function of adjustments made by guards in exchange for general compliance with regulation' by their prisoners.[1]

Some of the strategies mentioned by participants in our focus-group discussions should be regarded as perfectly legitimate for use within a liberal democratic society. Strategies such as persistence, argument and appeal to higher authority make a valuable contribution towards a healthy democracy even if they entail some pressure on the official. Indeed, they contribute to democracy precisely *because* they entail some legitimate pressure by citizens on officials. A growth in the use of such strategies by citizens in post-communist countries should be regarded as welcome evidence of liberation from the tyranny of an autocratic state. We might characterise them as 'legitimate' or 'democratic' methods of exerting pressure on officials.

Other strategies such as bribery or threats of violence cannot be regarded as making a positive contribution to a liberal democratic society. They are clearly 'illegitimate' or 'undemocratic' methods of exerting pressure on officials.

The use of contacts or 'networking' is more ambiguous. It can be inclusive or exclusive. It can spread information widely to those that need it, which is consistent with liberal democratic concepts of the free flow of information and equal access to it. But it can also spread special favours within a closed, restricted and privileged circle. Such unequal access to officials may in fact be a more or less regular occurrence in Western democratic practice, but it remains inconsistent with democratic principles of openness and equality.

In this chapter we look at the strategies used by citizens in their dealings with street-level officials. Thomas Lancaster and Gabriella Montinola have complained that despite their theoretical advantages for a study of corruption, 'cross-national studies using surveys are rare' because 'respondents may be unwilling to provide this information for fear of incriminating themselves. Thus, surveys tend to elicit general perceptions of the incidence of corruption in particular countries, and perceptions may differ from reality.'[2] Vito Tanzi also points out that corruption surveys have tended to focus on perceptions, which may differ from reality.[3] This concern that respondents may be unwilling to provide information applies with even greater force to survey research into the strategies that citizens themselves employ than it does to survey research about their treatment by officials. For citizens to report that an official asked for a bribe is an *allegation*. But for citizens to report that they themselves offered a bribe is a *confession*.

As we shall show, it is certainly true that perceptions of corruption do differ systematically from the reality. Public perceptions of the strategies that ('other' or 'typical') citizens generally use to influence officials are interesting in themselves, even when—or perhaps especially when—they differ from the reality of personal experience. But the reality is also important, and the difference between perceptions and reality cannot be demonstrated without measuring both. So here, as throughout our study, we have investigated both perceptions and experience and looked at the difference between them. We felt able to do that because our initial round of focus-group discussions indicated that citizens were surprisingly willing to talk about their own, or their family's, actual use of contacts, presents and bribes to influence officials, even though these discussions were being video-taped. Setting such behaviour within the wider context of discussing interactions with officials, which involved so much more than presents and bribes, may have helped. So in the more structured interviews of our large-scale surveys we paid great attention to question wording and sequence in order to reach questions about personal experience in as natural a context as possible. In particular, we only put questions about personal experience long after we had allowed respondents to voice their perception that such behaviour was quite frequent, 'normal', or even 'standard operating procedure' for bureaucratic encounters.

Moreover, we put questions about eight different citizen strategies for influencing street-level officials, both 'democratic' and 'undemocratic' strategies. So questions about the use of contacts, presents and bribes occurred in the context of a wider range of strategy questions. This was partly designed to relax the respondents. But our questions about legitimate and democratic strategies for dealing with officials were not just a cloak for sensitive questions about the use of illegitimate and undemocratic strategies. The more legitimate or democratic strategies are not so 'glamorous' as to capture the imagination either of commentators or the public itself. But as our focus-group discussions indicated so strongly and convincingly, it is these unglamorous and unexciting strategies that are nonetheless the predominant modes of actual behaviour in real interactions between ordinary citizens and street-level officials in post-communist Europe.

HOW CITIZENS IN FOCUS-GROUPS DISCUSSED STRATEGIES FOR DEALING WITH OFFICIALS

The actual phrases used in the focus-group discussions provide a valuable tool for interpreting and evaluating these different strategies. They not only describe, they also interpret. They have distinctly moral overtones. Without any external prompting they convey the discussants' own positive and negative feelings about strategies.

PASSIVE ACCEPTANCE

Frequently, citizens felt they had been forced to accept the actions (or the inaction) of officials whether they liked it or not. Passive acceptance was not a heroic strategy. Perhaps it hardly merits the title of a 'strategy' at all. But citizens were frequently forced to use it.

Sometimes that meant nothing worse than a boring wait for attention. 'Why people have to wait there for half a day beats me.'(Ol 2) 'There are long queues there and you have to wait. That is what I hate the most. They simply waste your time.'(HK 1) Sometimes the wait was longer. 'I must say that the attitude of all the officials there was wonderful. The only disadvantage was that they do not have a duty to solve individual cases within 30 days as it used to be in the past.'(Pra-B 1)

Sometimes it meant going from office to office. 'Whenever I go to an official I feel very unhappy…they always send me to another office located God knows where. So that in the end you get nothing settled.'(Br-A 1)

Sometimes it meant a refusal to help on that day. 'I went to the Broumov Labour Exchange…It was 4.30pm and they closed at 5pm. The official in charge started telling me how long it took them to switch off computers and that he had to refuse to register my case. He kept on talking and closing time was approaching. So I packed up all my documents and left.'(HK 2)

But sometimes it appeared worse than that. 'I clearly understood from the very beginning that it would not do any good…I came there, turned round, and went home.'(Striy 4) 'Circumstances made me give up, because if somebody else were in my position…it is no wonder why there are structures of force, racket, batons.'(Ya 4) 'For a couple of years now cattle has been regularly stolen from our farm at home. We call the police, but they do not do anything about it…How are we to live?'(Stral 6) 'My son [a Crimean Tatar] came back from the army three months ago. He is not a citizen of Ukraine. There is no record in his passport that he is a citizen of Ukraine. But he served anyway. I can give you lots of examples like this. They make our children go on active service.'(Se 5) In the previous chapter we quoted the story told by a Bulgarian Gypsy woman whose daughter had allegedly been raped and abducted and who reported that the police had demanded 'petrol money' before they would start searching for her. That sad story continued with her passive acceptance: 'I did not have the money so I went on my own.'(Stral 5)

ARGUMENT

Argument could be highly effective. 'I succeeded in persuading them. Maybe they were in a good mood. It was just after lunch.'(Do 5) One Czech said that when his wife was stopped for speeding 'she paid on the spot. But then there came a call from the inspectorate. So then I went there myself. I told them we had paid. I even had the receipts. The clerk looked in the computer. "I have no confirmation here", he says, "that it was collected on the spot." And he wanted proof. I said "Here it is. I am showing it to you here. I am not going to give it to you since I can see what a mess it is here. It could get lost and I would have to pay again. I am just showing the receipt. Copy the numbers—like which officers were there, who gave us the receipt. They will have to know, or the receipts are a sham. But I am not giving it to you. We simply paid and that is it." So then he apologised. He would find out himself.'(Ol 5) A Bulgarian used arguments equally effectively in a similar but more serious situation: 'They wanted me to pay a tax twice for the same thing. I went to the Ministry of Finance and I had all my necessary documents. I was determined not to pay the same tax twice. And I made it!'(So-A 7)

PERSISTENCE

Argument could verge into a strategy of persistence. If officials could 'make unnecessary problems and impose unnecessary delays in order to get money or a present for solving them', as was so often alleged, then clients could impose extra work on hard-pressed officials merely by taking up their time.[4] 'First you have to argue with them for two months.'(Do 5) 'You must stick to your guns, not let them persuade you that it cannot be done or that the fault is yours.'(HK 6) 'You keep coming to the official long enough, till he says he cannot stand you any longer, so he signs it.'(Ho 1) One woman had her own version of the biblical tale of the poor widow and the unjust judge: 'I drop in there every week and when they see me at the door they say to themselves: "Oh God, she is here again, give it to her and get rid of her."'(Pra-B 6)

But persistence was not always so successful. 'I have been to him several times. He closes the door in my face. Even pushed me once.'(Stral 5) 'For two months I have been going there, but receive no money.'(Ku 4) 'We have not received any [children's] allowances so far. My child is two.'(Te 7) 'We wanted to launch a Crimean Tatar television…Every day the official says "tomorrow", "the day after tomorrow".'(Se 4)

ABUSE OR THREATS

Sometimes, however, argument verged into abuse or threats. 'You have to know how to bite. Otherwise there is no way you can survive now.'(Ky-A 6) After the police asked to see a little boy's passport because he was a dark-skinned Tatar, his mother said she angrily 'phoned the KGB and asked: "Who are you trying to catch?…We are not in Moscow, we are in Ukraine, on our own land!"'(Se 6) 'I had to throw a hysterical fit. Then they gave it to me.' (Kh 2) 'When a person enters the office and opens the door with his leg, then the official knows that this is a tough one to deal with. And they will at once give away everything the person wants.'(Ky-A 1) 'So eventually being threatened, they find the money.'(Stral 8)

APPEALS TO HIGHER OFFICIALS OR ELECTED POLITICIANS

Appeals to more senior administrators or to elected politicians were another possibility. 'Address an official on a higher rung of the ladder. He will criticise the official on the lower rung and some measures will be taken.'(So-B 7) 'Automatically you have to go to a higher authority if you find out that you are getting less than you should, or if you suspect that something went wrong.'(Pres 2) 'If you visited some chiefs, you would probably receive something.'(Vo 5) Citizens could 'go higher' (HK 6), 'up the ladder'(Ho 2), to 'her superior'(Br-B 7), to 'the MP Boncho Rashkov'(Te 1), to 'the village soviet'(Ni 1), to 'the region executive office'(Vo 1), to 'the mayor'(Pra-A 7), to 'the minister'(Ol 3), or even to 'the Supreme Council [the Parliament of Ukraine]'.(Ky-A 6) But one target of appeals was no longer available: 'It was easier when there was the First Secretary of the Party City Committee. Now there is no power like that.'(Kh 3)

Some focus-group participants would not try an appeal until they had exhausted all other possibilities. 'You really have to be very angry to go and see their superior. I would only do it as a last resort.'(Pra-A 2) There was also some fear that an appeal might backfire. 'There is honour among thieves…and since the Bulgarian has common sense, he would rather keep quiet or, if he is able, find another way to solve the problem.'(Ya 2) But others reported some success. 'My daughter's friend had problems relating to alimony for her child. She went to the court hearings several times but the child's father simply would not pay. Nothing forced him. And so she started writing to the Presidential Office, to Parliament, and I cannot remember the third institution she turned to…and then the ice broke, the ice broke.'(Pra-B 1)

CONTACTS

Officials could be approached through a contact. 'In order to get to any of our authorities, you have to be brought to them on a tray.'(Striy 3) 'If someone intercedes on your behalf, then the question will be resolved.'(Ho 2) 'Almost everybody does it this way. I am convinced that this is the only way to settle things quickly, through contacts.'(NZ 4) 'You do not stand a chance if you do not have friends.'(Ol 4)

Contacts in senior positions were obviously useful. 'I have a friend in the higher echelons. That is why I managed to get the money. Otherwise I might have been expecting my money to this very last day.'(Ya 2) 'I wasted my time [visiting the customs office] six or seven times...They gave me the run-around very tediously for a long time. I got sick and tired of all this. I went and found a friend who is high enough up over them all, brought him there...[and] he broke through literally in about five minutes.'(Kh 4)

But low-level contacts with street-level officials, just some familiar person in the local office, could be useful too. 'I have been exchanging a flat between Prague and Brno and I have to say that without knowing some people at the office in Brno it would have taken a lot longer. If I had not known the person there I would have waited say five to six weeks, maybe seven, and this way it was ready in two or three days.'(Pra-B 5) 'I went to a social welfare office...and I was lucky because I have many former classmates from the elementary school there and that helped me.'(Pres 5) And in the small Bulgarian town of Straldja 'we know each other—half the people from Straldja are your relatives, the other half are friends...if you need something special...look for a friend who is able to help you at the moment. That is very common.'(Stral 4)

Although contacts could be useful on their own, they were often discussed in connection with bribery. 'I know roughly the price, plus the friend in the appropriate position.'(So-B 2) 'I had the best entrance exam results, but they only admitted people according to their contacts...my mum...knew someone there who knew the dean. Money was even involved.'(NZ 8) Even contacts themselves might require payment in the new market economy of post-communist Europe. 'Of course, acquaintances would not do anything for you without money either.'(Se 6) Our large-scale survey findings confirmed this view. With very little variation across countries, 69 per cent told us that people who 'used a contact and got what they wanted' would 'feel obliged to give a present to their contact'. A further 20 per cent said it would depend on the circumstances, and only 11 per cent thought they would not feel obliged to give a present to their 'contact'.

PRESENTS AND BRIBES

It is difficult to draw a clear line between a present and a bribe. We might distinguish between, on one hand, a small gift, freely given out of gratitude, after an official had provided a service—surely a 'present'?—, and on the other hand, a large gift, given under duress, before the service had been provided—surely a 'bribe'? We shall return to such distinctions in the next chapter. For the moment it is enough to note that focus-group discussions included many spontaneous comments about many different kinds of gifts offered to officials in many very different circumstances. Sometimes they were refused. More often the tale was of gifts accepted or even of gifts demanded.

Such presents or bribes could vary from a box of chocolates or a packet of coffee to a gift of money. 'Whenever my wife was in hospital, I would give flowers to the staff—flowers as a token of gratitude.'(So-B 5) 'I must say I did bring coffee for that lady after she had done things for me.'(Kh 2) 'I have given a token at an office. Nothing much financially. Not that. Just a little token.'(Pres 2) 'When a person treats you well there is nothing wrong with giving him or her a bottle of champagne, a box of candy, or a chocolate bar when you have a chance.' (Striy 1)

But often gifts were of money or were expensive presents. 'With money you can do everything, and very fast.'(Ol 4) 'When you bring money, he will have time. You have done yourself a favour.'(Ky-A 3) 'There was this guy and he says: "Look, miss, I will pay you for half an hour's work." She just wrote it there—it took five, ten minutes.'(Ol 2) 'If you have the money you are treated as a human being.'(Ku 1) And 'money as a rule is not "coupons" [Ukrainian temporary currency].'(Ky-B 4) 'People give dollars. Well, you are unlikely to bring butter now, or potatoes.'(Sh 4)

The size of the required gift was often specified by the gift taker. 'If a bureaucrat has even a slight chance to make something on you, he will do everything in order to get it from you.'(Ky-A 4) 'If you do not bring anything…if you do not grease, you will not go anywhere.'(Kh 3) 'Not a single case can be solved without a bribe.'(Ky-A 7) 'Now they [doctors] look you in the pocket, in the hand. You have to give them something and then they examine you.'(Ku 7) 'With doctors you know how to act and to give. They tell you beforehand…With policemen [also] things are defined. They tell you how much they want.'(So-A 7) 'Maybe you wanted to, maybe you did not want to, but they took it from you. They tell you a specific sum.'(Kh 6) 'Now, anywhere you go, they can even tell you how much, whom to give it to, and for what sort of matters.'(Ho 1) 'They would be better to have a price list.'(Sh 5)

In fact, the Ukrainian press frequently carried 'price lists' for the bribery of street-level officials. A typical example from the press in

Donetsk listed prices, mainly in US dollars.[5] It included US$30–50 for a good exam mark in local colleges and universities (though with a 'group option' as low as US$10 per student and a premium rate of US$80 for students who did not pay until they had already failed the exam). Law-enforcement officers were listed as charging much more: only $10–50 to avoid a speeding ticket, but $40–200 for escorting a drunk driver home without filing a report, rising to $10,000 for issuing a verdict of 'not guilty' without good reason. (Even that was cheap, of course, compared to the figures given in John T. Noonan's well-authenticated 'price list' for bribing elite officials in the USA.)[6]

But such price lists are very misleading in one important respect. They imply a situation in which clients pay bribes for illegal favours. What clearly emerges from our focus-group discussions and surveys is that clients frequently pay bribes to street-level officials in order to secure legal rights, not illegal favours.

OTHER STRATEGIES: KNOWLEDGE AND 'PSYCHOLOGY'

There were a very few references in our focus-group discussions to forming a protest group, or going to court. More frequently participants mentioned knowledge-based strategies, which ranged from checking up on the law to 'knowing the ropes'. Finally, there was a miscellaneous set of other strategies, mainly concerned with personal appearance and behaviour, and frequently described by focus-group participants as using 'psychology'—strategies such as an unusual degree of politeness or even a pleasant smile that anticipated friendship rather than reflected it. 'I try to agree with the [official], find some common interest. I start to talk, just by the way, about children or something and they usually swallow the bait and once we get on this level it is easy to sort it out with them.'(Pra-A 3) 'It depends on sex-appeal or on psychology, yes just that, how to talk the policeman round.'(KH 7)

One particularly attractive and smartly dressed young woman who arrived at a Bulgarian discussion group in a new sports car claimed that she had never paid a fine or a monetary bribe to the police. 'So far I have not paid a single penalty. When they stopped me I started deviating their attention…"Let us go and have a cup of coffee, I said"…I might call that coffee friendly.'(Ya 5) An older woman in the same discussion responded wryly. 'Your youth is your advantage. If they stopped me, even if I offered them whisky, they would not be lenient to me.'(Ya 6)

But too much style could be bad psychology. A woman in a Czech discussion group remarked that 'when I got dressed up and was wearing something better than the women [officials] there, everything went wrong'.(Pra-A 3)

DIFFERENT STRATEGIES FOR DIFFERENT OBJECTIVES: FAIR TREATMENT OR FAVOURS

Bribery was the strategy most frequently mentioned in our discussion groups in all four countries—in 26 per cent of relevant text units in the Czech Republic, 36 per cent in Slovakia, 35 per cent in Bulgaria and 42 per cent in Ukraine. It was also the most frequently denied. But other strategies were also mentioned frequently—including contacts, argument (especially in the Czech and Slovak Republics), and appeals to higher authority (especially in Ukraine).

Table 4.1. Focus-group references to coping strategies—by whether seeking rights or favours

	Czech Republic seeking rights or favours?		Slovakia seeking rights or favours?		Bulgaria seeking rights or favours?		Ukraine seeking rights or favours?	
	rts %	favs %	rts %	favs %	rts %	favs %	rts %	favs %
use of passive acceptance	25	12	26	7	28	12	25	3
use of persistence, argument, appeals	40	17	35	14	27	11	30	5
use of contacts	11	15	5	25	15	37	8	21
use of bribes	18	42	22	55	30	60	28	73
deny use of bribes	4	10	8	7	7	3	3	5
% use of bribes – deny use of bribes	+14	+32	+14	+48	+23	+57	+25	+68

Note: Percentages are percentages of relevant 'text units' in the focus-group discussions, not percentages of participants. A single text unit could answer several questions, or give several answers to the same question. Consequently, percentages of text units in different categories usually sum to a little over 100 percent.

In these discussions, strategies were clearly related to objectives. In every country strategies of passive acceptance, along with the more active but 'democratic' strategies of persistence, argument or appeal, were mentioned much more frequently in connection with attempts to get *fair treatment* than to get favours. Conversely, the 'undemocratic' strategies of contacts and bribes were mentioned much more frequently in connection with attempts to get *favourable treatment.* (Table 4.1) 'Do you mean you need to pay only when you are doing something illegal?' asked the moderator in our Sholomia discussion. 'I think when everything is legal people pay less' came the response.(Sh 2) Even in Ukraine, where bribes were mentioned in 28 per cent of text units that concerned obtaining legal rights, they were mentioned in almost three times as many (73 per cent) of the text units that concerned obtaining favours.

DIFFERENT STRATEGIES IN GOSSIP AND PERSONAL EXPERIENCE

As the focus-group discussions moved from general gossip through hypothetical scenarios to reports of personal experience, the nature of the discussion changed sharply. (Table 4.2) First, the balance between seeking rights and seeking favours changed. As compared to general gossip, more personal statements focused much more on seeking legal rights and much less on seeking favours. In parallel with this, references to different coping strategies also changed. Bribes were always mentioned much less (and usually denied rather more) in personal statements than they were in general gossip. The use of contacts was also mentioned rather less frequently in personal statements than in gossip.

Conversely, passive acceptance was mentioned more in personal statements than in gossip. More importantly, other more active but 'democratic' strategies like persistence, argument or appeal were mentioned twice as frequently in personal statements as in general gossip and hearsay.

Overall, therefore, there was a striking contrast between the repertoire of coping strategies discussed in general gossip and that reported in personal experience.

Since the number of assertions of bribery always fell as the conversation moved from general gossip to specific personal statements and denials usually increased, the net difference between the frequency of assertions and denials of bribery fell very sharply. The fall was particularly sharp in the Czech Republic. When people were gossiping in general terms, net assertions of bribery were about as frequent in Slovakia and Bulgaria as in Ukraine, and only around 10 per cent less in the Czech Republic. But when people began to talk about their personal experiences, net assertions of bribery were only half as frequent in Slovakia and Bulgaria as in Ukraine, and they sank almost to zero in the Czech Republic.

Table 4.2. Focus-group references to coping strategies—in gossip and personal experience

	Czech Republic in gossip or experience?		Slovakia in gossip or experience?		Bulgaria in gossip or experience?		Ukraine in gossip or experience?	
	gossip %	exp %	gossip %	exp %	gossip %	exp %	gossip %	exp %
use of passive acceptance	10	18	14	19	21	31	16	18
use of persistence, argument, appeals	11	28	18	29	15	27	16	32
use of contacts	20	16	10	10	23	17	12	10
use of bribes	36	16	47	29	42	27	46	33
deny use of bribes	7	13	9	15	3	9	5	4
% use of bribes – deny use of bribes	29	3	38	14	39	18	41	29

Note: percentages are percentages of relevant 'text units' in the focus-group discussions, not percentages of participants.

These focus-group discussions suggest that Czechs lacked much direct experience of corruption despite their enthusiasm for talking about it. In his review of allegations of high-level corruption, Steve Kettle argued that the Czech Republic was 'a country where people love to see a conspiracy behind any apparently simple event'.[7] Our focus-group findings are consistent with large-scale USIA surveys carried out in 1998–99 which asked people how they formed their impressions about corruption: Were their impressions based on reports in the media or on their own personal experience, or the experiences of their family and friends? Only a third in Bulgaria and Slovakia, but almost twice as many in the Czech Republic, said they based their impressions of corruption mostly on reports in the media rather than on direct experience.[8]

Particularly in the Czech Republic, but also in Slovakia, some comments in focus-group discussions actually combined a general assertion that bribery occurred locally with a specific denial of any personal experience of it. 'I would not try it, but I know people who have done it.'(HK 2) 'Not from our own experience, rather from what I hear.'(Ol 4) 'Everybody waits for something to be slipped into his or her pocket, a bribe...[but] I would never bribe anybody, I would not know how...Am I really supposed to add to their salaries if I want something settled?'(Pres 6)

In Slovakia, actual confessions to experience of bribery were more frequent than in the Czech Republic. Some were, in the donor's eyes at least, not a bribe but 'just a little token'.(Pres 2) From the standpoint of the official, however, even tokens might add up. As one participant put it: 'My cousin cannot praise it enough, being a customs officer. He says: "Yesterday I brought home slippers for the whole family. I get so many chickens that I do not know where to put them. I need a second fridge." These are tokens for customs clearance.'(Zv 5) Slovaks also listed monetary bribes quite explicitly, especially bribes to the traffic police and the health services. 'Sometimes [the police] give you a penalty without a receipt. Sometimes this satisfies both parties. This has already happened to me.'(Br-B 9) Bribery to get medical attention was mentioned particularly frequently. 'Special [maternity] deliveries—paid-for, fast, painless. And naturally the attitude of nurses to those patients was different.'(Zv 1)

Most personal confessions to bribing the Bulgarian police involved real or imaginary traffic offences: 'I had enclosed in my passport 1,000 levs...He took 200 levs...and recommended a brush-up course of driving for me.'(So-A 5) Once again, health care was the other main focus of experience of bribery. 'In my room I saw it. Doctors took money from those in the beds next to mine.'(Ku 5) But experience of bribery was not restricted to dealings with police and health workers. '[My friend's] son was about to join the army. His boy went to the barracks but he was asked to make his choice. He is serving in the army at a distance of [only] 15 km from Sofia. Every two or three days he comes home. But that has its price, too. I think the boy enjoys serving in the army, and it goes to show that bribing is based on reciprocity.'(So-B 3)

In Bulgaria as in the Czech and Slovak Republics there was also some experience of bribes being unnecessary or even being refused when offered. Especially in small villages, Bulgarians reported that 'people know each other here. Bribes are not expected.'(Te 1) There were also some tales of Bulgarian officials refusing to accept bribes, which even surprised and slightly disconcerted those who had offered them. 'I underwent two operations at the Medical Academy in Plovdiv. I was ready to pay, but the doctor I ran into turned down my money offer...Upon leaving I hinted about money, but he felt pained. Then he accepted, most unwillingly, a bottle of grape-brandy as a token of gratitude...Now I am not sure what is going on there.'(Ya 4) But there was a darker side to some tales of bribes refused. In one Sofia discussion group a university lecturer reported: 'I know the price is 300 dollars, but I have not given any mark without examining the student. So I have become the black sheep among my fellow-lecturers and they have become nasty towards me.'(So-B 5)

Every group discussion in Ukraine, apart from the one with the Crimean Tatars, produced specific personal confessions about the actual use of presents and bribes. Sometimes it clearly was for a favour. 'There was another instructor who had a tariff—a bottle of vodka for [an undeserved pass in] the mid-term test.'(Kh 1) Sometimes it was at least partly out of gratitude and relief. 'I had an operation last year, a professor did it...We all knew, the patients talked about it, that he only took things after the operation.'(Ky-A 1) But on many other occasions, the tales told in focus-group discussions clearly indicated extortion—a point to which we return in the next chapter.

No doubt our focus-group participants held something back. We do not suppose that they revealed all. But it is remarkable how much they were willing to say in front of the video-cameras at our focus-groups. Partly that reflected the expertise of our focus-group moderators, all of whom had extensive experience in leading group discussions. But it also reflected the openness of the participants themselves. Most did not seem over-inhibited by the long years of life under communism. On the contrary, they frequently seemed to revel in their new freedom to criticise the state—joking on one occasion that 'you must turn off the cameras now' before they grinned at the camera, named names and made detailed allegations of corruption against a senior local politician. Of course, the opposite danger is that people will tell extravagant but untruthful stories to impress their fellow-participants or to please the investigators. There was a sharp difference between allegations made in general terms and those based on more personal experience. In the Czech Republic general gossip in the focus groups about widespread corruption simply did not correspond to more personal accounts of experience and behaviour. But by contrast, the discrepancy between general allegations and personal experience was less elsewhere, and it was much less in Ukraine. It seems unlikely that this reflected greater inhibitions, more fear, or less openness in the Czech Republic than elsewhere. This has important implications: the difference between Czech and Ukrainian experience of interacting with officials was actually greater than was implied by focus-group responses to more superficial questions about the general climate of corruption.

PUBLIC PERCEPTIONS OF THE STRATEGIES NEEDED TO DEAL WITH OFFICIALS: GOSSIP AND HEARSAY

Basing our survey questionnaire on the citizen strategies that emerged in these focus-group discussions, we asked: 'Suppose a person asks an official for something to which he/she is *entitled by law*. Is it likely or not likely that he/she would accept what the official decides even if he/she remains dissatisfied?' We then followed that question with a battery of seven others: 'To get a successful outcome, is it likely or not likely that he/she would...

- *behave more pleasantly* than normal towards the official?
- *argue* with the official or keep going back [to see them]?
- *appeal to a higher official*?
- *appeal to an elected representative* on a local council or in parliament?
- approach an official through a *contact*?
- offer a *small present*?
- offer *money or an expensive present*?'

Together with *passive acceptance* that makes a menu of eight possible strategies.

Answers reveal general perceptions, what for brevity we may call 'gossip'. In public perceptions, the most likely strategy was using a contact (85 per cent), closely followed by behaving more pleasantly than normal (82 per cent) and offering a small present to the official (79 per cent). (Table 4.3) An appeal to a higher official or arguing with officials came next. Offering money or an expensive present (65 per cent) came slightly ahead of passive acceptance. Sadly, for a set of new democracies, the notion of an appeal to an elected representative, whether local or national, came at the bottom of the list (46 per cent).

Table 4.3. Perceptions of likely coping strategies

	Average	Czech Republic	Slovakia	Bulgaria	Ukraine
	%	%	%	%	%
More likely than not that a person seeking something to which he/she is entitled by law would...					
approach an official through a contact	85	76	87	86	90
behave more pleasantly than normal	82	67	78	93	91
offer a small present	79	62	80	84	91
appeal to a higher official	75	72	67	82	78
argue with the official or keep going back	68	75	70	63	65
offer money or an expensive present	65	44	62	72	81
accept official's decision even if dissatisfied	61	55	59	76	55
appeal to an elected representative	46	37	40	56	50

Notes: 'Don't know', 'mixed/depends' etc. answers were recorded if given spontaneously, but never prompted; they have been excluded from the calculation of percentages.

Strategies listed by average frequency.

Public perceptions of the likely use of money or expensive presents (to get no more than a legal entitlement) ranged sharply from 44 per cent in the Czech Republic through 62 per cent in Slovakia and 72 per cent in Bulgaria to 81 per cent in Ukraine. Public perceptions of the use of contacts and small presents also ranged from a minimum in the Czech Republic to a maximum in Ukraine, though cross-national differences were smaller than for large presents. Unusually pleasant behaviour and appeals both to higher officials and elected representatives were also thought more likely in Ukraine than in the Czech Republic. Conversely, the use of argument and persistence was thought more likely in the Czech Republic than in Ukraine.

By an average margin of 28 per cent the public thought citizens were now less likely than in communist times passively to accept an unsatisfactory decision by an official. Conversely, the public thought citizens were more likely than in the past to use every one of the other strategies. (Table 4.4) By margins of around 55 per cent respondents thought their fellow-citizens were now more likely to use contacts and small presents to influence officials. By smaller but still substantial margins they thought their fellow-citizens were also more likely to use argument, appeals to higher officials and gifts of money or expensive presents.

Table 4.4. Perceptions of changing strategies

	Average	Czech Republic	Slovakia	Bulgaria	Ukraine
	% more likely now – % less likely now				
Compared to the period (under communism), do you think it is now more likely or now less likely that people in (your country) would...					
approach an official through a contact?	+58	+49	+69	+46	+67
offer a small present?	+51	+25	+60	+53	+67
argue with the official or keep going back?	+38	+55	+33	+37	+28
appeal to a higher official?	+37	+47	+30	+47	+23
offer money or an expensive present?	+32	0	+34	+41	+51
behave more pleasantly than normal?	+13	–12	+9	+31	+25
appeal to an elected representative?	+9	–4	–6	+27	+17
Average perceived change in active strategies	+33	+23	+33	+40	+40
accept official's decision even if dissatisfied?	–28	–44	–21	–12	–36

Notes: 'Don't know' answers were recorded if given spontaneously, but never prompted; they have been excluded from the calculation of percentages.

Strategies listed by change in use.

The phrase '(under communism)' was replaced by 'during the Soviet period' in Ukraine; and by 'before 1989' elsewhere.

The phrase '(your country)' was replaced by the name of the country in which the interview took place.

Other surveys confirm our finding that a large majority of the public throughout post-communist Europe felt there had been a rise in 'the level of corruption and taking bribes' since the end of communism.[9] If correct, such perceptions point to a more individualistic rather than a more democratic post-communist society. 'Once you needed friends in court, whereas now you need a lot of money as well. And if you have the money, you need friends at court so that you should know to whom to offer the bribe. The system has become more complicated.'(So-A 7)

In very broad terms, the public in every country had the same perception of change since the end of communism. But there was some evidence that where life was getting more difficult, citizens were perceived as 'trying harder' to influence officials by whatever means they could (as judged by the average perceived change in the use of all seven active strategies).

Public perceptions of the increasing use of such illegitimate strategies as contacts, presents and bribes were much greater in Ukraine than in the Czech Republic—18 per cent greater in Ukraine for contacts, 42 per cent for small presents and 51 per cent for gifts of money or expensive presents. There also appeared to be a perceived trend towards the use of ingratiating behaviour and appeals to elected officials in Bulgaria and Ukraine that was not evident in the Czech or Slovak Republics.

Conversely, public perceptions of the increasing use of the legitimate strategies of argument and appeals to higher officials was much greater in the Czech Republic than in Ukraine—24 per cent greater in the Czech Republic for appeals to higher officials, and 27 per cent for the use of argument.

PERSONAL EXPERIENCE OF USING DIFFERENT STRATEGIES: REPORTED BEHAVIOUR

While perceptions of the 'typical' strategies used by their fellow-citizens are an important psychological fact, our focus-group discussions implied that citizens' actual behaviour was likely to be very different from these perceptions. Thus, much later in the survey interviews we asked respondents about their own (or their family's) actual experience of dealing with officials 'in the last few years'. After asking several other questions about these experiences of interacting with officials we then asked: 'Thinking over these personal experiences of dealing with officials in the last few years, did you or your family usually, sometimes, rarely, or never have to...'—after which we enumerated the same eight citizen strategies for dealing with officials that we had already used in our question about perceptions.

By focusing on the frequency with which people had used these strategies we hoped to stir memories and get a more accurate account than might be obtained by a simple 'yes/no' question format. In addition, this question format also encouraged respondents to admit to actions that they normally condemned and avoided but occasionally committed.

Reports of personal experience produced a very different ranking of strategies from that indicated by perceptions. (Table 4.5) Instead of being second last on the list, passive acceptance now appeared at the top. However unlikely it appeared as the hypothetical strategy for a typical citizen, however lacking it might be in charisma, it was nonetheless the most frequent strategy in citizens' actual reported experience. It is not a heroic finding but it is a very plausible one. On average, 87 per cent admitted that they had, at least on rare occasions, passively accepted an official's decision even though they remained dissatisfied.

Table 4.5. Experience of using strategies

	Average	Czech Republic	Slovakia	Bulgaria	Ukraine
	%	%	%	%	%
Personally used strategy in the last few years...					
accept official's decision even if dissatisfied	87	85	85	92	86
behave more pleasantly than normal	82	67	82	93	85
argue with the official or keep going back	77	78	79	76	76
approach an official through a contact	52	40	67	44	59
appeal to a higher official	44	36	38	47	53
offer a small present	42	23	56	33	57
offer money or an expensive present	24	11	31	19	36
appeal to an elected representative	20	15	18	19	27

Notes: 'Don't know', 'mixed/depends' etc. answers were recorded if given spontaneously, but never prompted; they have been excluded from the calculation of percentages.

Strategies listed by average frequency.

Conversely, approaching an official through a contact had topped the list in public perceptions of likely strategies. But barely half admitted that they had done so, even rarely, in the last few years. Over three-quarters reported that they had behaved more pleasantly than normal, or argued with an official. Ingratiating behaviour or argument and persistence were in fact more frequent, if less memorable, strategies than approaching an official through a contact.

Less than half had appealed to a higher official and only one-fifth had appealed to an elected politician. The number who had exercised their democratic right of appeal to an elected politician still came last in actual experience as it had in perceptions. But in actual experience the use of small presents and large bribes came close to last. Well under half had offered a small present to an official and less than a quarter had offered money or an expensive present. Only an appeal to an elected politician was used less frequently than gifts of money or expensive presents.

Thus, although the use of argument and offers of bribes (money or expensive gifts) were rated about equally likely in terms of perceptions, argument had actually been used by over three times as many citizens in practice.

In reports of personal experience, unlike general perceptions of the behaviour of their fellow-citizens, Ukrainians were almost as likely to have argued with officials as Czechs. In personal experience Ukrainian citizens still reported much greater use of contacts, presents and bribes than Czech citizens. But in their own personal experience, unlike perceptions of their fellow-citizens, Ukrainian use of contacts, presents and bribes was rivalled by that in Slovakia. So while Slovakia was close to the Czech Republic in the imagination of its citizens, it was closer to Ukraine in their actual behaviour. Slovak self-images conflicted with Slovak experience, nor was this likely to be due to some quirk in our data. Using slightly different questions, but nonetheless questions about confessed behaviour rather than perceptions, USIA surveys also indicate that actual experience of bribe giving was considerably higher in Slovakia than in Bulgaria.[10]

Table 4.6. Experience of using strategies 'more than rarely'

	Average	Czech Republic	Slovakia	Bulgaria	Ukraine
	%	%	%	%	%
Personally used strategy '*more than rarely*'...					
accept official's decision even if dissatisfied	69	69	64	78	65
behave more pleasantly than normal	64	42	59	83	72
argue with the official or keep going back	50	51	55	41	52
approach an official through a contact	31	21	42	20	40
offer a small present	25	11	34	15	39
appeal to a higher official	21	18	17	21	27
offer money or an expensive present	13	6	17	7	24
appeal to an elected representative	9	7	7	6	16

Notes: 'Don't know', 'mixed/depends' etc. answers were recorded if given spontaneously, but never prompted; they have been excluded from the calculation of percentages.

Strategies listed by average frequency.

Perhaps the numbers who used a strategy 'more than rarely' provides a better indication of their frequency of use. (Table 4.6, Fig. 4.1) The

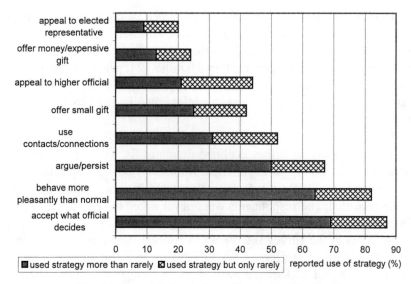

Fig. 4.1. The public's actual use of strategies (displayed by
frequency)

rank ordering of different strategies is scarcely changed but the percentages are much reduced and it is these reduced percentages that tell us about the numbers of citizens for whom such strategies were a fairly frequent or 'normal' part of their dealings with officials. Only when a strategy is used 'more than rarely' can it become part of the 'nature' of relationships with officials, part of the norm rather than a deviant exception. 'More than rarely':

- two-thirds of the public had behaved in an ingratiating way towards officials or passively accepted unsatisfactory decisions;
- half had used argument or persistence;
- a third had approached officials through a contact;
- a quarter had offered small presents, though only 13 per cent offered money or expensive presents (USIA figures for the numbers in Bulgaria, Slovakia and the Czech Republic who said they had actually 'had to pay a bribe in order to receive a social service to which they were entitled' are close to our figures for the numbers who had offered money or expensive presents 'more than rarely');
- a fifth had appealed to higher officials but only a tenth had appealed to elected representatives.

Given that 65 per cent had thought it more likely than not that citizens seeking a legal entitlement would have to offer money or expensive presents to officials, it is remarkable that only 24 per cent confessed to ever having done so in the last few years, and only 13 per cent 'more than rarely'. Enough confessed to offering money or an expensive present, ranging up to 36 per cent in Ukraine (24 per cent 'more than rarely'), to constitute more than a trivially small and deviant minority. But the level of confessions was much less than implied by the level of public perceptions.

That matches the evidence from our focus-group discussions that references to the use of bribes declined dramatically when the discussion switched from gossip to experience. Moreover, our survey interviews, unlike our focus-group discussions, were held in private, they were not video-recorded, and respondents were never asked to specify the names, times or places associated with bribes. So there was very little reason for respondents in the survey interviews to conceal their use of such strategies. That further reinforces our conclusion that the discrepancy between gossip and experience owes more to exaggerated gossip than to dishonest under-reporting of personal experience of using contacts, presents and bribes.

COMBINATIONS OF STRATEGIES

The use of contacts, presents and bribes easily dominates our attention. Such strategies are important, and they produce by far the most dramatic stories in group discussions or in-depth interviews. But it is equally important to remember that for the majority of citizens in every one of our four countries, dealing with officials more often meant trying hard to be pleasant even to unpleasant officials, pleading, arguing and persisting where possible, and ultimately accepting unsatisfactory treatment where that did not work.

But citizens could, and did, use more than one strategy in their dealings with officials. The norm was a combination of strategies not an obsession with one alone. Indeed, some strategies naturally went hand in hand with others—the use of contacts, presents and bribes for example. Those respondents who had more frequent dealings with officials than others were likely to have more frequent experience than other citizens of using every strategy—from passive acceptance and unusually pleasant behaviour through argument to contacts and bribes. Consequently, the correlation matrix of the frequency with which citizens used different strategies was entirely positive.

There is no evidence of exclusive alternatives. Nonetheless, there are some clear patterns. Some combinations of strategies were more frequent than others. There were particularly high correlations, ranging from 0.39 up to 0.72:

- between the use of passive acceptance and unusually pleasant, ingratiating behaviour towards officials;
- between the use of argument and appeals—whether to higher officials or elected politicians;
- between the use of contacts, small presents and large bribes.

A factor analysis identifies three factors: a *contacts, presents and bribes factor* centred on offering small presents (factor loading 0.90); an *argument and appeals factor* centred on appeals to higher officials (factor loading 0.84); and a *more passive factor* centred on passive acceptance (factor loading 0.85) but also including ingratiating behaviour.

There was only one cross-correlation exceeding 0.30 that linked a strategy to two different factors. The strategy of argument or persistence was primarily linked to the argument and appeals factor (factor loading 0.63), but it was also linked, though to a much lesser extent, to the passive factor (factor loading 0.31). Argument could include putting a diffident, tentative, persuasive and polite case to the official as well as more strident or threatening behaviour.

INFLUENCES ON CITIZENS' CHOICE OF STRATEGIES

What influenced citizens' choice of strategies for dealing with officials? Did different kinds of people have different strategy profiles? Or did different experiences with officials encourage citizens to adopt different strategies for dealing with them?

THE IMPACT OF SOCIAL BACKGROUND

In their ground-breaking study of émigrés from the Soviet Union, DiFranceisco and Gitelman found that those with a higher level of education made more use of contacts, while those with a lower level of education were more likely to offer bribes.[11] Education, in combination with type of agency approached, seemed to be of higher significance than other factors such as gender, age and area of residence. 'How Soviet citizens attempt to influence actively the implementation of policy seems to vary according to two factors: their own education and the particular agency involved. Regional differences are not as great as might be supposed. Sex and age are not important in differentiating styles of confronting and dealing with the bureaucracy.'[12]

Our survey confirmed the relatively weak impact of social background on strategies for dealing with officials, though in the disorder of post-communist Europe we found that even the impact of education was slight. Certainly the highly educated were more active in every respect except using ingratiating behaviour. They used arguments and appeals, as well as contacts, presents and bribes more than the less well educated. That is clear disproof of any prior expectation that education might make citizens more 'virtuous'. Clearly it did not. If anything, it made them less virtuous. But the impact of education in our surveys was small—5 or 6 per cent at most. We also found only slight differences between the profiles of strategies used by men and women, by those who lived in big cities and those who lived in smaller towns and villages, or by those with party preferences for socialist, communist or market-oriented parties.

In our survey, those on low incomes were a little (8 per cent) less likely to use contacts frequently (i.e. 'more than rarely'). But in keeping with their lack of income they were also marginally less likely to use presents or bribes and very slightly more likely to try unusually pleasant behaviour which cost nothing. In the end, the poor were also 9 per cent more likely to end up frequently accepting unsatisfactory treatment. That fits with the recurrent stories told in our focus-group discussions by people who had not offered presents or bribes simply because they could not afford them. But however plausible these patterns may be, our surveys suggest that even income had only a slight impact on citizens' choice of strategies for dealing with officials.

Age had rather more impact. The young were more likely than the old to use every strategy. (Table 4.7) Age differences on passive acceptance, abnormally pleasant behaviour and appeals to politicians were slight. But the young were 13 per cent more likely to argue, 16 per cent more likely to use contacts, and twice as likely to offer either small presents or large bribes. The young were just generally more active than the old in their attempts to cope with officials. Since the new generation was significantly more inclined to use contacts, presents and bribes than the old, the use of such strategies was clearly not a decaying legacy from the past. Indeed the greater prevalence of such democratically illegitimate strategies amongst the young fits the perception that corruption had increased during the transition from communism.

Table 4.7. The impact of youth on choice of strategies

	accept but not satisfied	behave unusually pleasantly	argue/ persist	appeal to higher official	appeal to elected politician	use contact	offer small present	offer money etc.
	Percentage who used each strategy frequently, that is, 'more than rarely'							
	%	%	%	%	%	%	%	%
By age:								
if under 30	71	66	55	24	11	37	31	18
if 30–44	68	64	52	22	10	34	27	14
if 45–59	69	64	49	21	9	30	24	13
if 60 and over	68	62	42	17	7	21	17	8
impact of youth	+3	+4	+13	+7	+4	+16	+14	+10

Note: Percentages in this table are the average of the percentages in the four countries, and the impact figures therefore show the average impact within countries.

Of course, the old were likely to have retired on low incomes. On average across the four countries in our survey, 24 per cent of the under-30s complained that their family income was not enough to live on. So did 27 per cent of the 30 to 44-year-olds and 32 per cent of the 45 to 59-year-olds, but the figure rose to 39 per cent amongst the over-60s. The age profile of income was particularly sharp in Bulgaria and Ukraine. But we have already found that income in itself did not have a very strong impact on citizens' choice of coping strategies and the age profile of income is not sufficient to explain the impact of age on choice of coping strategies.

Job status also varied with age. For one reason or another an average of 45 per cent of the under-30s in our surveys did not have a job. That dropped to just 17 per cent amongst 30 to 44 year olds before rising again to 31 per cent amongst 45 to 59 year olds and then reaching 94 per cent amongst the over-60s. To a degree, lack of a job linked the young and old in contrast to the middle-aged.

Jobs meant more than money. They integrated people into work-based networks of contacts. Job status did have clear, though limited, effects upon choice of coping strategies. The self-employed and pensioners differed from employees in opposite ways. Compared to employees, the self-employed were 12 per cent more likely than employees to use contacts, while pensioners were 13 per cent less likely to do so. To a lesser extent, the self-employed were also more likely to use argument, presents and bribes, while pensioners were less likely to use any of these.

But it is also evident from our findings that the various different reasons for not having a job also had implications for citizens' choice of coping strategies. Students, housewives and the 'temporarily' unemployed—as well as pensioners—also lacked jobs. Unlike pensioners, the choice of coping strategies among these other non-employed groups differed remarkably little from that of employees. It was specifically pensioner status, not just lack of a job, that had an impact on choice of strategies for dealing with officials.

THE IMPACT OF FREQUENT DEALINGS WITH OFFICIALS

The extent and nature of citizens' dealings with officials had a much greater influence than any of these social characteristics on the profile of strategies that the public used in their dealings with officials. The sheer quantity of interactions with officials made an impact. Those who had frequent dealings with officials were more likely to report that they had regularly used every one of the eight strategies. That was almost a tautology and yet not quite a tautology, since frequent interactions with officials seemed to increase the use of some strategies more than others.

Table 4.8. The impact of frequent dealings with officials on choice of strategies

	Percentage who used each strategy frequently, that is, 'more than rarely'							
	accept but not satisfied %	behave unusually pleasantly %	argue/ persist %	appeal to higher official %	appeal to elected politician %	use contact %	offer small present %	offer money etc. %
By frequency of dealing with officials...								
if frequently	75	68	68	36	13	42	34	23
if occasionally	72	67	53	23	10	34	28	14
if rarely	64	60	42	14	7	25	19	10
impact	+11	+8	+26	+22	+6	+17	+15	+13

Note: Percentages in this table are the average of the percentages in the four countries, and the impact figures therefore show the average impact within countries.

(Table 4.8) Frequent dealings with officials had least impact on the use of abnormally pleasant behaviour or appeals to elected politicians. Conversely, it had most impact on the use of argument and persistence (boosted by 26 per cent) and on appeals to higher officials (boosted by 22 per cent). It also had an intermediate impact on the use of contacts, presents and bribes. Familiarity in dealing with officials therefore seemed to teach the ability to argue, more than anything else.

THE IMPACT OF ILL-TREATMENT BY OFFICIALS

However, the character, as well as the extent, of citizens' dealings with officials also had an influence. In the face of unfair treatment they tried harder at almost every strategy that might be effective. Those who complained that they were 'rarely or never' treated 'fairly' by officials were around 13 per cent more likely to use contacts, presents or bribes and 22 per cent more likely to argue. (Table 4.9, Fig. 4.2) At the same time, they were also somewhat more likely to try using abnormally pleasant behaviour or appealing to a higher authority. Even so, they also reported more frequent occasions on which they simply had to accept the official's decision even though they remained dissatisfied.

Table 4.9. The impact of unfair treatment on choice of strategies

	Percentage who used each strategy frequently, that is, 'more than rarely'							
	accept but not satisfied	behave unusually pleasantly	argue/ persist	appeal to higher official	appeal to elected politician	use contact	offer small present	offer money etc.
	%	%	%	%	%	%	%	%
By experience of fair treatment:								
if rarely or never	76	69	61	29	13	36	32	22
if sometimes	76	72	61	26	11	39	32	16
if usually	63	58	39	17	8	22	19	10
impact	+13	+11	+22	+12	+5	+14	+13	+12

Note: Percentages in this table are the average of the percentages in the four countries, and the impact figures therefore show the average impact within countries.

By contrast, those who said they had frequently enjoyed 'specially favourable' treatment differed little from those who had never enjoyed it. This contrast implies that the impact of unfair treatment *on strategies* was much greater than the impact of strategies *on favourable treatment*.

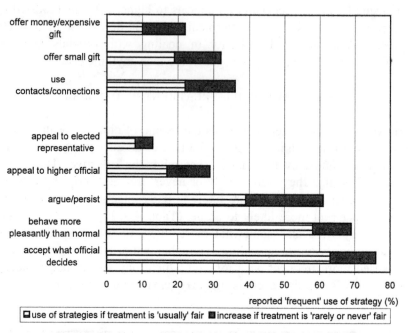

Fig. 4.2. The impact of unfair treatment (strategies displayed by category)

One feature of the impact of unfair treatment is worth noting. Even intermittent unfair treatment had a sharp impact on all strategies. But frequent unfair treatment had little or no additional impact except on offering 'money or an expensive present'. That hints at the possibility of a 'curvilinear' response to unfair treatment. Beyond a certain point the frequency or intensity of unfair treatment may cease to encourage citizens to 'try harder' to influence officials and may eventually discourage them. We return to this curvilinear response model at greater length in Chapter 6 when we look at the treatment and response of ethnic minorities, especially Gypsies.

THE IMPACT OF KNOWLEDGE

Whether people 'knew their rights' under the law could affect how well citizens coped with officials. So, also, could a rather different kind of knowledge—how well they knew their way around the bureaucracy, or even how well they knew the bureaucrats.

On average, 46 per cent of the public felt they 'usually knew what they were entitled to by law' in their dealings with officials in recent years, and 18 per cent felt they 'usually did not know'. The rest were less sure, or less consistently sure, about whether they knew their rights or not. Levels of knowledge about citizens' rights were much higher in the Czech and Slovak Republics than in Bulgaria or Ukraine. Not surprisingly, those with a higher level of education were far more likely to claim that they were 'usually' aware of their rights (about 20 per cent more), as were those on relatively high incomes.

Table 4.10. The impact of knowledge about legal rights on choice of strategies

	Percentage who used each strategy frequently, that is, 'more than rarely'							
	accept but not satisfied	behave unusually pleasantly	argue/ persist	appeal to higher official	appeal to elected politician	use contact	offer small present	offer money etc.
	%	%	%	%	%	%	%	%
By whether usually knew legal rights: if usually...								
knew	63	61	50	22	9	30	24	13
not quite sure	75	67	50	19	8	33	24	12
did not know	79	69	46	22	11	34	30	17
impact	−16	−8	+4	0	−2	−4	−6	−4

Note: Percentages in this table are the average of the percentages in the four countries, and the impact figures therefore show the average impact within countries.

But what concerns us here are the consequences of such knowledge. 'When they see that you do not know anything about the matter, they put you in your place straight away. But when someone is able to prepare the groundwork…and makes it clear they know what it is all about, the official's attitude changes.'(Pra-B 1) 'There is a rule: the more you are informed the less corrupt the official in front of you.'(So-A 7)

Those who felt they usually 'knew their rights' under the law were 16 per cent less likely to end up accepting an unwelcome decision. (Table 4.10) But apart from being somewhat less likely to behave in an abnormally pleasant way towards officials, they did not use very different strategies from those who seldom felt they knew their rights. On the other hand, they were around 12 per cent more satisfied in their dealings with officials. They presumably achieved a better outcome by using the same strategies more effectively rather than by using different strategies—not so much more frequent arguments as better arguments, for example.

Knowing officials is a very different kind of knowledge, with rather different causes and consequences. On average, two-thirds of the public had usually not known anyone in the office when they had dealt with officials in recent years. A fifth had usually known someone in the office but not the particular official they had to deal with. Rather less had usually known the relevant official personally. Even though the public in Bulgaria and Ukraine were far less likely than the public in the Czech and Slovak Republics to 'know their rights' they were just as likely to 'know someone in the office' and even more likely to 'know the relevant official'. Income had considerably less effect on knowledge of officials than on knowledge of rights, while settlement size was a stronger influence. Those living in the small towns and villages were about 16 per cent more likely to know their officials than those living in the capital or larger towns. 'Certainly we are locals here. We know each other, went to school together, or just know each other.'(Stral 7)

The *consequences* of knowing officials were different from the consequences of knowing your rights. One participant in the focus-group discussion in the Bulgarian village of Tenovo claimed: 'People know each other [here]. There are no bribes here.'(Te 4) Despite that claim, it seems from our large-scale surveys that knowing officials in general facilitated bribery rather than discouraging it, whatever may or may not have happened in the village of Tenovo.

Significantly, knowing the relevant official made very little difference to citizens' choice of strategies. It was knowing 'someone else in the office' that had a much greater impact, and the impact was greatest on the use of contacts. Presumably the 'someone else in the office' often acted as a contact themselves, introducing the client and their problems to a relevant official whom the client did not know personally. Knowing someone in the office (but not the relevant official) increased the use of contacts by 20 per cent, increased the use of small presents by 14 per cent, and increased the use of money or expensive presents by 6 per cent. (Table 4.11) That contrasts very sharply with the impact of knowledge about legal rights, which *reduced* the use of all three by about 5 per cent.

Again, knowing someone in the office *increased* the chances of having to accept an unsatisfactory outcome by 5 per cent, whereas knowledge of legal rights *reduced* it by 16 per cent. Those who usually 'knew an official in the office' were not on the whole any more satisfied than others about their dealings with officials, while knowledge of legal rights increased satisfaction by around 12 per cent. For the general public in their day-to-day interactions with street-level officials it seems both cheaper and better to know your rights than to know an official (though the opposite might well be true for high-level criminal activity and 'grand' corruption).

Table 4.11. The impact of acquaintance with officials on choice of strategies

	Percentage who used each strategy frequently, that is, 'more than rarely'							
	accept but not satisfied %	behave unusually pleasantly %	argue/ persist %	appeal to higher official %	appeal to elected politician %	use contact %	offer small present %	offer money etc. %
By whether usually knew anyone in the office: if knew...								
another official	75	71	56	24	13	46	36	18
relevant official	65	63	49	23	13	31	25	15
no one	70	63	49	19	7	26	22	12
impact	+5	+8	+7	+5	+6	+20	+14	+6

Note: Percentages in this table are the average of the percentages in the four countries, and the impact figures therefore show the average impact within countries.

In fact, it was clear from our focus-group discussions that using personal contacts was not always a very pleasant experience for the general public. 'I am a medical woman, I am friends with the dentist and the nurse. And yet I have got to invite them to a coffee shop and treat them. I wonder what people without connections can do.'(Ya 5) 'Some time ago my father had to be placed in hospital. A doctor, an acquaintance of ours, approached us and said: "I can do something for you. It will be very difficult but you have to pay for each day, since your father is not military"—I am speaking about the military hospital—"and you have to pay for the food, medicine, stay, treatment, for everything." It actually became a game of nerves. And it was a question of 30,000 levs. A year and a half ago that was quite a sum.'(So-B 8) With friends and acquaintances like these, they might feel, who needs enemies?

THE IMPACT OF DEALING WITH DIFFERENT KINDS OF OFFICIAL

It would have been far too time-consuming to ask respondents in detail about their interactions with different kinds of official. The patience of our respondents would have been exhausted long before we reached the end of the interview. But we know whether each respondent had any personal experience of dealing with 13 specified types of official, and we know what kinds of strategies they used. Of course, most citizens had dealt with several kinds of official and some citizens had dealt with many kinds of official, so we cannot divide the public into separate categories, each of which dealt exclusively with only one kind of official. Nonetheless, if those respondents who dealt with one particular kind of official (no doubt in addition to various others) reported an unusual tendency to use a particular strategy, it seems reasonable to link that strategy to that type of official, although technically it could be no more than a statistical coincidence.

In the event, those who had dealt with customs officials were the most likely to report frequent use of arguments, appeals, contacts, presents and bribes. They were particularly distinctive in terms of their use of presents and bribes. Compared to those who had dealt with pensions officials, for example, those who had dealt with customs officials were 15 per cent more likely to have used contacts, 17 per cent more likely to have offered small presents, and 13 per cent more likely to have offered money or an expensive present. Those who had dealt with the police were the next most likely to have used contacts, presents and bribes.

Multiple regression provides a better way to estimate the unique impact of dealings with each particular type of official after excluding the concurrent effects of dealing with other officials. Although in a large survey such as ours, many of the regression coefficients proved statistically significant, we shall restrict our attention to those that indicated at least a 10 per cent impact. These multiple regressions estimated that dealings with customs officials increased the use of contacts by 10 per cent, the use of small presents by 16 per cent, and the use of money or expensive presents by 11 per cent.

But there were very few other impacts greater than 10 per cent. Multiple regressions only highlighted the impact of dealing with housing officials on stimulating argument, the impact of dealing with health officials on stimulating abnormally pleasant behaviour, and the impact of dealing with contracts officials on stimulating argument and reducing abnormally pleasant behaviour.

THE IMPACT OF ATTEMPTED EXTORTION

The impact of attempted extortion was particularly strong. Although Michael Lipsky argues that clients nearly always have some means of influencing their relationship with street-level bureaucrats, he also points out that 'the relationship is by no means a balanced one' and that it is 'primarily determined by the priorities and preferences of the street-level bureaucrats', not by their clients.[13] So it appears. Those who complained that officials had asked them directly for a gift tried harder at all strategies. They were between 28 and 34 per cent more likely to report using contacts, presents and bribes. (Table 4.12, Fig. 4.3) But they were also around 14 per cent more likely to report using abnormally pleasant behaviour or appeals to higher officials, and 21 per cent more likely to report frequent arguments. In the end they were also 10 per cent more likely to accept an unsatisfactory outcome.

Table 4.12. The impact of extortion on choice of strategies

	Percentage who used each strategy frequently, that is, 'more than rarely'							
	accept but not satisfied %	behave unusually pleasantly %	argue/ persist %	appeal to higher official %	appeal to elected politician %	use contact %	offer small present %	offer money etc. %
By whether an official in the last few years ever asked directly for money or a present, or seemed to expect something. If official...								
asked directly	72	70	62	29	13	54	50	33
seemed to expect	76	71	59	27	11	40	33	19
neither	62	57	41	15	7	20	13	5
impact	+10	+13	+21	+14	+6	+34	+37	+28
By how often officials made unnecessary problems in order to get money or a present for solving them. If...								
frequently	80	76	71	35	13	49	43	26
rarely	72	67	55	22	10	32	25	12
never	60	56	36	13	6	20	13	6
impact	+20	+20	+35	+22	+7	+29	+30	+20

Note: Percentages in this table are the average of the percentages in the four countries, and the impact figures therefore show the average impact within countries.

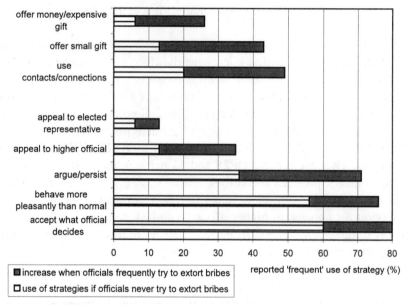

Fig. 4.3. The impact of attempted extortion by 'unnecessary
problems'
(strategies displayed by category)

Those who complained that officials had frequently made unnecessary problems for them in order to extract bribes, also tried harder at every possible strategy that might achieve a successful outcome. But the impact of officials making problems to extract a bribe was significantly different from the impact of officials asking directly for a bribe. Officials 'making unnecessary problems' had slightly less impact on their clients' use of contacts, presents and bribes, though it still increased their use by between 20 and 30 per cent. At the same time, however, it had far more impact on the use of abnormally pleasant behaviour (boosted by 20 per cent instead of only 13 per cent), appeals to higher officials (boosted by 22 per cent instead of 14 per cent), and especially on the use of argument (boosted by 35 per cent instead of only 21 per cent). There is another way of looking at this contrast. Direct requests from officials for gifts increased offers of small presents by almost twice as much as it increased the use of argument. But making unnecessary problems for clients increased the use of argument by more than it increased the use of small presents. Officials who caused unnecessary problems to get bribes clearly incensed the public even more than those officials who openly and directly asked for bribes.

Table 4.13. The impact of different problems on choice of strategies

	accept but not satisfied %	behave unusually pleasantly %	argue/ persist %	appeal to higher official %	appeal to elected politician %	use contact %	offer small present %	offer money etc. %
	Percentage who used each strategy frequently, that is, 'more than rarely'							
If officials...								
were incapable, lazy, uninformative	73	66	55	23	10	33	26	14
wanted money etc.	78	81	63	38	18	51	54	41
caused no problems	49	49	23	10	5	14	8	3
impact of incompetence etc.	+24	+17	+32	+13	+5	+19	+18	+11
impact of extortion	+29	+32	+40	+28	+13	+37	+46	+38

Note: Percentages in this table are the average of the percentages in the four countries, and the impact figures therefore show the average impact within countries.

The choice of strategies adopted by citizens was related to the different problems caused by officials. There was very little difference between the strategies adopted by citizens who were troubled by incompetent, lazy or uninformative officials. So we have averaged the strategy profiles for citizens who were troubled by such officials. But collectively they differed significantly from the strategies adopted by citizens who had been troubled more frequently by officials who sought bribes. The impact of dealing with incompetent, lazy or uninformative officials on citizens' acceptance of unsatisfactory outcomes (24 per cent) was almost as great as the impact of dealing with officials who wanted money or presents (29 per cent).

But dealing with incompetent, lazy or uninformative officials boosted argument by 32 per cent and had much less impact on any other strategy, though it boosted the use of abnormally pleasant behaviour, contacts and small presents by around 18 per cent.

By contrast, dealing with officials who wanted money or presents had most effect on the use of small presents, which was boosted by 46 per cent. It also boosted the use of money or expensive presents by 38 per cent—raising the level from 3 per cent amongst those who experienced no problems with officials, to 41 per cent amongst those who were most troubled by officials seeking presents. In addition to that, dealing with avaricious officials boosted the use of every strategy more, often much more, than did dealing with merely incompetent, lazy or uninformative officials. (Table 4.13, Fig. 4.4)

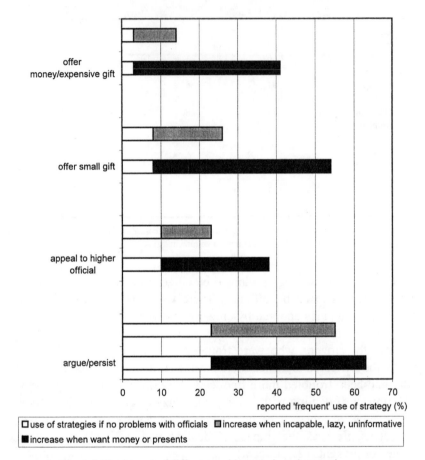

Fig. 4.4. The impact of different problems (selected strategies displayed)

ALL STRATEGIES CORRELATE WITH CITIZEN DISSATISFACTION

Our evidence suggests that all the strategies reviewed in this chapter were means of coping with unsatisfactory treatment at the hands of officials. No doubt some people enjoyed the exercise of their skills in argument, the mobilisation of their networks of contacts, or the frisson of power they got from using bribes to manipulate underpaid officials. But such citizens seem to be the exception, not the rule. In post-communist Europe citizens were as 'underpaid' as officials—or even more so. Despite the popular suspicion that their fellow-citizens were happy to achieve their ends by using these various strategies, every one of the eight strategies we studied was used more by those who described their experiences with officials as 'unsatisfactory' than by those who described them as satisfactory. (Table 4.14) Thus the frequency of using any of these eight strategies correlated with dissatisfaction rather than with satisfaction.

Table 4.14. The impact of unsatisfactory experiences on choice of strategies

| | Percentage who used each strategy frequently, that is, 'more than rarely' | | | | | | | |
	accept but not satisfied %	behave unusually pleasantly %	argue/ persist %	appeal to higher official %	appeal to elected politician %	use contact %	offer small present %	offer money etc %
By whether, on the whole, personal experiences of dealing with officials in the last few years were satisfactory.								
if unsatis- factory	81	72	70	33	14	39	33	21
if satisfactory	64	60	41	17	7	28	21	11
impact	+17	+12	+29	+16	+7	+11	+12	+10

Note: Percentages in this table are the average of the percentages in the four countries, and the impact figures therefore show the average impact within countries.

Dissatisfaction correlated most strongly with the use of argument and persistence ($r = 0.30$) or appeals to higher officials ($r = 0.23$). But dissatisfaction also correlated significantly with the use of abnormally pleasant behaviour and with the use of contacts, presents and bribes ($r = 0.16$ on average). Dissatisfaction correlated less with any of these citizen strategies than with the mere fact of unfair treatment ($r = 0.50$) but the correlations with citizen strategies were high nonetheless.

Those who felt dissatisfied with their experience were 29 per cent more likely to have engaged in frequent argument, 16 per cent more likely to have appealed to higher officials, and around 11 per cent more likely to have used abnormally pleasant behaviour, contacts, presents or bribes. There is no evidence here that citizens actually enjoyed any of the strategies for influencing officials. Such strategies were forced upon them.

CONCLUSION: INCREASED ARGUMENT, NOT BRIBERY, IS THE MAIN RESPONSE TO ILL-TREATMENT

Our findings suggest that the strategies used by citizens in their dealings with officials owed more to the officials than to the citizens. All strategies were responsive strategies, and all strategies correlated with citizen dissatisfaction.

Citizens' own characteristics had relatively little impact on the strategies they used in dealing with officials. But citizens' experience of unfair treatment and attempted extortion had much more effect upon the strategies they adopted. Unfair treatment correlated moderately with more frequent use of almost all citizen strategies. Extortion correlated particularly strongly with the use of contacts, presents and bribes, but also with greater use of argument or appeals to higher officials. (Table 4.15)

Table 4.15. Correlation between choice of strategies and experience

Correlations:	accept but not satis fied r x100	behave unusually pleasantly r x100	argue/ persist r x100	appeal to higher official r x100	appeal to elected politician r x100	use contact r x100	offer small present r x100	offer money etc. r x100
with unfair treatment	9	15	17	16	12	12	17	17
with officials making problems	15	18	33	29	17	34	37	35
with officials asking for gifts	8	12	22	21	13	34	37	33
with unsatisfactory experience	18	13	30	23	14	15	16	17

Note: All the correlations are statistically significant at the 1 per cent level.

Before we move on in the next chapter to focus more narrowly on bribery and extortion we need to emphasise the significance of more '*democratically legitimate*' strategies for coping with officials—especially the use of argument and persistence.

Of all the strategies that citizens used, their use of argument and persistence was the most sensitive to ill-treatment. It came third on the list of most frequently used strategies, beaten only by passive acceptance and abnormally pleasant behaviour. It held that position amongst those who had to deal with incompetent, lazy or uninformative officials. It held that position even amongst those who had to deal with officials who asked for bribes, and it held that position even more securely amongst those who dealt with officials who made unnecessary problems in order to get bribes. Extortion did stimulate the use of presents and bribes but it also stimulated argument and persistence. When extortion entailed the creation of unnecessary problems, it stimulated argument and persistence *even more* than it stimulated the use of presents and bribes.

According to Richard Lotspeich, 'anecdotal evidence from many different sources shows that payoffs to state officials for a wide variety of services' are 'ubiquitous' in post-communist Europe 'and have been for some time'.[14] John T. Noonan concedes that anecdotal evidence indicates that in all places and at all times, some people use bribery. Indeed, Noonan admits that the perception that 'everybody does it' is one of the most frequent arguments against moral condemnation of bribery and that it leads to the conclusion that reform is impossible.[15] But it is, he claims, 'essentially a quantitative argument, and its failure to produce quantitative data is its first deficiency'.[16]

So it is significant that our evidence supports Noonan rather than Lotspeich. Our evidence suggests that although occasional bribery of street-level bureaucrats in post-communist Europe is widespread, the most frequent strategies used by the public to combat unhelpful officials are not bribery but ingratiating behaviour, persistence and argument. These '*democratically legitimate*' strategies do not provide engaging anecdotes, but good anecdotes are often, by their nature, about the exceptions rather than the norms of everyday life. Even in our study, participants' gossip and anecdotes do suggest that 'everybody does it' all the time—but their convincing reports of their own actual experience do not.

NOTES

1 Lipsky, *Street-Level Bureaucracy*, 57.

2 Lancaster and Montinola, 'Towards a Methodology for the Comparative Study of Political Corruption', 193–4.

3 Tanzi, 'Corruption around the World', 577.

4 Lipsky, *Street-Level Bureaucracy*, 58.

5 *Tiurma i volya* (21 January 1999) and *Donbass* (19 January 1999), quoted by *Corruption Watch* 2, no. 3(24) (3 February 1999).

6 Noonan, *Bribes*, 708–9.

7 Kettle, 'Of Money and Morality', 39.

8 Smeltz and Sweeney, *On the Take*, 8.

9 Rose and Haerpfer, *New Democracies Barometer 5*, 33 and 58.

10 Smeltz and Sweeney, *On the Take*, 10.

11 DiFranceisco and Gitelman, 'Soviet Political Culture', 612.

12 DiFranceisco and Gitelman, 'Soviet Political Culture', 611.

13 Lipsky, *Street-Level Bureaucracy*, 59.

14 Lotspeich, 'Crime in the Transition Economies', 577.

15 Noonan, *Bribes*, 685.

16 Noonan, *Bribes*, 693.

CHAPTER 5

WILLING GIVERS?

Umit Berkman presents a particularly useful and comprehensive 'conceptual framework'[1] for explanations of 'bureaucracy and bribery' based on five major factors. These are related to:

- (C) the *bribe-giving clients* (C1: their values and norms; C2: the importance of the benefits to them; C3: their financial situation; and C4: their calculation of the risk involved);
- (O) the *bribe-taking officials* (O1: their values and norms; O2: the importance of the benefits to them; O3: their financial situation; O4: their position and tenure within the organisation; and O5: their calculation of the risk involved);
- (A) the *corrupt act itself* (A1: the nature of the corrupt act, e.g. expediting or distorting; A2: the demand for the corrupt act; A3: the supply of decision-making positions; A4: the number of collaborators needing to be brought together);
- (I) the *institution* where the bribery takes place;
- (E) the wider *national environment* within which both organisations and individuals operate.

In this chapter we focus on the behaviour of clients, on bribe giving rather than on bribe taking. We look at how clients' behaviour is conditioned by 'the nature of the corrupt act' (A1), especially whether it is designed to obtain a legal right or a favour, and we set clients' behaviour in the context of the wider national environment (E). But we focus primarily on the 'values and norms' of clients (C1) and 'the demand for the corrupt act' (A2)—and on the tension between these two powerful forces.

The 'values and norms' of clients (C1) are expressed in their approval of, excuses for, or condemnation of bribery. From the perspective of the client, 'the demand for the corrupt act' (A2) is often literally a 'demand' by an official for a bribe. It would be simplistic to expect that clients' behaviour should reflect nothing more than their values and norms. But it would be equally wrong to dismiss the importance of clients' values and norms merely because they do not dictate behaviour completely. Instead, we attempt to weigh the impact of clients' values against the impact of their experience of attempts at extortion by officials.

Did clients' values matter at all? Or was extortion the only influence? In the previous chapter we found that attempted extortion clearly had a considerable impact on the strategies used by citizens. But there was scope for values to have some impact even if they did not completely determine behaviour. Some citizens offered presents or bribes even when officials neither made demands nor caused unnecessary problems, and some citizens resisted extortion while others submitted to it.

Even when clients did submit to extortion, it is by no means obvious that they did so gladly. No doubt some were happy to give a bribe because it provided a quicker solution. But others no doubt submitted to extortion with anger, reluctance and resentment. To what extent were givers willing or unwilling givers? To what extent, in the language of the church, were their gifts to officials 'free-will offerings' or enforced 'tithes'? Feelings and subjective interpretations are important both in terms of the political disaffection that may be generated by corruption and in terms of the likely degree of public support for reform. Behaviour itself is only part of the story, albeit an important part.

A MORAL IMPERATIVE TO OBEY THE LAW?

Since bribing officials was unambiguously illegal in all four countries, and even small presents could be construed as bribes in law, respect for the law should have a bearing on attitudes towards using presents to influence officials. But respect for the law had not been encouraged by decades of communist government. The public in the former Soviet Union, for example, was notoriously intolerant and authoritarian[2] but not necessarily very law-abiding. Authority, morality and law were separated from each other much more clearly under the Soviet regime than in Western Europe. Insofar as they were intended to be applied at all, Soviet laws were the embodiment of state power, not the embodiment of a universal morality or public opinion. Worse, they were applied, or not applied, quite arbitrarily. To a significant degree Soviet laws were merely part of the propaganda battle with Western liberal democracy rather than codes to be rigidly followed, whether convenient to Soviet officials or not. 'The accepted approach...seemed to be, if the first law does not work, pass another one', even if the new law was no more respected and no more effective than the previous one.[3] It was the changing Party Line rather than the Law, which had to be respected. Thus Gorbachev's emphasis on a 'law-bound state' in the 1980s was a radical idea in the Soviet context, though it seemed banal in a Western liberal context. And if the Soviet regime did not respect the law, there was no reason why its citizens should do so either.

Central Europe had a shorter and less intense experience of communism, with rather less emphasis on the Party and somewhat more on the law. Reflecting that difference in traditions, we found that people in Ukraine were almost twice as likely as people in the Czech Republic to say that people 'should ignore or avoid' the law if they considered it was 'very unreasonable or unjust'. But by their own account, 59 per cent in Ukraine felt they should 'try to ignore or avoid' laws which they felt were 'very unreasonable or unjust'. (Table 5.1) A large majority in Ukraine simply did not equate law with morality. By contrast, less than a third of the public in the Czech Republic felt it was right to ignore unreasonable laws.

Table 5.1. Should people obey or ignore an unreasonable or unjust law?

	Average	Czech Republic	Slovakia	Bulgaria	Ukraine
	%	%	%	%	%
They should try to ignore or avoid it	44	32	47	37	59

Note: 'Don't know', 'mixed/depends', etc. answers were recorded if given spontaneously, but never prompted; they have been excluded from the calculation of percentages.

Despite its shared experience of the Czechoslovak period, however, the Slovak public in the 1990s took a view mid-way between that in Ukraine and that in the Czech Republic. Bulgarians came closer than Slovaks to the Czechs in their declared respect for the law—though that may have reflected the post-election euphoria and the unusual and temporarily high level of support for their new government in Bulgaria.

PUBLIC CONDEMNATION OF THE USE OF CONTACTS, PRESENTS AND BRIBES

We asked whether people considered 'the use of money, presents, favours or contacts to influence officials':

(i) 'bad for (the country), and for those involved?'
(ii) 'bad for (the country), but unavoidable for people who have to live here?'

or did they...

(iii) 'prefer it that way, because when you need a favour from an official, you can get it?'

'Bad for (the country), and for those involved?' This first option corresponded to the simple and unqualified condemnation of these practices that was expressed by some participants in our focus-group discussions. 'I do not approve of bribes.'(Do 3) There are many reasons for condemning bribery and corruption. Some would no doubt condemn bribery as inherently sinful, on a par with lying, cheating and stealing. Bribery does not appear explicitly on the Judaeo-Christian tradition's list of the Ten Commandments but it is not far removed from them. Indeed, to those within that tradition, Noonan argues that 'bribery violates a divine paradigm'.[4] From an economic perspective, Donatella Della Porta and Alberto Vannucci condemn bribery on the grounds of rationality and efficiency rather than morality.[5] Democratic theorists condemn it on the grounds that it offends their concept of 'equality of treatment' of citizens by the state—a view that was well expressed in one focus group: 'Corruption causes a distinction [but] every citizen is equal before any administrative official...That is what equality should mean.' (So-A 6) Another focus-group participant condemned the practice because it offended their concept of fairness to officials rather than fairness to citizens: 'It often happens that an unhelpful [official] gains even more than the one who is willing to help.'(Br-B 6)

Because there are so many disparate reasons for condemnation we use the term 'condemnation' without restricting it by adding the adjective 'moral'. But irrespective of its basis, condemnation of bribery is a key element of the 'values and norms' held by many citizens.

'Bad for (the country), but unavoidable for people who have to live here?' The second option combines condemnation of corruption with

some excuse for those who practice it. Noonan lists the five most frequent arguments against moral condemnation of bribery. We met (and rejected) one in the previous chapter: 'Everybody does it.' More relevant here is another, rather different, argument on Noonan's list: that 'It is necessary to do it.'[6] Noonan's own reading of the evidence 'does not show that bribery is necessary but that it has been thought to be necessary'.[7] Necessity was certainly a very frequent excuse under communism and it remains quite frequent under post-communist regimes. Konstantin Simis argues that bribery was certainly necessary during the declining years of the Soviet system. From anecdotal evidence, press reports, and his own experience of Soviet life he concluded that 'the Soviet Union is infected from top to bottom with corruption'. But 'this does not mean that the average Soviet citizen is immoral'. Rather, the Soviet citizen would 'lie to a representative of the government administration but be truthful and honest in relations with friends and neighbours; be happy to steal twenty packs of cigarettes from a tobacco factory where he worked but not steal a penny from another person'. With respect to corruption, 'if he did not pay bribes his family would not have meat, he would be forced to wait five or six years before a telephone was installed, he would remain for years with his large family in a single room in a communal apartment'. The Soviet citizen gave all these bribes 'without any burden on his conscience'. Well aware that he was breaking the law, he 'did not consider his actions immoral'. 'This double standard resulted from the complete alienation of the Soviet individual from governmental power.'[8]

Ending the Soviet system clearly did not solve the problem. Even when citizens were no longer completely alienated from power collectively with regard to electing a government, they were not necessarily in a powerful position individually with regard to street-level officials. According to some of our focus-group participants: 'You cannot do anything another way in this situation.'(Ho 2) Despite Simis's assumption that his fellow-citizens did not consider it immoral (though he clearly did not condone it himself), focus-group participants often combined condemnation with excuse, excuse with condemnation. 'I object to things like this...someone may force it out of you in a way...but I am basically against it, things should work even without gifts, those people are there to help, they are paid for it, its their duty.'(Br-B 6) It was possible even to excuse takers as well as givers: 'I think that the majority of those who take bribes are also compelled to do that because they do not get [enough] salary.'(Striy 5)

'*I prefer it that way, because when you need a favour from an offi-cial, you can get it.*' This third option expresses a positive preference, even approval, for bribery and corruption. Some participants in focus-group discussions openly expressed such sentiments. 'The main thing is the result.'(Striy 3) 'In any situation, whatever amount of money [the citizen] pays, it is normally more important that the problem is solved than that money is paid for it.'(Striy 5) Others argued that presents might usefully encourage flexibility. 'One person needs a passport in two months and someone else in two days. For the first person it is not so important as to have to give a gift, but for someone else it may be crucial if he/she needs it immediately.'(HK 3)

Faced explicitly with these three options, relatively few in our sur-veys expressed a positive preference for a corrupt system, but a large minority was willing to excuse it. (Table 5.2) On average, 39 per cent were willing either to excuse or approve corruption—rather less in the Czech Republic but more than that in every other country. Nonetheless, an absolute majority in every country, never less than 58 per cent nor more than 69 per cent, unreservedly condemned the use of money, pres-ents, favours, and contacts to influence officials.

Table 5.2. Public 'values and norms'

	Average	Czech Republic	Slovakia	Bulgaria	Ukraine
	%	%	%	%	%
Which comes closest to your view about the use of money, presents, favours and contacts to influence officials?					
it is bad for (the country) and for those involved	61	69	60	58	58
it is bad for (the country), but unavoid-able for citizens	30	25	28	34	31
I prefer it	9	7	12	8	11

Notes: 'Don't know', 'mixed/depends', etc. answers were recorded if given spontaneously, but never prompted; they have been excluded from the calculation of percentages.

The phrase '(the country)' was replaced by the name of the country in which the interview took place.

At this level of values and norms there was little evidence of any distinctive national cultures in our surveys. Our evidence here is consis-tent with findings drawn from the recent World Values Survey: in every one of the 33 countries where the question was put to the public, 'majority opinion classified accepting a bribe in the course of one's duties as never justified'.[9] Similarly, in USIA surveys covering Eastern and Western Europe during 1998–99, an overwhelming majority in every country said that taking a bribe in the course of a person's duties could never be justified. More specifically, in these USIA surveys the average level of outright condemnation in Bulgaria, Slovakia and the Czech Republic was almost the same as the average in Britain, France, Germany and Italy.[10] Cross-nationally, Noonan is right to claim that corruption is 'universally shameful' even if the majority against it is less than total anywhere.[11]

But putting the question in another way elicited greater—and more variable—public support for a system of presents and favours. We offered a choice between an austere Weberian system[12] where 'officials never accept presents and never do favours for people', and one where 'officials sometimes accept presents and in return do favours for people'. It was a hard choice, and to some extent an unreasonably hard one. Truly Weberian systems are hard to find in the real world, though Vito Tanzi claims Canada, New Zealand and Scandinavia may come close.[13] More important, a Weberian system is cold and unattractive. It is not a universally acknowledged standard of perfection. It is certainly not our standard of perfection. Citizens' top preference might be a system in which officials did not take bribes but still did favours for clients out of human kindness. But we did not offer that option. We deliberately posed the question in such a way that presents and bribes were pictured as the price to be paid for flexibility and consideration—a choice between two evils, not between evil and virtue.

Table 5.3. Public preferences for a reciprocal system of presents and favours

	Average	Czech Republic	Slovakia	Bulgaria	Ukraine
	%	%	%	%	%
Which would you prefer, a system where officials: (i) never accepted presents and never did favours for people? or (ii) sometimes accepted presents and in return did favours for people?					
prefer system of presents and favours	29	9	19	41	48

Note: 'Don't know', 'mixed/depends', etc. answers were recorded if given spontaneously, but never prompted; they have been excluded from the calculation of percentages.

Was that a price worth paying? For the Czechs it was not. Only 9 per cent in the Czech Republic favoured a system of reciprocal presents and favours. The Weberian model of a well-oiled but inhuman machine was the ideal for the overwhelming majority in the Czech Republic, as it was for four-fifths in Slovakia. But it was not nearly so popular in Bulgaria or Ukraine where almost half the public opted for a system of reciprocal presents and favours. (Table 5.3)

A PERMANENT PART OF OUR COUNTRY'S HISTORY AND CULTURE?

Berkman's scheme includes the impact of 'the wider national environment' (E). We have outlined four models for the impact of history and national culture. Some might feel that the use of money, presents and favours was part of their country's national tradition, part of their culture—not perhaps a valued part of their culture, but an inescapable part (the *'dead hand of history'* model). If so, there was not much that could be done about it.

But there were some other obvious historical explanations for the scale of corruption in Central and Eastern Europe. It might be blamed on the legacy of communism. If so, it could be expected to fade away as the communist system was progressively dismantled (the *'fading legacy'* model).[14] Ironically, in communist circles corruption was once viewed as a 'bourgeois legacy' that would fade away as society moved towards communism.

Alternatively, it could be blamed on the transition itself, with all the economic and moral chaos that accompanied it (the perverse variant of the *'escape from domination'* model). Leslie Holmes's argument that 'the very nature of post-communism encourages corruption'[15] hints at a one-way transition to a higher level of corruption. He optimistically presents some reasons for anticipating that the season of corruption, inaugurated by the transition, may come to an end:

- 'many of those who break the law in order to make wealth in its earliest stages subsequently want the law to protect and legitimise their gains';
- as post-communist economies recover from 'free-fall', 'officials who currently engage in corrupt practices primarily out of survival instincts' will desist;

- better pay for law-enforcement officers may help;
- 'legislation is gradually improving';
- 'the role of the media and of critical civil society more generally could play a positive role in bringing corruption to heel'.[16]

But Holmes adds that this 'optimistic scenario' is only a possibility not a prediction, still less a certainty. Nonetheless, insofar as corruption is mainly the product of a period of transition, then it is at least possible that it might fade away as and when a new and more orderly era emerges.

Ivan Krastev claims that 'in the context of post-communist politics...the majority of the public sees corruption as a direct result of market reforms'.[17] We asked the public to respond to the following question: 'Is the use of money, presents, favours and contacts to influence officials in your country

(i) a product of the communist past (the *'fading legacy'* model)?

(ii) a product of moral crisis in a period of transition (the *'escape from domination'* model)? or

(iii) a permanent part of your culture (the *'dead hand of history'* model)?'

Table 5.4. A product of the crisis of transition, or a permanent part of the country's culture?

	Average	Czech Republic	Slovakia	Bulgaria	Ukraine
	%	%	%	%	%
The use of money, presents, favours and contacts to influence officials in (your country) is...					
a product of moral crisis in a period of transition	43	31	30	49	62
a permanent part of (the country's) culture	36	46	47	34	16
a product of the communist past	22	23	23	17	23

Notes: 'Don't know', 'mixed/depends', etc. answers were recorded if given spontaneously, but never prompted; they have been excluded from the calculation of percentages.

The phrase '(your country)/(the country's)' was replaced by the name of the country in which the interview took place.

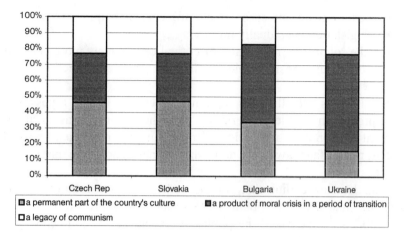

Fig. 5.1. Corruption–a product of moral crisis in a period of
transition?

On average, the culprit most frequently named by the public was 'the moral crisis of the transition'. (Table 5.4, Fig. 5.1) But there were sharp cross-national variations. People in the Czech and Slovak Republics were the most willing to accept that corruption was 'a permanent part' of their country's culture. By contrast, only 34 per cent in Bulgaria and a mere 16 per cent in Ukraine saw it as a permanent part of their culture and most people in Ukraine blamed it on the moral crisis of the transition.

This pattern of opinion might surprise some outside observers, perhaps many. Surely, they would argue, Ukrainian corruption is the product of a centuries-old 'culture of corruption'. Robert Service claims that in the old Soviet Union, of which Ukraine, along with Russia, formed the core: 'Always, there was a need to bargain and fiddle in order to make life tolerable…It was influenced by practices inherited from the three centuries of tsarism and its imprint remains on politics and society.'[18] But our findings would not surprise internal observers such as Ivan Krastev. No doubt there was some legacy from the past. But the Ukrainian public did not attribute current levels of corruption primarily to that historical or cultural legacy. They blamed it primarily on the moral crisis of the transition. Their view is perhaps closer to the more complex view expressed by Richard Paddock, which emphasises the power of the present to revive the flagging traditions of the past. According to Paddock, 'the practice of bribery dates back at least 450 years, to the time of the first czars'. It was complemented by the 'servile psychology' of the people, and 'despite Stalin's efforts to stamp it out, bribery survived communist rule to flower in the past eight years under gangster capitalism'.[19]

Our Ukrainian respondents' perception that corruption could be attributed more to the transition than to any cultural/historical legacy is consistent with their perception of rapidly falling standards of political and administrative behaviour. In Chapter 3 we found that, by a margin of 66 per cent, the public in Ukraine thought most of their politicians and street-level officials now behaved worse than they had under communism. That was backed up by many comments in our Ukrainian focus-group discussions that attributed declining standards to the fact that officials no longer lived in fear of the Party. The Ukrainian public certainly believed that corruption had 'flowered' during the transition. Such a very recent fall in the standards of behaviour of politicians and officials could not reasonably be attributed to a 'permanent national culture'. The public in fact explicitly attributed it to the post-communist 'transition'. Right or wrong, the people we interviewed in Ukraine were at least consistent in their views.

Conversely, we found that public perceptions of economic chaos during the transition were much less in the Czech and Slovak Republics than in Bulgaria and Ukraine. The sense of crisis was much less and the chaos of transition was a less obviously available scapegoat for the levels of public-sector corruption that the public thought existed in the Czech and Slovak Republics.

Table 5.5. Why the public thinks clients are more willing to give gifts now

	Average	Czech Republic	Slovakia	Bulgaria	Ukraine
	%	%	%	%	%
Since the end of communism:					
officials expect more	50	34	45	64	56
people push harder for special favours	31	45	33	19	28
people are *not* more willing to give money	11	10	13	11	11
people are more able to pay	8	11	9	6	5

Note: Respondents were asked to compare the present with the communist period, defined as 'during the Soviet period' in Ukraine, and by 'before 1989' elsewhere.

We asked why clients might now be more willing to use presents and bribes than under communism. On average, the most popular explanation was that officials expected more gifts now (50 per cent). In Bulgaria and Ukraine, two or three times as many blamed officials as blamed their clients. In Slovakia as well, more blamed officials than their clients, though the margin was not so great. Only in the Czech Republic was clients' 'pushing harder for special favours' the most popular explanation. (Table 5.5)

We also asked why clients might be *less* willing to use presents and bribes than under communism. Berkman's conceptual scheme listed 'the client's financial situation' (C3) as one influence on bribe giving. Overall, that proved to be the most frequent reason given for any decline in willingness to give bribes. On average, the most popular explanation for clients' reduced willingness to offer gifts was simply that they were 'less able to pay now'(44 per cent). The proportion that put forward that explanation reached 64 per cent in Ukraine. (Table 5.6) In Bulgaria also, twice as many cited inability to pay as cited any other reason. But in Slovakia clients' 'standing up more for their rights' rivalled inability to pay, and in the Czech Republic it was by far the most popular explanation (49 per cent).

Table 5.6. Why the public thinks clients are less willing to give gifts now

	Average	Czech Republic	Slovakia	Bulgaria	Ukraine
	%	%	%	%	%
Since the end of communism:					
people are less able to pay	44	36	44	33	64
people stand up for their rights more	30	49	36	18	17
people are *not* less willing to give money	16	5	9	40	11
officials do not have as much power over people	10	10	11	10	8

Note: Respondents were asked to compare the present with the communist period, defined as 'during the Soviet period' in Ukraine, and by 'before 1989' elsewhere.

The Czech public therefore explained both increased and decreased willingness to pay bribes in terms of *active citizens* taking the initiative, while the Ukrainian public explained both increased and decreased willingness to pay in terms of *passive citizens* being driven by forces beyond their control.

WOULD CITIZENS GIVE BRIBES IF ASKED, OR ACCEPT THEM IF OFFERED?

As a measure of the potential for bribery we asked whether the public would give bribes if asked, or take bribes if offered. To disentangle *inability* to pay from *refusal* to pay we were careful to include the qualifying phrase 'if you could afford it' in our question about whether people would pay bribes. We asked: 'If you had an important problem, and an official asked you directly for money to solve it, would you:

(i) pay if you could afford it, or
(ii) refuse to pay even if you could afford it?'

Later we asked citizens to project themselves into the role of an official. 'Imagine that you were an official on a low salary, and a person who came to you with a problem offered you money or a present. Would you:

(i) be tempted to give better service, or
(ii) be offended by the offer?'

On both questions unusually large numbers (about 20 per cent) refused to give a straight answer and temporised by volunteering some kind of 'depends on circumstances' answer. But remarkably large numbers of people were ready to admit that they would submit to extortion if they had the resources, and that they would not be offended to receive offers themselves. By an average margin of 10 per cent they said they would pay a bribe rather than refuse (if asked directly and if they could afford it). The margin varied from 10 per cent in Slovakia up to 37 per cent in Ukraine. Only in the Czech Republic were they more likely (by a margin of 22 per cent) to refuse than to give. In behavioural terms that indicates a high level of willingness to submit to extortion. But it does not indicate willingness in the psychological sense of a 'free-will' gift. Submission is not an exercise in freedom.

Our focus-group discussions, particularly those held in Bulgaria, showed that the qualification to these findings, 'if you could afford it', might be important. 'The Bulgarian is used to offering presents when contacting an official. The official may ask for something [more than a present] as well, and you will give it, if you can afford it. In this case you will be attended very well.'(So-B 2) 'Sometimes you are sorry. I knew the price of my case in the hospital, but I did not have the money.' (So-B 2) 'When I was in hospital, a guy whose father had to undergo an operation was told he had to give 20,000 levs. He said he could afford only 10,000 levs. He could not give the money and two days later his father died.'(Te 5) 'I got refusals because I could not afford to pay.'(Stral-IDI 2) 'Roughly speaking all of us here cannot afford it. If you have enough money, you will not have any difficulties...lots of money can make it.'(Ya 2) So although they would not refuse 'if they could afford it', some might refuse to pay what the official asked simply because they could not afford to pay.

Nonetheless, the public's attitude to explicit extortion was remarkably submissive. Much larger numbers would give bribes if asked than had expressed an explicit preference for a system of 'presents and favours' (Table 5.7) and much larger numbers would give bribes if asked than had ever experienced explicit extortion. In the Czech Republic, for example, 93 per cent condemned the use of presents and bribes, 91 per cent stated a preference for a rigid Weberian system where officials never did favours for a client, and 98 per cent had never been asked directly for a bribe. Nonetheless, only 52 per cent would clearly and certainly refuse to pay a bribe, if asked. In Ukraine only 21 per cent were clear that they would refuse.

Table 5.7. Would give if asked, would take if offered

	Average	Czech Republic	Slovakia	Bulgaria	Ukraine
		difference: % would pay – % would refuse			
	%	%	%	%	%
If you had an important problem and an official asked you directly for money and you could afford it, would you pay or refuse?	+10	–22	+10	+13	+37
		difference: % tempted – % offended			
	%	%	%	%	%
Imagine you were an official on a low salary and clients offered you money or a present, would you be tempted to offer better service or be offended by the offer?	–8	–25	–8	–20	+17
difference between submission to extortion and temptation					
	+18	+3	+18	+33	+20

Note: Since an average of around 20 per cent on both questions volunteered the reply that it 'would depend upon the circumstances' we have not excluded them from calculations of percentages. 'Don't knows' have been excluded as usual, however.

By their own account, citizens were significantly more likely to refuse to accept a bribe than to refuse to give a bribe. The pressures of extortion were more powerful than the pressures of temptation—at least in the imagination of the public. Perhaps for those who condemn bribery, it seems less hypocritical to submit to extortion than to temptation. By an average margin of 8 per cent (25 per cent in the Czech Republic) they said they would be offended by the offer of a bribe. More would be offended than tempted in Slovakia and Bulgaria also. But in Ukraine, 48 per cent would be tempted and only 31 per cent offended.

Only a third in the Czech Republic, Slovakia and Bulgaria, along with half the public in Ukraine, were ready, without equivocation, to accept bribes if offered.

FEELINGS ABOUT GIVING BRIBES: HAPPY, ANGRY, WORRIED, OR ASHAMED?

In Chapter 3 we found that a majority of the public in every country thought that *officials who accepted* 'money or a present' would be most likely to feel 'happy' rather than 'angry, worried or ashamed'. But the public suspected that many of their fellow-citizens would also be happy enough if they got what they wanted by giving bribes. In every country a majority thought that *clients who gave* 'money or a present to an official and got what they wanted' would be most likely to feel 'happy' rather than 'angry', 'worried' or 'ashamed'. The pleasure of success would outweigh the cost of the bribe. (Table 5.8)

Table 5.8. Perceptions of clients' feelings about giving gifts

	Average		Czech Republic		Slovakia		Bulgaria		Ukraine	
	%	%	%	%	%	%	%	%	%	%
A: People would be most likely to feel...										
B: But if they thought very few others gave bribes they would then be most likely to feel...										
	A	(B)	A	(B)	A	(B)	A	(B)	A	(B)
happy	59	(23)	50	(15)	63	(18)	66	(36)	55	(22)
angry	18	(29)	25	(36)	23	(37)	13	(20)	11	(24)
worried	10	(20)	7	(15)	5	(14)	11	(16)	18	(34)
ashamed	13	(28)	18	(34)	8	(31)	11	(29)	16	(20)

Note: 'Don't know', 'mixed/depends', etc. answers were recorded if given spontaneously, but never prompted; they have been excluded from the calculation of percentages.

Indeed, in our focus-group discussions participants sometimes expressed their own pleasure at a successful outcome achieved by bribery: '[Under communism], if they told you "no" then you went away and it was "no". Now you give someone a bribe and you go away and it is "yes". I think it is easier now. Now you go with money right away, give it to someone, and they solve your problem…It is more expensive, but it is easier.'(Kh 2) One woman, whose brother had died a vagrant, was told by an official 'We are not giving you any kind of death certificate.' 'What could I do? I brought champagne, chocolate, mandarin oranges, some candy…I gave her the plastic bag. She said: "Thank you. Wait five minutes. Everything will be done. No problem." I am happy, glad, because they gave [the certificate] to me.'(Kh 4) 'Officials were ready to break the rules. It was profitable for all of us.'(Striy-IDI 1) 'What I usually do is ask how much. Then I go to another official and try him, and so on, until I finally pick the one that has demanded the least. I pay after the official has provided the service to make sure my job will be done for me.'(So-IDI 3) This last quotation incidentally indicates that even payments given afterwards could reflect extortion or bribery rather than gratitude in any meaningful sense.

But a large minority in our surveys did think their fellow-citizens would be 'angry', 'worried' or 'ashamed'. Some people in our focus groups felt unhappy on moral grounds: 'I am ashamed to give…I am not ashamed to thank somebody…I am ashamed to give a bribe.'(Striy 3) But others felt it was simply undignified and degrading to give bribes and that giving bribes left them in a powerless position. 'You have to take up your cross, go there, give presents. When the official wants he takes it, but when he does not want it, he does not. I feel dependent and helpless.'(Stral-IDI 1)

If bribe-giving clients 'thought very few other people gave such things to officials', however, the public considered such clients would be much less likely to feel 'happy'. In these circumstances, the percentage expected to feel 'happy' dropped from 59 per cent to 23 per cent. In every country, this new situation would increase bribe givers' 'anger', their 'worry', and their 'shame'—but not by the same amount in each country. In Ukraine 'worry' increased more than anything else. In every other country 'shame' increased more than anything else, most of all in Slovakia where it increased by 23 per cent compared to an increase of only 4 per cent in Ukraine. In their perspectives on bribe givers, as in their perspectives on bribe takers, Ukrainians' views were uniquely characterised by fear rather than shame.

PUBLIC EXPERIENCE OF ACTUALLY GIVING PRESENTS AND BRIBES TO OFFICIALS

So a majority in every country condemned the use of presents and bribes to influence officials. But at the same time, a plurality in every country except the Czech Republic said they would pay a bribe if asked. These were hypothetical questions, however. What had they actually done?

In the previous chapter we found that 42 per cent had offered a small present to an official in recent years and 24 per cent had offered money or an expensive present. We explore that experience of giving presents and bribes in more detail now.

There was a sliding scale of giving. Almost all of those who had offered 'money or an expensive present' had offered 'small presents' as well. Conversely, the more frequently citizens offered small gifts to officials, the more likely they were to also offer large gifts of 'money or an expensive present' in addition. Amongst those who had 'never' offered a small present, less than 2 per cent had offered a large one; amongst those who had 'rarely' offered a small present, 35 per cent had also offered a large one; amongst those who had 'sometimes' offered a small present, 65 per cent had also offered a large one; and amongst those who had 'usually' offered a small present, 86 per cent had also offered a large one.

Giving was a habit. Gifts to officials could be quite frequent, especially in Slovakia and Ukraine. In Ukraine, 39 per cent admitted giving a small present 'more than rarely' in recent years, and 24 per cent had given money or an expensive present 'more than rarely'. Indeed, 13 per cent in Ukraine said that they 'usually' gave a small gift and 8 per cent that they 'usually' gave a large one when dealing with officials in Ukraine. Similar findings emerged from focus-group discussions in Ukraine. 'For this half-year, two times.'(Ky-B 1) 'For my family for the last half-year of time, five times probably, not less.'(Ky-B 3) 'I also had to do it frequently.'(Ky-B 4) For a significant minority of households in Ukraine, gifts to officials had become a budget item.

A DIFFERENCE BETWEEN PRESENTS AND BRIBES? THE SIGNIFICANCE OF SIZE, TIMING AND MOTIVATION

In principle we might wish to distinguish between 'presents' and 'bribes'. Noonan distinguishes between the four categories of 'bribes, gifts, tips and contributions'. In his scheme, gifts are 'not given by way of compensation or by way of purchase…no obligation is imposed'. 'Freely given, the gift leaves the gift-taker free.'[20] According to Zelizer, 'tips' are 'legally optional, informally bestowed, the amount unspecified, variable and arbitrary'.[21] 'Bribes' are a necessary part of the transaction with the official, while 'tips' are purely voluntary. The payment is a 'bribe' only when the official will refuse to provide the service if the 'bribe' is not paid. We might add a further important distinction here. If the client is paying for a favour to which they are not legally entitled, then that is a straight 'bribe'. But if the client is paying for a service to which they are legally entitled, then that is not only 'bribery' but 'extortion' as well.

Rose-Ackerman distinguishes between 'bribes, gifts, prices and tips' on two grounds.[22] First, are they given in return for what she calls a 'quid pro quo'? (The *Oxford English Dictionary* translates this Latin tag into the much more evocative 'something for something'.) Second, are they given 'to agents or to principals'? In a restaurant, the bill is paid to the 'principal', the owner, which makes it a 'price', while the 'tip' is paid to the 'agent', the waiter. Similarly, speeding tickets are paid to the 'principal', the state, which makes it a 'price', while 'bribes' are paid to the 'agent', the traffic policeman. Rose-Ackerman's definitions can be set out in tabular form, as in Table 5.9.

Table 5.9. Rose-Ackerman's definition of bribes

	given in return for something	no explicit return
payment to principal	price	gift
payment to agent	bribe	tip

In her view, gifts and tips are commonly regarded as acceptable: 'The definition of bribes and gifts is a cultural matter…if behaviour labelled "corrupt" by some observers is nevertheless viewed as acceptable gift giving or tipping within a country, it should simply be legalised and reported'—though she adds that 'culture is dynamic and constantly changing'.[23] She also argues that many 'bribes' could be converted into 'prices' by converting 'agents' into 'principals'. 'Bribes' to state-employed doctors could be converted into 'prices' charged by self-employed private-sector doctors, for example. But as long as services remain within the public sector, all officials or state employees are, by definition, merely 'agents' of the state, and all the unofficial payments that they take directly from clients are 'bribes' rather than 'prices'.

Since it is difficult to tell by observation whether a gift is given in expectation of a return ('something for something') it is often necessary to infer it. Hence, there are other common ways of distinguishing between 'presents' and 'bribes' on the basis of such inferences. One is *size*: a small gift is a 'present' or a 'token' while a large gift is a 'bribe'.[24] The inference is that a small gift is too small for the giver to expect anything significant by way of a return. It cannot therefore be a 'something for something'. It must be merely a mark of politeness or appreciation. Another criterion is *timing*: 'bribes' are given beforehand, 'tips' or 'tokens of appreciation' are given afterwards. Here the inference is that after the interaction between client and official there is nothing to be bought. The client is free to give or not give as much or as little as they wish, and it is too late for the official to alter the level of service to match the size of what must now, by inference, be merely a 'tip'.

But these fine distinctions are a good deal easier to make in theory than in practice. Even the most objective of these criteria is less clear-cut than it at first appears. Whether a gift is *large or small* is a matter of subjective judgement. The distinction between clients' *rights or favours* is often obscure and subjective, and, surprisingly perhaps, it is never quite certain whether a gift is given *before or after* a service is rendered.

The 'devil is in the detail' and in the perceptions of those who would classify gifts as 'presents' or 'bribes'—whether these are the officials and clients involved, or outside observers. From the inside there may even be an element of moral hypocrisy: 'I give (or take) tips and tokens, but you give (or take) bribes', or 'I pay bribes only to get what I am legally entitled to get for free, but you pay bribes to get illegal favours and advantages.' The distinction between 'prices' and 'bribes' is eroded when hospitals in post-communist countries charge clients for drugs or hospital services. Between 84 and 95 per cent of the public in the four countries we surveyed thought that people who went 'to a doctor or a hospital' in their country were 'legally entitled to get treatment without any official charge'. When they were charged for treatment they often did not know whether they were contributing to hospital funds (which might, at a stretch, be construed as a 'price' despite the legal entitlement to free health care) or contributing to the pockets of individual health-care staff. Even when they knew that the payment went directly into the pockets of health-care staff, some citizens took the view that they were simply paying a salary that the state had failed in its duty to pay.

The definition of 'large' and 'small' gifts is notoriously subjective. Senior civil servants in Western countries such as Britain have ended up in prison for accepting 'small' gifts from friends who happened to be very rich and very generous businessmen. In one notorious Scottish case the 'small' gifts included a luxury bungalow.[25] Conversely, the Ukrainian law *On Fighting Corruption*, for example, defines 'bribes' to include small gifts and favours such as a ride in a private car or a bottle of whisky—a definition so tight that it would obscure our findings, and so tight that it has, in the view of some Ukrainians, hindered rather than helped the fight against corruption.[26]

The distinction between gifts given before and after a service ignores the elementary fact that human beings anticipate, especially in routine social settings. The waiter anticipates, quite rightly, that especially good service will frequently (if not always) lead to an especially good tip. The client who regularly goes to the same restaurant anticipates that the lack of a good tip on one occasion might lead to worse service on the next. Those who 'tip' their doctor or their dentist in post-communist Europe are in a very similar situation.

The combination of the voluntary or involuntary nature of a gift, along with its size and timing, may provide a less ambiguous classification of 'presents' and 'bribes'. A small gift, voluntarily given afterwards, comes close to being an unambiguous 'tip' or 'present'. Conversely, giving a large gift before the official has provided a service comes close to being unambiguous bribery and, if it is given under pressure, unambiguous extortion.

We found evidence that money or expensive presents, given in advance, are usually payments designed to influence officials to give favours or to avoid causing unnecessary difficulties. Whether given 'voluntarily' or not, such gifts are not signs of gratitude or politeness. 'I gave him 20 dollars and he signed it…I did it in order for him to receive me and sign everything sooner…Yes, just to make him give me a reference. I paid him, got a permission for a subsidy and that was it.'(Striy 2) 'That office works fine. If I pay some extra money they have it ready for me in an instant.'(HK 4) 'The assistant who was to pin the university entrance-exam marks on the wall…was given money and she made mistakes deliberately in the computer. Later, if things became serious, she would confess: "I am sorry, I have made a mistake." The student was already admitted. He could not be expelled. And she could not be fired.'(So-B 1)

Many who admitted offering a 'small present' claimed they had done no more than that and they denied ever giving 'money or an expensive present'. Small gifts given afterwards might be considered more an act of human politeness or gratitude than a bribe to influence the official. 'There are situations where [an official] does not ask or demand anything from you, but you do it for him just out of gratitude.'(Striy 3) Most people would consider that a modest box of chocolates or a bunch of flowers presented to the nurses as a patient left a hospital was such an act of politeness or gratitude. 'If the doctor did an operation, rescued a person from death, and his relatives…bring a box of sweets, a bottle of cognac and flowers, that is not a bribe.'(Kh 6) 'It would not be very decent not to offer chocolates or a bottle of something as gratitude after you have had a major operation.'(So-B 4) 'A box of candy, with gratitude because he has done his job.'(Kh 5) So we might identify small gifts with presents and large gifts with bribes.

But that distinction may be too sharp. In our focus-group discussions even the gift of 'a box of candy' shaded imperceptibly from gratitude into extortion and bribery. 'I had to do it…Just to make the bureaucratic machine work faster, I brought a box of candy.'(Striy 4) 'I am not buying him [the official], I am just giving him something for his work, because he is achieving something there, he does everything faster.'(Ni 2) Even 'gratitude' itself is an elastic concept in the minds of some citizens. 'He is very sick, my son, he misses a lot of school. So purely from gratitude I give something to the teachers, so that they will compromise.'(Kh 2) Boxes of candy soon become bottles of brandy, while 'voluntary' gifts were often 'voluntary in form but extorted in content', as the Party would have said. 'I had to get the external passport and I needed it urgently. Then [the official] says: "You want it to be done faster, take a bottle of cognac and go to the militia." He told me the name and said that I had to tell the militia officer that I came from such-and-such and put the bottle right on the table. I came and as soon as he saw the bag he understood why I had come…I put the bag on the table. Then the militia officer told me to come the next day to get the passport.'(Ho 4) Such gifts are voluntary only in form.

There was also a strong element of extortion even in gifts given 'after' problems had been solved. In our surveys we asked: 'When people give something to an official before their problem has been solved, is that usually because:

(i) 'the official asks for something' (explicit extortion)?
(ii) 'officials expect rewards even if they do not ask directly' (implicit extortion)?

(iii) 'people feel it would be impolite not to give something' (politeness)? or

(iv) 'people want to give something?' (gratitude)?

Then we asked a similar question about clients giving something to an official 'after their problem has been solved', with a similar set of possible answers except that we reworded the fourth option slightly:

(iv) 'people just want to express thanks for the help they have received' (gratitude)?

and we added a fifth:

(v) 'people feel they might need help again from the same official' (anticipation)?

Table 5.10. Perceived motivations for giving–by timing of gift

	Average		Czech Republic		Slovakia		Bulgaria		Ukraine	
	%	%	%	%	%	%	%	%	%	%
	Given before or after their problem has been solved?									
	bef	aft	bef	aft	bef	aft	bef	aft	bef	aft
officials ask for or expect rewards (extortion)	69	34	58	27	65	27	77	35	77	47
might need help again (anticipation)	—	23	—	20	—	30	—	25	—	18
impolite not to offer (politeness)	19	13	25	20	22	11	11	9	17	14
people want to give/express thanks (gratitude)	12	30	17	33	13	32	11	32	7	21

Note: 'Don't know', 'mixed/depends', etc. answers were recorded if given spontaneously, but never prompted; they have been excluded from the calculation of percentages.

Timing had little connection with *politeness*. A few more, but only a few, thought politeness was more likely to be the motivation if the gift was given before (19 per cent) rather than afterwards (13 per cent). But *gratitude* was linked in the public mind to gifts given afterwards. On average, 30 per cent thought gratitude was the most likely motivation if the gift was given after the problem had been solved, but only 12 per cent if the gift was given beforehand. In every country people thought gratitude was two or three times more likely to be the motivation when the gift was given after the problem had been solved. (Table 5.10) Conversely, *extortion* was strongly linked in the popular imagination to gifts given beforehand. It was chosen by 69 per cent as the main reason for gifts given beforehand but only by 34 per cent as the main reason for gifts given afterwards. Nonetheless, by a small margin it was still the most popular explanation for gifts given afterwards.

But the simplistic distinction between extortion motivating gifts given beforehand balanced by gratitude motivating gifts given afterwards was further clouded once we took account of *anticipation*, the possibility that clients might look to the future. An average of 23 per cent thought the main motivation for gifts given afterwards was the fear that the client might need help in the future from the same official and therefore could not afford to take the risk of disappointing or offending them now. Taking both simple extortion and this complex anticipatory variant of extortion together, extortion was only a little less likely to be the motivation for gifts given afterwards than for gifts given beforehand. (Fig. 5.2)

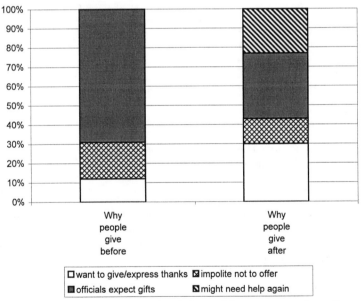

Fig. 5.2. Even presents given 'afterwards' are not expressions of gratitude

People thought their fellow-citizens were far more likely (by a margin of 45 per cent) to offer gifts to officials beforehand—even when these citizens sought 'something to which they were entitled by law'. But in their reports of their own behaviour, citizens were almost as likely to have offered gifts afterwards as beforehand. The timing of these gifts correlated with their size. By a margin of 29 per cent, those who had offered 'money or expensive presents' had more often offered their gifts beforehand. Conversely, by a margin of 19 per cent, those who had only offered 'small presents' said they had more often given them afterwards. (Table 5.11) Yet the correlation was far from perfect. Over a third of those who claimed they had only offered 'small presents' to officials admitted that they had usually done so 'before the official had solved their problem', which suggests there was some element of bribery even in the giving of some supposedly 'small' presents.

Table 5.11. Perceptions and experience of gift timing

	Average	Czech Republic	Slovakia	Bulgaria	Ukraine
		difference: % 'before' – % 'after'			
	%	%	%	%	%
Perceptions: When people seeking their legal rights give money, a present or a favour to the official, would they usually give before or after the official has dealt with their problem?	+45	+52	+56	+24	+51
Experience: If you or your family ever gave money, a present or a favour to the official, was that usually before or after the official dealt with your problem?	+6	+3	+12	–20	+29
amongst those who had given money etc.	+29	+36	+31	+6	+41
amongst those who had only given small presents	–19	–4	+8	–35	+12

Note: Since an average of 20 per cent (higher in Bulgaria and Ukraine) volunteered the reply that it 'would depend upon the circumstances' we have not excluded them from calculations of percentages. 'Don't knows' have been excluded as usual, however.

DID 'VALUES AND NORMS' AFFECT BEHAVIOUR?

We have found that a majority of the public in every country condemned 'the use of money, presents, contacts, or favours to influence officials' as being 'bad for (the country), and bad for those involved'. Yet many would give a bribe if asked and significant numbers had done so. So did condemnation really matter? Were clients' 'values and norms' significant? Or did their answers merely express ritual condemnation without much thought or much relationship to their actual behaviour? And if 'values and norms' were significant, were they equally significant in all countries? Or was bribe taking value-driven in some countries yet extortion-driven in others?

THE IMPACT OF 'VALUES AND NORMS' ON WHETHER CITIZENS 'WOULD GIVE' OR 'WOULD TAKE' BRIBES

Although the questions about whether citizens 'would give' or 'would take' bribes are only hypothetical, it is nonetheless significant that they correlated with values and norms. Also significant is the fact that the degree of correlation varied cross-nationally.

Those citizens who condemned the use of presents and bribes were much more inclined to refuse to pay them, and much less tempted to accept them. On average, condemnation doubled the rate of *resistance to paying bribes*. (Table 5.12) Although some of our percentages are based upon fairly small numbers of respondents within countries, they suggest that condemnation increased resistance to paying bribes by 36 per cent in the Czech Republic, by 30 per cent in Slovakia, and by 29 per cent in Bulgaria—but only by a mere 3 per cent in Ukraine.

Similarly, condemnation doubled *resistance to accepting bribes*. It increased the numbers who would be offended by the offer of a bribe by around 33 per cent or more in the Czech and Slovak Republics and Bulgaria, and even by 18 per cent in Ukraine.

Thus although condemnation had almost no effect upon willingness to submit to extortion in Ukraine, it had a significant effect upon willingness to accept bribes. That seems to indicate a degree of moral sensitivity combined with a sense of powerlessness in the face of authority within Ukraine.

Table 5.12. Would refuse to give or take bribes—by values

	Average	Czech Republic	Slovakia	Bulgaria	Ukraine
		Would refuse to pay a bribe if asked			
	%	%	%	%	%
If respondent says bribing street-level officials is...					
bad for (the country) and for those involved	48	67	48	51	27
bad for (the country) but unavoidable for people	36	53	38	31	23
preferable, because you can get favours	24	31	18	22	24
	Would be offended by the offer of a bribe				
	%	%	%	%	%
If respondent says bribing street-level officials is...					
bad for (the country) and for those involved	63	71	61	73	45
bad for (the country) but unavoidable for people	46	49	49	53	33
preferable, because you can get favours	33	38	26	40	27

Notes: 'Don't know', 'mixed/depends', etc. answers were recorded if given spontaneously, but never prompted; they have been excluded from the calculation of percentages.

The phrase '(the country)' was replaced by the name of the country in which the interview took place.

THE IMPACT OF 'VALUES AND NORMS' ON ACTUAL EXPERIENCE OF OFFERING GIFTS

Condemnation also correlated with reports of actual behaviour. In practice, condemnation increased the numbers who had never given even a *small present* to an official in recent years by an average of 24 per cent—by 37 per cent in the Czech Republic, by 18 per cent in Slovakia, and by 29 per cent in Bulgaria, though by only 10 per cent in Ukraine. Condemnation also increased the numbers who had never given *money or an expensive present* by an average of 19 per cent—by 23 per cent in the Czech Republic, by 20 per cent in Slovakia, and by 26 per cent in Bulgaria, though by only 7 per cent in Ukraine. (Table 5.13)

Values and norms therefore did matter. They mattered in terms of actual reported behaviour as well as in terms of what people 'would do' in hypothetical situations. They mattered in every country, though significantly less in Ukraine than elsewhere.

Table 5.13. Never gave presents or bribes—by values

	Average	Czech Republic	Slovakia	Bulgaria	Ukraine
		Never gave even a *small present*			
	%	%	%	%	%
If respondent says bribing street-level officials is…					
bad for (the country) and for those involved	62	81	45	74	46
bad for (the country) but unavoidable for people	48	64	33	60	35
preferable, because you can get favours	38	44	27	45	36
impact of clients' values	+24	+37	+18	+29	+10
	Never gave *money or an expensive present*				
	%	%	%	%	%
If respondent says bribing street-level officials is…					
bad for (the country) and for those involved	79	91	73	87	66
bad for (the country) but unavoidable for people	70	84	60	77	60
preferable, because you can get favours	60	68	53	61	59
impact of clients' values	+19	+23	+20	+26	+7

Notes: 'Don't know', 'mixed/depends' etc. answers were recorded if given spontaneously, but never prompted; they have been excluded from the calculation of percentages.

The phrase '(the country)' was replaced by the name of the country in which the interview took place.

THE IMPACT OF ATTEMPTED EXTORTION

Large numbers said they would pay a bribe 'if asked directly' and 'if they could afford it'. But what happened in practice? How many of those who had real experience of attempted extortion did actually submit to it?

There was in fact a remarkable similarity between the rates of submission to extortion amongst those (just over half the sample) who had actually experienced it, and the percentages of the whole sample who said they 'would' do so in the hypothetical situation that they 'were asked' for a gift. (Table 5.14) Both the hypothetical percentages (based on the entire public) and the actual percentages (based on those who had actually been asked or made to feel that something was expected) who had actually given something averaged around 59 per cent. Both ranged from around 38 per cent in the Czech Republic up to 74 per cent in Ukraine.

Table 5.14. Hypothetical and actual rates of giving compared

	Average %	Czech Republic %	Slovakia %	Bulgaria %	Ukraine %
Amongst all respondents:					
would pay if asked and could afford it	57	37	57	58	74
Amongst those who said officials had asked for or expected something:					
had actually given something, large or small	60	39	68	58	74

Note: 'Don't know', 'mixed/depends', etc. answers were recorded if given spontaneously, but never prompted; they have been excluded from the calculation of percentages.

Even those who condemned the use of presents and bribes might have to submit to extortion. '[Officials] want to use you...they want to use their position as a source of income.'(Kh 4) 'Until I gave a bribe he would not see me.'(Striy 2) 'To have a job at the school I have to give up my salary...For this whole year, if not longer, I will be earning money for them [those who appointed her].'(Striy 5) 'They make you feel you should go down on your knees, bring a bottle or offer 500 levs, just so the staff will pay attention to you.'(So-A 5) 'They put you in a situation that you have to.'(Ho 6) 'Five hundred crowns—otherwise she would not treat her.'(Br-B 7) 'When my wife went to the maternity ward, the obstetrician said 3,000 crowns for treatment and 1,000 for the delivery. I felt it would be better that he would take care of her...I felt her life was at stake.'(Br-B 4) None of this shows much public enthusiasm for giving presents or bribes. Willing givers perhaps, but resentful givers nonetheless.

Our analysis of coping strategies in Chapter 4 showed that pressure from officials had a powerful influence on actual giving by clients. On average, a direct request for bribes raised the rate of giving either small or large presents by about 40 per cent. Thus the impact of direct extortion on increasing rates of giving was greater than the impact of values and norms (i.e. condemnation) on reducing them. Unlike the impact of values and norms, the impact of extortion was greater in Ukraine than in the Czech Republic. (Table 5.15)

Table 5.15. Gave presents and bribes—by experience of extortion

	Average	Czech Republic	Slovakia	Bulgaria	Ukraine
Had given a *small present*...					
	%	%	%	%	%
if officials asked directly	67	48	67	64	87
if officials seemed to expect something	57	37	65	56	71
if neither	26	12	40	16	35
impact of extortion	+41	+36	+27	+48	+52
Had given *money or an expensive present*...					
	%	%	%	%	%
if officials asked directly	51	33	60	46	64
if officials seemed to expect something	35	20	38	33	47
if neither	11	3	18	6	16
impact of extortion	+40	+30	+42	+40	+48

Note: 'Don't know', 'mixed/depends', etc. answers were recorded if given spontaneously, but never prompted; they have been excluded from the calculation of percentages.

Officials making unnecessary problems in order to extort bribes had a similar impact on rates of giving, and its impact in Ukraine was at or above average.

So although citizens' condemnation of bribery had relatively little effect on their actual behaviour in Ukraine, officials' attempts at extortion clearly had at least as much effect in Ukraine as anywhere else.

We can usefully summarise our findings up to this point by calculating (Pearson) correlation coefficients between giving presents and bribes on the one hand, and condemnation or extortion on the other. In a highly compressed way these correlation coefficients show what we have already discovered from the more detailed cross-tabulations. On average, across all four countries, values and norms correlated moderately with willingness to give bribes, with willingness to take bribes, and with actual giving—though slightly more with willingness to take than with anything else. By contrast, extortion correlated only weakly with willingness to take, rather more with willingness to give, and far more with actual giving. (Table 5.16) So these correlations imply that:

- *willingness to take* bribes was dominated by *norms and values* (which were twice as powerful an influence as experience of extortion);

- *willingness to give* bribes was influenced about equally by *norms and values* on the one hand, and by experience of *extortion* on the other;
- *actual giving of bribes* was dominated by *extortion* (which is twice as powerful an influence as personal norms and values).

Table 5.16. Correlations between values, extortion and giving or taking bribes—averages

	Correlation with 'would accept if offered' r x 100	Correlation with 'would pay if asked' r x 100	Correlation with 'had given bribes' r x 100
with 'bribes are bad'	−19**	−16**	−18**
with 'prefer rigid system'	−23**	−9 *	−15**
with 'officials asked for, or expected, bribe'	12**	16**	35**
with 'officials made unnecessary problems'	10**	13**	36**

Note: r x 100 is (Pearson) correlation coefficient times 100. ** = significant at 1 per cent level, * at 5 per cent level.

'Had given bribes' coded: 0 = not, 1 = only small present, 2 = money or expensive present

'Would pay' coded: 0 = refuse, 1 = depends on circumstances, 2 = would pay if asked

'Would accept' coded: 0 = would be offended by offer, 1 = depends on circumstances, 2 = would be tempted to accept

'Prefer rigid system' coded: 0 = prefer reciprocal presents and favours, 1 = prefer no presents, no special help

'Bribes bad' coded: 0 = prefer flexible system, 1 = unavoidable, 2 = bad for country and those involved

'Officials asked for, or expected, bribes' coded: 0 = neither, 1 = expected, 2 = asked directly

'Officials made unnecessary problems to get bribe' coded: 0 = never, 1 = rarely, 2 = frequently (i.e. usually/sometimes)

Cross-nationally, condemnation sharply reduced bribe giving in Bulgaria, Slovakia and the Czech Republic but had much less influence in Ukraine. Its correlation with bribe giving declined in power from minus 0.25 in the Czech Republic to minus 0.09 in Ukraine. (Table 5.17) Correlations with preferences for a rigid Weberian system (no presents, no special help) showed a broadly similar pattern—highly significant in every country except Ukraine.

By contrast, the correlation between bribe giving and extortion was strong in all four countries, averaging 0.36 across the four countries—and Ukraine was exactly on the average.

Table 5.17. Correlations between values, extortion and giving bribes—within countries

	Average	Czech Republic	Slovakia	Bulgaria	Ukraine
Correlation between 'had given bribes'...	r x 100	r x 100	r x 100	r x 100	r x 100
and 'bribes are bad'	–18**	–25**	–17**	–21**	–9*
and 'prefer rigid system'	–15**	–16**	–17**	–21**	–4
and 'officials asked for, or expected, bribe'	35**	33**	26**	43**	39**
and 'officials made unnecessary problems'	36**	36**	40**	37**	33**

THE INDEPENDENT EFFECTS OF VALUES AND EXTORTION: A REGRESSION ANALYSIS

Indeed, the correlations between bribe giving and extortion were so strong in every country that they raise the question whether anything else had any real independent impact. To test this we can calculate multiple regressions predicting bribe giving from a combination of personal values and experience of extortion. (Table 5.18)

On average, these regressions confirm that clients' values and norms were the predominant influence on their hypothetical *willingness to take bribes* 'if offered'. Even in Ukraine, values had as much influence as extortion on willingness to take. They confirm that clients' values had as much influence as extortion on their hypothetical *willingness to give bribes* 'if asked'. They also confirm that extortion was the dominant influence upon *actual bribe giving* in all countries.

But these regressions also show that clients' values had an independent though smaller influence on actual bribe giving in every country except Ukraine. This pattern is illustrated in Figure 5.3. The rising bars in Figure 5.3 are much higher on the left than on the right (illustrating the dominant impact of extortion). But they are also somewhat higher towards the back (illustrating the smaller, but independent, impact of clients' values and norms).

The regressions also show that the influence of clients' norms and values on their actual bribe giving declined from a peak in the Czech Republic, through somewhat lower levels in Slovakia and Bulgaria, and then dropped sharply in Ukraine—where it was certainly weak and, by standard statistical tests, insignificant.

Table 5.18. Multiple regression estimates of the independent impacts of values and extortion

	Average Beta x 100	Czech Republic Beta x 100	Slovakia Beta x 100	Bulgaria Beta x 100	Ukraine Beta x 100
Predicting 'had given bribes'					
'bribes are bad'	–13**	–19**	–15**	–14**	–5
'official asked for, or expected, bribe'	34**	31**	26**	41**	38**
RSQ	15	15	9	20	15
Predicting 'would give if asked'					
'bribes are bad'	–15**	–18**	–18**	–21**	–4
'official asked for, or expected, bribe'	14**	16**	5	11**	22**
RSQ	6	7	4	6	5
Predicting 'would be tempted to accept'					
'bribes are bad'	–19**	–20**	–22**	–22**	–12**
'official asked for, or expected, bribe'	10**	6	9**	11**	13**
RSQ	5	5	6	7	3

Notes: Betas are the 'standardised regression coefficients' or 'path coefficients' in the multiple regressions.
** = significant at 1 per cent level.
RSQ is the 'squared multiple correlation' x100, or 'percentage of variation explained'.

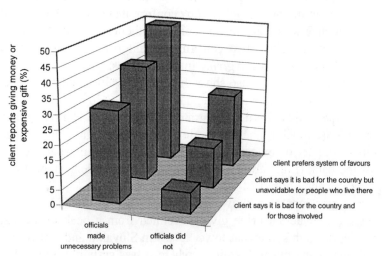

Fig. 5.3. The joint impact of citizens' values and extortion on giving bribes

CONCLUSION: EXTORTION ALWAYS WORKS, BUT VALUES SOMETIMES MODERATE ITS IMPACT

Our evidence does not support the view that the people were the source of corruption, pressing their bribes and their demands for favours upon reluctant officials. But there remains the question whether the people were truly 'willing givers'. That a majority were 'willing to give if asked, and if they could afford it' is not in doubt. But were they truly willing to give or merely willing to submit, reluctantly and resentfully, to extortion by street-level officials?

It is a question of some practical, as well as theoretical, importance. If ordinary people are the victims of extortion by officials then it may be possible to reduce public-sector corruption by reforming the administration in one way or another. Reform would then 'go with the grain' of public opinion and win public support. But if citizens are contented accomplices in petty corruption then reform is likely to be more difficult and less effective. It would then be necessary to reform the people as well as to reform the administration.

People in Ukraine especially were very keen to picture themselves as victims of extortion. But that self-image was tarnished somewhat by our finding that 61 per cent in Ukraine would be tempted to accept a bribe 'if they were themselves an official on a low salary'. Although a large majority of Ukrainians condemned the use of bribes, an unusually large number in Ukraine rejected the concept of a rigid Weberian system of 'no presents, no favours'.

Our multiple regression analyses suggest that extortion was the dominant influence on bribe giving in all countries. But personal values and norms (i.e. condemnation of bribery) had an independent and significant, though smaller, impact in every country except Ukraine. Bribe giving in Ukraine was therefore driven by extortion and not much hindered by personal values, while personal values bred strong resistance to extortion in other countries. On our evidence, citizens in Ukraine were certainly 'passive victims' even if they were not quite 'willing victims'. Their behaviour was influenced far more by the actions of officials than by their own values.

In the absence of extortion, however, few citizens who condemned the use of bribes actually offered them to officials. Amongst those citizens who *both* condemned the use of bribes *and* had never come across officials who made 'unnecessary problems' in order to extract bribes from them, only 3 per cent in the Czech Republic, 4 per cent in Bulgaria, 9 per cent in Slovakia, and 13 per cent in Ukraine confessed that they or their family had ever offered 'money or an expensive present' to an official at any time in 'the past five years'. Over that period of time, the 13 per cent in Ukraine is not negligible, but it is not large. In the absence of pressure from officials, behaviour did not contradict principle to a great extent.

It was the frequency and effectiveness of extortion—the combination of officials' greed and citizens' submissiveness—which produced high levels of bribery despite contrary norms and values. In the Czech Republic only 19 per cent had experienced such attempts at extortion 'more than rarely', while amongst those who condemned bribery only 16 per cent had submitted to it when it occurred. In Ukraine, at the other extreme, 42 per cent had experienced such attempts at extortion 'more than rarely', and amongst those who condemned bribery 44 per cent had submitted to it when it occurred. Thus in Ukraine there was over twice the frequency of extortion by officials, and almost three times as much readiness to submit to it. Ukrainian citizens who gave bribes were not so much willing to give, as willing to submit.

NOTES

1 Berkman, 'Bureaucracy and Bribery', especially 1347 and 1353–4.
2 Miller, White and Heywood, *Values and Political Change in Post-Communist Europe*, 155.
3 Goldman, *Environmental Pollution in the Soviet Union*, 31.
4 Noonan, *Bribes*, 705.
5 Della Porta and Vannucci, 'The Perverse Effects of Political Corruption'.
6 Noonan, *Bribes*, 685.
7 Noonan, *Bribes*, 693.
8 Simis, *USSR: The Corrupt Society*, 298–300.
9 Gilman and Lewis, 'Public Service Ethics', 520.
10 Smeltz and Sweeney, *On the Take*, 9.
11 Noonan, *Bribes*, 702.
12 Weber, *The Theory of Social and Economic Organization*.
13 Tanzi, 'Corruption around the World', 587.
14 Holmes, 'Corruption and the Crisis of the Post-communist State', 276.
15 Holmes, 'Corruption and the Crisis of the Post-communist State', 285.
16 Holmes, 'Corruption and the Crisis of the Post-communist State', 288–9.
17 Krastev, 'Dancing with Anticorruption', 58.
18 Service, 'Russia's Putrefying Corpse'.
19 Paddock, 'Greasy Palms Are Rampant in Russia'.
20 Noonan, *Bribes*, 695.

21 Zelizer, *The Social Meaning of Money*, quoted in Rose-Ackerman, *Corruption and Government*, 96.

22 Rose-Ackerman, *Corruption and Government*, 92–93.

23 Rose-Ackerman, *Corruption and Government*, 110.

24 Pasuk and Sungsidh, *Corruption and Democracy in Thailand*, 154, quoted in Rose-Ackerman, *Corruption and Government*, 92.

25 Gillard and Tomkinson, *Nothing to Declare*.

26 Vasyl Kostytsky MP, *Delovaya Odessa* (11 December 1998), quoted in *Corruption Watch* 1, no. 21 (23 December 1998).

CHAPTER 6

'TRY HARDER' OR 'GIVE UP': THE CHOICE FOR ETHNIC MINORITIES?

Any liberal democratic regime must aim to treat all its citizens fairly and equally. Previous chapters have shown that many individual citizens throughout post-communist Europe did not feel that they—as individuals—could get fair treatment from state officials without the use of contacts, presents and bribes. Here we address the specifically ethnic rather than the purely individual dimension to these complaints. An ethnically diverse liberal democracy must be particularly sensitive to the question of whether citizens from different ethnic backgrounds are treated fairly and equally—and not only as participants in political processes but also in their personal dealings with state officials.

In the nineteenth century, Central and Eastern Europe was ruled by imperial states characterised by ethnic diversity. But the multiethnic character of European states was reduced by the progressive collapse of the Ottoman, Romanov and Habsburg Empires. It was further eroded by the atrocities of Nazi occupation and by the 'ethnic cleansing' and revision of state borders that followed the Nazi defeat. It was brought to a new low by the post-communist break-up of Yugoslavia, Czechoslovakia and the Soviet Union. Together, these events conspired to produce a set of states that now come much closer to the model of a 'nation state'[1]—or to use the more explicit terms favoured by Todor Zhivkov's Bulgarian regime, a 'one-nation state' or even a 'single-nation state'. (In 1985, Politburo member Milko Balev is reported to have announced: 'Comrades! The People's Republic of Bulgaria is a one-nation state.')[2]

Yet despite all of these upheavals, the states of Eastern Europe are still not truly 'single-nation states'.[3] Changes in the ideology of the regime, and the fluidity of ethnic self-identification, make all statistics on Gypsies, Turks, Rusyns, Moravians and others a lot less rigid than one might suppose. The 'size' of an ethnic minority within a country is sufficiently subjective and psychological for it to increase or decrease quite rapidly without any physical change in the individuals who live there. Nonetheless, it is clear that by any definition the nationalist goal of 'single-nation states' has not in general been achieved. Even the mini-states of the new millennium cannot avoid their past as provinces of empires. There are substantial minorities in most parts of Central and Eastern Europe who do *not* regard their nationality and their citizenship as synonymous.

Moreover, the countries of Central and Eastern Europe are now committed to the ideology of liberal democracy, an ideological commitment that is reinforced by the economic attractions of EU membership. Both that ideology and the institutions of the EU assert the right to freedom of movement. 'Single-nation states' are an unnatural beast and particularly so in an era of rapid communications and freedom of movement. They cannot be maintained without coercion, and the nationalist goal of 'single-nation states' in Europe, East or West, is therefore likely to recede whenever ethnic violence abates. How European states treat ethnic minorities is therefore a matter of continuing, and indeed growing, importance. It is not a nineteenth-century problem that has since been solved by the break-up of existing European states or the rearrangement of borders. It is a twenty-first-century problem that can only be addressed in terms of citizens' rights—or even in terms of residents' rights.

In broad terms we wish to investigate the extent to which officials behaved differently towards different ethnic groups in post-communist Europe. That broad question immediately prompts a number of supplementary questions. We know that when people were gossiping rather than reporting personal experience they exaggerated their problems as individuals in dealing with officials. Perhaps the same might be true for the specifically ethnic dimension to bureaucratic encounters. To what extent, therefore, did people suspect that officials would behave differently towards different ethnic groups? And how did these suspicions compare with the extent to which different ethnic groups actually reported different treatment?

Conversely, we are also interested in the extent to which different ethnic groups behaved differently towards officials. To what extent did a local concentration of an ethnic minority affect the way different ethnic groups behaved? Was the minority more confident and secure in minority areas? Was the titular nationality less confident and secure in those minority areas?

Finally, it is all too easy to confuse ethnic differences with area effects. There may be, for example, a Crimean rather than a Tatar perspective, a Transcarpathian (Zakarpatian) rather than a Rusyn perspective. So we also touch on the question of whether, and to what extent, apparently 'ethnic' effects were merely 'area' effects?

A GENERAL CURVILINEAR MODEL OF RESPONSE TO STRESS

One model that may be particularly useful for understanding the treatment and behaviour of ethnic minorities in post-communist Europe is the curvilinear model of response to stress. This model suggests that a moderate amount of stress increases activity (to overcome the problem causing the stress), while a greater amount of stress reduces activity (because despair, depression and hopelessness set in).

As a psychological theory of individual behaviour this curvilinear model can be traced back to Yerkes and Dodson's experiments at the start of the last century.[4] It is also closely related to psychological theories of 'learned helplessness' which suggest that after a series of disappointments or failures, people come to believe that failure is inevitable and stop trying.[5] But this is a model with remarkably wide application in the social sciences. In a monumental, if now unfashionable, work, world historian Arnold Toynbee used it to explain the development, decay and

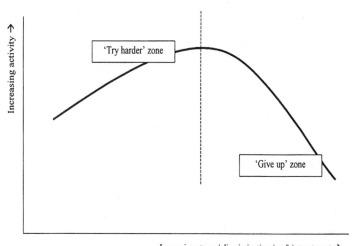

Fig. 6.1. The curvilinear model of response to stress

collapse of civilisations throughout history.[6] In his view, civilisations developed vigorously only when the pressures upon them were neither 'too slight to be stimulating' nor 'so strong that their effect is crushing'.[7] In sociology and political science, studies of the unemployed, from Jahoda, Lazarsfeld and Zeisel's classic 1930s survey of *Marienthal* to Schlozman and Verba's more recent *Insult to Injury*, have repeatedly found that while the threat of unemployment may breed activism and industrial unrest, long-term unemployment merely leads to inactivity, passivity and withdrawal.[8]

Such a model might also explain some of the patterns underlying citizens' choice of strategies for dealing with street-level officials. A very simplified schematic version is shown in Figure 6.1. As the degree or the frequency of discrimination or unfair treatment increases, the model suggests that citizens will first of all 'try harder' to overcome their difficulties. Within what might be called the '*try harder zone*', citizens may increase their use of some or all strategies which they hope will influence officials. But this model suggests that, beyond a certain point, an increasing degree or frequency of unfair treatment may lead citizens to 'give up'. Within this '*give up zone*', the use of some or all strategies may start to decline again.

Our analysis in Chapter 4 suggested that the vast majority of citizens were located in the 'try harder zone'. As they reported increasing frequencies of unfair treatment their use of all strategies increased. Some citizens claimed that they had 'rarely or never' received 'fair treatment'. They tended to use most strategies as frequently as those who were only intermittently ill-treated by officials. But the fact that they did not respond even more vigorously provides at least a hint that they were close to the boundary between the 'try harder' and 'give up' zones. We can find further evidence of a curvilinear response to unfair treatment if we separate out the few respondents who claimed they had 'never' received fair treatment in that time. These very few (4 per cent on average, ranging from 1 per cent in the Czech Republic to 13 per cent in Ukraine) but *very unfairly treated* respondents do in fact appear less active than those who had intermittently received unfair treatment. Compared to the intermittently ill-treated, the most ill-treated report less use of ingratiating behaviour (7 per cent less) as well as less use of contacts (19 per cent less), small presents (10 per cent less), and bribes (2 per cent less).

Things could be worse for some citizens. Some at least of those who reported that they had 'never' received fair treatment were no doubt complaining about the frequency rather than the intensity of unfair treatment. The response of some at least of those who reported that they had 'never' received fair treatment may have been constrained by perceptions that they had simply been unlucky so far. For them, the repertoire of reasonable responses might be defined by what they judged to be the more typical experience and responses of their fellow-citizens.

This curvilinear model might apply more strongly where the degree of unfair treatment was more extreme than that suffered by the vast majority of our respondents. It might also apply more strongly when a group of citizens were all likely to suffer relatively unfair treatment, so that they did not regard their own experience as unique or atypical. If only a random 4 per cent of isolated and unfortunate individuals were located in the 'give up zone' then their existence and behaviour might only be of methodological or psychological interest. They would not constitute a politically important fact. But the curvilinear model might not only be more powerful but also more socially and politically significant if its effects were concentrated within self-conscious groups and/or within groups that lived together in close proximity. Members of such groups would exchange stories of unfair treatment. Then the 'ecological effect' and its associated 'super-additivities' (as outlined in Chapter 1) would come into play as the ill-treatment of one citizen affected the attitudes of other members of the same group.

Ethnic minorities are the most obvious example of such groups. They are relatively self-conscious compared to other social groups. What happens to one member of an ethnic group sends ripples of identification and reaction throughout that group. Moreover, ethnic minorities in post-communist Europe tend to be concentrated into particular towns or regions within countries—and in some cases into ghetto areas within these towns and regions. If the curvilinear model applied to any groups we should expect it to apply to ethnic groups. Ethnic groups which experienced moderate levels of discrimination and unfair treatment might be particularly sensitive to that treatment and respond by 'trying harder'. Ethnic groups whose members experienced higher levels of discrimination and unfair treatment might be so demoralised individually and collectively by that experience that they might 'give up' and withdraw into inaction or avoidance strategies, minimising their interaction with officials.

Because they are so easily identified, discrimination against ethnic minorities is particularly visible—both to the minority itself and to the wider national and international community. It is therefore a particularly sensitive political issue in a way that discrimination or unfair treatment of a similar number of randomly selected and isolated individuals would not be. In the light of recent ethnic conflicts, ethnic discrimination is an even more sensitive issue in Eastern Europe than in Western Europe.

EIGHT DIVERSE MINORITIES

Our findings in this chapter are based on our nationally representative samples supplemented by special additional samples in areas where ethnic minorities were concentrated. These additional samples were not restricted to the ethnic minorities themselves because we were also interested in the reactions of the so-called titular nationalities living in ethnic minority areas.

We interviewed additional samples of 325 respondents in 'Hungarian minority' areas of Slovakia, 347 in 'Turkish minority' areas of Bulgaria, 300 in Crimea, and 300 in Transcarpathia (the 'Zakarpatska oblast').

In Slovakia, the additional ethnic minority area sample was carried out with randomly selected representative samples in areas where, according to the 1991 census, ethnic Hungarians were in the majority (the '*okres*' of Dunajská Streda and Komárno) or where the population was divided about equally between Hungarians and Slovaks (Galanta, Nové Zámky, Levice, Rimavská Sobota, and Trebišov). In Bulgaria, the additional ethnic minority area sample was carried out with randomly selected representative samples around Kurdjali (Kurdzhali), where the 1992 census indicated 65 per cent were Turks, Razgrad (48 per cent Turks), Turgovishte (34 per cent Turks), Slistra (33 per cent Turks), and Shoumen (29 per cent Turks). Kurdjali was the site of two well-publicised Constitutional Court decisions over the election of a Turkish mayor in 1996.[9] In Ukraine, the two minority area samples comprised one quota sample of 100 ethnic Ukrainians, 100 Russians and 100 Tatars in Crimea, and a second quota sample of 100 Ukrainians, 100 Rusyns and 100 Hungarians in Transcarpathia.

Combining these 'ethnic minority area' samples with our country-wide samples gives a total of 6,050 interviews.

We have generally accepted each respondent's own description of their ethnic identity. Since ethnic self-descriptions can change rapidly in response to events (and have done so recently in, for example, Bulgaria), self-descriptions seem the most appropriate basis for a study of perceived discrimination. The only exception is that within Bulgaria we have merged the relatively few self-described 'Bulgarian Muslims' with the much more numerous self-described 'Turks' to provide a larger ethnic minority sample and to simplify the analysis. With the additional interviews in minority areas, our survey design produced enough interviews to let us investigate the opinions and experience of eight ethnic minorities and contrast them with the four titular nationalities:

- in the Czech Republic—ethnic Czechs, plus Moravians;
- in the Slovak Republic—ethnic Slovaks, plus Hungarians;
- in Bulgaria—ethnic Bulgarians, plus Turks and Gypsies/Roma;
- in Ukraine—ethnic Ukrainians, plus Russians, Tatars, Rusyns, and Hungarians.

The table in the appendix to this chapter sets out the numbers of interviews with each of these 12 ethnic groups—the four 'titular nationalities' and the eight 'ethnic minorities'.

In terms of history and status, the ethnic minorities in this analysis are diverse, and their interactions with officials could be expected to reflect that diversity. There is likely to be a difference, both in their treatment by officials and in the ethnic minority's own behaviour, between a relatively wealthy minority and a desperately poor minority, between a respected minority and a feared or despised minority, between a culturally similar minority and a culturally alien minority.

Some minorities were regarded as 'ex-imperial', formerly dominant ethnic groups now left behind in the 'near-abroad' by the shrinking borders of Hungary, the Ottoman/Turkish state, or Russia. Tatars and Gypsies were regarded as 'alien' although not ex-imperial. To many in the titular nationality, Moravians and Rusyns were regarded as no more than 'exotic' variants of the titular nationality, bent on making a distinction without a difference. (The phrase 'exotic Ukrainians' comes from Andrew Wilson.)[10]

MORAVIANS IN THE CZECH REPUBLIC

In our survey almost no one outside Moravia, and only a minority of 21 per cent within it, described their 'ethnic group/nationality' as Moravian. A majority of them claimed to speak 'Moravian' at home. They were more likely than ethnic Czechs to live in a village, to lack higher education, to identify with the Catholic Church, and to claim that their income was 'not enough to live on'—though the differences between ethnic Moravians and Czechs were relatively small.

ETHNIC HUNGARIANS IN SLOVAKIA

For some years after Slovakia's independence, its leaders were continuously troubled by the fears of Hungarian secession.[11] A liberal treaty with Hungary on the treatment of minorities was offset by actions that 'contradicted both the spirit and the contents of the treaty',[12] actions that included a new law prescribing prison terms to people who organised public rallies 'with the intention of subverting the country's constitutional system, territorial integrity, or defence capability'.[13] In its original form, the president vetoed this law. As a statement of the government's attitude towards the Hungarian minority it could not be undone, however. Western critics of Slovak democracy highlighted its treatment of the ethnic Hungarian minority, but in a longer perspective it was also easy to depict Slovaks as victims.[14] Compared to Slovaks, ethnic Hungarians in Slovakia were somewhat more likely to live in a village and to lack higher education—as others have noted.[15] But the main differences were cultural and political. Over 90 per cent of the ethnic Hungarian minority spoke Hungarian at home and 63 per cent preferred to vote for a minority Hungarian nationalist party.

Conversely, our previous study of post-communist values found that 40 per cent of ethnic Slovaks would 'ban' Hungarian minority parties in Slovakia if they could.[16] When a memorial to the Slovak co-founder of Czechoslovakia was defaced with Hungarian graffiti in August 1999, the formerly governing and nationalist-inclined MDS (Movement for a Democratic Slovakia), now in opposition, promptly blamed the minority Hungarian Coalition Party.[17] There was continuing antagonism on both sides.

TURKS IN BULGARIA

Since independence from the Ottoman Empire in 1878, Bulgarian state policy towards its Turkish/Muslim minority has been erratic. Governments have lurched between policies of cultural pluralism and compulsory assimilation. Under the post-communist democratic regime, religious or ethnically based political parties were officially banned but actually existed under the guise of parties committed to the 'rights and freedoms' of individual citizens.[18] Post-communist governments have been relatively liberal, though other Bulgarian politicians have not. In retrospect, according to Petar-Emil Mitev, 'Zhivkov's regime appears liberal or at least timidly nationalistic in comparison with the new nationalists'.[19]

In our survey ethnic Turks were more likely than ethnic Bulgarians to live in a village. (Under the Ottomans, it was the ethnic Bulgarians who lived in the villages and rural areas.) Ethnic Turks were also relatively poor, unemployed, and uneducated. Attempts in the 1980s to eradicate the Turkish language were counter-effective[20] and almost all the Turks in our survey now claimed to speak Turkish at home. As regards religion, 94 per cent identified themselves as Muslims. Two-thirds preferred to vote for a party that stood for the rights of ethnic minorities.

GYPSIES/ROMA IN BULGARIA

According to the census, Gypsies are the second largest ethnic minority in Bulgaria. In fact, official statistics on Gypsies are under-estimates because Gypsies/Roma frequently claim to be members of the dominant nationality—often as a means of self-protection.[21] That is true throughout Eastern Europe. In the Czech Republic, for example, 'Roma who claim Romany nationality represent less than 12 per cent of the total Roma population' according to Jiřina Šiklová and Marta Miklušaková.[22]

At home, 71 per cent of Gypsies in our Bulgarian sample spoke Romany and only 16 per cent Bulgarian. In religion they were divided fairly evenly between Muslims, Orthodox and unspecified 'Christians'. Unemployment amongst Gypsies was very high. Although unemployment was twice as high amongst ethnic Turks as amongst ethnic Bulgarians, it was almost five times as high amongst Gypsies; and while 42 per cent of ethnic Bulgarians and 54 per cent of Turks complained that their family income was 'not enough to live on', that figure rose to 88 per cent amongst Gypsies.

Surprisingly, perhaps, only 18 per cent of Gypsies preferred a party representing ethnic minorities while a greater number (29 per cent) preferred a socialist or communist party. The orderly communist regime had forced them to live in settled accommodation. But their socialist voting preferences in the mid-1990s reflected their extreme poverty. It also reflected their unusually strong opposition to restitution, for which they had good reason: 16 per cent of ethnic Bulgarians but none of the Gypsies in our survey told us that their family had benefited from the restitution process. The communist regime had tried to end the Gypsies' nomadic ways by settling them on land seized from private landowners, and in the post-communist era 'disputes between ethnic Bulgarians and

Gypsies often flared up in villages as ex-owners claimed their land back'.[23] For Gypsies, an old injury (forced settlement) was now superseded by a new one (forced eviction).

By the 1990s Bulgarian Gypsies had become 'even more marginalised than in the past, despised by almost everybody regardless of whether they were Christians or Muslims'.[24] And, we might add, injured by both the communist regime and its anti-communist successor. Recognising these problems the Bulgarian government signed an agreement with a number of Roma organisations in April 1999, known as the *Framework Program for Equal Integration of Roma into Bulgarian Society.*[25]

Gypsies were also desperately poor and disliked in other countries than Bulgaria. Defending plans to 'wall in' a tenement block of Romany families in the northern Bohemian town of Ústí nad Labem, for example, Mayor Ladislav Hruska said the plan was 'not racially motivated' but just intended to 'separate the decent people from those who are not'.[26] Only a few hundred Czech Gypsies survived the Nazi occupation but Gypsies were moved from Slovakia to the Czech lands after the war and now number about 300,000.

Unfortunately we do not have enough interviews with Gypsies for reliable analysis of their opinions in any other country than Bulgaria. But it is likely that our findings about Bulgarian Gypsies are indicative of their treatment elsewhere in Central and Eastern Europe. Indeed, their treatment may be worse elsewhere. The fact that we were able to interview so many in Bulgaria and so few elsewhere implies greater social exclusion elsewhere. So it might be more accurate to interpret our findings about Bulgarian Gypsies principally as findings about Gypsies rather than as findings about Bulgaria.

RUSSIANS IN UKRAINE

Early fears of major conflicts between ethnic Russians and Ukrainians in an independent Ukraine have not been realised. Ethnic Russians in Ukraine are only a 'numerical' rather than a 'psychological' minority.[27] The most popular TV newscast in Ukraine is still *Vremya*, produced by ORT Moscow, and in eastern and southern Ukraine *Vremya* is as popular as in Russia itself.[28] Empirical evidence suggests that ordinary ethnic Russians and Ukrainians do not in fact feel very different from each other.[29] Other ethnic conflicts in Ukraine are more acute even if less potentially catastrophic. There has been more pressure and more progress towards autonomy for Crimea and Transcarpathia than for those mainland areas of southern and eastern Ukraine where there are high concentrations of ethnic Russians.[30]

TATARS IN CRIMEA

Crimea (or 'Krym') is a much-disputed territory. Russia annexed it in 1783 during the reign of Catherine the Great.[31] It was transferred from Russia to the Soviet Republic of Ukraine as recently as 1954. To some Russians it is still Russian rather than Ukrainian territory. That applies to ethnic Russians in Crimea as well as in Russia: a 1995–96 USIA survey found that 59 per cent of ethnic Russians within Crimea felt that their territory should belong to Russia rather than to Ukraine.[32]

There are also older claims on its soil. In 1944, ten years before Ukraine acquired Crimea, Stalin deported 269,000 Crimean Tatars to Central Asia for alleged collaboration with the Nazi occupiers. The USSR Supreme Soviet condemned this deportation in 1989. The Tatars were subsequently allowed to trickle back and in 1991 the Medjlis (the executive of the Tatar Assembly or Kurultai) claimed that 'Crimea is the national territory of the Crimean-Tatar people, on which they alone possess the right of self-determination'.[33] But the return of the Tatars after half a century was not universally welcomed. By 1998 Tatar leader Mustafa Dzhemilev complained, at a rally to mark the 54th anniversary of their deportation, that the 250,000 Tatars who had returned faced 'a disastrous situation without rights', that many had no jobs or housing and that 70,000 had not even acquired Ukrainian citizenship.[34] In opposition to the locally dominant ethnic Russians, however, Tatars sometimes found themselves in an alliance of convenience with the central Ukrainian authorities in Kyiv. For example, only 8 per cent of the Tatars in the 1995–96 USIA Crimean survey felt Crimea should belong to Russia, while 54 per cent felt it should belong to Ukraine.

RUSYNS AND HUNGARIANS IN TRANSCARPATHIA

Transcarpathia also has a much disputed history. Now formally 'Zakarpatia' or the 'Zakarpatska oblast', it has from time to time been called 'Transcarpathia', 'Transcarpathian Ukraine' or 'Carpatho-Ukraine'—each title often carrying a weight of political baggage. (We use the term that is most familiar in the English language but without any political implications.)

Transcarpathia was only added to Ukraine by the Soviet-Czecho-slovak treaty of 1945, having previously been within the Habsburg Empire until 1918 and within Czechoslovakia until 1938. In the 1990s, the originally anti-Habsburg 'Rusyn movement, thought dead and bur-ied in 1945, has revived'[35] and ethnic identities have shifted. As many as half of those who were once classified as ethnic Ukrainians in Tran-scarpathia now identify themselves as wholly or partly Rusyn.

The small minority of ethnic Hungarians in Transcarpathia is concen-trated along its western border. In Andrew Wilson's view, 'Kyiv has played divide-and-rule between Rusyns and Hungarians in Transcar-pathia, with some success'.[36]

ETHNIC MINORITIES IN UKRAINE

Despite their generally good inter-personal relations, our survey reveals some sharp cultural differences between ethnic Russians and Ukrainians within Ukraine, notably on education, religion, and language. Ethnic Russians are more likely to have higher education and much less likely to live in a village. Insofar as they are religious, both Russians and Ukrainians are Orthodox, but the Russians are twice as likely as Ukrainians to be irreligious. Amongst those who are religious, ethnic Ukrainians are four times as likely as ethnic Russians to say they are 'Ukrainian Orthodox' as distinct from 'Russian Orthodox' or simply 'Orthodox'. Almost all ethnic Russians, but less than a third of ethnic Ukrainians, speak Russian at home. In economic terms ethnic Russians are less distinctive, however.

But the greatest differences within Ukraine are between ethnic Rus-sians and Ukrainians on the one hand, and Tatars, Rusyns and Hungari-ans on the other. A majority within each of these five groups claim to speak their own ethnic language at home, for example, but the Tatar and Hungarian languages clearly differ much more than Russian or Rusyn from standard Ukrainian. No Ukrainian-language speaker, for example, would have very great difficulty reading the Rusyn-language version of the 'Declaration on the occasion of the celebratory announcement of the codification of the Rusyn language in Slovakia'.[37]

Minority Rights Group (MRG) International claims that 'since the 9th century Rusyns have belonged to the Greek Catholic Church, but under Soviet rule this was outlawed'.[38] Although the majority of Rusyns in our survey describe their religious affiliation as Orthodox, a large mi-nority (28 per cent) identified themselves as Catholic, mainly 'Greek

Catholic', and remarkably few disclaimed any religious affiliation at all. Similarly, most Transcarpathian Hungarians in our survey also claimed a religious affiliation, though they divided two to one between Catholics and Protestants, with very few Orthodox. Moreover, Hungarian Catholics, unlike Rusyns, were divided more evenly between the Greek and Latin rites. Tatars were overwhelmingly Muslim.

In economic terms, Rusyns, and more especially Hungarians, felt much more satisfied with their incomes than ethnic Ukrainians, while Tatars felt much less satisfied. But Tatars, Rusyns and Hungarians in our survey were all far more committed than ethnic Ukrainians to the principle of restitution, even though Tatars felt they had not yet gained much from it.

NEGATIVE ATTITUDES TOWARDS ETHNIC MINORITIES: CROSS-COUNTRY AND CROSS-MINORITY COMPARISONS

Petra Kovacs has classified post-communist countries on a 'scale of ethnic climate' based in part on national policy as expressed in domestic legislation and adherence to international agreements. The Czech Republic is located towards the 'inclusive' end of her scale, Bulgaria and Slovakia towards the 'exclusive' end, and Ukraine close to the 'ambiguous' centre.[39] But that classification reflects the ethnic homogeneity of the Czech Republic and the liberalism of Czech governments rather than the prejudices of the Czech public.

In a cross-country survey for the *Los Angeles Times-Mirror* respondents were asked about unspecified 'other ethnic groups' in general. The numbers who felt that they did not 'have much in common with people of other ethnic groups' provides one indicator in general inter-ethnic alineation. By that measure ethnic alineation was low in Ukraine, moderate in Bulgaria and higher in the Czech and Slovak Republics—though even there it was less than in such West European countries as Britain, Spain and Italy.[40]

That survey also asked whether people had favourable or unfavourable feelings about specific ethnic minorities living within their country. Attitudes to Gypsies were most unfavourable in the Czech and Slovak Republics where 94 per cent reported unfavourable feelings. In Bulgaria 77 per cent were unfavourable to Gypsies, though that was about the same as in Germany and less than in Hungary. (There was no question about Gypsies in Ukraine.) Jews were regarded with disfavour by 29 per cent in the Czech and Slovak Republics, and by 24 per cent in Ukraine, but by only 13 per cent in Bulgaria—though even the Czech and Slovak figures were exceeded in Germany and Poland.

In Bulgaria 43 per cent also reported unfavourable feelings towards the Turkish minority—though that was significantly less than in Germany and about the same as French attitudes towards its North African minority. In the Czech and Slovak Republics (taken together since separate figures were not published) 60 per cent had unfavourable feelings towards ethnic Hungarians living within their borders—similar to German feelings about ethnic Poles in Germany.

These *Times-Mirror* surveys therefore suggest that:

- From Spain to Bulgaria, feelings towards Gypsies were uniquely unfavourable. Although we only have direct survey evidence on the treatment of Gypsies in Bulgaria, we should bear in mind that public feelings about Gypsies were even less favourable elsewhere, especially in the Czech and Slovak Republics.
- The level of antagonism towards Jews was very much less widespread and generally less intense, though it was relatively high in Germany, Poland and Russia—all outside the scope of our investigation, however.
- Bulgarian feelings towards Turks, and Czech or Slovak feelings towards Hungarians had their counterpart in Western Europe, notably in German feelings towards Turks and Poles (which were reciprocated by the Poles), and French feelings towards North Africans.

In short, while there were problems of ethnic antagonism in post-communist Europe, which might well be reflected in the treatment of ethnic minorities by officials, these problems varied sharply from group to group and they were not unique to Eastern Europe.

Finally, there is another similarity between ethnic relations in Western and Eastern Europe that has important implications for bureaucratic behaviour: positive feelings towards the ethnic Russian minority within Ukraine (and, conversely, towards the ethnic Ukrainian minority within Russia) echoed the positive feelings towards the Scottish minority within the UK. On *Times-Mirror* figures only 8 per cent within Ukraine had unfavourable feelings about the ethnic Russian minority, which was about the same as the numbers in Russia who had unfavourable feelings towards the Ukrainian minority—and very similar to the 6 per cent within the UK who had unfavourable feelings towards the Scots. (Feelings towards the Welsh and Irish minorities within the UK were significantly more antagonistic.)

If these feelings were translated into patterns of bureaucratic behaviour towards ethnic majorities and minorities in post-communist Europe we might expect to find:

- *no difference* between the treatment of Ukrainians and Russians within Ukraine;
- *only slight discrimination* against Jews;
- *greater discrimination* against Turks in Bulgaria and Hungarians in Slovakia;
- *severe discrimination* against Gypsies.

Of course, a well-run Weberian bureaucracy would provide fair treatment even to unpopular ethnic minorities. The personal prejudices of officials would be held in check by their professional norms. But the alternative is that street-level bureaucrats may be out of tune with high-level government policy. Their attitudes towards Gypsies 'are the most problematic...They often contend that the empathy and enlightened views of national officials are naïve and idealistic, for they are rarely matched by actual experience with the Roma'.[41]

In our survey of officials (described more fully in later chapters) we asked about the behaviour of their ethnic minority clients 'in their own experience'. By a margin of 41 per cent they described Gypsies as 'more' rather than 'less' 'rude and abusive' compared to other clients. At the same time they said that all other ethnic minorities were less 'rude and abusive' than their other clients.

Zoltan Barany claims that 'the overwhelmingly negative societal attitudes toward the Roma are strongly reflected in the implementation of policies, enlightened though those policies may be'. 'While the minister of the interior might order county police captains to follow anti-discrimination regulations in law enforcement, it is up to the policeman on the street to arrest those attacking the Roma and to close down restaurants displaying "No Gypsies Allowed" notices.' But 'more often than not the policeman shares the anti-Romani biases of the general population'.[42]

Similarly, the local mayor in Ústí nad Labem rejected orders from the regional council and central government to halt construction of the wall to fence off local Gypsy housing in his town, and pressed ahead to complete it.[43]

SUSPICIONS OF ETHNIC DISCRIMINATION

Suspicions of ethnic discrimination would be important even if they did not reflect reality. So, to what extent did people think that ethnicity would affect the relationship between citizens and officials? To what extent did different ethnic groups have different views on this question?

Table 6.1. Perceptions of ethnic discrimination

	officials treat their own na- tionality	officials treat Gypsies	officials treat Jews	officials treat (*specified minority*)
		% 'better' – % 'worse'		
	%	%	%	%
Within Czech Rep:				*spec min:*
views expressed by...				Slovaks
ethnic Czechs	+52	–47	+7	–3
ethnic Moravians	+24	–42	–1	0
Within Slovakia:				*spec min:*
views expressed by...				Hungarians
ethnic Slovaks	+59	–54	+8	–12
ethnic Hungarians	+55	–56	–14	–40
Within Bulgaria:				*spec min:*
views expressed by...				Turks
ethnic Bulgarians	+58	–50	+13	–13
ethnic Turks	+54	–54	–14	–11
Gypsies	+66	–78	+29	–20
Within Ukraine:				*spec min:*
views expressed by...				Tatars/Russians
ethnic Ukrainians	+49	–58	–9	–21/+19
ethnic Russians	+41	–55	–19	–27/+6
ethnic Tatars	+45	–58	–9	–57/+42
ethnic Rusyns	+52	–60	–30	–28/+1
ethnic Hungarians	+59	–58	–15	–24/+12
Average:	+51	–56	–4	

Notes: Ethnicity defined by each respondent's own self-description of their 'nationality/ethnic group'.

Figures based on augmented samples, including the additional booster samples in minority areas. See appendix.

We asked respondents whether they thought officials would treat a client 'of the same nationality as the official, better or worse than they treat most other people?' Although some felt officials did not discriminate either way, a very large majority in almost every ethnic group felt that officials treated clients of their own nationality better than others. (Table 6.1) Typically, by a margin of over 50 per cent, people said officials treated their own nationality 'better' rather than 'worse'. Amongst Gypsies this margin of suspicion reached 66 per cent.

One participant in the focus-group discussion we held in the ethnically Turkish Bulgarian town of Kurdjali claimed that 'if you have money you are treated as a human being. Otherwise—a Turk, a Gypsy or a Jew—you do not get served or even close to that.'(Ku 1)

In our surveys we asked specifically how the public in each country thought their officials would treat clients who were (i) Gypsies/Roma or (ii) Jews. Despite the comment in our Kurdjali focus group, speculation about the treatment of Jewish clients was erratic, unclear and probably uniquely ill-informed. There are few Jews left in Eastern Europe after the Nazi Holocaust. But very large majorities in every ethnic group felt that officials treated Gypsy clients worse than others. By margins of at least 42 per cent, and usually over 50 per cent, every ethnic group said Gypsy clients were treated worse than others. In Bulgaria, the margin of suspicion ran at 50 per cent amongst ethnic Bulgarians and 54 per cent amongst Turks, but reached 78 per cent amongst Gypsies themselves.

Then we repeated the question again, now focusing on ethnic minorities of particular significance within particular countries. Within the Czech Republic we asked about the treatment of Slovak clients. Neither Czechs nor Moravians thought officials discriminated much with respect to Slovak clients, and the very few ethnic Slovaks that we interviewed in the Czech Republic actually thought they were treated better than other clients.

Within Slovakia we found a consensus across ethnic groups that officials treated ethnic Hungarian clients worse than others, but these perceptions of discrimination varied in degree. By a margin of 40 per cent the Hungarian minority itself thought Hungarians were treated worse than others. But amongst Slovaks that margin fell to only 12 per cent.

Within Bulgaria there was a consensus across all ethnic groups that officials treated Turkish clients worse than others. But the margins were small—only 13 per cent amongst ethnic Bulgarians and 11 per cent amongst Turks themselves, though rising to 20 per cent amongst Gypsies who seem to have projected some of their own perceptions of ill-treatment onto Turkish clients.

Within Ukraine, there was a consensus across all ethnic groups that officials treated Ukrainian and Russian clients better than others, and that they treated Tatar clients worse than others. However, the margins varied both according to the ethnicity of the client in question and the ethnicity of the observer. By a large margin both Russians and Ukrainians thought Ukrainians were treated better than others were. By smaller margins both ethnic groups also thought that Russians were treated better than others were.

Tatars had distinctive views. They were amongst the most likely to allege that officials discriminated in favour of ethnic Ukrainians. More strikingly still, they were by far the most likely to allege that officials discriminated in favour of ethnic Russians (by a margin of 42 per cent). Indeed, Tatars were the only ethnic group to allege more discrimination in favour of Russians than in favour of Ukrainians—no doubt reflecting the tensions between Tatars and the locally dominant Russians in Crimea. As might be expected, Tatars were by far the most likely to allege that officials discriminated against Tatars. But the very high margin of 57 per cent amongst Tatars, over twice as high as amongst any other ethnic group, indicated a remarkable degree of polarisation of suspicion between Tatars and others about the way that officials were thought to treat Tatars.

We also asked whether arguing with an official, appealing to a higher official or giving money and presents would be more effective 'if the client were the same nationality (ethnic group) as the official', or would nationality 'make no difference'? Only around two out of five respondents said ethnicity would make a difference to the effectiveness of clients' arguments or appeals. Rather fewer respondents, less than a third on average, thought ethnicity would make a difference to the effectiveness of giving money and presents to officials. Ethnic minorities were consistently more inclined than the titular nationality to think that ethnicity would make a difference, however.

Altogether, these findings indicate a very widespread suspicion of ethnic discrimination. It was voiced particularly by ethnic minorities, but not only by them. Indeed, there was a consensus across ethnic groups, whether majority or minority, that officials were likely to discriminate on ethnic grounds.

ACTUAL EXPERIENCE OF BIASED TREATMENT

How far was this suspicion upheld by experience? To what extent were people from different ethnic groups actually disadvantaged? To what extent did they report actual experience of different treatment at the hands of officials?

Most respondents said that they or their family had in fact dealt with officials at some time in the last few years. But amongst some ethnic groups—not all of them minorities, however—a significant number reported no contact with officials. In the Czech and Slovak Republics almost everyone had had some dealings with officials, irrespective of whether they came from the titular nationality or from the ethnic minorities. In Ukraine, the minority Tatars reported more contact with officials than did the ethnic Ukrainians or Russians. If anyone avoided contact with officials in Ukraine it was the dominant Ukrainians and Russians rather than the minorities. In Bulgaria, the Turkish and Gypsy minorities were at least three times more likely than ethnic Bulgarians to report no contact with officials.

Table 6.2. Ethnic patterns of useful knowledge

	usually knew legal rights %	usually knew someone in office %
Within the Czech Rep: views expressed by...		
ethnic Czechs	52	31
ethnic Moravians	44	41
Within Slovakia: views expressed by...		
ethnic Slovaks	53	41
ethnic Hungarians	50	47
Within Bulgaria: views expressed by...		
ethnic Bulgarians	39	31
ethnic Turks	29	31
Gypsies	8	15
Within Ukraine: views expressed by...		
ethnic Ukrainians	46	40
ethnic Russians	40	40
ethnic Tatars	39	24
ethnic Rusyns	61	45
ethnic Hungarians	59	51

Notes: Ethnicity defined by each respondent's own self-description of their 'nationality/ethnic group'.

Figures based on augmented samples, including the additional booster samples in minority areas. See appendix.

Were ethnic minorities more or less aware of their legal rights, as compared with the titular nationality? Were they more or less likely to have friends and acquaintances 'in the office'? Our evidence is mixed. Moravians, ethnic Hungarians in Slovakia and ethnic Turks in Bulgaria were all less likely than the titular nationality to feel that they 'knew their rights' when they met officials. But ethnic Turks were as likely as the titular nationality to 'know someone in the office', and both the

Moravians and Hungarians were actually more likely to do so. Overall, therefore, these ethnic minorities' greater knowledge of officials offset their relative lack of knowledge about their rights. (Table 6.2)

Tatars, and more especially Gypsies, on the other hand, were not just less likely than the titular nationality to know their rights. They were also less likely to know an official in the office. Gypsies, for example, were 31 per cent less likely than ethnic Bulgarians to know their rights and also 16 per cent less likely to know someone in the office. So these two minorities were unambiguously disadvantaged by lack of knowledge.

How well had ethnic minorities been treated? We asked about 'your own or your family's personal experience of dealing with officials in the last few years—approximately the last four or five years. Did these officials usually, sometimes, rarely or never: (i) treat you and your family as equals? (ii) give you or your family fair treatment?'

It is important to reiterate here that the question about experience of equal treatment was neither about equality between citizens nor about perceived equality between ethnic groups (which could not be answered from the personal experience of an individual), but about equality of respect between the citizen and the official. However, although the *question* was not about equality between ethnic groups, the *pattern of answers* could tell us whether ethnic groups were treated equally. If answers to the question varied across different ethnic groups, then this variation would indeed indicate unequal treatment of different ethnic groups.

There were some very obvious and important differences between experiences of treatment in different countries which we have discussed in earlier chapters. But within countries, ethnic minorities nearly always complained more than titular nationalities about the way officials had treated them.

As a simple index of good treatment, we can take the percentage that said they had 'usually' been well treated minus the percentage that said they had 'rarely or never' been well treated. In terms of *'equality of respect'*, that index shows that every ethnic minority except Hungarians in Ukraine were more likely than the titular nationality to complain—especially the Turks (by 36 per cent) and Gypsies (by 72 per cent). In terms of complaints about *'unfair'* treatment, the index shows that every ethnic minority except Russians complained considerably more than the titular nationality. (Table 6.3, Fig. 6.2) Again, that was especially true for Turks (by 28 per cent) and Gypsies (by 58 per cent). But it also applied to Tatars, Rusyns, ethnic Hungarians in Ukraine and Slovakia, and even to self-described ethnic Moravians in the Czech Republic.

Table 6.3. Experience of ethnic discrimination

	treated with respect 'as equals'		treated fairly		official asked for or expected a bribe	
			% 'usually' – % 'rarely or never' (difference from titular nationality)			
	%	%	%	%	%	%
Within Czech Rep: views expressed by...						
ethnic Czechs	+32	***	+61	***	45	***
ethnic Moravians	+18	(–14)	+47	(–14)	57	(+12)
Within Slovakia: views expressed by...						
ethnic Slovaks	+3	***	+43	***	67	***
ethnic Hungarians	–9	(–12)	+23	(–20)	73	(+6)
Within Bulgaria: views expressed by...						
ethnic Bulgarians	+19	***	+23	***	45	***
ethnic Turks	–17	(–36)	–5	(–28)	59	(+14)
Gypsies	–53	(–72)	–35	(–58)	22	(–23)
Within Ukraine: views expressed by...						
ethnic Ukrainians	–22	***	–19	***	70	***
ethnic Russians	–25	(–3)	–19	(0)	66	(–4)
ethnic Tatars	–31	(–9)	–41	(–22)	69	(–1)
ethnic Rusyns	–31	(–9)	–41	(–22)	91	(+21)
ethnic Hungarians	–18	(+4)	–36	(–17)	90	(+20)

Notes: Ethnicity defined by each respondent's own self–description of their 'nationality/ethnic group'.

Figures based on augmented samples, including the additional booster samples in minority areas. See appendix.

Compared to the titular nationality, most ethnic minorities also reported greater experience of *extortion* by officials who explicitly or implicitly solicited bribes: Turks 14 per cent more than the titular nationality, Rusyns and Hungarians in Ukraine over 20 per cent more, and even Moravians 12 per cent more than Czechs. But there were exceptions. Officials reportedly sought bribes from Tatars no more than from Ukrainians, and from Gypsies 23 per cent less than from ethnic Bulgarians. The relative poverty of these groups may have offset (or more than offset) the tendency for officials to pressure ethnic minorities more than majorities. Conversely, the relative affluence of Rusyns and Hungarians in Ukraine may have increased the tendency for officials to at least 'expect' if not 'directly ask for' a bribe or a present.

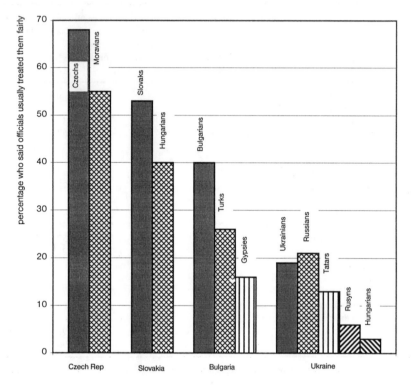

Fig. 6.2. Second-class citizens? The ethnic experience of fair treatment

COMPARATIVE INTERNATIONAL PERSPECTIVES

Ethnic minorities were even more inclined than titular nationalities to claim that officials in their country were 'more corrupt than officials in most East European countries'—Moravians 13 per cent more, ethnic Hungarians in Slovakia 18 per cent more, Tatars 12 per cent more, and Rusyns 16 per cent more. (Bulgarian citizens found the comparison with the rest of Eastern Europe more difficult, and unusually large numbers gave a 'don't know' response.)

Conversely, ethnic minorities were generally less likely than titular nationalities to regard international pressure on their government to reduce corruption (including the suspension of international aid and investment) as 'unacceptable interference in their country's internal affairs'—Moravians 17 per cent less, ethnic Hungarians in Slovakia 12 per cent less, Tatars 15 per cent less, and ethnic Hungarians in Ukraine 10 per cent less. Only two ethnic minorities (Russians and Rusyns) reacted against international pressure more strongly than the titular nationality, and then only slightly more.

ETHNIC VALUES AND NORMS

Even if it is not 'politically correct' to do so, we must ask whether different ethnic groups had different values and norms. In particular, did ethnic minorities have a different moral perspective on giving and taking bribes?

Seven of the eight ethnic minorities proved less inclined than the titular nationality to condemn bribery as 'bad for the country and for those involved'. Gypsies and Tatars were particularly inclined to excuse it as 'bad but unavoidable', while the Hungarian minorities were particularly inclined to defend it as 'preferable'.

It could be argued that willingness to *give bribes* might be more a matter of survival than of morals, a reaction to oppression rather than a truly autonomous choice. But willingness to *take bribes* indicates choice and preference more than submission to forces beyond the individual's control.

Again there were sharp and important differences between countries, which we have discussed already. But within Bulgaria, Turks and Gypsies were both much more willing than the titular nationality to give bribes, and much more tempted to accept them. Except for Russians and Rusyns within Ukraine, all ethnic minorities were at least somewhat more willing than the titular nationality both to give and to take bribes. (Table 6.4)

Table 6.4. Ethnic willingness to give or take bribes

	would pay if asked (difference from titular nationality)		would be tempted to accept if offered (difference from titular nationality)	
	%	%	%	%
Within Czech Rep: views expressed by...				
ethnic Czechs	36	***	34	***
ethnic Moravians	44	(+8)	49	(+15)
Within Slovakia: views expressed by...				
ethnic Slovaks	55	***	44	***
ethnic Hungarians	71	(+16)	49	(+5)
Within Bulgaria: views expressed by...				
ethnic Bulgarians	55	***	35	***
ethnic Turks	84	(+29)	63	(+28)
Gypsies	80	(+25)	64	(+29)
Within Ukraine: views expressed by...				
ethnic Ukrainians	75	***	63	***
ethnic Russians	71	(–4)	60	(–3)
ethnic Tatars	87	(+12)	71	(+8)
ethnic Rusyns	72	(–3)	49	(–14)
ethnic Hungarians	84	(+9)	75	(+12)

Notes: Ethnicity defined by each respondent's own self-description of their 'nationality/ethnic group'.

Figures based on augmented samples, including the additional booster samples in minority areas. See appendix.

ETHNIC BEHAVIOUR

What had they done in practice? Did different ethnic groups actually report giving more or fewer bribes? Did they differ in terms of the many other strategies that might be used to influence officials? Across the range of citizen strategies for dealing with officials, every ethnic minority except Gypsies had been at least as active as the titular nationality and usually more active, typically by around 10 per cent. (Table 6.5)

Ethnic minorities did not differ greatly from titular nationalities in terms of mere passive acceptance nor in terms of unusually pleasant behaviour. But every ethnic minority except Turks and Gypsies reported that they had argued more often than the titular nationality—Moravians by only 3 per cent and Hungarians in Ukraine by only 5 per cent, but ethnic Hungarians in Slovakia by 8 per cent, Rusyns by 11 per cent and Tatars by 16 per cent. In sharp contrast, Turks had argued 4 per cent less than the titular nationality, however, and Gypsies 10 per cent less. (Fig. 6.3)

Table 6.5. Strategies used by ethnic minorities (at least rarely)

	Accepted	Were more pleasant than usual	Argued	Appealed to higher official	Appealed to elected politician	Approached official through a contact	Gave a small present	Gave money or an expensive present	(difference from titular nationality)
	%	%	%	%	%	%	%	%	%
Within Czech Rep: behaviour of...									
ethnic Czechs	85	66	78	35	14	39	23	10	***
ethnic Moravians	88	72	81	46	21	54	25	17	+7
Within Slovakia: behaviour of...									
ethnic Slovaks	85	80	77	37	17	65	53	28	***
ethnic Hungarians	87	86	85	48	27	73	69	48	+11
Within Bulgaria: behaviour of...									
ethnic Bulgarians	91	93	75	48	19	44	32	16	***
ethnic Turks	91	93	71	54	34	56	49	34	+9
Gypsies	95	87	65	30	9	27	28	8	−11
Within Ukraine: behaviour of...									
ethnic Ukrainians	85	86	78	54	26	60	58	37	***
ethnic Russians	88	88	78	60	33	60	59	37	+2
ethnic Tatars	90	99	94	72	42	73	65	32	+11
ethnic Rusyns	88	95	89	66	22	77	62	41	+8
ethnic Hungarians	90	95	83	66	31	79	70	53	+11

Notes: Ethnicity defined by each respondent's own self-description of their 'nationality/ethnic group'. Figures based on augmented samples, including the additional booster samples in minority areas. See appendix.

In this table, the 'difference from titular nationality' is the average difference in use of the 7 active strategies, excluding passive acceptance.

There were greater differences on recourse to appeals. Every ethnic minority except Gypsies reported that they had appealed to higher officials more often than the titular nationality—Turks by only 6 per cent, Moravians in the Czech Republic along with ethnic Hungarians in Slovakia by 11 per cent, Rusyns and Hungarians in Ukraine by 12 per cent, and Tatars by 18 per cent. But unlike every other minority, Gypsies had appealed to higher officials 18 per cent less than the titular nationality.

Most ethnic minorities had also appealed to their elected representatives more often than the titular nationality, Turks and Tatars especially. But Gypsies had appealed to their elected representatives 10 per cent less often than the titular nationality.

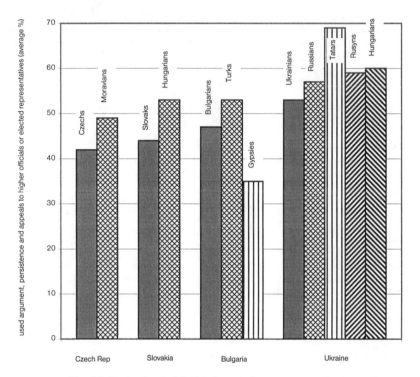

Fig. 6.3. Trying harder? I: Ethnic use of argument, persistence and appeals

Russians had used contacts to the same extent as Ukrainians, but other ethnic minorities were up to 19 per cent more likely than the titular nationality to have approached officials through a contact—except for Gypsies who had used contacts 17 per cent less than the titular nationality.

Russians had also used small presents to much the same extent as Ukrainians, but other ethnic minorities had used them up to 17 per cent more often than the titular nationality—except for Gypsies who had used them very slightly less. Russians had also used bribes of money or expensive presents to the same extent as Ukrainians. But other ethnic minorities had used them up to 20 per cent more than the titular nationality—except for Gypsies and Tatars who had used them less (despite the Tatars being the most willing to give bribes 'if asked' and 'if they could afford it'). (Fig.6.4)

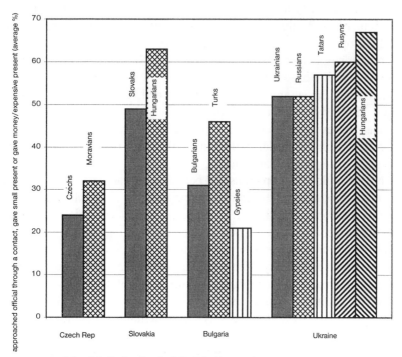

Fig. 6.4. Trying harder? II: Ethnic use of contacts, presents and bribes

Gypsies were therefore unique. They alone, of all the ethnic minorities we investigated, displayed unambiguous characteristics of hopelessness, exclusion and 'giving up'. Most other ethnic minorities simply 'tried harder'. They used a variety of active strategies significantly more than the titular nationality. No minority other than Gypsies ever used any such strategy significantly less than the titular nationality.

Of course, many of those who had used contacts, presents and bribes only admitted to doing so 'rarely' in recent years. If we restrict attention to those who admitted using these strategies 'more than rarely', the numbers obviously go down. But ethnic patterns remain broadly similar.

THE 'ECOLOGICAL EFFECT': THE IMPACT OF CONTEXT

The design of our survey allows us to contrast the opinions and behaviour of both ethnic Slovaks and ethnic Hungarians in Slovakia as a whole, with the opinions and behaviour of these ethnic groups within 'Hungarian minority areas'. Similarly, we can contrast the opinions and behaviour of both ethnic Bulgarians and Turks in Bulgaria as a whole with their opinions and behaviour within 'Turkish minority areas'.

Comparison is more difficult in the Czech Republic and Ukraine because nearly all ethnic Moravians in our survey lived in Moravia, nearly all Tatars in Crimea, and nearly all Rusyns and Hungarians in Transcarpathia. Similarly, most ethnic Russians lived in southern and eastern Ukraine. But even in the Czech Republic and Ukraine we can still look at the effects on the titular nationalities, if not on the ethnic minorities, of living in different social contexts.

Context could affect opinions and behaviour in various ways. First, and most obviously, there is the ethnic context itself. In areas where an ethnic minority was concentrated, even if it did not form a local majority, its local concentration could affect the opinions, perceptions and behaviour of individuals—both those drawn from the ethnic minority itself and those drawn from the titular nationality. The ethnic minority might be more confident than in other areas, and the titular nationality less confident.

But in addition, ethnic minority areas sometimes differed from other areas in ways that were only coincidentally (and thus misleadingly) related to ethnicity. Pure area-effects could then be mistaken for ethnic-effects. We can illustrate this with a very simple example. Regions close to state borders brought people into closer and more frequent contact with customs and passport officials, irrespective of ethnicity. Minorities with friends and relatives across the border—Turks in Bulgaria, Tatars in Ukraine, ethnic Hungarians in Slovakia and Ukraine—dealt with customs and passport officials much more than the titular nationality. But that misleadingly over-emphasises the significance of ethnicity itself. Within Ukraine, 36 per cent of ethnic Hungarians compared to only 12 per cent of ethnic Ukrainians had personally dealt with customs officials in recent years. But within the border *oblast* of Transcarpathia where those ethnic Hungarians were concentrated, 28 per cent of ethnic Ukrainians had also dealt with customs officials. So what appeared to be an ethnic effect on propensity to interact with customs officials was mainly an area effect, the result more of geography than of ethnicity.

CONTEXT AND INFORMATION

There was no evidence that the titular nationality lacked knowledge of their rights within minority areas, nor that they lacked useful contacts amongst officials in these places. Indeed, if anything, the titular nationality seemed better informed in minority areas than it did elsewhere. Perhaps, of course, it was just more nervous and alert to its interests in minority areas.

In Slovakia as a whole, ethnic Slovaks claimed to 'know their rights' no more than ethnic Hungarians. But within Hungarian minority areas, 11 per cent more Slovaks than Hungarians claimed to 'know their rights'. Similarly, in Slovakia as a whole, ethnic Slovaks were 10 per cent less likely than ethnic Hungarians to claim they usually knew 'someone in the office'. But within Hungarian minority areas, Slovaks claimed to know 'someone in the office' more often than ethnic Hungarians.

In Bulgaria as a whole ethnic Bulgarians were 9 per cent more likely than Turks to claim they usually 'knew their rights'. But within Turkish minority areas, ethnic Bulgarians were 18 per cent more likely than Turks to claim such knowledge. In Bulgaria as a whole, ethnic Bulgarians claimed they usually knew 'someone in the office' slightly less often than Turks. But within Turkish minority areas, ethnic Bulgarians claimed this knowledge 13 per cent more often than Turks.

In the more Russian areas of Ukraine, ethnic Ukrainians were a little more likely than Russians to claim that they 'knew their rights'. In Crimea, the numbers of both Ukrainians and Russians who claimed to 'know their rights' increased by over 10 per cent, and that put both of them ahead of the Tatars. Transcarpathia was the sole exception to this rule of the titular nationality's extra sensitivity in ethnic minority areas. In Transcarpathia ethnic Ukrainians felt relatively well informed about their rights compared to Ukrainians in the rest of Ukraine but they still did not feel as well informed as ethnic Rusyns and Hungarians.

CONTEXT AND SUSPICION

There was a recurrent tendency for the titular nationality to perceive less discrimination against the minority if they themselves lived within a minority area. (Table 6.6) Significantly, the ethnic minorities themselves did not concur.

In Slovakia as a whole, for example, ethnic Slovaks felt that officials treated Hungarians worse than others (though larger numbers of ethnic Hungarians felt so too). But within the Hungarian minority areas of Slovakia, ethnic Slovaks did not feel that officials treated Hungarians worse than others (though ethnic Hungarians still did feel they were treated worse). Thus, in Slovakia as a whole, ethnic Hungarians were 24 per cent more likely than Slovaks to perceive official discrimination against Hungarians; but within Hungarian areas, ethnic Hungarians were 40 per cent more likely than Slovaks to perceive ethnic bias against Hungarians. So, within ethnic minority areas, perceptions of discrimination by officials against Hungarians were almost twice as polarised between the ethnic minority and the titular nationality as in the rest of the country.

Table 6.6. The impact of context on suspicion

	Do officials treat specified nationalities better or worse than they treat most other people? % 'better' – % 'worse'	
	Views about the treatment of ethnic Hungarians in Slovakia	
views expressed by...	views expressed in Slovakia as a whole	views expressed in Hungarian minority areas within Slovakia
ethnic Slovaks	−15	0
ethnic Hungarians	−39	−40
	Views about the treatment of ethnic Turks in Bulgaria	
views expressed by...	views expressed in Bulgaria as a whole	views expressed in Turkish minority areas within Bulgaria
ethnic Bulgarians	−14	−1
ethnic Turks	−11	−10
	Views about the treatment of ethnic Tatars in Ukraine	
views expressed by...	views expressed in south and east Ukraine as a whole	views expressed in Crimea
ethnic Ukrainians	−24	0
ethnic Russians	−30	−11
ethnic Tatars	na	−59

Note: In this table, figures for Slovakia and Bulgaria as a whole are based on our country-wide representative samples, excluding the additional booster samples in minority areas.

Similarly, in Bulgaria, both Turks and Bulgarians felt that officials treated Turks worse than others. But while ethnic Bulgarians in Bulgaria as a whole were actually 3 per cent more likely to suspect officials of anti-Turkish bias than were the Turks themselves, ethnic Bulgarians living in Turkish areas were 9 per cent less likely than Turks to suspect officials of ethnic discrimination against Turks.

In Ukraine as a whole, all ethnic groups felt that officials treated Tatars worse than others. In particular, by a margin of 30 per cent, ethnic Russians in the south and east of Ukraine suspected officials of discriminating against Tatars. But within Crimea, that margin fell to only 11 per cent amongst ethnic Russians. Similarly, by a margin of 24 per cent, ethnic Ukrainians in the south and east of Ukraine alleged that officials discriminated against Tatars; but within Crimea, ethnic Ukrainians felt that officials treated Tatar clients no worse than others. So the difference between Ukrainian and Tatar perceptions of anti-Tatar discrimination was 35 per cent in the south and east of Ukraine as a whole, but soared to 59 per cent within Crimea.

CONTEXT AND EXPERIENCE

The actual personal experience of our respondents did not support the view that ethnic bias varied according to context. Within the Czech Republic, Czechs reported that they were treated 'fairly' and 'as equals' to the same extent in Bohemia and Moravia. Within Slovakia, ethnic Hungarians complained more than Slovaks about their treatment by officials—but to the same extent within ethnic minority areas as in the country as a whole. Within Bulgaria, ethnic Turks complained more than ethnic Bulgarians—but to the same extent within ethnic minority areas as in the country as a whole. Ethnic Ukrainians actually complained about their treatment more in Ukrainian areas than in Russian areas.

Moreover, there was an almost consistent tendency for the titular nationality to complain less about extortion in minority areas. The only exception was Transcarpathia. In terms of their experience of extortion, therefore, ethnic differences within minority areas were generally greater than in the country as a whole and, paradoxically, it was the ethnic minorities that seemed relatively disadvantaged in the very areas where they were most numerous. Thus the fact that the titular nationality's perception of anti-minority discrimination faded in ethnic minority areas probably reflected a psychological reaction by the titular nationality, a less generous and more apprehensive posture by them, rather than an accurate perception of more favourable treatment of the ethnic minority in those areas. The titular nationality's apprehension was itself an important psychological fact, however, even if it was a delusion.

CONCLUSION: MOST ETHNIC MINORITIES ARE LOCATED IN THE 'TRY HARDER' ZONE, BUT GYPSIES IN THE 'GIVE UP' ZONE, AND TURKS ON THE BOUNDARY

We found pervasive suspicions that officials were guilty of ethnic bias against their clients. These suspicions were voiced particularly by ethnic minorities, but not only by them. Even the titular nationalities thought that officials discriminated against minorities. Such feelings of discrimination are an extremely important fact in political life, irrespective of their objective basis. Even if they had no objective basis at all they would be a political problem that required a solution. Politically, it is important that ethnic justice not only 'be done', but that it 'be seen to be done', and a widespread suspicion of ethnic discrimination is a real political problem in itself.

By themselves such suspicions are not proof of discrimination, however. They certainly tell us something about the psychology of the citizens, but not necessarily anything about the actual behaviour of officials. To what extent was the pervasive suspicion of ethnic discrimination justified?

The answer is inevitably complicated by the diversity of ethnic minorities. Our evidence suggests that there was real discrimination against clients from ethnic minorities but also that the degree or severity of that discrimination varied sharply. Reports by respondents from different ethnic groups about their own personal experience as individuals confirmed that officials had treated clients from different ethnic groups differently. But on average the scale of ethnic discrimination revealed in these personal experiences was much less than that implied by the pervasive suspicion of ethnic discrimination. On the other hand, the scale of ethnic discrimination revealed in these personal experiences varied from nothing at all against the Russian minority in Ukraine to a very high level of actual discrimination against Gypsies. The evidence from reports of actual experience is that officials not only discriminated *against ethnic minorities* but also discriminated sharply *between ethnic minorities*.

Conversely, different ethnic groups behaved differently towards officials. We looked at a wide range of detailed strategies for dealing with officials. But more important than the detail was whether different ethnic groups engaged more or less actively in a whole range of strategies for influencing officials. In broad terms the strategic option was between activism and resignation, between 'trying harder' and 'giving up'.

Despite the diversity of ethnic minorities, most of them seemed more active than the titular nationality. Ethnic Russians behaved much like ethnic Ukrainians, but most other ethnic minorities compensated for their minority status by engaging more than the titular nationality in a wide range of strategies to influence officials—unusually pleasant behaviour, argument, appeals to higher officials or elected representatives, approaching officials through contacts, and offering presents or bribes. Ethnic minorities generally followed a 'try harder' strategy. The titular nationalities themselves echoed that broad strategy of compensatory activism, of 'trying harder', by paying special attention to their rights and special attention to personal contacts with officials when they themselves lived in ethnic minority areas.

The only clear exception was Gypsies/Roma, who used every one of the strategies for dealing with officials (except passive acceptance) less, and often far less, than the titular nationality. Of all the ethnic minorities, only Gypsies clearly displayed the characteristics of hopelessness, alienation, exclusion, and 'giving up'.

The approximate locations of each ethnic group in terms of the 'curvilinear response to stress' model are shown in Figure 6.5. Ethnic minorities are located by the extent to which they suffered more 'unfair' treatment than the titular nationality (taken from Table 6.3 and measured horizontally) together with the extent to which they adopted more active response strategies than the titular nationality (taken from Table 6.5 and measured vertically).

Ethnic Russians in Ukraine were located at almost the same point as the titular nationality. Since most other ethnic minorities suffered more unfair treatment and responded with more active strategies than the titular nationality, they are located in the 'try harder zone'. Since Gypsies suffered extreme levels of unfair treatment and responded with less active strategies than the titular nationality they are clearly located in the 'give up zone'. But we have placed the Turkish minority in Bulgaria just over the boundary into the 'give up zone' even though it used more active strategies than the titular nationality. That is because it reported more unfair treatment than Hungarians and Tatars yet responded with no more, indeed slightly fewer, active strategies. Thus ethnic Turks seem to be located just at the point where the response curve peaks and begins to fall. It would be foolish to attribute too much precision to such calculations, but Figure 6.5 does provide a useful summary and interpretation of our principal findings about the treatment and response of ethnic minorities.

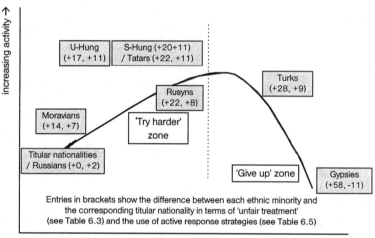

Fig. 6.5. Locating ethnic minorities on the curvilinear model of response to stress

Did suspicions of ethnic discrimination, or even the experience of it, really matter? They certainly seemed to influence attitudes towards officials, towards reform, and towards international intervention. Ethnic minorities were more inclined than titular nationalities to view officials in their country as 'more corrupt than officials in most East European countries'. They were generally less likely to regard international pressure on their government to reduce corruption (including threats to suspend international aid or investment) as 'unacceptable interference in their country's internal affairs'.

But more importantly, fair and equal treatment by officials lies at the heart of a truly democratic system. Ethnic discrimination by officials is only one aspect of unfair or unequal treatment of citizens by officials in post-communist Europe. But it is an important one, and it is incompatible with the concept of a 'complete' democracy, rather than a merely 'consolidated' democracy.

APPENDIX

Table 6.A1. The ethnic samples

Self-described ethnic group/ nationality	Number drawn from the representative country-wide sample N	Number drawn from the minority–area sample N	Total number of interviews N
Czech Republic			
Czechs	866	0	866
Moravians	95	0	95
Slovakia			
Slovaks	905	181	1,086
Hungarians	113	137	250
Bulgaria			
Bulgarians	1,299	174	1,473
Turks	144	149	293
Gypsies	62	24	86
Ukraine			
Ukrainians	881	200	1,081
Russians	258	100	358
Tatars	3	100	103
Rusyns	3	100	103
Hungarians	0	100	100

Notes: Although all the interviews in the Czech Republic were drawn from a country-wide representative sample, nearly all respondents who described themselves as 'Moravian' lived in the two Moravian regions of the Republic.

Included with the 'Turks' in Bulgaria are 34 self-described 'Bulgarian Muslims'.

NOTES

1 Miller, White and Heywood, *Values and Political Change in Post-Communist Europe*, 268–301.

2 Eminov, *Turkish and Other Muslim Minorities of Bulgaria*, 14.

3 Harris, 'New European Countries and Their Minorities', 301–20.

4 Yerkes and Dodson, 'The Relation of Strength of Stimulus to Rapidity of Habit Formation'.

5 Matute, 'Learning and Conditioning', 92–4.

6 Toynbee, *A Study of History*, 123–6.

7 Toynbee, *A Study of History*, 126.

8 Jahoda, Lazarsfeld and Zeisel, *Marienthal*; Schlozman and Verba, *Insult to Injury*.

9 Neuburger, 'Bulgaro-Turkish Encounters', 13–14.

10 Wilson, *Ukrainian Nationalism in the 1990s*, 165.

11 Bacova, Homisinova and Cooper, 'Questions Connected with the Reform of Public Administration in Slovakia in Regard to the Nationally Mixed Areas'.

12 Fisher, 'Backtracking on the Road to Democratic Reform', 30.

13 Fisher, 'Slovakia Heads towards International Isolation', 23–4.

14 Teleki, 'Loss and Lack of Recognition'.

15 Gabzdilova, 'Quality and Structure of Education of the Slovak Population in Relation to Ethnic Differentiation'.

16 Miller, White and Heywood, *Values and Political Change in Post-Communist Europe*, 165.

17 *RFE/RL Newsline* 3, no. 171, part 2 (2 September 1999).

18 Ganev, 'Bulgaria's Symphony of Hope', 129–130; Krastev, 'Party Structure and Party Perspectives in Bulgaria'.

19 Mitev, 'The Party Manifestos for the 1994 Bulgarian Elections', 77.

20 Eminov, *Turkish and Other Muslim Minorities of Bulgaria*, Chapters 1, 4 and 5.

21 Snavely and Chakarova, 'Confronting Ethnic Issues', 314 and 316.

22 Šiklová and Miklušaková, 'Denying Citizenship to the Czech Roma', 64.

23 Tomova, 'Gypsy-Bashing', quoted in Eminov, *Turkish and Other Muslim Minorities of Bulgaria*, 118.

24 Eminov, *Turkish and Other Muslim Minorities of Bulgaria*, 119.

25 Danova, 'Roma Calls for Inclusion Are Heard in Bulgaria', 17.

26 *RFE/RL Newsline* 2, no. 105, part 2 (3 June 1998); Traynor, 'Czech Gypsies Fear Ghetto Wall'.

27 Churilov and Koshechkina, 'Public Attitudes in Ukraine', 194.

28 *USIA Opinion Analysis* (2 February 1999): 1.

29 Miller, White and Heywood, *Values and Political Change in Post-Communist Europe*, 276–79; Golovakha, Panina and Churilov, 'Russians in Ukraine', 69, in Shlapentokh, Sendich and Payin, *The New Russian Diaspora*.

30 Wilson, *Ukrainian Nationalism in the 1990s*, 163–168; Kuzio and Wilson, *Ukraine: Perestroika to Independence*, 191–202 on separatism, but especially 191–4 on Crimea, and 195–7 on Transcarpathia.

31 Reid, *Borderland*, 177.

32 *USIA Opinion Analysis* (15 March 1996), 7.

33 Kuzio and Wilson, *Ukraine: Perestroika to Independence*, 192.

34 *RFE/RL Newsline* 2, no. 94, part 2 (19 May 1998).

35 Wilson, *Ukrainian Nationalism in the 1990s*, 165.

36 Wilson, *Ukrainian Nationalism in the 1990s*, 166.

37 Magocsi, *A New Slavic Language is Born*, x for the Rusyn version of the declaration, xi for the English and Slovak versions, 19–47 for the history of the Rusyn language.

38 MRG International, *Minorities in Central and Eastern Europe*, 2.

39 Kovács, *A Comparative Typology of Ethnic Relations*, 28.

40 Los Angeles Times-Mirror, *The Pulse of Europe*, question Q113.

41 Barany, 'Ethnic Mobilisation and the State', 323; see also Barany, 'Orphans of Transition'.

42 Barany, 'Ethnic Mobilisation and the State', 323.

43 *RFE/RL Newsline* 3, no. 169, part 2 (31 August 1999); *RFE/RL Newsline* 3, no. 170, part 2 (1 September 1999); *RFE/RL Newsline* 3, no. 201, part 2 (14 October 1999).

CHAPTER 7

STREET-LEVEL BUREAUCRATS: CAUGHT BETWEEN STATE AND CITIZEN

Junior officials work at the interface between state and citizen. That is not a comfortable position in post-communist Europe. As we have seen, the public accuses officials of treating citizens unfairly and soliciting presents or bribes to solve their clients' problems. At the same time officials are often badly paid, under-resourced, and under-valued by the state.

Given these criticisms it would be odd not to allow officials to speak for themselves. The obvious procedure is to interview a sample of post-communist officials about their relationships with their clients. But such studies still seem rare. Interview-based studies of officials' democratic or ethical values are more frequent, both in post-communist Europe and elsewhere. Some have looked at support amongst officials for technocratic rather than democratic rule in newly democratising countries.[1] Others have interviewed senior civil servants[2] or legislators about ethical standards.[3] Stewart, Sprinthall and Siemienska interviewed local officials in post-communist Poland about their reaction to hypothetical stories or scenarios containing ethical dilemmas.[4] Kutuev and Svintsitsky have interviewed officials in post-communist Kyiv about their autonomy in decision making.[5]

But however interesting and important values and orientations may be, we know that they differ from behaviour. None of these studies combines an analysis of officials' values with reports of their actual dealings with clients. Lancaster and Montinola's complaint,[6] echoed by Tanzi,[7] that surveys tend to seek only 'general perceptions of the incidence of corruption' for fear that respondents may be unwilling to 'incriminate themselves' seems even more true for studies of officials than for studies of their clients.

But although it may be difficult to interview officials about their relations with clients it is sufficiently important to be worth the attempt. We interviewed quota samples of street-level officials to complement our surveys of the public in post-communist Europe. In each country we aimed to interview 60 street-level officials within each of five broad institutional categories: health care, education, welfare offices, the police, and legal services. More precisely, we aimed for 20 interviews within each of three specific occupations in each institutional category:

- doctors, nurses, and hospital administrators (in health care);
- university teachers, university administrators, and schoolteachers (in education);
- officials in pensions, benefits, and housing offices (in welfare offices);
- traffic police, ordinary police, and police administrators (in the police);
- court officials, customs officials and passport officials (in legal services).

From our focus-group discussions it was already clear that these represented the face of the state to the public, irrespective of whether they might all be technically classified as officials or civil servants.

Since our interviewers usually exceeded their targets and produced 1,307 interviews in total, we have down-weighted the data to get the equivalent of exactly 20 interviews in each specific occupation in each country. That eliminates any bias due to interviewing a different mix of officials in different countries.

On average, 22 per cent admitted that they had been members of the Communist Party. The figure was lowest in the Czech Republic which had carried through the most severe 'lustration' or 'ideological cleansing' process, and highest in Bulgaria where the former Communist Party had been much more successful at reinventing itself in the post-communist era and protecting former party members. More immediately, the officials that we interviewed were always more favourable than the public towards their incumbent government, though to varying degrees in different countries. By an average margin of 6 per cent, officials said they generally 'supported' rather than 'opposed' the incumbent government and its policies. But by a margin of 20 per cent on average, the public said they 'opposed' rather than 'supported' the government. That difference was reflected in many specific assessments of government policy.

Our main focus, however, is not on the past or present political orientations of officials so much as on their attitudes towards their work and on their relationships with their clients. In particular we look at officials:

- *as citizens* themselves—in relation to other officials;
- *as employees*—in relation to the state;
- *as officials*—in relation to their clients.

Further, we look at how their experience 'as employees' affected the way they behaved 'as officials' towards their clients.

OFFICIALS 'AS CITIZENS'—IN RELATION TO OTHER OFFICIALS

Officials were citizens themselves. Each of them had to deal with other officials in their role as citizens as well as in their role as officials. Teachers got stopped by traffic police, traffic police fell ill and had to go to hospital, and so on. So before we asked officials about their interactions with their clients, we asked them about their own perceptions and experience as citizens interacting with other officials.

Table 7.1. Comparative perceptions of the behaviour of politicians or street-level officials

	Average	Czech Republic	Slovakia	Bulgaria	Ukraine
		% 'better now' – % 'worse now'			
	%	%	%	%	%
How do most politicians behave now?					
views expressed by the public	−31	−23	−51	+15	−66
views expressed by officials	−11	+21	−37	+21	−50
difference: officials − public	+20	+44	+14	+6	+16
How do most street-level officials behave now?					
views expressed by the public	−20	+4	−24	+7	−66
views expressed by officials	−2	+33	−9	+15	−45
difference: officials − public	+18	+29	+15	+8	+21

Note: 'Don't know' answers were recorded if given spontaneously, but never prompted; they have been excluded from the calculation of percentages.

Officials were somewhat less critical than the public about trends in the behaviour of politicians and officials since the end of communism. (Table 7.1) On this, the polarisation of opinion between officials and the public was greatest in the Czech Republic and least in Bulgaria.

Table 7.2. Comparative perceptions of the need to bribe various types of official

	views expressed by the public %	views expressed by all officials %	views expressed by 'very similar' officials	
			%	('very similar' defined as indicated below)
Likely that the client would need to offer money, a present or a favour to...				
hospital doctors	81	82	64	hospital doctors
state ministry officials	81	81	69	benefits officials
customs officials	75	78	61	customs officials
university staff	68	71	48	university teachers
court officials	72	70	46	court officials
local-government officials	68	67	44	benefits officials
police	67	66	50	traffic police
schoolteachers	39	42	26	schoolteachers
Average of the above	*69*	*70*	*51*	
members of parliament	70	65	na	na
local councillors	60	54	na	na
private sector	55	51	na	na

Notes: 'Don't know', 'mixed/depends' etc. answers were recorded if given spontaneously, but never prompted; they have been excluded from the calculation of percentages.
na = not available.

But just as many officials as members of the general public (about 70 per cent) alleged it was more likely than not that even a client who approached an official 'seeking something to which he/she was entitled by law' would 'have to offer money, a present or a favour to get help'. Officials took a significantly less critical view of similar officials—but only of *very* similar officials. (Table 7.2) When hospital doctors were asked about hospital doctors, schoolteachers about schoolteachers, or customs officials about customs officials, and so on, the numbers who said presents or bribes were likely to be necessary went down from 70 per cent to 51 per cent on average. But at the same time, even slightly different professions were highly critical of each other:

- 75 per cent of nurses (compared to only 64 per cent of doctors) said it would be necessary to give something to a hospital doctor;
- 68 per cent of schoolteachers (compared to only 48 per cent of university teachers) said it would be necessary to give something to university staff;
- 84 per cent of passport officials (compared to only 61 per cent of customs officials) said it would be necessary to give something to customs officials.

But overall, the striking thing about officials' perceptions of other officials was not that they were occasionally a little less critical than the public. Rather, it was the similarity between the perceptions of the public and of officials themselves. While officials defended those who did exactly their own job, they remained remarkably critical of officials in general.

If they needed help 'to solve an important problem', officials themselves were just as willing as the general public to give money to an official 'if they were asked directly and could afford it'. The level of willingness to submit to extortion varied sharply across the four countries, but within each country the replies of officials mirrored those of the public remarkably closely. Differences between the public and officials within each country were so slight as to be insignificant.

Table 7.3. The knowledge, fair treatment and satisfaction bonuses for officials

	Average	Czech Republic	Slovakia	Bulgaria	Ukraine
		% amongst officials – % amongst the public			
	%	%	%	%	%
usually knew their legal rights	+14	+5	+14	+19	+20
usually knew someone in the office	+14	+4	+20	+13	+18
usually treated fairly	+10	+6	+10	+3	+23
experience with officials was satisfactory	+6	+5	+4	0	+16

Note: 'Don't know', 'mixed/depends' etc. answers were recorded if given spontaneously, but never prompted; they have been excluded from the calculation of percentages.

In their personal experience, however, officials clearly had some advantages over other citizens when dealing with officials. As might be expected, officials felt more knowledgeable than the public. Officials were 14 per cent more likely than the public to feel that they 'knew their rights', and also 14 per cent more likely to report that they 'knew someone in the office'. This 'knowledge bonus' for officials was slight in the Czech Republic (5 per cent), but it ranged between 16 and 19 per cent elsewhere. (Table 7.3)

Officials were also more likely than the public to report that they had actually been treated 'as equals', 'fairly' or even 'favourably' when they took their own problems to other officials. This 'good treatment bonus' for officials was fairly small in Bulgaria and the Czech Republic, but officials were 10 per cent more likely than the public to report fair treatment in Slovakia, and 23 per cent more likely than the public in Ukraine.

'On the whole', officials themselves were also more satisfied than the public with their actual treatment at the hands of officials though never by more than a few percentage points—except, once again, in Ukraine where officials were 16 per cent more satisfied than the public. On every indicator, therefore, officials in Ukraine scored significant advantages over the general public when they themselves had to take their problems to officials. These advantages were more variable and usually smaller in the other three countries.

OFFICIALS 'AS EMPLOYEES'—IN RELATION TO THE STATE

On average, 40 per cent of officials claimed it was 'impossible to live on their official salary'. (A further 28 per cent that it was 'possible, but very difficult'.) The numbers that said it was 'impossible' ranged from only 16 per cent in the Czech Republic to over 60 per cent in Bulgaria and Ukraine. (Table 7.4) Moreover, 49 per cent of officials in Ukraine (though very few elsewhere) said their salaries were 'rarely or never' paid 'in full and on time'.

Some admitted that they had 'another source of income than their official salary', but they were not always the worst paid. About a quarter of all officials—ranging from 10 per cent in the Czech Republic to 40 per cent in Ukraine—claimed *both* that they could not live on their salary *and* that they had no other source of income.

Even their badly paid jobs were insecure in Bulgaria and Ukraine, where a quarter said they thought they 'might lose their job because of job cuts in the next year or two' and over half thought it would then be 'very difficult or impossible' to find another suitable job. Where salaries were worst, both job security and the availability of alternative employment were also worst.

Table 7.4. Economic problems of officials

	Average	Czech Republic	Slovakia	Bulgaria	Ukraine
	%	%	%	%	%
cannot live on salary	40	16	23	62	60
rarely or never paid on time and in full	14	2	2	3	49
cannot live on salary *and* no other income	25	10	15	35	40
very likely to lose job through cuts	17	7	8	23	29
very difficult or impossible to get another job	39	33	20	50	52

Note: 'Don't know', 'mixed/depends' etc. answers were recorded if given spontaneously, but never prompted; they have been excluded from the calculation of percentages.

Table 7.5. The economic bonus for officials

	Average	Czech Republic	Slovakia	Bulgaria	Ukraine
		% amongst officials – % amongst the public			
	%	%	%	%	%
family income not enough to live on	−14	−6	−10	−25	−15
family living standard has got 'much worse'	−12	−5	−12	−8	−24

Note: 'Don't know', 'mixed/depends' etc. answers were recorded if given spontaneously, but never prompted; they have been excluded from the calculation of percentages.

But life was tough for everybody in Bulgaria and Ukraine, not just for officials. In fact, according to our surveys, life was easier for officials than for their clients. (Table 7.5) Officials were less likely than the public to complain that their 'family income was not enough to live on' or that their family living standard had got 'much worse' over the last five years. Indeed, precisely where life was toughest for everybody, the comparative advantages of being an official were the greatest. Averaging these two comparative indicators of economic stress, the relative economic advantage of officials over the public ranged from only 6 per cent in the Czech Republic up to 20 per cent in Ukraine.

Compared to the public, therefore, officials had done better out of the transition from communism. Or perhaps it would be more accurate to say that officials had not done as badly as the rest of the public out of the transition. Not surprisingly, therefore, officials were more positive than the public about their country's move towards a market economy. (Table 7.6) Although support varied sharply from country to country, officials were 17 per cent more likely than the public to support the move to a market economy in principle. To a markedly lesser degree, officials were also a little more likely than the public to say that the transition to a market economy had been 'handled well', especially in the Czech and Slovak Republics.

Table 7.6. Comparative support for the transition to a market economy

	Average	Czech Republic	Slovakia	Bulgaria	Ukraine
	% amongst officials – % amongst the public				
	%	%	%	%	%
The transition to a market economy was…					
right in principle	+17	+20	+13	+14	+19
handled well	+7	+12	+11	+3	+3

Note: 'Don't know', 'mixed/depends' etc. answers were recorded if given spontaneously, but never prompted; they have been excluded from the calculation of percentages.

Table 7.7. Job preferences and expectations of officials

	Average	Czech Republic	Slovakia	Bulgaria	Ukraine
	%	%	%	%	%
Working for a private or foreign company, or as self-employed?					
would prefer it	26	27	23	25	30
expect it to happen within next five years	15	12	9	17	20

Note: 'Don't know', 'mixed/depends' etc. answers were recorded if given spontaneously, but never prompted; they have been excluded from the calculation of percentages.

On average, 26 per cent of officials said they would prefer to be self-employed or work for a private or foreign company rather than continue in the public sector. But only 15 per cent expected to make the switch within the next five years. So despite their no doubt well-founded complaints about their public-sector jobs, most officials in every country could not see much better prospects for themselves in the private sector. (Table 7.7) Preferences for leaving the public service did not vary much cross-nationally. But expectations of a move out of the public service were higher in Bulgaria and Ukraine where their public-sector jobs were the worst paid and the least secure.

OFFICIALS 'AS OFFICIALS'—IN RELATION TO THEIR CLIENTS

Officials recognised that they had problems in relation to their clients. By a margin of 10 per cent on average, they said that the relationship between the public and officials had deteriorated rather than improved since the end of communism. There was a very clear perception of improvement in the Czech Republic but it was offset by perceptions of deterioration in Slovakia and a particularly sharp deterioration in Ukraine. (Table 7.8) In Bulgaria views were mixed, though slightly negative.

Table 7.8. Officials' perceptions of the trend in the relationship between citizens and officials

	Average	Czech Republic	Slovakia	Bulgaria	Ukraine
	%	%	%	%	%
Compared to (communist times), the relationship between the public and officials is...					
better now	30	46	28	26	21
worse now	40	24	48	32	55
no different	30	30	24	41	24
better – worse	−10	+22	−20	−6	−34

Notes: 'Don't know' answers were recorded if given spontaneously, but never prompted; they have been excluded from the calculation of percentages.

The phrase '(communist times)' was replaced by 'during the Soviet period' in Ukraine, and by 'before 1989' elsewhere.

A PRIORITY TO HELP CLIENTS?

From a British perspective, Fred Ridley accuses 'continental European advisors with a constitutional or administrative law background' of putting too much stress on the 'rule of law'. 'Though respect for the law—assuming it is not authoritarian law—is important, it is insufficient in the relationship between official and citizens. Unless accompanied by sympathetic attitudes and a degree of discretion—a human rather than a lawyer's approach—individual cases will be treated in a bureaucratic manner and individual problems, all different, are as likely to be made worse as to be resolved.'[8]

We asked officials whether their 'top priority' when a client came to them with a problem was...

(i) 'to apply the laws and regulations as they are without question';
(ii) 'to do what is fair and reasonable, but no more than that' for the client; or
(iii) 'to help the client as much as possible'.

Table 7.9. Officials' perceptions of the service provided by other officials and by themselves

	Average	Czech Republic	Slovakia	Bulgaria	Ukraine
		% 'more/better now' – % 'less/worse now'			
	%	%	%	%	%
Compared to (communist times)...					
own ability to help clients	+25	+35	+28	+26	+8
most street-level officials behave	–2	+33	–9	+15	–45
rating of themselves – rating of 'most officials'	+27	+2	+37	+11	+53

Notes: 'Don't know' answers were recorded if given spontaneously, but never prompted; they have been excluded from the calculation of percentages. On average, 35 per cent said their ability to help clients had not changed since communist times and 29 per cent that the behaviour of street-level officials had not changed. They have been included in the calculations.

The phrase '(communist times)' was replaced by 'during the Soviet period' in Ukraine, and by 'before 1989' elsewhere.

By default, this third option implied doing something more than what was merely fair and reasonable. Nonetheless, half the officials indicated that it was their priority to give the maximum help to their clients, with roughly a quarter opting for each of the other alternatives. There was little variation between countries although, for what it is worth, it was in Slovakia and Ukraine, where officials perceived the sharpest deterioration in relations between officials and clients, that they put the greatest personal priority on helping their own clients.

By an average margin of 25 per cent, officials said that they personally were now able to help their clients more, not less, than in the past. However, that margin ranged down from 35 per cent in the Czech Republic to a mere 8 per cent in Ukraine. Understandably, perhaps, officials were more positive about themselves than about officials in general. But the gap between their ratings of their own performance and their ratings of other officials was remarkably large and varied. (Table 7.9) It was greatest in Ukraine where officials, even if only by a small margin, thought their own ability to help clients had improved, yet where these same officials alleged, by a margin of 45 per cent, that the behaviour of 'most officials' had actually deteriorated. Similarly, in Slovakia officials felt, by a large margin, that their own ability to help had improved, yet on balance they alleged that the behaviour of 'most officials' had deteriorated.

Table 7.10. Officials' complaints about their problems in providing a service for clients

	Average	Czech Republic	Slovakia	Bulgaria	Ukraine
	%	%	%	%	%
equipment inadequate	44	33	30	48	65
funds inadequate for clients' legal rights	76	63	71	78	90
too many instructions and guidelines	64	61	69	57	69
prefer more discretion, not more instructions	67	69	55	78	67

Note: 'Don't know', 'mixed/depends' etc. answers were recorded if given spontaneously, but never prompted; they have been excluded from the calculation of percentages.

Officials complained that the state did not provide them with the means to satisfy their clients. Just under half complained that they did not have enough equipment (computers etc.) to get their work done efficiently—about a third in the Czech and Slovak Republics, but half in Bulgaria and two-thirds in Ukraine. Two-thirds complained that they were subject to 'too many instructions and guidelines' and wanted more 'freedom and discretion to decide how to do their job'. Worst of all, a majority of officials in every country, ranging from 63 per cent in the Czech Republic up to 90 per cent in Ukraine, complained that they did not have sufficient funds to give clients 'their legal rights'. (Table 7.10)

To some degree, officials accepted the democratic principle that their function was to serve the public. Despite the long tradition in Central and Eastern Europe of accountability to the state rather than to the people, the overwhelming majority of officials (82 per cent) accepted that the public should be directly involved, in one way or another, in assessing their performance. Cynically, perhaps, the old Soviet regime had encouraged a 'culture of complaining' as a system of controlling street-level officials at least after the decree of 1967, though it had much earlier roots.[9] Newspapers had their own complaint departments. Every official institution had its complaint book, the so-called red book or '*krasnaia kniga*', where complaints about badly behaved officials could be lodged. Officials feared such complaints as they were reviewed on a regular basis and could get the official into trouble even if they had little or no impact on high policy.

Table 7.11. Officials' views on accountability to the public

	Average	Czech Republic	Slovakia	Bulgaria	Ukraine
	%	%	%	%	%
Public opinion should be involved in assessing the performance of street-level officials...					
by means of surveys and questionnaires	46	44	48	51	41
by means of public meetings	18	8	12	21	30
by writing letters of complaint	15	23	16	15	9
by other means	3	2	2	3	3
not at all	18	22	22	10	17

Note: 'Don't know', 'mixed/depends' etc. answers were recorded if given spontaneously, but never prompted; they have been excluded from the calculation of percentages.

The top preference of street-level officials was for public monitoring by means of 'surveys and questionnaires'. (Table 7.11) Support for surveys averaged 46 per cent and was fairly uniform across countries. Officials were much less enthusiastic about 'public meetings' or 'letters of complaint', and the balance of their support for public meetings or letters of complaint varied considerably. Support for public meetings rose steadily from a mere 8 per cent in the Czech Republic to 30 per cent in Ukraine. Conversely, support for letters of complaint declined from 23 per cent in the Czech Republic to a mere 9 per cent in Ukraine. These differences may reflect the long Soviet and pre-Soviet Russian tradition of expressing public opinion, insofar as it could be expressed at all, through (often carefully controlled) public meetings. The Russian Empire's tradition of democratic institutions, slight though it was, centred on the sixteenth- and seventeenth-century *'Zemskii Sobor'*—public meetings modelled on the church's ecclesiastical councils and aiming at a clear consensus and unanimity rather than liberal-democratic compromise or disagreement.[10]

JUSTIFYING EXTRA PAYMENTS FOR HELPING CLIENTS

Even though their top priority was to give their clients the maximum of help, a majority of officials also felt that their clients should do something in return. A majority of officials felt that clients should pay something extra, directly to the official, if they got special help. As one client alleged in a Bulgarian in-depth interview: 'They all expect, not if it is routine, but if it is something special, they expect you to bribe, give something.'(Te-IDI 2)

Table 7.12. Officials' willingness to justify extra payments from clients

	Average	Czech Republic	Slovakia	Bulgaria	Ukraine
	%	%	%	%	%
If an official solved a client's problem faster than normal then the official would be...					
right to ask for something	9	5	10	9	13
right to ask for, or at least accept, something	53	40	51	56	64
If an official did some extra work to solve a client's problem then the official would be...					
right to ask for something	16	11	14	19	18
right to ask for, or at least accept, something	60	53	59	61	67

Note: 'Don't know', 'mixed/depends' etc. answers were recorded if given spontaneously, but never prompted; they have been excluded from the calculation of percentages.

Not 'all' officials admitted such feelings. But 53 per cent thought it would be right to at least 'accept something if offered' for solving a client's problem 'faster than normal'. Also, 60 per cent thought it would be right to at least 'accept something if offered' in return for 'extra work' to solve a client's problem. Indeed, 16 per cent of officials thought it would even be 'right to ask for something' from the client in such circumstances.

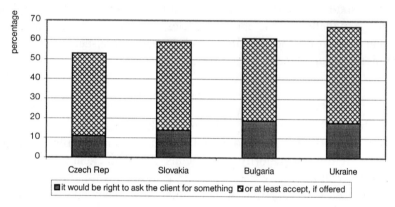

Fig. 7.1. Officials justify informal payments by clients for 'extra' work

This sense of moral justification was most prevalent in Ukraine where roughly two-thirds of officials expressed support for the idea. It was least prevalent in the Czech Republic where only 40 per cent justified extra payments for 'faster work' and 53 per cent for 'extra work'. (Table 7.12, Fig. 7.1)

EXPERIENCE OF CLIENTS' STRATEGIES

Officials reported that their clients used various strategies towards them with different frequencies. A simple indicator is the percentage of officials who said their clients used a strategy frequently—that is 'usually' or 'sometimes', in contrast to 'rarely' or 'never'.

Significantly, the frequencies with which officials reported that their clients had used these various strategies correlated exactly (in rank order) with the frequencies with which the public confessed that they had used them towards officials. Both sides told the same story. (Table 7.13) Officials corroborated what the public had told us already. For the majority of officials most of the time, dealing with clients primarily meant confronting clients who used abnormally pleasant behaviour, argument and persistence—and ultimately clients who remained dissatisfied but accepted the official's decision. In the experience of officials, as in the claims of the public, their clients' use of appeals, threats of violence or gifts of money and expensive presents were much less frequent.

Table 7.13. Clients' strategies viewed from above (and below)

	Average		Czech Republic	Slovakia	Bulgaria	Ukraine
	%	(%)	%	%	%	%
According to officials, clients 'frequently' (i.e. more than 'rarely')…						
accepted their decision even when dissatisfied	82	(69)	84	79	87	79
were friendly just to get better treatment	77	(64)	80	80	78	69
argued	54	(50)	37	52	61	66
approached the official through a contact	43	(31)	43	54	50	26
offered the official a small present	30	(25)	24	43	23	30
appealed to a superior official	27	(21)	30	21	22	35
threatened violence	13	(na)	12	11	17	13
offered money or an expensive present	10	(13)	7	14	9	11
appealed to an elected politician	8	(9)	8	3	6	14

Notes: 'Don't know', 'mixed/depends', etc. answers were recorded if given spontaneously, but never prompted; they have been excluded from the calculation of percentages.

Figures in brackets are the frequencies with which the public said they had used these strategies in their dealings with officials.

(na): Although officials were asked how frequently they had personally been 'threatened with violence' by their clients, the public themselves were not asked whether they had personally threatened officials with violence.

At the top of the list, 82 per cent of officials said clients had frequently 'accepted their decisions even when they were dissatisfied with them'. But 77 per cent of officials also said clients had frequently 'behaved in a friendly way just to get better treatment', while 54 per cent reported that clients had frequently 'argued' with them. Somewhat smaller numbers of officials reported that clients had frequently 'approached them through a contact' (43 per cent), offered 'a small present' (30 per cent) or appealed over their head 'to a superior official' (27 per cent). Relatively few reported that their clients had frequently 'threatened violence' (13 per cent), offered 'money or an expensive present' (10 per cent), or appealed to 'an elected politician' (8 per cent).

However, 37 per cent of officials said they personally had been 'threatened with violence', and 27 per cent that they had been offered 'money or an expensive present', at least on rare occasions.

As with citizens' claimed use of different strategies, there were particularly high positive correlations, ranging up to 0.55:

(i) between officials' experience of clients using argument, threats and appeals;

(ii) between officials' experience of clients using contacts, presents and bribes.

In the experience of officials, however, the correlation between abnormally pleasant behaviour and passive acceptance was only 0.18 (compared to 0.39 in citizens' reports of their own activities). In the experience of officials, the correlation between passive acceptance and anything other than abnormally pleasant behaviour was close to zero, and nearly always negative. Citizens who had problems with officials were more likely than others both to argue and to remain dissatisfied in the end, for example. But for officials, the experience of clients who frequently argued and threatened tended to obliterate their perception that their clients had often, in the end, to accept their judgement while remaining dissatisfied.

A factor analysis of officials' experience of their clients' strategies identified three factors. First, a contacts, presents and bribes factor centred on offering small presents (factor loading 0.86). Second, an argument, threats and appeals factor centred on appeals to higher officials (factor loading 0.79). Third, a more passive factor centred on passive acceptance (factor loading 0.83). There were no cross-correlations exceeding 0.30 between a strategy linked to two different factors. These were very much the same three factors that emerged from our analysis of the public's reports of their own behaviour towards officials. The core strategies were exactly the same, and the factor loadings very similar.

So, just as citizens had indicated that they tended to use contacts, presents and bribes in combination, officials tended to report experience of all three together or of none. The same could be said for the package of appeals, threats and arguments, and for the combination of abnormally pleasant behaviour and passive acceptance.

BADLY BEHAVED CLIENTS?

Twice as many officials as ordinary citizens alleged that 'on the whole' clients behaved badly towards officials. Overall the numbers were small, just 13 per cent amongst officials and 7 per cent amongst the public. However, both sides indicated that clients behaved worse in Ukraine: 19 per cent of officials and 13 per cent of the public said clients in Ukraine behaved badly 'on the whole'.

Of course, many individual clients might behave badly towards officials even if clients behaved well 'on the whole', and even though few officials felt their clients had behaved badly 'on the whole', officials still had criticisms to make. Just as the public thought the behaviour of officials had deteriorated since the end of communism, so officials felt that clients' behaviour had deteriorated. Clients were not only more likely to complain, which might, in some respects, be a positive trend, they were also more likely to offer bribes. (Table 7.14) By an average margin of 50 per cent, officials said their clients were now more, rather than less, likely to complain compared to communist times. By an average margin of 38 per cent, officials said that their clients were now more, rather than less, likely to offer money, presents or favours.

Table 7.14. Officials' experience of trends in their clients' behaviour

	Average	Czech Republic	Slovakia	Bulgaria	Ukraine
		% 'more now' – % 'less now'			
	%	%	%	%	%
Compared to (communist times)...					
clients complain	+50	+67	+55	+62	+17
clients offer money, presents or favours	+38	+4	+47	+65	+31

Notes: 'Don't know' answers were recorded if given spontaneously, but never prompted; they have been excluded from the calculation of percentages.

The phrase '(communist times)' was replaced by 'during the Soviet period' in Ukraine, and by 'before 1989' elsewhere.

There were large cross-national differences, however. Czech officials reported a particularly sharp increase in complaints but hardly any increase in offers of gifts. Slovak and Bulgarian officials reported a sharp increase in both. Ukrainian officials reported a much greater increase in presents and bribes than in complaints.

What type of client behaviour irritated street-level officials most? Officials cited 'rude or abusive' behaviour by clients as 'having the worst effect on relations' with officials, although it was relatively infrequent. But it was closely followed by clients who assumed that they 'could get their way by offering money or presents' and by clients who simply had 'excessive expectations'. By contrast, clients' complaints and confusion, though relatively frequent, caused very little resentment amongst officials. (Table 7.15)

Table 7.15. Clients' most irritating faults

	Average	Czech Republic	Slovakia	Bulgaria	Ukraine
	%	%	%	%	%
The worst influence on relations with the public is clients who…					
behave rudely or abusively towards officials	31	42	15	36	33
think they can get what they want by bribery	28	21	37	22	32
have excessive expectations	27	24	30	30	23
complain too much	8	4	9	9	11
go to the wrong office	6	10	11	3	2

Note: 'Don't know', 'mixed/depends' etc. answers were recorded if given spontaneously, but never prompted; they have been excluded from the calculation of percentages.

Officials put attempts by clients to influence them by offering gifts high up on their list of annoying client behaviour, even if not in top place. Yet a majority of officials were prepared to justify accepting 'extra payments' from clients. But perhaps it was the way some bribe givers behaved, rather than bribe giving itself that damaged relations with officials? One way of resolving this apparent inconsistency is to see how the criticism that clients 'behave badly towards officials' correlates with officials' experience of their clients' use of different strategies.

Of the nine strategies we investigated, five correlated significantly with officials' perceptions that clients 'on the whole behave badly towards officials'. (Table 7.16) The strongest correlation was with the frequency of threats of violence ($r = 0.20$). Less than 8 per cent of officials who had never experienced threats, but over 22 per cent of those who had even 'rarely' experienced threats, said clients on the whole behaved badly. Threatening behaviour was sometimes used as an excuse, rivalling that of temptation, for accepting bribes. Commenting on an opinion poll indicating that tax officers were amongst the most corrupt officials in Ukraine, the deputy head of the tax department in Donetsk was reported as saying:

> Naturally, one cannot deny that there are some people in the taxation administration bodies who break the law due to consideration of their own advantages. However, the taxmen's work cannot be taken apart from the general situation in the state. Who else is under such pressure of temptation as employees of taxation services? On the other hand, where bribery does not work, threats and often violence are used.[11]

Table 7.16. The correlation between clients' strategies and officials' criticisms

	Correlation with whether official says 'clients behave badly' r x 100
Correlation with experience of clients who frequently...	
threatened violence	20 **
argued	18 **
appealed to a superior official	12 **
appealed to an elected politician	12 **
offered money or expensive presents	3
approached the official through a contact	2
offered small presents	−1
accepted the official's decision even when dissatisfied	−4
behaved in a friendly way just to get better treatment	−8 *

Note: ** means significant at 1 per cent level, * means significant at 5 per cent level.

The impact of argument was more progressive but more clients used it with greater frequency, which led to a correlation of 0.18. There were somewhat weaker correlations between officials' criticisms of clients and their experience of clients appealing to higher officials or elected politicians ($r = 0.12$).

There was also a negative correlation—weaker, but still just significant—between criticisms of clients and officials' experience of being subject to abnormally pleasant behaviour. So officials warmed slightly to abnormally pleasant behaviour but reacted strongly against clients using arguments and threats.

But the use of contacts, presents and bribes produced an ambiguous response. On balance, the frequency of such experiences left officials neither more nor less positive about clients' behaviour.

These correlations confirm officials' claims that rude or abusive client behaviour annoyed them most. But they cast some doubt on officials' claims that clients' attempts to use money to exert influence annoyed them almost as much.

HOW DID THEIR EXPERIENCE 'AS EMPLOYEES' AFFECT OFFICIALS' RELATIONSHIPS WITH CLIENTS?

Apart from the obvious and important cross-national differences, how did the relationship between officials and clients vary? We looked at how officials' social characteristics and experience 'as employees' affected a number of key indicators summarising the nature of their relationships with their clients. These key indicators include officials':

(i) reports on their clients' behaviour;
(ii) priorities in dealing with clients;
(iii) perceptions of constraints on their ability to help clients;
(iv) willingness to justify taking gifts from clients;
(v) perceptions of trends in relationships with clients.

THE IMPACT OF SOCIAL BACKGROUND

The social background of officials had relatively little impact on their relations with clients. We found only slight differences between officials who lived in large towns and those who lived in small towns or villages. Once we controlled for cross-national differences (important because the Czech and Slovak officials in our survey tended to live in smaller settlements than the Bulgarian or Ukrainian officials), no difference between officials in more or less urban locations reached as much as 10 per cent on any of these indicators of relationships with clients.

In general, we also found only slight differences between the better-educated officials and the less well educated. As might be expected, better-educated officials were 19 per cent more likely to want 'more freedom and discretion' and 'fewer instructions' about how to do their job. Less obviously, though plausible enough in retrospect, better-educated officials were 10 per cent less likely to face frequent arguments from clients and only half as likely to face frequent threats of violence. But all other differences between the better-educated officials and the rest were small.

Female officials were 14 per cent more likely to give priority to helping their clients as much as possible, and 13 per cent less likely to give priority to strict application of the laws and regulations. At the same time, they were more pessimistic about the trends in their ability to help their clients. They faced fewer threats of violence from their clients, but they also got less frequent offers of small presents, and they were 10 per cent less likely to get frequent offers of money or expensive presents. Since relatively few officials of either gender got offers of money or expensive presents, that meant male officials were almost three times as likely as female officials to get such offers frequently.

We looked for evidence of a distinctive 'post-communist generation' of officials. We extracted those officials who had been students rather than employees in communist times, and divided the remainder into younger officials (aged under 40) and older (aged 40 and over). This three-way split correlated strongly with confessed Communist Party membership. Only 1 per cent of the former students admitted ever having been members of the Party. But amongst the rest, 14 per cent of the younger and 34 per cent of the older officials admitted Communist Party membership at some time in the past. So this three-way split really does tap the notion of a 'post-communist generation' of officials.

But only two of our indicators of relations between officials and clients varied by as much as 10 per cent across these three categories. Moreover, both hinted at nostalgia for the past rather than different relations with clients in the present. Compared to the post-communist generation of ex-students, the older, communist-era officials were 23 per cent more likely to feel they could offer clients less help now than in communist times and 15 per cent more likely to feel that their relationship with clients had deteriorated. But all other differences were small. Communist and post-communist generations of officials were easily identifiable but they did not have very distinctive priorities in dealing with their clients. In particular, they did not have distinctive attitudes as to whether it was right to accept gifts from clients in return for special help. Perhaps that reflects the formalism of party membership for many officials in the past. But it also suggests that the post-communist generation of officials did not have significantly different bureaucratic values in terms of service to clients.

THE IMPACT OF INSTITUTIONAL CULTURES

Specifically job-related characteristics had far more impact than any social background factors on the attitudes and behaviour of officials towards their clients. Let us start with the particular institutions in which they worked—the health services, education services, welfare services, police services and our more heterogeneous category of 'court, customs and passport' services, which we shall call 'legal services' for brevity. Almost without exception, the institution employing the official proved to have a significant impact on indicators of relations with clients. (Table 7.17, Fig. 7.2)

Those who worked in the *health services* were the most likely to feel that their relationship with clients had deteriorated since the end of communism. Health-service employees were 18 per cent less likely than average to put their priority on strictly applying the laws and regulations, and 19 per cent more likely to put their priority on helping their clients as much as possible. However, they were particularly likely to complain about a lack of funds and to feel that they could give clients less help now than under communism. They were the most likely to get frequent offers of small presents from clients, and were 15 per cent more willing than the average official to justify accepting extra payments from clients for 'extra' work. They were also relatively positive about the overall behaviour of their clients.

Those who worked in the *education services* were distinguished most by their wish for more freedom and discretion to do their job. Compared to the average official they put 17 per cent more weight on freedom and discretion. Conversely, they were also less likely than the average official to give priority to strictly applying the laws and regulations. They were especially likely to complain about lack of resources. They were somewhat more willing than average to justify taking payments from clients for 'extra' or 'faster' work. Very few reported that their clients frequently threatened them with violence. Like those in the health services they were relatively positive about the overall behaviour of clients.

Those who worked in the *welfare services* were distinguished most by the tendency of their clients to argue with them (13 per cent more than average) and by their relatively negative view about the overall behaviour of clients (almost twice as negative as the average official). They were more likely than average to prefer more detailed instructions and guidelines to do their job. They were the least willing to justify taking extra payments from clients for 'faster' or 'extra' work.

Table 7.17. Distinctive institutional cultures

	Average %	in health services %	in education services %	in welfare services %	in police services %	in legal services %
Officials' experience: clients...						
frequently argued	54	43	48	67	60	53
frequently threatened violence	13	9	5	15	23	11
frequently offered small presents	30	39	27	27	28	30
frequently offered money etc.	10	13	7	6	13	13
behaved badly, on the whole	13	7	8	23	13	15
Officials' priorities						
to apply the laws and regulations	27	9	18	25	45	42
to be fair to the client	24	23	30	23	20	22
to help clients as much as possible	49	68	52	52	35	36
Officials' perceptions of constraints on their ability to help clients						
lack adequate funds	76	83	84	73	72	68
want more freedom and discretion	67	71	84	59	64	57
Officials' justifications for taking gifts						
right to accept for 'extra' work	60	75	67	52	55	52
right to accept for 'faster' work	53	64	60	43	49	48
Officials' perceptions of trends in relationships with clients						
less able to help clients now	31	41	32	35	20	26
relationships with clients worse now	57	64	52	58	57	54

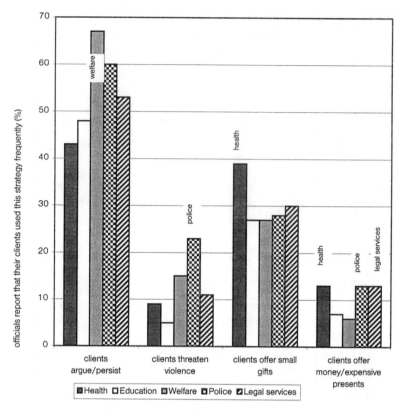

Fig. 7.2. Institutional patterns of client behaviour

Those who worked in the *police services* were distinguished most by the tendency of their clients to threaten them with violence. The police were almost twice as likely as the average official to report frequent threats of violence from clients. They were also 18 per cent more likely than the average official to give priority to strict application of the laws and regulations, and 14 per cent less likely to give priority to helping their clients. Relatively few of the police felt less able to help than in the past, but nonetheless they were no more optimistic than others about the trends in their relations with clients.

Those who worked in our somewhat heterogeneous category of *legal services*—officials working for the courts, customs and passport services—were also distinguished most by the high priority they put on strictly applying the law (15 per cent above average). Conversely, they put a relatively low priority on helping their clients as much as possible

(13 per cent below average). They were also the least inclined to demand more freedom and discretion to do their job.

THE IMPACT OF SPECIFIC OCCUPATIONS WITHIN INSTITUTIONS

In addition to these sharp differences between institutions there were also sharp differences *within institutions*, which reflected the specific occupation of the official. On every indicator there was a difference of more than 10 per cent across the three specific occupations within some institutional category. (Table 7.18) Of course, we are now contrasting quite small sub-samples of not much more than 80 interviews within each specific occupation. But it is not statistically probable that more than a few of these differences could be dismissed as accidents of sampling.

Within the health services: Doctors were the least likely (and hospital administrators the most likely) to feel that they were less able to help clients now than under communism, or that their relations with clients had deteriorated since communist times. Doctors and administrators differed by 29 per cent on their perceptions of trends in their own ability to help clients, and by 12 per cent on their perceptions of more general trends in relations between clients and officials.

Doctors and nurses gave about 13 per cent more weight than administrators to helping their clients as much as possible, and correspondingly less weight to strictly applying the laws and regulations. Doctors were also the most likely to want more freedom and discretion to do their job—26 per cent more than nurses.

Nurses were the most willing to justify taking gifts in return for 'extra' or 'faster' work—up to 19 per cent more so than administrators. But doctors came close behind nurses in that respect. It was doctors, not nurses, who received the most frequent offers of gifts from clients. Doctors were twice as likely as nurses or administrators to report that clients frequently offered them small gifts, and much more than twice as likely to report frequent offers of money or expensive gifts.

Within the education services: Schoolteachers were 21 per cent more likely than university teachers to give priority to helping their clients as much as possible, though they were also 10 per cent more pessimistic about the trends in their ability to do so. They were the most positive about the overall behaviour of clients, indeed as positive as doctors. At the same time, schoolteachers were also at least 11 per cent more likely than any university staff to justify accepting gifts from clients 'for extra

Table 7.18. Sharp differences between specific occupations within the same institution

	Average %	Health doctors nurses admin			Education univ teach univ admin schoolteach			Welfare pensions benefits housing			Police traffic ordinary admin			Legal services courts customs passports		
		D %	N %	A %	UT %	UA %	S %	P %	B %	H %	T %	O %	A %	Crt %	Ctm %	P %
Officials' experience: clients frequently...																
argued	54	32	46	50	44	46	52	63	65	73	67	57	55	55	58	45
threatened violence	13	13	9	5	5	2	7	8	19	18	27	24	18	10	14	9
offered small presents	30	57	33	27	36	26	19	31	22	27	37	21	25	20	38	33
offered money etc.	10	21	7	11	10	7	5	6	6	5	21	10	6	11	21	5
behaved badly	13	3	9	7	11	10	3	16	26	27	12	14	13	17	9	17
Officials' priorities																
to apply the law	27	5	4	17	21	22	10	21	30	24	50	43	41	40	50	35
to be fair	24	23	23	23	35	31	24	14	25	31	19	16	26	17	23	26
to help clients	49	72	73	60	44	47	65	65	45	45	31	41	33	43	27	39
Officials' perceptions of constraints on their ability to help clients																
inadequate funds	76	79	85	85	86	79	85	62	66	89	67	79	69	77	62	67
want more discretion	67	85	59	71	84	81	89	54	54	70	63	63	65	65	50	55
Officials' justifications for taking gifts																
OK for 'extra' work	60	78	80	67	64	61	75	43	52	59	66	53	46	49	52	54
OK for 'faster' work	53	65	73	54	59	54	67	35	41	52	62	40	46	38	48	59
Officials' perceptions of trends in relationships with clients																
less able to help now	31	24	46	53	28	30	38	28	29	45	15	27	21	26	29	21
relationships worse now	57	59	62	71	53	53	50	57	62	55	42	69	58	58	48	54

work'. Paradoxically, however, university teachers were twice as likely as schoolteachers to report frequent offers of either small or large gifts from their clients.

Within the welfare services: There were sharp differences between housing and pensions officials. Housing officials reported 10 per cent more frequent arguments with clients than those who dealt with pensions and benefits, and they were 11 per cent more negative about the overall behaviour of clients. They were over twice as likely as pensions officials to report frequent threats of violence. They put 17 per cent more priority than pensions officials on being 'fair but no more than that', and 21 per cent less on helping their clients 'as much as possible'. They were 27 per cent more likely than pensions officials to complain about lack of funds to give clients their legal rights, and 16 per cent more likely to demand more discretion to do their job. They were over 16 per cent more willing than pensions officials to justify taking gifts from their clients in return for 'extra' or 'faster than usual' work.

Within the police services: Traffic police were the most likely to put priority on strictly enforcing the laws and regulations. But compared to the administrators who worked in police offices, traffic police were also 20 per cent more willing to justify taking gifts from clients in return for 'extra' work. Traffic police uniquely combined authoritarian attitudes towards their clients with a lack of discipline, and even a degree of moral indulgence, with respect to themselves.

Traffic police were also 12 per cent more likely than police administrators to report that their clients frequently argued with them, and one and a half times as likely to report frequent threats of violence. Life was tough out on the road. Nonetheless, traffic police were the least pessimistic about the deterioration in their relations with their clients—and not just the least pessimistic amongst the police services but the least pessimistic amongst any group of officials. Given the frequency of arguments and threats from clients it seems a little paradoxical. But traffic police were also one and a half times as likely as administrators to report frequent offers of small gifts from clients, and three and a half times as likely to report frequent offers of money or expensive gifts. There were compensations as well as problems out on the road.

Within the legal services: Within the more heterogeneous category of court, customs and passport services, customs officials were the most distinctive. Like traffic police within the police service, customs officials were not only the most likely to put priority on strictly applying the laws and regulations but also the most likely to report that clients frequently offered them both large and small presents. Compared to passport officials, customs officials were 15 per cent more likely to put their priority on strict application of laws and regulations, and 12 per cent less on helping their clients as much as possible. Customs officials were 13 per cent more likely to report frequent arguments with clients, and one and a half times as likely to report frequent threats of violence. But they were also slightly more likely to report frequent offers of small presents, and over four times as likely to report frequent offers of money or expensive presents. Customs officials were markedly more positive than passport or court officials about the overall behaviour of clients.

THE IMPACT OF INADEQUATE SALARIES AND JOB PROSPECTS

We found clear evidence of institutional cultures. But the patterns associated with specific occupations highlight the significance of variable power-relations between officials and clients within different parts of the same institution.

Even more personal aspects of employment might also be important. We might expect that inadequate salaries and job insecurity might make officials less committed to their jobs and perhaps therefore less committed to treating their clients well.

Inadequate salaries: We can compare those officials who said it was possible to live on their salary with those who said that it was impossible. Those who said it was impossible were more sympathetic towards the problems of their clients. They were 10 per cent less likely to give priority to strictly applying the laws and regulations, and correspondingly more likely to give priority to being fair or helpful. But they were 20 per cent more likely to complain that they did not have enough resources to give their clients their legal rights. They were 11 per cent more likely to feel that their relations with clients had deteriorated since the end of the communist regime. At the same time, they were 10 per cent more willing to justify taking extra payments for 'faster' work.

Job insecurity: Compared to those who felt fully secure in their job, those who felt it was 'very likely' that they might lose their job through cuts in the next two years were 16 per cent more likely to complain that they did not have the resources to give their clients their legal rights. They were 14 per cent more likely to feel that they could help their clients less now than under communism, and 13 per cent more likely to feel that relations with clients had deteriorated since communist times.

The insecure, like the inadequately paid, were also 10 per cent more willing to justify taking extra payments for 'faster' work.

Job expectations: Officials who expected to be in the same job in five years' time (the '*stay-puts*'), and, more especially, those who expected promotion to a higher level within the same institution (the '*aspirants*'), might be more committed to their job and perhaps therefore more committed to their clients also. Conversely, expectations of a move out of the public sector (the '*quitters*') might make officials less committed to their current jobs and perhaps therefore less committed to treating their clients well.

In general, expectations of a switch to the private sector within the next five years seemed to have more influence than expectations of promotion. (Table 7.19) As might be expected, the 'stay-puts' were the least likely to want more powers of discretion and the most willing to accept more detailed instructions. They lacked ambition. Compared to these 'stay-puts', the 'aspirants' were a negligible 3 per cent more optimistic about trends in relations with clients. But by contrast, the 'quitters' were 16 per cent more pessimistic about deteriorating relations with clients, and twice as likely to take a negative view about the overall behaviour of clients.

Altogether, the 'aspirants' put most weight on strictly applying the law and were relatively complacent about the way clients were being served. They were almost twice as likely as the 'quitters' to put priority on strictly applying the laws and regulations. They were the least likely to put priority on helping clients, the least likely to complain about inadequate funds to give clients their legal rights, and the least likely to feel that their ability to help clients had declined since the communist regime.

The 'quitters' were over 16 per cent more willing than other officials to justify taking extra payments from clients in return for 'extra' or 'faster' work. They were also the most likely to report frequent offers of both large and small gifts from clients. Indeed, the 'quitters' were twice as likely to report frequent offers of money as the 'stay-puts', and seven times as likely to admit actually accepting money as the 'aspirants'. It is possible, of course, that the 'aspirants' were just especially careful not to admit to improper behaviour. But it is also possible that the 'quitters' were especially careless about observing the law.

Table 7.19. The impact of inadequate salaries and job prospects

	Can live on salary?		Likely to lose job?		Job expectations over next five years?		
	yes	no	very	not	same 'stay-puts'	higher 'aspirants'	private 'quitters'
	%	%	%	%	%	%	%
Officials' experience: clients...							
frequently argued	53	54	55	51	53	53	55
frequently threatened violence	8	15	10	11	11	16	15
frequently offered small presents	26	31	34	29	28	32	42
frequently offered money etc.	8	10	11	10	9	11	18
behaved badly, on the whole	11	16	14	14	10	14	20
Officials' priorities							
to apply the laws and regulations	33	23	27	28	27	32	18
to be fair to the client	18	25	26	20	21	27	34
to help clients as much as possible	49	52	47	52	52	41	48
Officials' perceptions of constraints on their ability to help clients							
lack adequate funds	61	81	87	71	74	70	88
want more freedom and discretion	67	67	66	70	65	74	76
Officials' justifications for taking gifts							
right to accept for 'extra' work	56	64	60	54	57	57	73
right to accept for 'faster' work	49	59	54	44	50	51	67
Officials' perceptions of trends in relationships with clients							
less able to help clients now	24	32	36	22	33	20	23
relationships with clients worse now	49	60	65	52	51	48	67

CONCLUSION: BENIGN AND PERNICIOUS
INSTITUTIONAL CULTURES

In this chapter we have looked at street-level officials' perceptions and attitudes from three different perspectives.

First, *as citizens themselves* street-level officials articulated many of the same complaints as other citizens. They were just as willing as the public to allege that officials in general took bribes, and only made an exception when asked about officials who did the same job as their own. But they enjoyed measurable advantages over other citizens, especially in Ukraine, when they themselves had to take personal problems to officials.

Second, *as employees* street-level officials complained about poor pay and job insecurity. But their complaints about inadequate salaries need to be put into perspective. Life was tough for everybody, and the public complained even more than officials about declining standards of living and inadequate family incomes.

Third, *as officials in relation to their clients* half the street-level officials that we interviewed put their priority on helping their clients as much as possible. The rest divided equally between wanting to do what was fair and reasonable or simply applying the laws and regulations strictly. Although generally positive towards clients, officials were particularly critical of rude, abusive, argumentative or threatening behaviour. Their attitudes towards attempts by clients to use contacts, presents and bribes were ambiguous, however. Overtly, they listed these attempts as being almost as annoying as rude or abusive behaviour, but they justified accepting 'extra payments' for special services to clients. A correlation analysis revealed that officials did not in fact react adversely to frequent offers of presents and bribes.

We have also looked at how officials' experience as employees affected their relationship with clients—both their experience of clients and their attitudes and behaviour towards clients.

First, there clearly was an institutional culture that, for example, put the top priority on helping clients in the health, education and welfare services, but put the top priority on strict application of the laws and regulations in the police and legal services. Second, the official's specific occupation or position within the institution also mattered. Doctors differed sharply from nurses (within health services), traffic police differed sharply from other police (within police services), and customs officials differed sharply from passport officials (within legal services). Third, we found that employment conditions and prospects, especially inadequate salaries, job insecurity and job expectations also had an impact on relationships with clients.

While the empirical pattern of relationships between officials and clients now seems reasonably clear, some questions of interpretation remain, and these have important implications for any strategies of reform.

Some aspects of what we have termed 'institutional culture' seem entirely positive and well worth preserving. It seems not only inevitable but also quite proper and appropriate that officials in health, educational and welfare services should give top priority to helping their clients as much as possible, while those in the police and legal services should give greater priority to strictly applying the laws and regulations.

But other aspects of institutional culture seem negative, inappropriate, and worth discouraging, even if they are quite natural and also to some degree inevitable. They have the character of an 'occupational disease' rather than an 'occupational skill'—typical, but unwelcome. (Fig. 7.3) The culture of gift taking in the health and education services, characterised by their unusual willingness to justify taking extra illegal payments from clients for 'extra' or 'faster than usual' work, does not seem so positive as their culture of helpfulness. In short, institutional cultures have both positive and negative aspects, some worth encouraging, others worth discouraging. Programmes to socialise new entrants into an institutional culture should consciously discriminate, therefore, between the positive and negative aspects of that institution's natural cultural tendencies.

But that raises the even more difficult question of whether these positive and negative aspects can easily be separated. The moralist might argue in favour of altruistic caring and helpfulness, without hope or expectation of reward. But the economist might see human behaviour more in terms of explicit or implicit bargaining and, in that perspective, helpfulness might go out of production if there was no market and no reward for it. No doubt reality lies somewhere in between. If the moralist's view prevailed completely there would be no correlation between caring and corruption. Conversely, if the economist's view prevailed the correlation between caring and corruption would be far stronger than it is.

In fact, those officials who gave top priority to the strict application of the laws and regulations were indeed the least likely to justify extra payments, presents or bribes. But the most likely to justify such extra payments were those who gave top priority to doing only what was 'fair and reasonable, no more'. Those who gave top priority to 'helping their

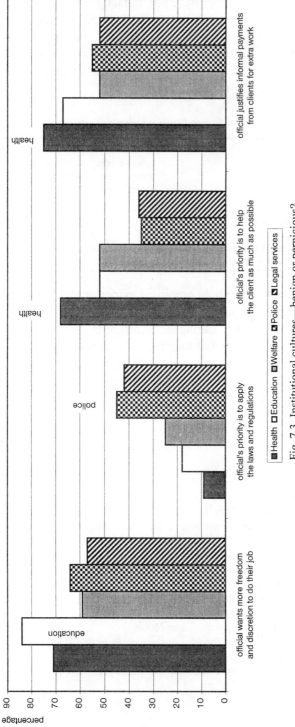

Fig. 7.3. Institutional cultures—benign or pernicious?

clients as much as possible' were not, in fact, the most inclined to justify 'extra payments'. (Table 7.20) It seems that rejecting the cold Weberian principle of strict, mechanical application of the laws and regulations does encourage a gift-taking culture. But it also seems that maximum concern for helping clients as much as possible tends to moderate rather than intensify that gift-taking culture.

Table 7.20. The connection between caring and gift-justifying cultures

	Official's attitude to gifts from clients:		
	right to accept something for 'extra' work	right to accept something for 'faster' work	Average
	%	%	%
If official's top priority is…			
to apply the laws and regulations	53	46	50
to do what is fair and reasonable, but no more	66	59	63
to help the client as much as possible	62	54	58

There is thus some slight empirical evidence that it may be possible, albeit difficult, to separate the positive and negative aspects of the 'I help, you pay' culture. Caring and corruption are loosely linked, not tightly and inevitably bound together. Those who reject what Fred Ridley calls the excessive 'continental European' over-emphasis on 'the rule of law' and who advocate instead what he calls the more 'sympathetic' and 'human' alternative, might be somewhat encouraged by that finding.

NOTES

1 Steel, Davenport, and Warner, 'Are Civil Servants Really Public Servants?'.
2 Lui and Cooper, 'Values in Flux'.
3 McAllister, 'Keeping Them Honest'.
4 Stewart, Sprinthall and Siemienska, 'Ethical Reasoning in a Time of Revolution'.
5 Kutuev, 'Public Service Ethos in Ukraine'; Kutuev and Svintsitsky, *Institutions of the Executive Power in Ukraine*.
6 Lancaster and Montinola, 'Towards a Methodology for the Comparative Study of Political Corruption', 193–4.
7 Tanzi, 'Corruption Around the World', 577.
8 Ridley, 'Civil Service and Democracy', 13.
9 Lampert, *Whistleblowing in the Soviet Union*.
10 Biryukov and Sergeyev, 'The Idea of Democracy in the West and in the East', 189; Biryukov and Sergeyev, *Russia's Road to Democracy*.
11 *Zhyzn* (4 July 1998), quoted in *Corruption Watch* 1, no. 9 (8 July 1998).

CHAPTER 8

WILLING TAKERS?

In this chapter we focus on how officials themselves viewed the use of presents and bribes, and why they accepted them. Once again, Umit Berkman's 'conceptual framework'[1] for 'bureaucracy and bribery' is a useful starting point. As summarised in Chapter 5, Berkman's framework was based on five major factors related to:

- (C) the *bribe-giving clients* (C1: their values and norms; C2: the importance of the benefits to them; C3: their financial situation; and C4: their calculation of the risk involved);
- (O) the *bribe-taking officials* (O1: their values and norms; O2: the importance of the benefits to them; O3: their financial situation; O4: their position and tenure within the organisation; and O5: their calculation of the risk involved);[2]
- (A) the *corrupt act itself* (A1: the nature of the corrupt act—expediting or distorting; A2: the demand for the corrupt act; A3: the supply of decision-making positions—that is, the availability of alternative officials whom clients may approach; A4: the number of collaborators needing to be brought together);[3]
- (I) the *institution* where the bribery takes place;
- (E) the wider *national environment* within which both organisations and individuals operate.

For an analysis of *bribe taking* rather than bribe giving, it is the factors related to officials rather than to clients that are most obviously relevant. We look at the impact of all the detailed factors listed by Berkman under the heading of 'bribe-taking officials' (O1–5). But we also take account of national culture and economic circumstances (E).

Our evidence in Chapter 7 suggests that the impact of distinctive institutional cultures (I) is important. In addition, we focus on 'the corrupt
act itself' (A), especially 'the demand for the corrupt act' (A2). From
the officials' perspective, this demand is expressed in the frequency of
offers and temptations from clients. In turn, that frequency may reflect
the bargaining power of officials—which derives from 'the supply of
alternative access points' (A3), and the official's particular position
within their organisation (O4).

According to Berkman, the connection between client demand for
corruption (A2) and the perceived bargaining power of officials may be
complex and, to a degree, even reciprocal: 'Clients may be more inclined to bribe public officials if they think that the organisation is corrupt and bribery is a sure way to have things done', and, reciprocally,
'such inclination may induce a weak official to accept and in time perhaps to ask for bribes'.[4]

Any empirical analysis of Berkman's model requires answers to some
sensitive questions. Surveys of citizens' perceptions of bribe taking are
not unusual. But there seems an understandable reluctance in survey interviews to ask officials directly even about *their own attitudes* towards
bribe taking. More especially, there seems to be a reluctance to ask officials directly whether, and if so how often, they themselves *have actually
taken* presents or bribes. Tim Ensor and Larisa Savelyeva, for example,
report that (unquantified) 'discussions with medical practitioners suggest
that for certain specialities in certain Kazakhstan hospitals a doctor might
obtain many times his official income. Yet little empirical work has been
done in this area'.[5] Louise Shelley and Anna Repetskaya provide a partial
exception to the rule. They interviewed five hundred inmates in a special
labour camp outside Irkutsk, which housed convicted former officials.[6]
But interviewing those already in prison for corruption gives no clue to
the incidence of corruption. It is logically impossible to research the factors that encourage one official to accept a bribe while another refuses, by
interviewing only those who have accepted.

We aimed to go beyond general questions about the use of presents
and bribes—beyond even such oblique questions as those that we reported in the previous chapter, about whether it would be 'right' for
some unspecified official to accept 'extra payments' in hypothetical circumstances. That is, we aimed to go beyond questions about *bribe-
taking values* to questions about actual *bribe-taking behaviour*. We
aimed to probe whether the officials we interviewed were personally
willing to accept gifts from clients, whether they had actually done so

recently and, if so, how often, and then to discover empirical evidence on why some officials had taken bribes while others had not.

But first, we review the factors that might possibly encourage or discourage bribe taking.

TEMPTATIONS, EXCUSES AND JUSTIFICATIONS

Temptations, excuses and justifications might all encourage officials to accept presents and bribes from their clients. So also might officials' perceptions, however mistaken, that their government was willing to turn a blind eye to the practice.

OFFERS FROM CLIENTS

Table 8.1. Frequent offers

	Average	Czech Republic	Slovakia	Bulgaria	Ukraine
		'more than rarely' in last few years			
	%	%	%	%	%
'A small present'					
officials report clients offered	30	24	43	23	30
public confess they themselves offered	25	11	34	15	39
'Money or an expensive present'					
officials report clients offered	10	7	14	9	11
public confess they themselves offered	13	6	17	7	24

Note: 'Don't know', 'mixed/depends', etc. answers were recorded if given spontaneously, but never prompted; they have been excluded from the calculation of percentages.

Officials reported that their clients used different strategies towards them with varying frequency. We focus here on their reports about just two of these strategies. On average, 30 per cent of officials said that their clients had frequently offered them 'a small present' and 10 per cent said that their clients had frequently offered them 'money or an expensive present'. (Table 8.1) On at least rare occasions, however, 67 per cent of officials had been offered 'a small present' and 27 per cent had been offered 'money or an expensive present'. The frequency of such offers must surely have tempted officials to accept, as well as providing the opportunity for actual acceptance. Perhaps the official might completely resist occasional offers but succumb, once in a while, to frequent offers. Or perhaps frequent offers would even make the official feel that it was 'normal' for clients to offer and officials to accept. As one client in a focus-group discussion put it: 'We have taught them this…we take them things…the first and the second bring something, and the third cannot avoid bringing something.'(Kh 3)

The percentage of clients who make frequent offers is not directly comparable with the percentage of officials who frequently receive them. Nonetheless, it is significant that both officials and their clients reported more frequent offers of presents and bribes in Slovakia and Ukraine than elsewhere. (In comparison with other countries, however, the frequency of offers reported by Ukrainian officials seems unusually low relative to the particularly high frequency of offers reported by Ukrainian citizens.)

EXCUSES AND JUSTIFICATIONS

Table 8.2. The basic cause of bribery

	Average	Czech Republic	Slovakia	Bulgaria	Ukraine
	%	%	%	%	%
Basic cause of bribery is 'greedy officials'					
views expressed by the public	39	37	30	39	48
views expressed by officials	13	15	16	7	12
difference: officials – public	−26	−22	−14	−32	−36
Basic cause of bribery is the poor pay of officials					
views expressed by the public	25	12	19	47	23
views expressed by officials	55	43	34	78	67
difference: officials – public	+30	+31	+15	+31	+44

Note: 'Don't know', 'mixed/depends' etc. answers were recorded if given spontaneously, but never prompted; they have been excluded from the calculation of percentages.

Officials had a ready set of excuses and justifications for accepting gifts from clients. They took a much more indulgent view than the public about officials' motivations for accepting presents and bribes. On average, 39 per cent of the public but only 13 per cent of officials blamed the practice of taking 'money or presents' from clients on the 'greed' of officials. (Table 8.2) Officials did not reciprocate by blaming clients. They were no more inclined (indeed slightly less) than the public to blame corruption on clients. But officials were 30 per cent more likely than the public to lay the blame on 'the government' because it 'does not pay officials properly'.

As we saw in the previous chapter, officials also had a self-flattering view about why clients generally offered gifts to them. They were around 12 per cent more likely than the public to attribute such gifts to clients' gratitude or politeness. A majority of officials thought it quite proper to accept unofficial payments from clients in return for 'some extra work' or for solving the client's problem 'faster than normal'.

PERCEPTIONS OF GOVERNMENT TOLERATION

Table 8.3. Officials' perceptions of government tolerance for bribe taking

	Average	Czech Republic	Slovakia	Bulgaria	Ukraine
	%	%	%	%	%
The government regards low-level officials' accepting money or expensive presents from ordinary people as…					
a corrupt practice which it must liquidate	46	54	47	48	36
unavoidable until it can pay better salaries	35	37	23	36	42
an informal way of charging for state services	19	9	30	16	22

Note: 'Don't know', 'mixed/depends' etc. answers were recorded if given spontaneously, but never prompted; they have been excluded from the calculation of percentages.

Speaking on television, President Leonid Kuchma claimed that corruption in Ukraine could be defeated by economic as well as administrative changes: 'If an official is paid appropriately…then I think he will have sufficient wisdom and will not deal with such matters as corruption.'[7] Such views were not always so openly expressed at the top. Nonetheless, over a third of officials felt that their government regarded officials' acceptance of 'money or expensive presents' from clients as 'unfortunate but unavoidable until it could pay officials better salaries'. A further one-fifth of officials even thought their government regarded bribe taking as 'an informal way of charging for state services and paying officials'. Less than half the street-level officials that we interviewed (indeed, only one-third in Ukraine) thought that their government viewed gift taking as 'a corrupt practice which it must liquidate'. (Table 8.3)

INSTITUTIONALISED CORRUPTION: SHARING WITH COLLEAGUES OR SUPERIORS

Mehmet Bac distinguishes between '*external corruption*' involving only 'the client and street-level bureaucrat' and the more deadly '*internal corruption*' involving a variety of officials and indeed various levels of official, 'transforming the organisation into an internal market of systematised sharing of corrupt proceeds'.[8] Such institutionalised corruption would encourage individual officials to participate. Indeed, it would make it difficult for individual officials to avoid accepting bribes. We asked those officials who had indicated that they were willing to accept a gift of 'money or an expensive present' whether they would: (i) be able to keep it; (ii) have to share it with their superiors; or (iii) have to share it with their colleagues but not with their superiors.

Gift taking seemed a relatively individual thing in the Czech and Slovak Republics where almost twice as many officials thought they would be able to keep such gifts for themselves as felt they would have to share them (though many said it would 'depend on the circumstances'). But gift taking had a more corporate flavour in Bulgaria where those proportions were reversed and where twice as many thought that they would have to share gifts as felt they would be able to keep them for themselves. In Ukraine, gift taking was not merely corporate but hierarchical. As in Bulgaria, almost twice as many officials thought they would have to share gifts as thought they could keep them for themselves. But in Ukraine, unlike Bulgaria, much of the sharing would have to be with superior officials. (Table 8.4)

Table 8.4. Institutionalised corruption—sharing with colleagues and superiors

	Average	Czech Republic	Slovakia	Bulgaria	Ukraine
	%	%	%	%	%
If you accepted money or an expensive present would you…					
be able to keep it?	27	33	36	16	23
have to share with colleagues only?	24	17	18	36	24
have to share with superiors?	5	2	3	1	15
it would depend on circumstances	44	48	43	46	39

Notes: Since 44 per cent volunteered a 'depends' answer these answers have not been excluded from calculations of percentages. 'Don't know' answers have been excluded as usual.

DOUBTS, FEARS AND INHIBITIONS

Doubts, fears and other inhibitions might discourage bribe taking. Officials' own norms and values tended to condemn bribe taking, and these are backed up by feelings of shame and by fears of punishment.

CONDEMNATION: 'BLACK' OR 'GREY'?

Arnold Heidenheimer distinguishes between '*black*' and '*grey*' corruption on the basis of public and elite opinion. 'Black' corruption comprises acts condemned by both public and the political or bureaucratic elite, while 'grey' corruption comprises acts condemned by only one side (usually the public) but defended or excused by the other (usually the elite).[9] Sceptics such as Peter deLeon claim that 'all corruption is grey' by that definition.[10] On the contrary, Michael Jackson and Rodney Smith contend that the literature on corruption suggests that the elite and the public tend to respond similarly to examples of political corruption, so that 'black' corruption is more frequent than 'grey'.

According to Jackson and Smith, however, 'no one until now has examined Heidenheimer's distinction using empirical evidence in a direct comparison of elite and public opinion'.[11] The attitudes of the public and the elite had been drawn from different surveys. They therefore asked the public and politicians in Australia to consider ten hypothetical scenarios that involved possibly 'corrupt' behaviour. Politicians proved more discriminating in what they condemned or excused, while the public saw the scenarios 'all of a piece' and were therefore more critical overall. Nonetheless, Jackson and Smith found that 'never does a clear majority of voters disagree with a clear majority of politicians'.[12] So there was little empirical evidence of truly 'grey' corruption. Ian McAllister's findings, also based on Australian data, are similar.[13]

We found that officials' values were less authoritarian but more law abiding than the public's. (This same combination of less authoritarian but more law abiding attitudes amongst the elite has also been reported in other post-communist countries[14] as well as in Britain and other Western counties.)[15] Officials were 11 per cent more likely than the public to reject the proposition that 'a strong leader with a free hand could solve the problems of our country'—a standard test of authoritarian values. But officials were also 18 per cent more likely than the public to say that people 'should obey' even a 'very unreasonable and unjust law'. (Table 8.5) (Both the public and officials were least authoritarian in the Czech Republic and the most authoritarian in Ukraine. But at the same time, both the public and officials were the most law abiding in the Czech Republic and the least law abiding in Ukraine. Ukraine combined relatively authoritarian with relatively lawless values.)

Table 8.5. Less authoritarian but more law-abiding

	Average	Czech Republic	Slovakia	Bulgaria	Ukraine
	%	%	%	%	%
A strong leader with a free hand could solve the problems of our country.					
views expressed by the public	42	26	31	50	60
views expressed by officials	31	16	25	30	52
difference: officials − public	−11	−10	−6	−20	−8
Even a very unreasonable or unjust law should be obeyed.					
views expressed by the public	56	68	53	63	41
views expressed by officials	74	86	71	72	66
difference: officials − public	+18	+18	+18	+9	+25

Note: 'Don't know', 'mixed/depends' etc. answers were recorded if given spontaneously, but never prompted; they have been excluded from the calculation of percentages.

Other things being equal, the fact that officials gave greater support than the public to obedience to the law should translate into greater condemnation of bribery. But it did not. The attitudes of officials were very similar to those of the public. On average, officials were less inclined than the public to condemn such actions as 'bad for the country and for those involved', but only by a negligible 5 per cent. (Table 8.6)

Table 8.6. Condemnation

	Average	Czech Republic	Slovakia	Bulgaria	Ukraine
	%	%	%	%	%
The use of money, presents, favours or contacts to influence officials is bad for the country and for those involved.					
views expressed by the public	61	69	60	58	58
views expressed by officials	56	71	59	55	39
difference: officials − public	−5	+2	−1	−3	−19

Note: 'Don't know', 'mixed/depends' etc. answers were recorded if given spontaneously, but never prompted; they have been excluded from the calculation of percentages.

On attitudes towards 'the use of money, presents, favours or contacts to influence officials', our findings are generally consistent with Jackson and Smith's. In every country except Ukraine a majority of officials as well as a majority of the public condemned the practice. In Heidenheimer's terms, the use of presents and bribes to influence officials was clearly 'black' corruption in these three countries.

But in Ukraine, officials were 19 per cent less likely than the public to condemn these actions. So while a majority of the public in Ukraine condemned the practice without reservation, a majority of officials did not. In Heidenheimer's terms, the use of presents and bribes to influence officials was therefore 'grey' corruption in Ukraine—an unusual occurrence according to Jackson and Smith's reading of the literature on corruption.

FEAR AND SHAME

Two-thirds of officials said that 'a person in a job like mine who did accept money or a present' from a client would be punished. On average, 29 per cent said they would suffer something 'more severe than confiscation' and a further 33 per cent that they would be 'dismissed'. This seems to imply that officials who took gifts might have reason to fear the consequences.

Table 8.7. Shame

	happy %	angry %	worried %	ashamed %
Public perceptions: An official who accepted money or a present would be most likely to feel...	65	2	21	12
Officials' claims: If they themselves accepted money they would be most likely to feel...	6	8	34	53
difference: officials claims – public perceptions	−59	+6	+13	+41

Note: 'Don't know', 'mixed/depends', etc. answers were recorded if given spontaneously, but never prompted; they have been excluded from the calculation of percentages.

What emotions would officials feel if they accepted a gift of 'money or an expensive present' from a client? Would they be most likely to feel 'happy, angry, worried or ashamed'? Over half the officials said they themselves would most likely feel 'ashamed' if they personally accepted such a gift, and another third said they would feel 'worried'. (Table 8.7) Only 6 per cent said they would personally feel 'happy'.

This is totally inconsistent with public perceptions of bribe-taking officials. Two-thirds of the public thought bribe-taking officials would feel 'happy' about it. Even if officials somewhat exaggerated their feelings of shame and fear, it seems likely that public perceptions of officials' feelings were wildly wrong. Fear and shame affected officials far more than the public realised.

CONFESSIONS

WILLINGNESS

There are many reasons why an official might accept a gift, and many reasons why they might refuse. There can be 'unwilling takers' (or at least 'reluctant takers') just as there are 'unwilling givers'.

One of the most frequent and most traditional excuses for taking bribes is poverty. It may be more than an excuse. When Shakespeare's Romeo persuades the apothecary to break the law to supply a lethal poison, the exchange goes thus:

Romeo: The world is not thy friend, nor the world's law:
              The world affords no law to make thee rich;
              Then be not poor, but break it, and take this.
Apothecary: My poverty, but not my will, consents.
Romeo: I pay thy poverty, and not thy will'.[16]

(Romeo later describes the bribe he paid as more poisonous than the chemical substance supplied by the apothecary—but that is a moralistic digression.)

Before asking officials to confess their actual experience of bribe taking we put two hypothetical questions about whether they would or would not accept a 'small present' or a large gift comprising 'money or an expensive present', if these were offered by a client. In addition, our questions inquired about the officials' motivations for accepting or rejecting a gift. Each question was intended to provide a 'willingness scale' running from the most unqualified and uninhibited willingness to accept ('I would *welcome* it as a token of thanks') to the most indignant and offended refusal ('I would *feel offended* and refuse').

Apart from a simple 'welcome' for a gift, the scale included mild reluctance, little more than a formality perhaps, expressed in the phrase:

'It would be *impolite to refuse.*' But it also included more intense reluctance, reflecting the position of Shakespeare's apothecary: 'I would reluctantly accept it because salaries are so low that I *could not afford to refuse.*' We may be somewhat sceptical of such answers in our survey—as Shakespeare's audiences are about the apothecary's words in the play—but they nonetheless seem to indicate more reluctance than 'welcoming' a gift or simply accepting one 'out of politeness'.

Similarly, there were two categories of refusal on the scale. First the indignant 'I would feel offended and refuse', which implies an internal, personal condemnation of gift taking; and second, a less specific, less indignant refusal: 'I would *refuse for other reasons.*' These might include fear of the penalties, or a salary so good that the gift held no great temptation, but this answer certainly did not include any element of revulsion.

On average, 47 per cent said they would accept 'a small present' if offered. Far fewer, an average of only 17 per cent, said they would accept 'money or an expensive present' if offered.

Table 8.8. Why officials say they would accept gifts

	Average	Czech Republic	Slovakia	Bulgaria	Ukraine
	%	%	%	%	%
If a client offered *'a small present'*...					
they would keep it as a token of thanks	20	11	24	33	11
it would be impolite to refuse	18	26	28	5	14
they could not afford to refuse	9	2	6	8	19
total accept	47	39	58	46	44
they would feel offended and refuse	17	14	11	24	19
they would refuse for other reasons	36	46	31	30	37
If a client offered *'money or an expensive present'*...					
they would keep it as a token of thanks	4	2	5	5	4
it would be impolite to refuse	4	4	6	3	5
they could not afford to refuse	9	3	7	10	16
total accept	17	9	18	18	25
they would feel offended and refuse	27	27	24	37	21
they would refuse for other reasons	56	65	59	45	54

Note: 'Don't know', 'mixed/depends' etc. answers were recorded if given spontaneously, but never prompted; they have been excluded from the calculation of percentages.

The numbers of officials who would accept a large gift comprising 'money or an expensive present' ranged from 9 per cent in the Czech Republic up to 25 per cent in Ukraine. But the cross-national variation in reasons for accepting was as striking as the variation in the totals willing to accept. (Table 8.8) There was a steady rise in the numbers who 'could not afford to refuse' both large and small presents from the Czech Republic through Slovakia and Bulgaria to Ukraine. Only 2 per cent of all officials in the Czech Republic 'could not afford to refuse' a small present and only 3 per cent a large one. But in Ukraine, 19 per cent of all officials said they 'could not afford to refuse' a small present and 16 per cent 'could not afford to refuse' a large one. So only a small minority of those officials who were willing to accept money or an expensive present in the Czech Republic would do so for reasons of necessity, less than half in Slovakia, but just over half in Bulgaria and almost two-thirds in Ukraine. That pattern mirrors the cross-national spectrum of economic deprivation.

THREE MEASURES OF CONFESSED ACCEPTANCE

Later we asked three questions, in quick succession, about officials' actual experience of gift taking:

- 'In the last few years—say the last five years—did you *ever accept* a present from someone whose problem you dealt with as part of your official duties?' Of those who gave a straightforward 'yes' or 'no' answer, 30 per cent said 'yes'.
- 'If you did accept something, was that *only after* you had solved the client's problem?' Despite the conditional phrasing, we put this question to all officials, including those who had originally denied accepting anything at all. In reply, 43 per cent now confessed that they had accepted something either 'before' (8 per cent) or 'after' (35 per cent) solving their client's problem.
- 'If you did accept something, was that *only a small present*— flowers, chocolates, or a bottle for example—or was it *something more* than that?' Again, despite the conditional phrasing, we put this question to all officials, including those who had originally denied accepting anything. In reply, 58 per cent now confessed that they had accepted either 'a small present' (53 per cent) or 'something more' (5 per cent)—almost twice as many as had originally confessed to accepting a present of any kind.

The numbers who confessed to accepting large gifts, or accepting them 'before' addressing their clients' problems, were larger in Slovakia and Ukraine. The number of refusals to answer, though never very large, was greater in Ukraine than elsewhere.

Of course, some may fail to confess what they have done (perhaps out of embarrassment) and others may confess to what they have not done (perhaps out of a desire to please the interviewer). We tried to minimise inaccuracy by placing these three questions in the middle of the interview, well after officials had recounted their own perceptions and experience as citizens giving presents and bribes to other officials to get help with their own problems. In fact, the three questions about actual bribe taking caused very little shock. The levels of 'don't knows/refusals' were low and dropped steadily across the three questions as they became less ambiguous. Moreover, interviewers' reports from pilot interviews suggested that officials were more concerned about the confidentiality of their party preferences (a reasonable concern in any formerly authoritarian country) than about the confidentiality of their confessions to gift taking.

Table 8.9. How officials' confessions emerged

	If answer to the initial question ('Did you accept a gift from a client recently?') was…		
	yes %	depends %	no %
Answers to question about size of gifts:			
confessed to taking 'only a small present'	85	93	36
confessed to taking 'something more'	14	3	0
did not accept anything, large or small	0	4	63
Answers to question about timing of gifts:			
accepted gifts but 'only after' solving the problem	77	83	14
'sometimes' accepted gifts 'before' solving the problem	22	6	2
did not accept anything, before or after	1	11	84

Although the numbers who confessed rose from 30 per cent to 58 per cent across these three questions, the answers were not as inconsistent as they at first appear. (Table 8.9) The apparent inconsistency arises from the ambiguity that surrounds the meaning of a 'present'. Over a third of those who initially denied accepting 'a present' later admitted that they had accepted 'a small present', but none of them admitted to accepting 'something more', and very few admitted that they had accepted even a small present 'before' solving the client's problem. Almost all of those who had given a 'depends what you mean' response to the first question, later admitted that they had taken something, but it was nearly always something small and few had accepted even a small present 'before' solving their client's problem. In sharp contrast, amongst those who readily admitted, in reply to our first question, that they had accepted a present, 14 per cent later admitted that they had accepted 'something more than a small present' and 22 per cent that they had accepted something 'before' solving their client's problem.

OPPORTUNITY AND MOTIVATION

Under our persistent questioning, the number of those who confessed to accepting gifts from clients (58 per cent) actually exceeded the number of those who had declared that they would accept a small gift if offered (47 per cent). But, significantly, the number of those who confessed to actually accepting 'something more' (5 per cent) was much smaller than the number of those who had said they were willing to accept a large gift 'if offered' (17 per cent).

Gift taking requires *opportunity* as well as motivation, however. Some officials had never accepted a gift simply because they had never been offered one. Large gifts were offered much less frequently than small ones. Of those who said earlier in the interview that they had 'never' been offered 'money or an expensive present', less than 1 per cent later confessed to accepting such a gift. Of those who reported getting such offers only 'rarely', 10 per cent confessed that they had accepted, and of those who had received such offers more frequently, 25 per cent confessed they had accepted.

But *motivation* itself also mattered. Only 1 per cent of those who had said they 'would refuse' a large gift comprising 'money or an expensive present' confessed to accepting one. Amongst those who would only accept because they 'could not afford to refuse', confessions rose to 13 per cent. Amongst those who would reluctantly accept out of 'politeness', confessions rose to 22 per cent, and amongst those who would 'welcome' a large gift 'as a token of thanks' from a grateful client, confessions rose to 39 per cent.

Motivation and opportunity operated jointly and *interactively*. (Table 8.10, Fig. 8.1) That is to say, the impact of motivation was greater amongst those officials who received such offers 'more than rarely'. Amongst such officials, confessions to actually taking large gifts differed by 59 per cent between the least willing and most willing. But, as we might expect, amongst officials who had 'rarely or never' received such offers, the impact of willingness on actual behaviour was only half as great.

Table 8.10. The joint and interactive impact of willingness and opportunity on gift taking

	If received offers		
	'more than rarely'	'rarely or never'	impact of opportunity
	% who had accepted 'something more' than a small gift		
	%	%	%
If officials claimed their attitude to an offer of 'money or an expensive present' would be to...			
welcome it as a token of thanks	59	31	+28
accept because it would be impolite to refuse	54	10	+44
accept because they could not afford to refuse	32	9	+23
refuse, but not be offended	12	1	+11
feel offended and refuse	0	1	−1
impact of degree of willingness	+59	+30	

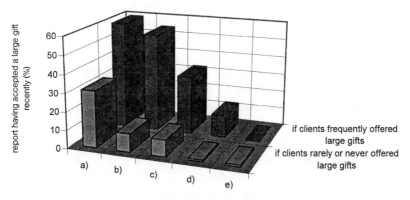

Fig. 8.1. Motive and opportunity—the joint impact on taking bribes
a) if official would welcome a large gift, b) if official would accept out of politeness, c) if official could not afford to refuse, d) if official would refuse but not be offended, e) if official would be offended by an offer

Conversely, opportunity had its greatest effect amongst the willing. Opportunity had very much less impact amongst those who had claimed they would refuse an offer without being offended by it—though they

were not entirely resolute in their refusals and could not entirely resist
temptation. Opportunity had no impact at all amongst those who said
they would be offended by such an offer—those officials really meant it
when they said they would refuse.

WHY DID SOME OFFICIALS ACCEPT WHILE
OTHERS DID NOT?

What influenced motivation? And what, apart from opportunity, affected the translation of motivation into actual behaviour? We looked at
the possible impact of a wide range of influences.

Many officials were clearly willing to accept presents and bribes 'if
offered'. But not all officials. Indeed, a majority claimed they would
refuse them. Why were some officials willing to accept presents and
bribes 'if offered', while others were not? Similarly, why did some officials actually accept them while others did not? The cross-national dimension was clearly important, whether that reflected national economic
conditions, long-term 'national cultures', or simply different cultures in
different institutions—the Czech health service as distinct from the
Ukrainian health service, for example.

But beyond these cross-national differences, were there important
within-country differences? More specifically, were there consistent
within-country tendencies that might unambiguously link certain types
of official to bribe taking? To focus on consistent within-country tendencies we carried out separate within-country analyses but present only
the results averaged across the four countries. That not only eliminates
any potential confusion between cross-national and within-country effects, it also directs our attention away from those within-country effects
which vary in direction from country to country, and towards more general and consistent within-country tendencies.

THE WEAK IMPACT OF SOCIAL BACKGROUND

Age, gender, education, religiosity, and a rural, urban or metropolitan
milieu reputedly indicate significantly different social and intellectual
'cultures' with pervasive influences upon individual behaviour. No
doubt that is true. But did these influences affect officials' willingness to
accept gifts, or their experience of actually taking them? Younger officials, for example, had been less exposed to communist influences and

might therefore think and behave differently from older 'communist-era' cohorts. But whether they represent a less corrupt or a more aggressively individualistic and acquisitive generation (or a self-cancelling mixture of the two) is an open question.

As we saw in the previous chapter, a 'post-communist generation' of officials is fairly easy to identify. But it proved no more distinctive on actual bribe taking than on other aspects of officials' views or experience. Old, young and 'post-communist' officials (as defined in the previous chapter) never differed by more than a negligible 4 per cent on their declared willingness to accept large or small presents 'if offered' by a client, nor on their confessions to actually taking them. For what it is worth, the 'post-communist' officials were very slightly more willing than the older generation to accept a large gift, yet very slightly less likely to have done so. What is absolutely certain from our data is that, in their approach to corruption, 'post-communist' officials did not represent a new wave of 'clean-hands'.

Male and female officials also differed little on whether they were willing to accept a present 'if offered' by a client, and only slightly more on whether they had actually accepted them. Female officials were about 8 per cent *more* likely than their male colleagues to confess to having accepted a gift of some kind, but it tended to be only a small gift. They were 4 per cent *less* likely than their male colleagues to admit having accepted a large gift. Divorced, separated and widowed officials were also very slightly more likely than others to admit receiving 'only a small present' but no more likely to admit receiving anything more than that.

Similarly, the most actively religious officials were about 5 per cent more likely to admit accepting a gift than those who 'never attended' a place of worship, but 4 per cent less likely to admit receiving a large one. Neither education nor residence in a large town or city had much influence on whether officials would accept presents 'if offered' by a client, nor on whether they had actually accepted one in recent years.

In short, social background had remarkably little influence, either on officials' willingness to take bribes or on their actually confessing to taking them.

THE WEAK IMPACT OF IDEOLOGY

Officials who opposed the move to a market economy, who favoured voting for a 'socialist or communist party', or who supported nationalist claims on neighbouring states' territories were all somewhat more willing than others to accept a large gift but scarcely any more likely to confess that they had actually done so. Thus, socialist and nationalist values also appear to have had little effect upon actually accepting gifts.

We found no correlation between generally authoritarian attitudes and a refusal to accept gifts. But a specific emphasis on strict observance of the law had some influence. Those officials who said people 'should obey even a very unreasonable or unjust law' were 12 per cent more likely to claim that they would refuse an expensive gift and 18 per cent more likely to claim that they would refuse a small gift. In the event, they were also 15 per cent less likely to confess to accepting a small gift, though they were scarcely any less likely to confess to accepting a large one.

So general ideology, like social background, had little influence upon willingness to accept gifts from clients, and even less influence on actual behaviour. Only a specific respect for the law had a significant influence.

THE IMPACT OF INSTITUTIONAL CULTURES

Table 8.11. The impact of institutional cultures on gift taking

	Average %	health services %	education services %	welfare services %	police services %	legal services %
'a small present'						
would accept	47	65	50	48	36	37
had accepted recently	58	78	58	59	47	47
'money or an expensive present'						
would accept	17	28	13	14	15	14
had accepted recently	5	9	3	2	6	2

Specifically job-related characteristics had far more impact than social background or ideology. Although Michael Lipsky argues that the relationship between street-level bureaucrats and their clients is 'primarily determined by the priorities and preferences of the street-level bureaucrats' he adds that 'the character and terms of the relationship are substantially affected by the limits of the [bureaucrat's] job'.[17] Within the benign context of his investigation, Lipsky chose to highlight the constraints imposed on American street-level bureaucrats by 'professional and bureaucratic standards of fairness and due process (notwithstanding the most outrageous tales of exceptions to the contrary)'.[18] In post-communist Europe it seems more relevant to highlight the less exceptional opportunities for outrageous behaviour that were provided by some jobs, rather than the constraints imposed by others.

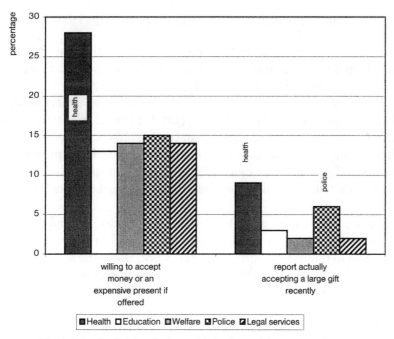

Fig. 8.2. Institutional attitudes and behaviour with respect to large gifts

Compared to the average across all services, health-service employees were 18 per cent more willing to accept a small gift 'if offered' and 11 per cent more willing to accept money or an expensive gift. Furthermore, they were also 20 per cent more likely to admit actually taking a gift recently and, although the absolute numbers were small, twice as likely as the average official to admit taking money or an expensive gift. (Table 8.11, Fig. 8.2)

Conversely, those who worked in our somewhat heterogeneous category of legal services (court, customs, and passport services) were 10 per cent less willing than the average official to accept a small gift 'if offered', and 11 per cent less likely to confess having done so recently.

Those who worked in the police services were 11 per cent less willing than average to accept a small gift 'if offered' and also 11 per cent less likely to confess they had accepted one recently. But, para-doxically, they came second only to health-service employees in con-fessing that they had recently accepted money or an expensive gift from a client.

THE STRONG IMPACT OF SPECIFIC OCCUPATIONS

In addition to these sharp differences *between* institutions there were also sharp differences *within* institutions, related to the specific occupa-tion of the employee. (Table 8.12, Fig. 8.3)

Within the health services: Hospital doctors were almost twice as likely as nurses or administrators to report that clients frequently offered them small gifts, and much more than twice as likely to report frequent offers of money or expensive gifts. Compared to hospital administrators, doctors were 24 per cent more willing to take a small gift 'if offered', and 19 per cent more likely to confess that they had accepted a gift re-cently.

Nurses were almost as willing as doctors to take gifts, and they were the most willing of all in the health services to justify extra informal payments in return for 'extra' or 'faster' work. But at the same time they were the least likely to confess they had actually accepted money or an expensive gift from a client. Only 2 per cent of nurses, compared to 16 per cent of doctors, had done so.

Within the education services: University teachers were 17 per cent more likely than schoolteachers to report that clients had frequently of-fered them small presents and twice as likely as schoolteachers to report offers of money or expensive gifts. Whatever the behaviour of their cli-ents, however, it was the schoolteachers rather than the university staff who were most likely to justify accepting gifts from clients and also the most likely to confess they had accepted some kind of gift recently. Yet they were like nurses in some respects. Although schoolteachers ac-cepted small gifts relatively frequently they seldom accepted money or expensive gifts. Within education, large gifts went mainly to university teachers.

Within the welfare services: Relatively few welfare officials of any kind admitted accepting money or expensive gifts.

Within the police services: Traffic police were about 14 per cent more likely than other police to report that clients frequently offered them gifts, and between two and three times as likely to report offers of money. In the event, traffic police were 19 per cent more likely than

Table 8.12. The impact of specific occupations on gift taking

	All	Health			Education			Welfare			Police			Legal services		
		doctors	nurses	admin	univ teach	univ admin	schoolteach	pensions	benefits	housing	traffic	ordinary	admin	courts	customs	passports
	%	D %	N %	A %	UT %	UA %	S %	P %	B %	H %	T %	O %	A %	Crt %	Ctm %	P %
'a small present'																
would accept	47	75	70	51	52	45	53	51	45	49	42	31	36	29	39	42
had accepted recently	58	89	75	70	59	50	67	59	62	56	56	37	49	44	48	49
'money or an expensive present'																
would accept	17	31	27	26	15	10	14	13	12	18	19	11	14	10	20	14
had accepted recently	5	16	2	10	5	1	1	1	3	3	12	2	5	1	6	0

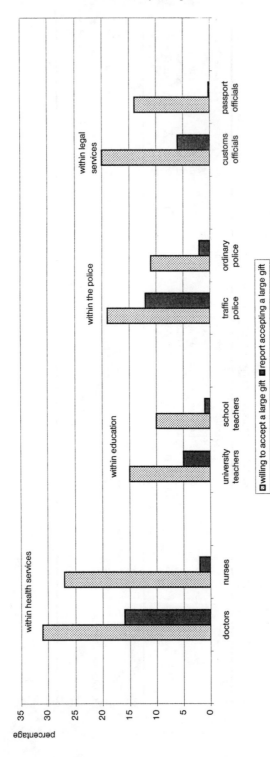

Fig. 8.3. Within institutions, occupations differ more in behaviour than in attitudes towards gift taking

ordinary police to confess that they had accepted a small present and six times as likely (12 per cent compared to 2 per cent) to confess accepting money or an expensive present.

Within the legal services (the more heterogeneous category of court, customs and passport services): Customs officials were the most distinctive. They were almost twice as likely as court officials to report frequent offers of both large and small presents. While they were only a little more likely than passport officials to be offered small presents, they were four times as likely to be offered money or an expensive present.

Customs officials had a lot in common with doctors and traffic police, while passport officials had more in common with nurses. Within our category of legal services those who confessed to actually taking money or an expensive gift from clients were limited almost exclusively to customs officials.

BARGAINING STRENGTH

It is difficult to believe that such narrowly defined occupations as traffic police or doctors had an 'institutional culture' that was distinct from the more general police or health-services culture. What these specific occupations had was *power and opportunity* vis-à-vis their clients. Indeed, doctors accepted bribes within an institution (the health service) which was broadly sympathetic to gift taking, while traffic police accepted bribes within an institution (the police) which was particularly unsympathetic to gift taking. Conversely, although nurses worked in an institutional culture that was sympathetic to gift taking, and although they came near the top of the list of those who had accepted small gifts, they came very low down the list of those that had accepted more than a small present.

All of this points to the significance of occupational opportunity and bargaining power rather than institutional culture in determining which officials actually took money or expensive gifts from their clients. The concept of an official's bargaining power vis-à-vis clients is encapsulated in Robert Klitgaard's famous equation:[19]

$$Corruption = Monopoly + Discretion - Accountability$$

It is also characteristic more of specific occupations than of countries or institutions.

THE IMPACT OF INADEQUATE SALARIES AND JOB PROSPECTS

More personal aspects of employment were also important. Inadequate salaries, job insecurity and future job prospects all had an impact. (Table 8.13)

Table 8.13. The impact of inadequate salaries and job prospects on gift taking

	Can live on salary?		Likely to lose job?		Job expectations over next five years?		
	yes	no	very	not	same 'stay-puts'	higher 'aspirants'	private 'quitters'
	%	%	%	%	%	%	%
'a small present'							
would accept	42	53	43	52	48	44	59
had accepted recently	51	62	52	65	57	51	69
'money or an expensive present'							
would accept	10	22	14	21	14	17	31
had accepted recently	6	4	4	4	5	1	7

Inadequate salaries: Amongst the four countries in our survey there is a clear spectrum of economic deprivation,[20] accentuated by recent economic decline,[21] that runs from the Czech Republic through Slovakia and then Bulgaria to Ukraine. Transparency International's *Corruption Perception Index*[22] now ranks these countries in the same order from relatively low levels of corruption in the Czech Republic, through intermediate levels in Slovakia and Bulgaria to the highest in Ukraine. That hints at a connection between corruption and economic factors. But not all of the data on corruption ranks these countries in order of the economic pressures upon them. On some of our own indicators, Bulgaria seems less corrupt than Slovakia, and a recent EBRD survey of over 3,000 firms in 20 transition countries suggests that firms in Slovakia and Ukraine pay bribes to officials more frequently than in either Bulgaria or the Czech Republic.[23]

But even if corruption were most widespread in the poorest country, that would not allow us to infer that, within countries, corruption was most widespread amongst the poorest officials. Making such an inference would be a perfect example of falling into the statistical trap of the 'Ecological Fallacy'[24] (see Chapter 1). As *Vilnu Ukrainu* put it rather well: 'Statistics offer no reason to believe that corruption is widespread only among low-paid civil servants...*on the contrary*.'[25] Indeed, well before the fall of communism, Aron Katsenelinboigen put forward 'three laws of Soviet corruption'. They were unfortunately based only on anecdote, gossip and hearsay, but the first of these laws is thought-provoking nonetheless: 'The higher the level of the person in the society, the greater the percentage of bribes in his total income.'[26] Paradoxically, we might suspect that although corruption may be most widespread in the poorest countries, corruption within countries is likely to be more widespread amongst the better-paid officials—or at least that the taking of larger bribes may be more widespread amongst the better-paid officials.

Our survey did not extend to the upper echelons of elite officials who salt away huge bribes in numbered Swiss bank accounts. But even within the ranks of street-level officials we found evidence of a complex relationship between inadequate salaries and accepting gifts from clients. Compared to those officials with adequate salaries, those who said they 'could not live on their salary' were 11 per cent more willing to accept a small gift 'if offered', and over twice as willing to accept money or an expensive gift.

Salary levels also influenced officials' reasons for being willing to accept gifts. Amongst well-paid officials, a majority (6 per cent) of the 10 per cent who were willing to accept money said they would 'welcome it as a token of thanks' or because it would be 'impolite to refuse'. But amongst inadequately paid officials, a majority (13 per cent) of the 22 per cent who were willing to accept money claimed they would accept only because they 'could not afford to refuse'.

In the event, inadequately paid officials were 13 per cent more likely to confess to accepting a small present. But in line with Katsenelinboigen's theory, the inadequately paid were not more likely than the better-paid to confess to accepting larger gifts, but actually slightly less. Unlike hospital doctors, traffic police or customs officials, the inadequately paid were notably willing to accept money or expensive gifts but they were not specially favoured by offers of such gifts from clients. They had motivation but not opportunity.

Job insecurity: Compared to those who felt fully secure in their job, those who felt it was 'very likely' that they might lose their job 'through cuts in the next two years' were 11 per cent more willing to accept a small gift. They were also one and a half times as willing to take money or an expensive gift 'if offered'. But although the insecure were 13 per cent more likely to confess having taken a small present recently, they were no more likely to confess having accepted money or an expensive present. In general, the impact of job insecurity was similar to that of inadequate pay but smaller in scale, perhaps because insecurity was only hypothetical while inadequate salaries were a real and present problem.

Job prospects: In general, prospects of a switch to the private sector sometime within 'the next five years' had more influence than prospects of promotion. Those who expected to quit the public sector were 13 per cent more willing than others to accept a small present, and twice as willing to accept a large one. They were twice as likely to report frequent offers of money as those who expected to stay in the same job. In the event, they were the most likely to confess accepting money. Conversely, those who expected promotion within the public sector were the least likely to confess accepting money—though that could reflect a lack of openness as well as a wish to avoid misdemeanours which might prejudice their chances of promotion.

THE IMPACT OF FEAR

While frequent offers from clients encouraged bribe taking, fear of punishment had the opposite effect. Compared to those who feared the penalty for being caught taking bribes would be 'dismissal', those who thought 'nothing' would happen were 42 per cent more willing to accept a small present and 34 per cent more likely to confess that they had actually done so recently. They were also 25 per cent more willing to accept money or an expensive gift, and four times as likely to confess that they had actually done so. (Table 8.14)

Table 8.14. The impact of fear of punishment on gift taking

	If thinks likely penalty for being caught taking money or a present from a client would be…		
	nothing %	severe penalty %	dismissal %
'a small present'			
would accept	71	40	29
had accepted recently	75	58	41
'money or an expensive present'			
would accept	33	12	8
had accepted recently	8	5	2

THE IMPACT OF A PERSONAL GIFT-JUSTIFYING CULTURE: CONDEMNATION OR JUSTIFICATION

Although it could be described as getting close to the end of the 'funnel of causality', we might expect that those officials who made excuses, defended, or even justified accepting extra payments or gifts from clients, would actually accept them more frequently than other officials.

Officials who thought their government regarded taking gifts as 'a corrupt practice, which should be liquidated' were 16 per cent less willing than others to accept a small present and 14 per cent less willing to accept an expensive one. They were also 18 per cent less likely to confess that they had actually taken a gift from a client.

Officials' own personal views about whether taking gifts from clients was 'bad for the country and for those involved' had a similar effect. Officials who preferred a strict Weberian system ('no presents, no favours') were 21 per cent less willing to accept small gifts, 15 per cent less willing to accept expensive ones, and 20 per cent less likely to confess that they had actually accepted a gift recently. (Table 8.15)

Table 8.15. The impact of perceived government tolerance and personal values on gift taking

	If thinks govt regards gifts as...		If officials regard gifts as...		If official prefers system...	
	corrupt	unavoidable etc.	bad	unavoidable etc.	without bribes and favours	with bribes and favours
	%	%	%	%	%	%
'a small present'						
would accept	40	56	38	58	40	61
had accepted recently	50	68	53	66	54	74
'money or an expensive present'						
would accept	9	23	11	25	13	28
had accepted recently	2	7	2	7	4	7

Compared to those officials who said it would be 'wrong' to accept payments from clients for 'extra work', those officials who said it would be 'right to ask' for such payments were 38 per cent more willing to take a small gift and 25 per cent more willing to take an expensive one. In the event, they were 46 per cent more likely to confess that they had actually taken a gift recently, and six times as likely to confess that they had actually taken an expensive one. (Table 8.16)

Officials who justified extra payments for 'faster than usual work' responded in a similar way.

Table 8.16. The impact of a gift-justifying culture on gift taking

	If the official thinks that for 'extra work' it would be…			If the official thinks that for 'faster than usual work' it would be…		
	right to ask %	right to accept %	wrong to accept %	right to ask %	right to accept %	wrong to accept %
'a small present'						
would accept	66	59	28	66	64	28
had accepted recently	75	70	39	70	73	42
'money or an expensive present'						
would accept	33	21	8	33	25	7
had accepted recently	12	6	2	12	6	2

A CAUSAL MODEL

In terms of Berkman's 'conceptual framework' our findings suggest that even a highly simplified model of bribe taking should take account of:

- national circumstances (E);
- institutional cultures or sub-cultures (I);
- the values and norms of officials as expressed in condemnation or justification (O1), their fear of punishment (O5), and the economic pressures upon them (O2, O3);
- the frequency of opportunities or temptations from clients (A2), which is related to the precise occupation of the official (O4) and the associated bargaining power of officials vis-à-vis their clients (A3, though also a function of O4 and I).

These influences fall naturally into a sequence of cause and effect. We take the country, the institution and the occupation of the official as given. Other factors depend on them. Economic pressures on officials reflect their particular occupations and the performance of their countries' economies. Their exposure to temptation and fear of punishment may reflect not only broad national cultures but also the particular institutional culture of the service in which they are employed and the bargaining power vis-à-vis clients which is associated with their very particular occupation within that institution. Condemnation or justification (often described by our focus-group participants as the official's 'personal culture') may reflect national, institutional and occupational cultures that encourage or discourage bribe taking. But this 'personal culture' may also reflect the economic pressures of inadequate salaries. Finally, whether officials are willing to accept a gift, and whether they confess to having accepted one recently, are likely to reflect their feelings about whether such behaviour is justified. But they may also reflect temptations, opportunities and fears as well as economic pressures.

That sequence implies a *three-stage 'recursive' causal model* defined by three sets of variables, with each set dependent, to a greater or lesser extent, on the preceding sets. Table 8.17 describes how we operationalised the variables in this model.

Table 8.17. Operationalisation of variables in the causal model

variables	operational definitions (coding)
Set 1.	
country	CZ, SLVK, BULG, UKR: 1 if in the respective country, 0 otherwise
institutions	1 if in the respective institution, 0 otherwise
occupations	1 if in the respective occupation, 0 otherwise
Set 2.	
economic pressure	LOWPAY: 1 = possible to live on salary, 2 = very difficult, 3 = not
	LATEPAY: 1 = always paid on time, 2 = usually, 3 = rarely or never
	POORPAY = LOWPAY + LATEPAY
opportunity	OFFER: 1 = clients never offered, 2 = rarely, 3 = sometimes, 4 = usually
fear	FEAR: 1 = 'nothing' would likely happen if official caught taking bribes, 2 = 'confiscated', 3 = 'more severe penalty', 4 = 'dismissal'
personal culture	JUSTIFY: 3 = right to ask for 'extra' payments, 2 = right to accept, 1 = neither
Set 3.	
willing to take gifts	WILLING: 4 = would welcome, 3 = accept out of politeness, 2 = could not afford to refuse, 1 = would refuse
had taken gifts recently	CONFESS: 3 = took more than a small gift from a client in recent years, 2 = took only a small gift, 1 = took nothing

With such a model, the dependence of each variable on all prior variables can be estimated using multiple regression. 'Standardised regression coefficients' or 'betas', which can range in size from zero to 1.0 (except in the most unusual and pathological circumstances where it is technically possible for betas to exceed 1.0) indicate the degree to which one variable influences another. For readability we eliminate the decimal point and report betas multiplied by 100.

INFLUENCES ON ECONOMIC PRESSURE, OPPORTUNITY, FEAR, AND GIFT-JUSTIFYING CULTURE

As might be expected, by far the best predictor of inadequate or late salaries was the country in which the official worked—and that proved a very powerful predictor. (Table 8.18)

Opportunities or temptations (i.e. officials' reports of frequent offers from clients) were far less predictable and cross-national differences were much smaller (though in earlier chapters we found greater cross-national differences in citizens' own reports of their frequent offers to officials). However, three occupations stood out for the frequency with which they reported clients offering gifts: traffic police, customs officials and hospital doctors—for whom the beta coefficient (strictly speaking, beta expressed as a percentage) was 16 for small gifts and 12 for large gifts. At the same time, institutions proved an insignificant influence on opportunities and temptations. There could hardly have been a clearer indication that frequent offers from clients reflected the bargaining power of specific occupations rather than a more general institutional culture.

By contrast, fear of punishment primarily reflected institutional cultures rather than specific occupations. It was exceptionally low in the health services (beta = −35) though not quite so low amongst hospital administrators as amongst doctors and nurses. It was also relatively low in the education services (beta = −12) but relatively high in police services (beta = +17).

Institutional cultures were also an important influence on gift-justifying culture, the values and norms of officials. Those who worked in the health service, particularly as doctors and nurses rather than as administrators, were very much more inclined to justify accepting extra payments from clients (beta = +28 for the health services, offset somewhat by beta = −9 for hospital administrators). To a much lesser extent, those who worked in the education services were also unusually inclined to justify 'extra payments' from clients (beta = +12). But although the police were particularly fearful of punishment, they were not particularly adverse to the principle of 'extra payments' from clients.

Table 8.18. Regressions predicting economic pressures, opportunities, fear, and a gift-justifying culture

	Economic pressure POORPAY beta x100	Opportunity/temptation OFFER(S) beta x100	OFFER(L) beta x100	Fear of punishment FEAR beta x100	Gift-justifying culture JUSTIFY beta x100
Occupations:	nurses 9**	doctors 16** traffic pol 7* customs off 6* schoolteach -8**	doctors 12** traffic pol 11** customs off 10**	hosp admin 11** customs off 9**	hosp admin -11** traffic pol 9**
Institutions:	legal -12** police -6*			health -35** education -12** police 17**	health 28** education 12**
Countries:	UKR 66** BULG 38** SLVK 9**	SLVK 18**	SLVK 7**	SLVK -13** BULG -10**	UKR 10** BULG 7*
RSQ:	38	7	4	19	7

Notes: Entries are 'betas' (x 100), i.e. standardised regression coefficients, calculated by SPSS-PC 'stepwise' regression. * means conventionally significant at the 95 per cent level; ** at the 99 per cent level. All variables from Set 1 were used as predictors. Those not shown had too little impact for inclusion in the 'stepwise' regression.

(S) = small gift, (L) = large gift, (money or an expensive present)

In sum, therefore: Economic pressure primarily reflected the *country* in which the official worked. Gift-justifying culture (values and norms) and fear of punishment primarily reflected the *institution* in which they worked. The frequency of opportunities and temptations (i.e. offers from clients) primarily reflected the bargaining power of *specific occupations* vis-à-vis clients.

INFLUENCES ON WILLINGNESS TO TAKE GIFTS, AND ON ACTUALLY ACCEPTING THEM

Table 8.19. Regressions predicting degree of willingness to accept, and actual acceptance of gifts

| | Model for degree of willingness to accept | | 3-stage model of confessions | 4-stage model of confessions |
	a *small* gift WILLING(S) beta x100	a *large* gift WILLING(L) beta x100	had accepted gift CONFESS beta x100	had accepted gift CONFESS beta x100
WILLING(S)			not used	30**
WILLING(L)			not used	16**
Gift-justifying culture:				
JUSTIFY	21**	14**	22**	13**
Economic pressure:				
POORPAY		8*		
Opportunity and fear:				
OFFER(S)	25**	not used	24**	18**
OFFER(L)	not used	25**	9*	
FEAR	–23**	–20**	–15**	
Occupations:				
hospital admin		7*		
court officials	–8*			
nurses			–10**	
Institutions:				
health services			16**	8**
police services	–8*			
Countries:				
UKR	–8*			
SLVK			8**	8**
RSQ:	25	17	26	37

Notes: All variables from Sets 1 and 2 were used as predictors.
(S) = small gift, (L) = large gift (money or an expensive present).

Officials' willingness to accept gifts was influenced most strongly by the opportunities or temptations provided by frequent offers from clients (beta = +25 for both large and small gifts). It was also influenced strongly by their personal gift-justifying culture (beta = +21 for small gifts and +14 for large). It was sharply reduced by fear of punishment (beta = –23 for small gifts and –20 for large). But inadequate or late-paid salaries had little or no statistically significant impact. (Table 8.19)

The pattern of influence underlying actual gift taking broadly mirrored the same pattern. But the health services were notable for actually taking gifts (beta = +16), though nurses less so than others.

A FOUR-STAGE MODEL

We can refine our causal model by treating 'willingness to accept' as an influence on actual acceptance—splitting our third and final set of variables into a third (willingness) and a fourth (actual acceptance). In this four-stage model (shown in the last column of the table), the predictability of gift taking, as measured by RSQ (the proportion of variance explained) rises from 26 per cent to 37 per cent, and the strongest influence on actual gift taking is willingness to accept either small gifts (beta = +30) or large gifts (beta = +16). Over and above the influence of willingness, however, there remains a significant additional influence from opportunity (beta = +18) and gift-justifying culture (beta = +13).

In terms of this four-stage model, the coefficients for economic pressure, fear of punishment, gift-justifying culture and opportunities/temptations in the last column of the table may be interpreted as their 'direct' effects on gift taking, over and above the effect of willingness, and any influence they may have through willingness. The coefficients in the second-last column may be interpreted as their 'full' or 'total' effects on gift taking ('direct' plus 'indirect').

THE CAUSES OF TWO DIFFERENT TYPES OF WILLINGNESS

So far we have treated our measure of willingness to accept gifts as a four-point scale that runs from (i) refusal, through (ii) reluctant acceptance because the official 'could not afford to refuse', then (iii) reluctant acceptance out of 'politeness', and finally to (iv) a completely uninhibited 'welcome'. In terms of its *consequences* for actual acceptance it makes some sense to treat willingness as a scale. As we noted earlier, the numbers of those who confessed to accepting 'money or an expensive present' rose from a mere 1 per cent through 13 per cent and 22 per cent to 39 per cent across this four-point scale.

On the other hand, in terms of its *causes* it makes a lot less sense to treat willingness as a scale. There are qualitative as well as quantitative differences between the different categories of willingness. Significantly, our regressions implied that inadequate or late-paid salaries had little or no significant influence upon our scales of willingness to accept gifts. But perhaps such economic pressures might have an influence upon willingness to accept gifts because the official 'could not afford to refuse', even if not on acceptance out of 'politeness' or on an uninhibited 'welcome'. That potential influence is obscured by placing willingness to accept gifts 'because they could not afford to refuse' in the middle of the scale of willingness—where it certainly fits in terms of its consequences but yet may not fit in terms of its causes.

Table 8.20. Regressions predicting two different types of willingness to accept, and actual acceptance of large gifts

	Models for two kinds of willingness to accept a large gift		3-stage model of confessions	4-stage model of confessions
	could not afford to refuse WILLING-CNAR(L) beta x100	welcome/ politeness WILLING-WP(L) beta x100	had accepted large gift CONFESS (L) beta x100	had accepted large gift CONFESS (L) beta x100
WILLING-CNAR(L)			not used	12**
WILLING-WP(L)			not used	30**
Gift-justifying culture:				
JUSTIFY	11**	10**	13**	7*
Economic pressure:				
POORPAY	25**			
Opportunity and fear:				
OFFER(L)		25**	31**	22**
FEAR	–12**	–16**		
Occupations:				
doctors			14**	10*
hospital admin		8*	9*	8*
traffic police			7*	8*
Institutions:				
education services	–8*			
RSQ:	11	13	17	24

Notes: All variables from Sets 1 and 2 were used as predictors. Those not shown had too little impact for inclusion in the 'stepwise' regression.

(S) = small gift, (L) = large gift (money or an expensive present).

To test this possibility we distinguished those who were willing to take large gifts 'out of politeness' or even 'welcome them as a token of thanks' on the one hand, from those who would accept them only 'because they could not afford to refuse them'. When we did this we found that the patterns of influence underlying these two kinds of willingness were radically different. (Table 8.20) A gift-justifying culture and fear of punishment had small but significant effects (in opposite directions, of course) on both kinds of willingness. But other influences affected only one kind of willingness:

'Could not afford to refuse'
- This first kind of willingness was influenced most strongly by inadequate or late salaries (beta = +25).
- However, the frequency of offers from clients had no statistically significant influence.

'Welcome' or accept out of 'politeness'
- The strongest influence on this second kind of willingness was temptations and opportunities as indicated by the frequency of offers from clients (beta = +25).
- However, inadequate or late salaries had no statistically significant effect.

In calculating these regressions we used dummy variables to indicate whether officials felt 'unable to refuse' (coded 1) versus any other answer (coded zero); and whether they were willing to 'welcome or accept out of politeness' (coded 1) versus any other answer (coded zero). It could be argued that this produces artifactual results particularly in the regressions predicting feelings of being 'unable to refuse'—because we are contrasting that feeling against a heterogeneous mixture of refusal-plus-even-greater-willingness to accept. Of course, there is some truth in that. The question is how much it distorts, or even manufactures, our findings. So we recalculated these regressions contrasting each variety of willingness simply against refusal, excluding from the analysis all those who would accept for reasons other than the one being investigated at the time. In fact, such recalculations make very little difference. The size of all coefficients (betas and RSQs) rises by 2 or 3 per cent but the pattern of influence remains unaltered.

Simple cross-tabulations of willingness against our indicators of inadequate salaries (LOWPAY and LATEPAY as defined above) confirm the conclusion that economic pressure affected only one kind of willingness to accept gifts. They are illustrated in Figure 8.4. The numbers that would 'welcome' a large gift or accept it 'out of politeness' did not increase across either indicator. But the numbers who 'could not afford to refuse' increased from 3 per cent to 16 per cent across our indicator of low pay and from 4 per cent to 26 per cent across our indicator of late pay.

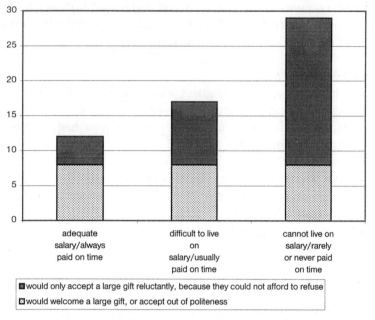

Fig. 8.4. Inadequate or late salaries only make officials more willing to accept large gifts 'reluctantly, because they cannot afford to refuse'

THE IMPACT OF DIFFERENT TYPES OF WILLINGNESS
ON ACTUALLY TAKING LARGE GIFTS

In the final version of our model we distinguish the two kinds of willingness and, for simplicity, we also restrict the model to the prediction of large gifts—which are far more likely to be bribes than presents. The pattern of influence underlying actually taking such large gifts was dominated by the opportunities or temptations provided by offers from clients (beta = +31). Personal gift-justifying culture had a smaller influence (beta = +13). Inadequate or late salaries had no significant influence at all.

In the four-step version of this final model, where willingness is treated as a potential influence on actual behaviour, the strongest influence on actually taking a large gift was relatively uninhibited willingness (beta = +30). Willingness based on the feeling that the official 'could not afford to refuse' had a marked but smaller influence (beta = +12). Over and above the influence of willingness, however, there remained a significant additional, direct influence from opportunity or temptation (beta = +22).

(Since the dependent variable for accepting gifts in this regression is dichotomous, it could be argued that we should have calculated these regressions using logistic rather than linear regression. We have used linear regression partly for consistency with earlier tables where it is the appropriate technique. But we have recalculated our results using logistic regression and our key conclusions remain unaltered, although the numerical sizes of all coefficients change.)

CONCLUSION: BARGAINING POWER RATHER THAN POVERTY LEADS TO BRIBE TAKING

Our final causal model of influences leading to the acceptance of large and expensive gifts is summarised in Figure 8.5. In the interests of simplicity and statistical robustness we have excluded from the diagram all pathways of influence with beta coefficients smaller than 10, even if they are statistically significant. Omitting such minor influences may cost something in terms of comprehensive description, but it does allow clear theoretical conclusions to emerge:

- *Flowing down the left-hand side* of the diagram there is a chain of influence that runs strongly from country through economic pressures to willingness to take large gifts, but only because officials feel they 'could not afford to refuse'. Significantly, this chain exerts a relatively weak influence upon actually taking large gifts from clients (beta = +12).
- *Flowing down the right-hand side* of the diagram is an entirely separate chain of causation that runs from specific occupations, through opportunities and temptations which reflect the bargaining power of these occupations vis-à-vis clients, and then on to uninhibited willingness to 'welcome' large gifts. Significantly, this chain exerts a far stronger influence upon actually taking large gifts from clients—partly through uninhibited willingness (beta = +30) but also through the additional direct influence of opportunities and temptations (beta = +22).
- *Flowing down the centre* of the diagram is a third chain of influence that runs strongly from institutions with their peculiar institutional cultures, through personal gift-justifying culture and fear

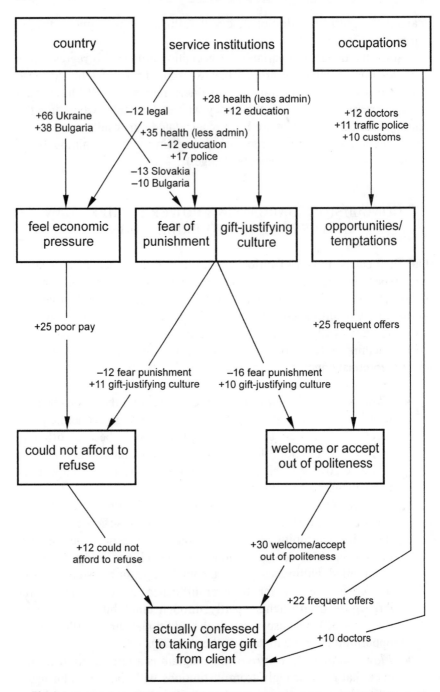

Fig. 8.5. A causal model for officials' confessions to taking large gifts from clients

of punishment, and then on to both kinds of willingness. Both the causes and the consequences of gift-justifying culture and fear of punishment are similar (though whatever is associated positively with a personal gift-justifying culture is associated negatively with fear of punishment).

What was the role of culture in gift taking? We can usefully distinguish between national, institutional and personal culture. There were some cross-national differences in attitudes towards gift taking. But the role of country within our model proved to be more relevant to economic than cultural differences, and it was through economic pressure rather than national culture that country had its primary impact on officials' willingness to accept gifts. Institutional culture, on the other hand, especially the culture of gift taking that pervaded the health services, had a direct impact on the personal gift-justifying culture of officials, in particular their willingness to justify informal charges for 'extra' or 'faster' service. In turn, that encouraged officials to welcome gifts from clients as tokens of presumed client gratitude (whether or not clients themselves actually felt grateful).

But directly or indirectly, whether we omit or include intervening variables in the model and whether we use linear or logistic regression, our analysis suggests that the predominant influence on street-level officials taking large gifts was not culture of any kind. Instead, our analysis points to the bargaining power of officials vis-à-vis their clients.

Economic pressures on officials encouraged them to express a willingness to accept large gifts but only because they 'could not afford to refuse', and that did not translate very well into actually taking large gifts. Perhaps the expression of willingness to take gifts because they 'could not afford to refuse' was itself more a comment on their poor salaries than on any realistic expectation of accepting large gifts. Perhaps the jobs that went with low salaries also went with such a weak bargaining position that they were indeed willing, but actually unable to 'collect'. Whatever the reason, being too poor to reject a bribe was a fairly weak predictor of actually taking bribes.

The pattern of confessions suggests that the core of gift taking, especially with regard to large or expensive gifts, is located in the frequency of offers from clients and in the specific occupations that presented certain officials with unusually frequent and unusually large offers. Some of these occupations (doctors perhaps) were at least consistent with the possibility of unusual levels of client gratitude, but others (traffic police and customs officials) quite unambiguously reflect the crude bargaining power of officials vis-à-vis their clients. The public did not feel especially grateful to traffic police or customs officials.

Both our quantitative and qualitative studies of the general public suggest that even clients' attitudes towards doctors owed more to a sense of powerlessness in the face of danger than to a sense of gratitude.

NOTES

1 Berkman, 'Bureaucracy and Bribery', 1347.
2 Berkman, 'Bureaucracy and Bribery', 1350.
3 Berkman, 'Bureaucracy and Bribery', 1353–4.
4 Berkman, 'Bureaucracy and Bribery', 1357.
5 Ensor and Savelyeva, 'Informal Payments for Health Care', 41.
6 Shelley and Repetskaya, 'Corruption Research among Convicted Government and Law-Enforcement Officials'.
7 *RFE/RL Newsline* 3, no. 206, part 2 (21 October 1999).
8 Mehmet Bac, 'The Scope, Timing and Type of Corruption', 102.
9 Heidenheimer, 'Perspectives on the Perception of Corruption'.
10 deLeon, *Thinking about Political Corruption*, 23, quoted in Jackson and Smith, 'Inside Moves and Outside Views', 24.
11 Jackson and Smith, 'Inside Moves and Outside Views', 27.
12 Jackson and Smith, 'Inside Moves and Outside Views', 34.
13 McAllister, 'Keeping Them Honest', 28.
14 Miller, White and Heywood, *Values and Political Change in Post-Communist Europe*, 199.
15 Miller, Timpson and Lessnoff, *Political Culture in Contemporary Britain*, Chapter 3: 'The Governing Perspective'.
16 Shakespeare, *Romeo and Juliet*, Act V, Scene 1.
17 Lipsky, *Street-Level Bureaucracy*, 59.
18 Lipsky, *Street-Level Bureaucracy*, 58.
19 Klitgaard, *Controlling Corruption*, 75.
20 EBRD, *Ten Years of Transition*, 213, 265, 205, and 281.
21 EBRD, *Ten Years of Transition*, 73.
22 Transparency International, *Corruption Perception Index 1999*.
23 EBRD, *Ten Years of Transition*, 125.
24 Miller, 'Quantitative Methods', 155.
25 *Za Vilnu Ukrainu* (4 April 1998), quoted in *Corruption Watch* (15 April 1998).
26 Katsenelinboigen, 'Corruption in the USSR', 233.

CHAPTER 9

A CULTURE OF CORRUPTION?
SUPPORT, PRIORITIES AND
PROSPECTS FOR REFORM

'*Now is the winter of our discontent*'[1]

Throughout our study we have focused on the relationships between citizens and street-level officials rather than on corruption for its own sake. Our study is located in the tradition of research on the democratic culture exemplified by such classics as Gabriel Almond and Sydney Verba's *Civic Culture,*[2] Daniel Katz et. al.'s *Bureaucratic Encounters,*[3] or Michael Lipsky's *Street-Level Bureaucracy,*[4] rather than in the equally distinguished but differently focused tradition exemplified by Arnold J. Heidenheimer's classic *Political Corruption.*[5]

Only if corruption figured significantly in the relationship between citizens and street-level officials would we have anything to say on the subject of corruption. In particular, it is only insofar as corruption figured significantly in the relationship between citizens and street-level officials that our consideration of proposals for reform includes proposals designed to suppress corruption.

Perceptions of high-level corruption were widespread and irritated citizens everywhere. But although we found that the need to offer presents and bribes to street-level officials was widely discussed by citizens in general terms, it was much less frequent in their reports of personal experience than in their gossip, hearsay or perceptions. In their own dealings with officials, corruption was not the only problem that confronted citizens. It was not even the most frequent nor the most annoying feature of their day-to-day interactions with officials in any of our four countries. In some countries (though not in others) corruption was hardly significant in actual bureaucratic encounters with street-level bureaucrats—even though it figured in media coverage of high-level politics and consequently in the public's imagination.

We need to keep corruption in perspective. That means we must consider a wider range of reforms that aim to improve the relationship between officials and their clients, whether or not they aim to suppress corruption—reforms that aim at producing *fair and satisfactory treatment* rather than reforms that aim exclusively at *eliminating corruption*. The concept of 'good governance' includes efficient, respectful, fair and considerate—as well as honest—administration.

Nonetheless, when citizens thought street-level officials were making unnecessary problems in order to extract presents and bribes it had an enormous impact on their levels of satisfaction. When it comes to reform, the suppression of corruption must certainly be one important objective even if it is by no means the only objective that we need to consider.

Moreover, corruption is no longer a purely internal issue. It affects foreign affairs as well as domestic stability. International organisations have turned less tolerant of corruption than once they were. The World Bank's *World Development Report 1997*, for example, pointed to 'a clear negative correlation between the level of corruption and both investment and economic growth'.[6] More importantly, going beyond intellectual analysis to the threat of international action (or inaction), a more specific World Bank report on Ukraine recently concluded that the level of corruption not only endangered local investment but threatened the flow of foreign aid and foreign commercial investment.[7] Naturally, international economic organisations are primarily concerned with the economic effects of high-level corruption, but they have increasingly recognised that pervasive low-level corruption amongst street-level bureaucrats has an economic as well as a social and political impact.

In this final chapter we look at expert proposals for reform. But should reform be left to the experts? Or does wider public opinion matter? We suggest that public attitudes to reform are always important in any system, but that public attitudes are especially important in a democratic system. Reforms that go against the grain of public opinion can be difficult to implement anywhere, but in a democratic system they may also have direct electoral consequences. We need look no further than the adverse public reaction to the introduction of the 'Poll Tax' in Britain for an example and a warning.[8]

The reactions of both the public and street-level bureaucrats are important. What measures of reform might 'go with the grain' of opinion amongst the public and/or street-level bureaucrats? What would be their priorities? How enthusiastically might they support different measures of reform? What measures of reform might be attractive to 'experts' but arouse opposition amongst significant sections of the public or street-level bureaucrats?

IS REFORM POSSIBLE?

Before we consider any specific proposals, we have to ask whether reform itself is possible at all. There is little point in discussing alternative proposals if the long-term and immutable culture of a society makes reform itself impossible. Here public opinion can be doubly important. A feeling of impotence can be self-justifying. Certainly, the public may sometimes believe that things are possible when they are not. But if people feel that nothing can be done, then they may well be right. Their hopelessness and apathy could be self-justifying. Without public hopes and expectations for a better future, positive change will be exceedingly difficult to achieve.

Few doubt that some managerial reform is possible. More training, better organisational structures, better offices and better equipment (especially more and better computers) and less paperwork are always likely to improve the business of governance even if they are expensive. The feasibility of managerial reform is not a major issue. The question of feasibility arises mainly in connection with corruption reform. Where there is a long historical/cultural tradition of corruption the 'dead hand of history' model implies that corruption reform is not possible.

However, the experience of Hong Kong since the 1970s refutes the notion of either an irresistible or immutable culture of corruption.[9] There, as in Singapore in the 1960s, a successful turnaround in corruption was achieved by a combination of 'commitment at the top, credible law enforcement by an independent agency operating under a strong statute, and reform of the civil service'—a reform programme which even succeeded in 'transforming citizens' beliefs and expectations'.[10] In that respect, culture itself was not merely overcome, it was changed.

Equating an immutable Chinese culture with corruption proved to be a racist misconception. Indeed, it was always doubtful whether there was anything uniquely Chinese about corruption in Hong Kong. Ex-pat British police officers were amongst the worst culprits.

Similarly, our own evidence suggests that the public in Central and Eastern Europe do not accept that they are imprisoned for all time in a uniquely East European culture of corruption. We asked our focus

groups for their views on what could be done to improve the relationship between citizens and officials. Very few comments in these discussions suggested that it was impossible to change the relationship. The
percentage ranged from zero in the Czech Republic to only 6 per cent in
Ukraine. In an earlier chapter we reported that only a third of the public
in our large-scale surveys were apathetically resigned to regarding 'the
use of money, presents, favours and contacts to influence officials' as 'a
permanent part of (their country's) culture'. We put the same question to
street-level officials and got almost exactly the same answer. Moreover,
both the public and officials rejected the notion of an unchangeable
culture most strongly in Ukraine, the country where change and reform
seemed most necessary.

Table 9.1. A permanent part of the country's culture?

	Average	Czech Republic	Slovakia	Bulgaria	Ukraine
	%	%	%	%	%
The use of money, presents, favours and contacts to influence officials in (your country) is a...					
product of moral crisis in a period of transition	43 (45)	31 (29)	30 (34)	49 (58)	62 (57)
permanent part of (the country's) culture	36 (34)	46 (47)	47 (43)	34 (31)	16 (13)
product of the communist past	22 (22)	23 (24)	23 (23)	17 (11)	23 (29)

Notes: 'Don't know', 'mixed/depends' etc. answers were recorded if given spontaneously, but
never prompted; they have been excluded from the calculation of percentages.
Figures in brackets are based on the replies by officials.
The phrase (your country) was replaced by the specific name of the country in which the interview took place.

Both the public and street-level officials most frequently interpreted
current levels of corruption as 'a product of moral crisis in a period of
transition'. (Table 9.1) To some extent they echoed the view of theorist
Umit Berkman that 'there seems to exist a relationship between the rate
of change of a social system and corruption...norms become blurred,
tolerance limits for deviance widen'.[11] Quite apart from the economic
chaos, this 'moral crisis in a period of transition' is likely to create a
surge in corruption—a 'season of corruption' perhaps. But the public's
remarkably self-conscious awareness of this phenomenon suggests that
the 'blurring of norms' and the 'tolerance for deviance' alleged by

Berkman is regarded by the public only as an exceptional response to exceptional times, and therefore that, at a deeper level, public norms and values remain intact. What is so self-consciously interpreted as a 'season of corruption' is less likely to inaugurate a 'step-function' change to a new and permanent 'climate of corruption'.

Indeed, a massive majority of the public in all four countries (most of all in Bulgaria) said that it would be possible to cut corruption 'greatly' if their government 'tried really hard' to do so. (Table 9.2) They felt their government could cut corruption at all levels both inside and outside the public sector. But they were most inclined to believe that their government could cut corruption amongst street-level officials (83 per cent on average) and least inclined to believe it could cut corruption amongst top private businessmen (72 per cent on average). This finding is confirmed by later USIA surveys in which the numbers who felt that corruption could at least be limited ranged from 80 per cent in Slovakia and 85 per cent in the Czech Republic up to 92 per cent in Bulgaria.[12]

Table 9.2. Would it be possible to cut corruption?

	Average	Czech Republic	Slovakia	Bulgaria	Ukraine
	%	%	%	%	%
If it tried really hard, the government could greatly reduce corruption amongst...					
officials who deal with ordinary people	83	82	81	88	80
top government officials	76	76	75	82	69
top businessmen	72	70	73	76	67

Notes: 'Don't know', 'mixed/depends' etc. answers were recorded if given spontaneously, but never prompted; they have been excluded from the calculation of percentages.

Question not asked in the officials' survey.

PERCEPTIONS OF GOVERNMENT COMMITMENT TO REFORM

It has become almost routine for political leaders in Central and Eastern Europe to castigate corruption amongst their officials. They do so in part because they recognise the truth of the claims by the World Bank or other international organisations such as the OECD or the EU and by important foreign governments, notably that of the USA, that public-sector corruption really does degrade economic performance and human rights. But in part they are driven to attack corruption by the claims themselves, irrespective of whether these claims are true or false and irrespective of whether they are based on scientific analysis or on intellectual fashion.

There is a degree of ambiguity in their pronouncements. While they publicly attack corruption themselves they clearly resent outside criticism. In September 1999, Russian foreign minister Igor Ivanov said his government would not accept 'the use of unverified facts to cast a shadow over our country'. He complained that coverage in 'some Western mass media is not about fighting corruption but rather targeted politics...certain circles do not want Russia to reclaim its role as a great power in the international arena'.[13]

But at least the appearance of some action against corruption has become necessary to impress foreign governments and investors and, more generally, to get or retain membership of the invisible but important 'international club'. In early January 1997, for instance, the president of the World Bank, James Wolfensohn, wrote to the Ukrainian president, Leonid Kuchma, criticising high-level corruption in the Ukrainian government.[14] Although Kuchma later complained that 'foreign media often largely exaggerate the scale of corruption in Ukraine',[15] a month after the World Bank letter he launched an anti-corruption campaign, claiming that the Ukrainian government was going to crack down on corruption 'which had infected a significant part of the state apparatus'.[16] Two ministers were fired. Ukrainian justice minister Serhiy Holovatyi produced evidence of corruption and abuse of office within the Justice Ministry. As a result, a deputy justice minister and several departmental heads lost their jobs. The 1995 law *On the Struggle Against Corruption* had proved ineffective and a new *National Programme for the Struggle Against Corruption* was approved in April 1997. Yet another decree, *On Fighting Corruption 1998–2005*, was signed by President Kuchma in April 1998.[17]

At a June 1997 Council of Europe conference in Prague, attended by justice ministers from each member state, Holovatyi said corruption threatened 'to undermine the fragile foundations of the emerging civil societies [in Central and Eastern Europe]...Having wielded tremendous administrative control over the lives and activities of their citizens, the members of the nomenklatura are now the virtually uncontrolled arbiters of the distribution and use of state property...the scope for fraud, corruption, and self-aggrandisement is broad, to put it mildly. The nomenklatura is not interested in serious economic and administrative reform because its members profit handsomely from the existing unregulated environment.' The economic implications of the link between organised crime and corruption were serious, he said, referring to 'increasing institutionalisation of corruption, enormous losses of revenue to state budgets, retardation of the development of the private sector, the monopolisation of certain aspects of economic activity, and pervasive unjust enrichment'. The Czech minister of justice also admitted that corruption was 'a serious problem' in the Czech Republic, not only in public administration but also in law enforcement and within political circles.[18]

The collapse of the Italian political system under the weight of corruption made a deep impression in Eastern Europe. At the top, politicians liked to identify with the Italian magistrates' 'Clean Hands' campaign. The term has been used in Ukraine at least since President Leonid Kuchma's September 1996 *Complex Target Programme for the Struggle against Criminality for the Years 1996–2000*. Ukraine even had a 'Clean Hands in Education' programme, though surveys of students indicated that high-school students' perceptions of corruption in education were growing rapidly.[19] During the Czech election campaign in June 1998, the Social Democratic Party (ČSSD) leader and future prime minister, Miloš Zeman, promised an 'Italian-style clean hands campaign' against corruption if his party won the election. He claimed that the 'Czech economic transformation has been unsuccessful' because the country was ruled by an 'economy of mafiosi'.[20] His predecessor, Václav Klaus, had been 'forced' to resign at the end of November 1997 amid allegations of corruption.[21] In Bulgaria, Prime Minister Ivan Kostov described officials in his country as 'corrupt, secretive and reluctant to give up power'.[22] Coalition 2000, formed shortly afterwards, linked the Bulgarian government with NGOs and international organisations in a broad anti-corruption campaign[23] and the Bulgarian press used the headline 'Filchev Imitates Clean Hands' to describe this campaign.[24] (Nikola Filchev was the Bulgarian attorney general.)

References to Italian corruption even cropped up in our focus-group discussions, though not always with such a 'politically correct' message. 'In Italy they talk about it in such a way that you feel there is corruption everywhere there, in contrast to Sweden where they do not talk about it that much, they do not trumpet it to the world…It is as if they wanted to make Italy yet more attractive so that more people go there for holidays.'(HK 3) 'But it is true that more judges are shot dead in Italy than here.'(HK 2)

Public pronouncements are not necessarily the same as private commitments, however. At a Paris conference in July 1998, Hryhory Omelchenko, who had actively promoted anti-corruption measures within the Ukrainian legislature, urged the World Bank to change its policy towards his country. 'Ukraine was given loans but reforms were not proceeding...and corruption was growing. Therefore, the money was wasted...In fact, the World Bank supports Ukraine's corrupt regime and assists growing corruption in principle...I put it bluntly at the conference: If international capital wants to help Ukraine clear itself from the metastasis of corruption they must stop giving money to it.'[25]

Omelchenko's views were echoed by a disillusioned press in which a typical comment was: 'Fighting corruption [has] remained at the level of claims and debates, party slogans and legislative changes...without just trials, just sentences and penalties. Little by little, the tone of the debate has deteriorated from calls for a wide-scale fight against corruption to the claim that corruption exists everywhere in the world...[and] therefore there is no point in trying to fight it.'[26]

The practice of Soviet leaders was to use anti-corruption campaigns 'to punish opponents, to strengthen the security forces, and to consolidate their personal power rather than to root out corruption' and the main effect was merely 'to increase public cynicism'.[27] In the post-communist era politicians promised much—on corruption as on other issues—but achieved far less than promised. According to Taras Kuzio: '...all candidates [in the 1994 Ukrainian presidential election] included populist slogans in their election manifestos against organised crime and corruption, which, if they had been elected, would have been difficult to implement.'[28]

Despite all the rhetoric, the laws and the presidential decrees, our surveys show that only a small minority of the public thought that their government was actually making a 'strong and sincere effort to combat corruption' of any kind—though the public was more inclined to believe their government was making a serious effort against corruption amongst street-level bureaucrats than amongst top government officials or businessmen. We put the same question to officials. Their views were broadly similar to those of the public. Only a small minority of officials thought their government was actually making a 'strong and sincere effort to combat corruption' of any kind. (Table 9.3, Fig. 9.1)

There were differences of degree between the perceptions of officials and the public, however. Street-level officials themselves were rather more inclined than the public to feel that their government was cracking down on corruption amongst low-level officials (average 34 per cent instead of 25 per cent). At the same time, street-level officials were less inclined than the public to feel that their government was cracking down on corruption amongst top officials or businessmen (only 12 per cent instead of 17 per cent). So three times as many street-level officials felt their government was targeting them as felt it was pursuing corruption at higher levels. It was a view that found some support in the press. According to the Ukrainian paper *Gorod*: '...corrupt officials of the top ranks are almost immune to prosecution, while judgements against petty bribe-takers who commit violations to survive are often too severe.'[29]

On one thing officials and the public concurred: both awarded the Bulgarian government top marks for being really serious about combating corruption. All Bulgarian governments since 1994–5 had been publicising their anti-corruption campaigns, but survey evidence from the end of 1996 indicated that the public had reservations about these campaigns up to that point. Twice as many Bulgarians believed corruption was most widespread amongst politicians as believed it was most widespread amongst street-level officials.[30] By contrast, our findings probably reflect the dramatic change of government shortly before our survey in Bulgaria. (For further details see Chapter 2.) Ivan Kostov, the leader of the new and as yet untainted government declared an 'all-out war on crime and corruption' and was widely believed to be more sincere in this than his predecessors.[31] This Bulgarian experience contrasted with the lack of a similarly dramatic break between the administrations of Prime Ministers Václav Klaus and Miloš Zeman in the Czech Republic, which operated 'as a kind of parliamentary coalition, albeit unusual and covert'.[32] It contrasted still more sharply with the continuity of government under President Leonid Kuchma in Ukraine and Prime Minister Vladimir Mečiar in Slovakia.

Within every country we found a fairly strong correlation (r = 0.25 in Bulgaria) between support for the government and public perceptions that it was sincerely fighting corruption. The fact that the new Bulgarian government got the top marks for fighting corruption was consistent with the fact that it was the only government in our survey for which a majority of the public declared their 'support'.

Table 9.3. Is the government making a sincere effort?

	Average %	Czech Republic %	Slovakia %	Bulgaria %	Ukraine %
The government is really making a strong and sincere effort to combat corruption amongst...					
officials who deal with ordinary people	25 (34)	18 (34)	22 (24)	41 (44)	18 (34)
top government officials	18 (13)	10 (11)	13 (12)	34 (24)	13 (7)
top businessmen	17 (12)	8 (7)	14 (12)	32 (20)	14 (10)

Notes: 'Don't know', 'mixed/depends' etc. answers were recorded if given spontaneously, but never prompted; they have been excluded from the calculation of percentages.

Figures in brackets are based on the replies by officials.

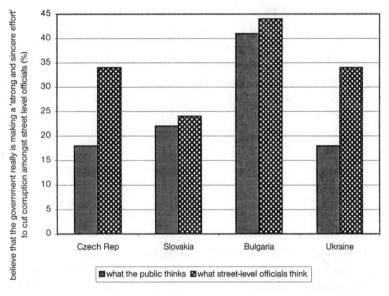

Fig. 9.1. A 'strong and sincere' effort by government to combat corruption amongst street-level officials?

EXPERT OPINION: SIX PRESCRIPTIONS

If they were serious about reform, however, what measures should governments take? Public administration experts have suggested a number of reforms that might be useful in post-communist Europe.[33] We can usefully group them under six headings:

- impose tighter control and stricter penalties;
- encourage officials, by salary increases or other means;
- improve administrative efficiency;
- empower citizens;
- improve openness and transparency;
- downsize the state.

1. IMPOSE TIGHTER CONTROL AND STRICTER PENALTIES

Politicians and senior officials in Eastern Europe frequently equate campaigns against corruption with stricter penalties. It is a very natural top-down viewpoint. One of the 'four fundamental objectives of reform' listed by Imre Verebélyi, Hungary's commissioner for the modernisation of public administration, is 'to make public administration lawbound. More serious legal consequences such as sanctions should prevent public officers, citizens and organisations from infringing the law, and internal and external control of public administration should be more regular'.[34]

Public administration experts distinguish sharply between laws and their implementation, especially in communist and post-communist countries. According to a SIGMA/OECD report, 'The bureaucracies in [Eastern Europe] are inherited from authoritarian regimes where the administration existed for the purpose of implementing the directives of a single ruling party which was intertwined and inseparable from the government. The socialist period had a legacy of regarding the law as a formal expression rather than an instrument to accomplish change.'[35] Vito Tanzi suggests that the problem of implementing anti-corruption legislation is severe even outside post-communist Europe. 'In the real world, relatively few people are punished for acts of corruption, in spite of the extent of the phenomenon' and this 'limits the role that penalties actually play in many countries'.[36]

In addition, communist laws often contradicted each other or were incomplete. Unfortunately, some of the new regimes, in their eagerness to reject their country's socialist legacy, have compounded these problems rather than solved them. There has been a 'scarcity of qualified personnel, intense political pressures, lack of accessible and reliable data, insufficient co-ordination and implementation mechanisms...and [even] where formal law-drafting requirements and co-ordination mechanisms are in place, actual practice lags behind somewhat'.[37] In different ways the communist legacy hindered both law-enforcement and law-drafting. Badly drafted post-communist laws further damaged the relationship between citizens and officials by leaving street-level officials with great scope for interpretation or causing confusion, sometimes, but by no means always, in order to extract bribes.

From an economic perspective, Susan Rose-Ackerman wishes to de-emphasise coercive measures and put more weight on structures of incentives: 'Enforcement and monitoring are needed, but they will have little long-term impact if the basic conditions that encourage payoffs are not reduced. If these incentives remain, the elimination of one set of "bad apples" will soon lead to the creation of a new group of corrupt officials and private bribe payers.'[38] Frank Anechiarico and James B. Jacobs seem to go further when they argue that a coercive approach to corruption control can 'make government ineffective'. But they agree that corruption 'must be condemned, investigated and punished', even if they regard structural reform as a higher priority.[39]

Despite her self-consciously economic perspective, even Rose-Ackerman pays considerable attention to coercive measures.[40] While 'structural reform should be the first line of attack in an anti-corruption campaign', she adds that 'the criminal law is the second basic part of a comprehensive strategy'.[41] Some countries do not criminalise bribe giving, others do not criminalise bribe taking.[42] Rose-Ackerman advocates a more even-handed approach except where indemnities are offered in return for giving evidence to the courts. (Protecting or even rewarding 'whistle-blowers' who expose corruption amongst their colleagues also has some relevance to stricter controls, though we place it under the heading of reforms to encourage 'openness and transparency'.)

2. ENCOURAGE OFFICIALS

Public administration experts recognise that encouragement may be at least as effective as coercion.

Adequate salaries might be one way to do that. Experts suggest that badly paid officials will be tempted to accept bribes or to desert the public service for better-paid jobs in private firms. In Ukraine the exodus of officials to better-paid jobs in private firms, together with the failure to recruit younger people, has resulted in a situation where only 15 per cent are younger than 30 years old.[43] A recent cross-country study for the International Monetary Fund (IMF) found a correlation between public-sector corruption and low salaries for officials (relative to private-sector wages in their own countries).[44] But the same study did not find a cross-time correlation between corruption and salary levels within countries.[45] A sharp short-term drop in officials' income may force them into corruption as a survival strategy, and in that case, promptly restoring previous salary levels might help to solve the problem. But on the other hand, low salaries in the longer term—what Timothy Besley and John McLaren call a 'capitulation wage regime'—may simply attract those who are willing to accept low salaries because the jobs provide an opportunity to extract unofficial payments from clients.[46] Only the corrupt will then apply to be tax officials. In that case, raising their salaries will not change their behaviour. The 1997 IMF study found that increasing officials' salaries without replacing personnel did not, in fact, appear to reduce corruption.[47]

In any case, there are other ways of encouraging officials. Public administration experts also advocate *improvements in officials' working conditions*. An SIGMA/OECD panel of management experts urged that 'foremost consideration must be given to changing negative working environments which can undo the accomplishments of training...this involves addressing the morale, pay systems and prestige of public employees'.[48] To keep officials and to provide them with incentives not to take bribes, Tony Verheijen and Antoaneta Dimitrova suggest not only better salaries but also more job security.[49] They urge efforts to rebuild mutual respect between civil servants and the public as a means of improving morale. Chavdar Popov suggests a need to 'maintain continuity and to create incentives' for officials.[50] Imre Verebélyi[51] and Emilia Kandeva[52] both emphasise the need for more job security and better promotion possibilities.

Another way to encourage junior officials in good behaviour is simply to *set a good example at the top*. Kandeva emphasises the importance of senior officials and politicians setting a good example at the top rather than simply harassing junior officials. Writing about 'top administrative officials' concerned with 'privatisation, restitution, land use, licensing [and] criminal justice', she claims that 'society expects a higher standard of moral integrity from people empowered to uphold the law and judge their fellow citizens'.[53] Conversely, a bad example at the top is likely to encourage corruption. Both street-level officials and the public are likely to regard large-scale corruption at the top as a moral justification for their own small peccadilloes at lower levels.

High-level corruption can do worse than merely set a bad example. Sometimes senior officials 'tolerate the petty corruption of subordinates to assure their complicity in a corrupt system'. Sometimes junior officials buy the silence of their superiors by sharing the bribes they collect from the public, and sometimes bribes are so institutionalised that they 'become a condition of employment, organised by superiors for their own gain'.[54] Hierarchical corruption is especially difficult to eliminate and is unlikely to be broken by attempted reforms at the bottom.[55] In a previous chapter we found quite striking evidence of such hierarchical corruption in Ukraine, though nowhere else: over a third of officials in Ukraine said that if they took 'money or an expensive present' from a client they would have to share the proceeds with their superiors.

3. IMPROVE ADMINISTRATIVE EFFICIENCY

We found that corruption is not the only, nor even the main, source of friction between citizens and officials in post-communist Europe. Experts suggest that government structures and responsibilities are fragmented, overlapping and poorly co-ordinated in many East European countries.[56] This not only leads to inefficiency and poor-quality administration but gives scope for unfair treatment,[57] for 'delays' and for 'abuse of discretion' as one businessman put it.[58] More generally, Paolo Mauro found such a high cross-national correlation between indices of *bureaucratic inefficiency* and *bureaucratic corruption* ($r = 0.79$) that he rolled them together into a single index for analysis purposes.[59]

Reforms that achieved greater bureaucratic efficiency would almost certainly reduce the incidence of corruption. So experts who argue the need for anti-corruption reforms usually argue the need for efficiency reforms as well.

But the converse does not hold. Even in relatively non-corrupt systems there may be good reasons to urge efficiency reforms. Although the British civil service was notoriously corrupt in the nineteenth century before the Northcote-Trevelyan reforms, in the 1970s and 1980s it was criticised for being inefficient even if it was remarkably honest by historical or international standards. Reforms were therefore introduced which aimed to increase efficiency even at the risk of some increase in corruption. The risk was real: the British Parliament's Public Accounts

Committee concluded that 'failings in integrity and probity had resulted from public service reforms' but the British government pushed ahead with its reform programme.[60] Efficiency reforms should not be viewed simply as a means to an end, they are desirable in themselves.

But in the post-communist context, what are ostensibly efficiency reforms can also be used as a useful cloak, a smoke-screen or a camouflage for anti-corruption measures. Juliet Gole praises a model developed at an East European Transparency International conference for focusing 'on improving municipal service delivery in addition to identifying and rooting out corruption', for focusing 'on positive ideas and suggestions rather than negative accusations that result in an uncooperative relationship between the administration and civil society'. A negative approach could be self-defeating: '...if one is fortunate enough to find an administration that is committed to fighting corruption within, then finger-pointing and whistle-blowing might only provide the opposition with political fuel for the fire' and discourage further attempts at reform.[61]

Less bureaucracy: Some experts argue for smaller, simpler, faster and more cost-effective public administration that performs the necessary public tasks with better-qualified and more stable personnel. The need for fewer forms, documents, certificates and permissions not only reduces or eliminates the possibilities for 'gate-keeping' officials to charge illicit tolls, it also provides a speedier, more efficient service and greater consumer satisfaction.

Better technical training is another 'efficiency' reform.[62] One contributor to the SIGMA/OECD report noted that while 'newly elected officials at the local level are often well-respected professionals in a particular field [they] know nothing of the operations of municipal government and its regulatory responsibilities'.[63] Others have complained that officials have 'little formal education in essential practices such as accounting, managerial techniques, computer programming, record keeping, interpersonal skills, etc.'.[64] But Verheijen and Dimitrova warn that training programmes and facilities in post-communist Europe have a tendency to open and close depending on who is in power.[65]

4. EMPOWER CITIZENS

Citizens can be empowered and their rights can be strengthened in a number of ways. Most obvious, perhaps, are better appeal and complaints procedures. In this connection, the appointment of ombudsmen to hear citizens' complaints might help.[66] A proposal to introduce one in the Czech Republic was voted down in parliament[67] and none had been established in any of our four countries at the time of our surveys.[68] Shortly afterwards, however, there were moves to establish the institution of ombudsman in Bulgaria.[69]

But appeals procedures are only one component of a 'citizen empowerment' approach. Michael Johnston argues that 'in countries where corruption is the exception, not the rule, reformers have several advantages. Anti-corruption laws, agencies and organisations are in place and enjoy broad-based support...government is broadly legitimate' and 'a range of familiar and well-tested options is at hand' focusing on 'institutional reform'. But where corruption is pervasive or 'systemic', reform is more difficult.[70] Then 'social empowerment—expanding and protecting the range of political and economic resources and alternatives open to ordinary citizens—is an essential part of any attack upon systemic corruption'. He adds that it is 'in no way a substitute for reforms at the organisational, personnel and administrative levels: indeed, [bottom up] social empowerment and [top down] macro-level policies must work together'.[71]

Citizens' rights can be reinforced by increasing their awareness of what they can legally claim as their rights.[72] In Britain that was the motivation for the *Citizens Charters* introduced by the Conservative governments of Margaret Thatcher and John Major and supported by the subsequent Labour government of Tony Blair. In Rose-Ackerman's judgement, 'it is easy to underestimate the importance of posters, fliers and videotapes that tell people what they can expect from honest officials and how to make a complaint' against dishonest ones.[73] Verheijen and Dimitrova suggest that 'citizen information seminars' may be useful in Eastern Europe as they have been in Latin America.[74]

Gole develops a more pro-active, bottom-up 'model for fighting corruption' based on a regional conference of Transparency International chapters in post-communist Europe.[75] That strategy involves attempts to *build a coalition of 'stakeholders'* with an interest in clean government, perhaps including some elements within the government, then using surveys, workshops, open forums and press conferences to raise public awareness of problems. It involves contrasting those parts of the bureaucracy which are performing badly with those that are performing well in order to transform blanket criticisms, which simply depress and enervate the public, into focused criticisms that invigorate and empower them. One example of many such local initiatives (for others see the *Coalition 2000 Newsletter*[76] in Bulgaria or the *UNCI Newsletter*[77] in Ukraine) is the public anti-corruption committee recently set up in Lviv as a voluntary non-profit organisation but with the backing of the regional state administration, the mayor's office, other local agencies and USAID. Its chairman, Professor Victor Hryshchuk of the Department of Law at Lviv State University, argues that the main solution to problems of low-level corruption is to ensure that citizens know their rights.[78]

But paradoxically, citizens can also be empowered by reforms aimed at officials. Officials can be made more aware of citizens' rights by means of *ethical training* (as contrasted with technical training) or by being forced to sign mandatory *'codes of conduct'*. Codes of conduct are currently very popular in the West. The 1996 OECD report *Ethics in the Public Service* noted that despite a trend from a 'public administration' ethos to a more 'managerial' ethos in Western countries, a majority of the OECD members had recently implemented new codes of conduct for officials.[79] It claimed the trend in the West was to avoid 'detailed controls' and rely more on a combination of 'broadly based codes of conduct' with greater transparency (including measures to encourage *'whistle-blowing'* and 'disclosure of financial and other interests by public servants').

Although 'economic analysis of corruption postulates that rational actors compare the benefits and expected costs of behaving corruptly', Peter Huang and Ho-Mou Wu follow Robert Klitgaard in arguing that 'changing attitudes about corruption can be effective as a tool for dealing with corruption'. They argue that this may be achieved amongst officials through 'education, codes of ethics, and organisational cultures'.[80] Barbara Kudrycha argues that codes of conduct for parliamentary deputies have 'instilled greater self-discipline' in Poland and form a natural basis for the application of other codes of conduct to civil servants and junior officials.[81] In Bulgaria, Kandeva has called for more attention to be given to ethics in the civil service.[82]

Verheijen and Dimitrova have suggested that new codes of ethics should be introduced and officials required to sign a declaration of conduct.[83] Transparency International claims that the act of signing specific declarations to honestly apply existing law can have a powerful psychological effect and a strong influence on actual behaviour even though it does not change the legal position at all. Transparency International uses the term 'islands of integrity' when those bidding for, and awarding, specific public-sector contracts sign such a declaration.[84]

All of these proposals aim to increase the moral pressure on officials, even what Huang and Wu term the 'remorse' which is associated with corrupt behaviour.

5. IMPROVE OPENNESS AND TRANSPARENCY

Experts also emphasise the importance of '*glasnost*', 'openness' and 'transparency' in local decision making.[85]

Rose-Ackerman quotes purchasing postage stamps in a post office as a simple example that combines the ideas of citizen empowerment and transparency. It highlights the importance of giving clients the choice of which official to approach (= 'empowerment') and ensuring that interactions between clients and officials take place in public (= 'transparency'). Any attempt by the post-office official to overcharge for stamps would be visible to bystanders and/or would simply prompt the client to move to another position on the counter.[86]

Procedures for informing the public should be routine, but they should also be flexible enough to accommodate 'scandals'. Verheijen and Dimitrova have suggested that the public should be involved in gathering information about abuse or misappropriation of power in official offices.[87] Customer surveys might be useful for routine complaints. 'Hot-line' anonymous phone access to investigating authorities might be useful for more serious 'scandals'. It is equally important to ensure that officials who come across scandalous behaviour or inefficient procedures within offices and organisations are encouraged to 'go public' without fear of personal consequences—what is often called 'whistle-blowing', though the term is sometimes used more widely to include citizen complaints as well.

Whistle-blowing has a positive image in Britain where there are moves to give greater protection to whistle-blowers following growing public awareness of too many scandalous 'cover-ups' in recent decades. In the USA the law not only protects whistle-blowers but pays their legal fees unless the courts judge their allegations 'frivolous, or brought mainly for purposes of harassment'.[88] But whistle-blowing may have a less positive image in post-communist countries after their long experience of 'snoopers and informers' working for the communist authorities. There needs to be a clear awareness of the difference between:

(i) 'going public' within a democratic and legitimate political system; and

(ii) 'spying for the authorities' under an imposed regime that lacks popular legitimacy.

The transition from the one perspective to the other is difficult and will take time, not least because the post-communist regimes themselves still lack full public legitimacy.

Rose-Ackerman claims that 'limiting low-level bureaucratic corruption is often in the interests of top officials who may try to enlist ordinary citizens in the effort'.[89] But when top officials in new regimes are widely criticised for their own alleged corruption they lack the legitimacy that is required in order to enrol the public in a crusade against low-level corruption. The Hong Kong reform experience began with high profile prosecutions of top British ex-pat police officers and followed through with efforts to ensure that all public complaints about corruption were investigated quickly without adverse consequences for those who complained. 'Hot-lines', staffed 24 hours a day, were used to give complainers anonymity if they lacked the confidence to identify themselves. But at the same time, statistics on the willingness of complainers to identify themselves were used to monitor public confidence in the anti-corruption campaign. Those who did identify themselves were guaranteed a response from the anti-corruption commission within 48 hours of their complaint.[90]

6. DOWNSIZE THE STATE

Finally, Rose-Ackerman also proposes 'programme elimination'.[91] She has in mind not only the elimination of over-costly and unnecessary prestige infrastructure projects but also the unnecessary subsidy programmes and, especially relevant to our concerns, the elimination of customs and tax 'checkpoints'. We might add police 'checkpoints' as well. Some of these may perhaps be absolutely necessary but their number could be reduced.

In the end, if the state proves incapable of delivering services honestly and efficiently it may be advisable to admit defeat and, in the words of British Thatcherites, 'roll back the state' by cancelling state programmes and privatising state services. Indeed, if post-communist states prove more corrupt and less efficient than Western states, then deregulation and privatisation should perhaps be carried much further than in the West, leaving Western states 'larger' and Western countries therefore more 'socialist' than post-communist states.

The transition from communism in Eastern Europe and the former Soviet Union was motivated largely by the perception that the state was incapable of running commercial enterprises honestly and efficiently. But deregulation and privatisation could be carried much further, right into the heart of the public sector and the bureaucracy. Many official regulations, forms, licences and permissions could be abolished not only to increase efficiency by avoiding unnecessary bureaucracy, but also in order to reduce the scope for officials to extort bribes and the incentives for frustrated clients to offer them. Daniel Kaufman found that small and medium businesses in Ukraine were overburdened by the time spent dealing with officials, much of it spent negotiating 'unofficial fees' or bribes. He recommends eliminating licences and permits apart from those absolutely necessary for health and safety purposes, cutting export controls, trading restrictions and price controls, and accelerating privatisation.[92]

But downsizing the state is not necessarily cost-free to clients, and it is precisely when it imposes costs as well as benefits that it becomes something other than an 'efficiency reform'. Only then does downsizing the state become controversial. It could mean *fewer officials and therefore fewer public services*. An SIGMA/OECD panel of management experts noted: 'One suggestion, made in the light of limited government resources, is to employ less workers [i.e. less officials] and pay those employed higher salaries.'[93] Estonian interior minister, Juri Mois, has recently proposed a plan to reform the police by increasing salaries but cutting numbers by 13 per cent overall and by 40 per cent in Estonia's second largest city, Tartu.[94] That means fewer police available for public protection—if, of course, that is actually the role of the police in Estonia.

Alternatively, state services could be retained within the public sector but made to act more like private businesses. At the extreme, formerly illegal activities can be legalised—as with the end of prohibition in the USA and elsewhere. If clients are already paying for faster or better public services—faster handling of passport applications or better access to medical services, for example—then Rose-Ackerman suggests that a *legal system of user charges* 'may be a reasonable second-best'.[95] At least it might introduce some transparency, rationality and equity into an obscure, capricious and unfair procedure. Having paid 'officially', clients might be encouraged to resist demands for 'unofficial' payments. The charges would allocate scarce resources in an orderly way. There would also be a degree of equity both between different clients who paid for the services they received, and between different officials who took payments for the services they provided (or were compensated by higher salaries funded by the user charges).

PUBLIC OPINION ON REFORM—AS EXPRESSED IN FOCUS-GROUP DISCUSSIONS

There is no shortage of plausibly argued expert proposals for reform. But do they have public support? In our large-scale structured interview surveys we forced the public to address most of the expert proposals outlined above. But that inevitably imposes a frame of reference on public opinion. So before looking at our survey findings on reform it may be useful to look at the natural, unprompted and unstructured views of the public as expressed in our focus-group discussions. Although these are inevitably less coherent and less 'tidy' (as well as possibly less 'representative') than the more structured opinions expressed in our large-scale surveys, some very clear patterns emerge. (Table 9.4)

Table 9.4. Reform proposals that emerged in focus-group discussions

	Average	Czech Republic	Slovakia	Bulgaria	Ukraine
	%	%	%	%	%
improve personal qualities of staff	29	29	32	24	31
better administrative organisation	22	46	18	15	9
better legal framework	20	21	15	15	29
stricter controls and penalties	16	4	20	22	16
better salaries	13	7	18	14	13
more informed/demanding citizens	6	0	3	17	4
reform would be impossible/ineffective	3	0	4	2	6
(total N)		(72)	(99)	(152)	(271)

Note: Percentages are percentages of relevant 'text units' in the focus-group discussions, not of participants. Because text units can include references to more than one topic percentages may add up to over 100 percent. The total number of relevant text units on which percentages are based is shown in brackets at the foot of each column.

There was a sharp difference between the reform proposals put forward in the Czech discussions and those elsewhere. Far more than anywhere else, focus groups in the Czech Republic concentrated on measures to improve administrative efficiency and organisation. That reflected the burden of the Czech public's complaints: at street level they found the Czech bureaucracy tedious and unhelpful rather than corrupt.

Conversely, discussion groups outside the Czech Republic put more emphasis on other reforms, reflecting the different nature of their complaints which were far more about extortion and rather less about mere time wasting. So discussion groups outside the Czech Republic gave more attention to better salaries for officials (to make extortion less necessary) and stricter controls and penalties on officials (to make it more dangerous).

Stricter controls and penalties were seldom mentioned in the Czech Republic but quite frequently elsewhere. Slovaks complained that: 'It is worse now than under the rule of communism...You could lodge even an anonymous complaint and now there is no one to complain to...Now [officials] are not afraid of anything.'(Do 4) One Slovak wanted 'really harsh conditions, strict sanctions...We would have to start from the top and proceed downwards.'(Pres 6) In Bulgaria, also, some participants complained about the lack of control since the fall of communism. 'There used to be some order.'(Ya 2) 'Now the situation is very bad, perhaps because we have no one to take our complaints to.'(Ya 1) 'There should be [more] control.'(So-A 3)

Ukrainians also emphasised the need for more control, even a need for more fear. In an earlier chapter we noted that Ukrainians frequently mentioned lack of fear as one reason for declining standards of official behaviour. But some went further when asked about possible reforms, explicitly advocating the reintroduction of more fear as a remedy for present ills. 'There should be power in the country.'(Kh 4) 'We lack discipline. There is no fear now.'(Striy 1) 'It is necessary that the official simply be afraid that he can lose his place.'(Ky-B 3) Against the great preponderance of such authoritarian sentiments there were only a few atypical remarks expressing reservations. 'Control can be strengthened, but that is not the way out.'(Ky-A 4) 'Sanctions will not do. They will be carried out by people who might perhaps have the same weaknesses.'(So-B 8) 'The innocent suffer.'(Ni 1)

Encouraging officials by increasing salaries was seldom proposed in the Czech discussions, but it was a popular suggestion in Slovakia: 'Insufficient salaries, that is the cause of all that bribing.'(Br-B 8) Sometimes there was special pleading, however: 'Doctors' remuneration should be quite different in my opinion...my husband is a doctor.'(Pres 8). But sometimes support for higher salaries was conditional: 'I think salaries should be raised in health care and in education...[but] not to all of them without any discrimination.'(Zv 9). Similarly in Bulgaria: 'Perhaps they are underpaid.'(So-A 4) 'If the inspectors within this system were well paid, they would not give way to tips of 500 or 5,000 levs. They would not be tempted so easily.'(So-A 1) But again, support for more pay was sometimes linked to performance: 'I think people should be paid according to their performance.'(So-B 4) Some Ukrainians also sympathised with underpaid officials: 'They have to live, they do not earn enough money, that is why they take bribes.'(Ni 3) 'If they received appropriate payment, they would work professionally in their positions and would not take bribes.'(Sh 4)

Improve administrative efficiency: Overall, the most frequent suggestion in our focus-group discussions was a better quality of official: between 24 and 32 per cent of relevant text units in each country mentioned it. The proposal was almost as vacuous as it sounds—but not quite. Certainly, comments about better officials were often tautologous: 'Pleasant people should work there. A private businessman would not hire a waitress or a shop assistant who would turn her back on a customer.'(Br-B 2) In Ukraine, especially, there were calls for officials to 'change their psychology'(Ho 1), for 'more responsible'(Ho 6) officials, for officials with more 'conscience'(Ho 3), more 'competence'(Kh 6), more 'understanding'(Vo 3), more 'culture'(Ky-B 5) and, what must surely be the ultimate in tautologies, for more 'honesty' amongst officials (Striy 3 and 4).

But other comments about better-quality officials had a less tautologous content. They suggested better systems of selection, more qualified entrants and more in-service training—including training in customer relations as well as in more technical matters. Selection could be improved by less 'nepotism'(So-B 1). The Czech and Slovak discussions especially, but others also, emphasised 'higher qualifications'(Pra-B 1) and 'better training'(Br-B 5). 'There is little professionalism…they are poor souls, typing with just one finger. Do not take this literally [but] I sometimes feel they must have studied at a special university for mentally handicapped students.'(Pra-A 7) Training in customer relations might also help: officials 'should be aware that those coming to them are their customers, not experts in filling out forms'.(HK 3)

In addition, 46 per cent of text units in the Czech Republic (though fewer elsewhere and indeed very few in Ukraine) explicitly mentioned the need to improve administrative efficiency and organisation. They complained about wasting too much time on filling out forms, going to offices and standing in queues. They proposed a better administrative structure, less bureaucracy, better-located offices, or simply longer opening hours. Individual departments were 'unable to communicate between themselves'.(KH 7) There was a need for 'longer opening hours'(Pra-B 4), for 'fewer useless forms'(KH 5). Slovaks made similar but less frequent suggestions for administrative reform: 'Less bureaucracy, more flexibility' (NZ 3, with noises of agreement from NZ 1 and NZ 2). The need for better premises was also mentioned: 'People cram in there and the clerk gets irritable...slightly more human conditions would do.'(Br-B 2) There were also a few similar suggestions in Bulgaria and Ukraine. 'There should be computers everywhere.'(Ya 5)

In focus-group discussions, demands for more information were generally inseparable from proposals to improve efficiency. 'At all these offices where most people have to go, there should be one person whose sole responsibility it is to provide information.'(Zv 4) A 'one-stop shop' such as they had enjoyed under communism could help. 'Formerly everything was in one place [at 'National Committees']. It was a well-established system and...people there knew their jobs.'(Br-A 2) 'They should tell you everything you need to bring the first time.'(Ky-A 6)

At first sight, the frequency of proposals for a *better legal framework* appears to provide a point of similarity between discussions in the Czech Republic and Ukraine. But in the Czech Republic, that meant 'simpler, more easily understandable'(Ol 4) and more stable laws—in other words, better laws were needed for efficiency reasons. In Bulgaria, too, there were references to simplifying the laws to improve efficiency. 'Legislation should be simplified and made clear to the people.'(So-A 7) 'Laws should be clear...At the moment I have the feeling we are ruled by decrees and regulations.'(So-A 1) But in Bulgaria there was also a plea for laws to replace anarchy, to fill a vacuum and thereby exert control over officials. 'There are no laws, they say. When will these laws be passed?'(Stral 6) There was some emphasis on simply enforcing obedience to the law. 'In a West European country, corruption is controlled...the penalty is serious...We all have to work towards creating a normal state, a law-abiding state.'(So-A 6)

Suggestions for improved legislation were also voiced in Ukraine. '[We have] no developed legislation.'(Ky-A 4) But two-thirds of the references to the law in Ukraine did not focus on this need for clearer, simpler and better-publicised laws. One-third consisted of complaints from Crimean Tatars (in our special Crimean focus group) that the laws of Ukraine were biased against them: '...discrimination against nationality'.(Se 4 and 5) More typically, however, the remaining third of Ukrainian suggestions for legal reform concerned enforcement rather than clarification. 'There should be organs that would make sure this law is followed.'(Kh 4) So while a better legal framework meant more efficiency in Czech discussions, it meant more coercion and more control in Ukrainian discussions.

Empower citizens: We found the most explicit references to empowering citizens in our Bulgarian focus groups. Bulgarians in particular viewed better-informed citizens in terms of citizens' rights rather than administrative efficiency, for example. 'There is a rule: The more you are informed, the less corrupt the official.'(So-A 7) 'When I know my legal rights…I can defend them and I can make demands.'(Ya 4)

Improve openness and transparency: Despite their popularity with experts, reforms centred on greater openness and transparency seldom emerged in our focus-group discussions. As we have indicated there were frequent demands for 'more information' but that was conceptualised in terms of citizens' needs as individual clients rather than as a control mechanism focused on officials.

Downsize the state: Focus-group suggestions for increased efficiency frequently mentioned the need for less paperwork: 'You do not need so many certificates in every country.'(Ky-A 2) They also mentioned fewer officials: '…above all, fewer bureaucrats'.(KH 4) Sympathetic attitudes towards officials' salaries were sometimes accompanied and combined with less sympathetic suggestions. Pay rises could be combined with stricter control or with a cut in the number of officials. 'Nothing terrible would happen if the official apparatus were cut back by two-thirds'(Ky-A 4) '…and raise the salaries of the ones who are left'.(Ky-A 5) Efficiency proposals certainly included 'downsizing the state' as well as other approaches such as better training or better office equipment.

In addition, complaints about the health service often implied that it might be better if the state reduced its role in health care by privatisation or by the introduction of user charges. We shall return to that issue later, but within our focus-group discussions such comments emerged mainly as complaints against the failure of the state to honour its responsibility to provide free health care, and only implicitly hinted at privatisation or user charges as proposals for reform.

A TEN-ITEM MENU OF REFORM: PUBLIC OPINION AND
THE REACTIONS OF STREET-LEVEL OFFICIALS

In our large-scale representative surveys we drew on the reform proposals that had emerged in expert prescriptions or in the focus-group discussions. We asked the public (and street-level officials) to rate ten items on a menu of reforms according to their effectiveness in 'ensuring that citizens get fair treatment from officials, without having to give them money or presents'. That menu included items that covered five out of the six categories of reform that we have identified in the expert literature:

1: Impose tighter control and stricter penalties
- 'stricter controls and penalties for officials?'
- 'stricter penalties for people who bribe officials?'

2: Encourage officials
- 'higher salaries for officials?'

3: Improve administrative efficiency
- 'better training for officials to give them the necessary knowledge and skills?' (This option was carefully worded to distinguish it very clearly from moral or ethical training.)
- 'fewer official forms and documents?'

4: Empower citizens
- 'better appeal and complaints procedures for citizens?'
- 'display the rights of citizens on notices in all offices?' (A 'Citizens' Charter' approach.)
- 'make all officials sign a code of conduct setting out how they should behave towards citizens?' (A version of 'ethical training' as distinct from 'technical training'.)

5: Improve openness and transparency
- 'more openness: require officials to explain their actions to citizens and the press?' (A Gorbachev-style *'glasnost'* strategy.)
- 'encourage officials to tell the public if they find things that are wrong in their offices?' (A 'whistle-blowing' approach.)

This menu did not include items reflecting reforms that fell into the sixth category, 'downsizing the state'. It did not include items about 'encouraging officials' by means other than salary increases, nor items about 'controls and penalties' imposed by international organisations. All of these were covered separately with specially designed questions. Nonetheless, the basic ten-point menu provides a good starting point for assessing the pattern of public support for different reforms.

First, we asked whether each of these ten reforms would be '*very effective* for improving the situation in (the country), *useful* though not very effective, *not necessary*, or *actually harmful*?' After going through the list item by item, we finally asked which of the ten would be 'the *single most effective* way of ensuring fair treatment for citizens?'

PRIORITIES: THE SINGLE MOST EFFECTIVE REFORM

Table 9.5. The most effective way to ensure fair treatment for citizens (ten-item menu)

	Average	Czech Republic	Slovakia	Bulgaria	Ukraine
	%	%	%	%	%
The single most effective reform would be…					
stricter controls/penalties for officials	33(13)	28	21	32	51
higher salaries for officials	18(42)	11	18	30	12
better training for officials	16(18)	21	26	12	6
fewer official forms/documents	8(11)	17	10	3	3
more openness/require officials to explain	7 (4)	7	6	6	7
make officials sign a 'code of conduct'	6 (5)	5	7	5	8
better appeal/complaints procedures	5 (3)	6	5	5	3
display citizens' rights in offices	4 (2)	3	3	3	5
encourage officials to expose wrongdoing	3 (1)	1	3	2	4
stricter penalties for clients who give bribes	2 (2)	2	2	3	2

Notes: 'Don't know', 'mixed/depends' etc. answers were recorded if given spontaneously, but never prompted; they have been excluded from the calculation of percentages.

Figures in brackets are based on the replies by officials.

Both street-level bureaucrats and the public put 'higher salaries', 'more training', and 'stricter controls and penalties' for officials above all

other proposed reforms—but not in the same order. (Table 9.5) Street-
level officials were 25 per cent more likely than the public to choose
'higher salaries'. Conversely, the public was 20 per cent more likely
than officials to choose 'stricter controls and penalties for officials'. Indeed, officials put 'higher salaries' at the very top of their list while the
public put 'stricter controls and penalties' at the very top of theirs.

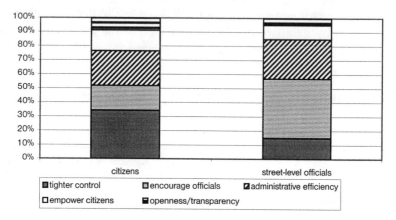

Fig. 9.2a. The public and officials have different priorities for
reform

It would have been very surprising if officials had not been somewhat more favourable than the public to 'higher salaries' and less favourable to 'stricter controls'. But the scale of the polarisation of opinion between the public and street-level officials is striking. It emerges
even more clearly if the ten menu items are grouped under our five standard categories of control, encouragement, efficiency, empowerment
and transparency. (Fig. 9.2a)

Equally striking is the way that priorities for reform vary across the
four countries. (Table 9.6, Fig. 9.2b) Again, grouping the ten menu
items under our five standard categories of control, encouragement, efficiency, empowerment and transparency, reveals:

- *amongst both officials and the public* much stronger priorities for
  'administrative efficiency' reforms in the Czech and Slovak Republics (average 40 per cent) than in Bulgaria or Ukraine (average
  13 per cent)

which is balanced by somewhat different patterns amongst officials and
the public:

Table 9.6. The most effective way to ensure fair treatment for citizens (five categories)

	Average %	Czech Republic %	Slovakia %	Bulgaria %	Ukraine %
The single most effective reform would be...					
tighter control	35(15)	30(12)	23(16)	35 (8)	53(22)
encourage officials	18(42)	11(26)	18(26)	30(69)	12(48)
administrative efficiency	25(28)	38(48)	36(38)	15(14)	9(14)
empower citizens	15(10)	14 (8)	15(15)	13 (6)	16(12)
openness and transparency	9 (5)	8 (6)	9 (6)	7 (4)	11 (5)

Notes: 'Don't know', 'mixed/depends' etc. answers were recorded if given spontaneously, but never prompted; they have been excluded from the calculation of percentages.

Figures in brackets are based on the replies by officials.

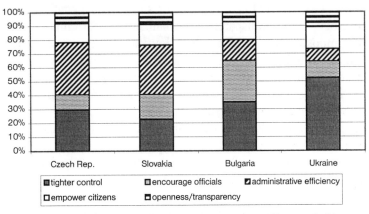

Fig. 9.2b. The publics in different countries have different priorities for reform

- *amongst officials*, much stronger priorities for 'encouragement' in Bulgaria and Ukraine (average 59 per cent) than in the Czech or Slovak Republics (average 26 per cent);
- *amongst the public*, a relatively strong priority for 'encouragement' in Bulgaria but a uniquely strong priority for 'stricter penalties and controls' in Ukraine (53 per cent).

Stricter control may or may not require new laws. Many countries have exemplary anti-corruption laws that have no impact on behaviour in the real world.[96] In a supplementary question we asked whether, in

order 'to stop officials taking money or presents', it was 'more important to: (i) pass new, stricter laws; or (ii) enforce existing laws more
strictly?' A narrow majority of the public (58 per cent) and a two-thirds
majority of officials (66 per cent) opted for stricter enforcement rather
than new laws. Cross-nationally, support for stricter enforcement was
greatest in Ukraine, both amongst the public and amongst officials.

REFORM PACKAGES

When the OECD recently asked governments about 'the most effective
anti-corruption measures', it found, despite the wording of its enquiry,
that 'most countries cited more than one type of mechanism'.[97] Although only 15 OECD countries participated in the survey, 9 countries
opted for strict 'law enforcement', 6 for strict 'management and financial controls', 5 for 'transparency mechanisms', 5 for empowering citizens by imposing 'codes of conduct, [ethical] training and guidelines'
on officials, and 2 for adequate 'remuneration' of officials.[98] Although
that indicates the usual governmental emphasis on coercive measures, it
also indicates some awareness that no single reform can provide a
'magic bullet' to eliminate corruption.

Experts usually advocate twin or multi-track strategies of reform
rather than placing too much faith in any single 'magic solution'.[99]
Fairly typically, Transparency International's Peter Eigen advocates a
package of measures to reduce corruption:[100]

- comprehensive anti-corruption legislation, enforced by an independent agency, with effective deterrents/penalties; *and*
- adequate salaries for officials; *and*
- a clear and demonstrable commitment by political leaders; *and*
- simplification of procedures in areas of activity most prone to
  corruption; *and*
- empowerment of the people by open debate, a free press, and accountability.

The public was sophisticated enough to agree with public administration experts that there could be no quick or simple 'magic bullet'
solution. Both focus-group discussions and expert opinion stressed the
importance of some mixture of encouragement, control and citizen information. When forced to choose, citizens and officials specified their

priorities. But in principle, all of these reforms could be pursued simultaneously. They are not exclusive alternatives, and public opinion recognised that.

When asked whether each of the reforms on our ten-point menu would be 'very effective', 'useful', 'not necessary', or 'actually harmful', both the public and street-level bureaucrats typically declared that several reforms, not just one, would be 'very effective'. Half the public rated at least five of the ten items on our menu as 'very effective'. Street-level officials were more discriminating, but over half of them rated at least four of the ten items as 'very effective'. Every one of the ten reforms on the menu was rated 'very effective' by at least a third of the public and by at least a quarter of street-level officials. (Table 9.7, Fig. 9.3)

Table 9.7. Reform packages: very effective reforms

	Average	Czech Republic	Slovakia	Bulgaria	Ukraine
	%	%	%	%	%
The reform would be 'very effective':					
stricter controls/penalties for officials	77(51)	73	66	86	81
fewer official forms/documents	63(64)	72	68	61	52
better training for officials	54(58)	59	59	65	34
better appeal/complaints procedures	53(41)	51	52	64	43
more openness/require officials to explain	49(33)	43	43	58	51
display citizens' rights in offices	46(33)	40	46	53	46
stricter penalties for clients who give bribes	45(41)	44	35	61	40
make officials sign a 'code of conduct'	42(28)	34	37	46	50
encourage officials to expose wrongdoing	40(26)	33	32	53	42
higher salaries for officials	37(61)	22	32	68	24

Notes: 'Don't know', 'mixed/depends' etc. answers were recorded if given spontaneously, but never prompted; they have been excluded from the calculation of percentages.

Figures in brackets are based on the replies by officials.

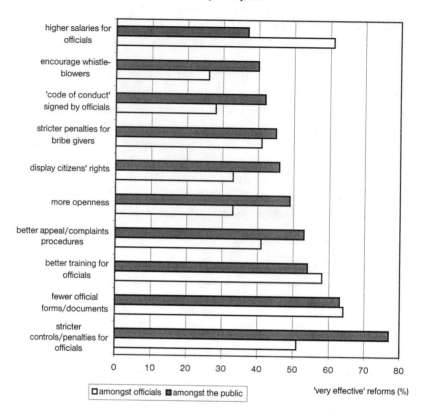

Fig. 9.3. Public support for a multi-track approach (reforms
displayed by degree of public support)

Rated by their effectiveness rather than by their priority, stricter
controls and penalties on officials once again topped the public's list of
reforms. But quite dramatically, higher salaries for officials slipped from
second to last place on the public's list when they rated reforms according to whether they would be 'very effective' rather than the 'single
most effective' reform. That was because those citizens who rejected
higher salaries as their first choice tended to rate it as ineffective. By
contrast, the public rated many other reforms as 'very effective' even
when they did not opt for them as the 'single most effective' reform. For
example, an average of 45 per cent thought 'stricter penalties for clients'
who offered bribes would be 'very effective' although only a mere 2 per
cent nominated this as the 'single most effective' reform.

The public put 'fewer official forms and documents' second on their
list of 'very effective' reforms. Street-level officials put higher salaries

near the top of their list of 'very effective' reforms, but only slightly ahead of better technical training, and slightly behind 'fewer official forms and documents'.

There were sharp differences between officials and the public—but only on some specific reforms. Officials and the public differed little on the effectiveness of administrative efficiency reforms such as 'fewer forms and documents' or 'better technical training' for officials. More surprisingly, they differed little on the effectiveness of stricter penalties for clients. Indeed, officials were slightly less inclined than the public to penalise clients. But officials gave considerably more support than the public to higher salaries (as 'very effective') and considerably less support than the public to stricter controls and penalties.

In addition, officials were somewhat less enthusiastic than the public about a whole range of other reforms—better appeals and complaints procedures, the display of citizens' rights in offices, a mandatory code of conduct for officials, more openness, and encouragement of whistle-blowers.

Amongst the public, a factor analysis of public attitudes to reform produces three factors, which we might usefully term:

(i) an *administrative efficiency factor* centred on better technical training for officials, but including better appeals procedures, fewer official forms, and, less clearly, higher salaries for officials;

(ii) a *citizens' rights factor* centred on more openness and accountability to the media, but including the display of citizens rights in offices, encouragement of whistle-blowers, and a mandatory code of conduct for officials;

(iii) a *controls and penalties factor* centred on stricter penalties for clients who offered bribes but also stricter control of officials.

There is one surprise in these factor analysis results—namely, that 'better complaints and appeals' procedures lie close to the heart of the administrative efficiency factor and are unrelated to the citizens' rights factor. Perhaps we should conceptualise complaints and appeals procedures in terms of a smoothly running administrative machine rather than in terms of empowering citizens. Conversely, of course, and more in line with our thinking so far, the factor analysis suggests that 'codes of conduct' for officials should not be conceptualised as part of a well-run administrative machine but rather as a device for empowering citizens.

Amongst street-level bureaucrats, a factor analysis produces a very similar but not quite identical factor structure. There are two slight differences between the structures of attitudes amongst officials and the public:

- first, amongst officials, support for higher salaries is less strongly linked to the administrative efficiency factor and linked rather more strongly (and negatively) to the citizens' rights factor;
- second, amongst officials, support for whistle-blowers is less strongly linked to the citizens' rights factor and as strongly linked to the coercion and control factor.

The contrast between these two factor analyses implies that officials view both higher salaries and the encouragement of whistle-blowers in a somewhat different light from the public. The public view higher salaries in a less confrontational light as a measure designed to improve public administration, while officials view higher salaries more as part of a confrontation between their privileges and citizens' rights. Conversely, citizens view whistle-blowers primarily as contributing to openness and citizens' rights, while officials consider them as an instrument of coercion as well as a contributor to citizens' rights.

RESISTANCE TO REFORM

In the context of such widespread approval for so many different reforms, perhaps we should draw attention to the numbers who opposed a reform by describing it as 'not necessary' or 'actually harmful'. This indicates more than lack of enthusiasm for a reform. It indicates actual rejection and perhaps implies a degree of resistance to certain reforms—reforms which 'go against the grain' of opinion amongst a significant section of the public or street-level bureaucrats. (Table 9.8, Fig. 9.4)

Public resistance to reform: Overall, higher salaries topped the list for public antipathy. 'Even if they got more money, they would behave in the same way.'(Br-A 6) In our surveys, higher salaries for officials were opposed in this way by about one-third of the public in every country except Bulgaria. In our focus-group discussions there was also considerable opposition to higher salaries for officials, and Bulgaria was no exception. (Our focus-group discussions, unlike our surveys, took place before the dramatic change of government in Bulgaria.) 'I do not think the explanation lies only in the low salaries. Salaries will be raised, and they will become corrupt again...there are no moral values.'(So-A 6) 'The appetite grows in the course of eating.'(So-B 8) Remarkably, public opposition to higher salaries for officials was greater than public opposition to stricter penalties for clients who gave bribes, which took second place on the list of reforms opposed by the public.

Table 9.8. Resistance to reform

	Average	Czech Republic	Slovakia	Bulgaria	Ukraine
	%	%	%	%	%
'Unnecessary' or 'actually harmful' reforms:					
encourage officials to expose wrongdoing	19(34)	26(51)	26(38)	12(22)	12(27)
make officials sign a 'code of conduct'	19(32)	24(45)	20(25)	21(33)	12(27)
more openness/require officials to explain	12(25)	16(36)	17(28)	9(20)	6(17)
stricter penalties for clients who give bribes	20(23)	19(30)	20(20)	14(15)	26(25)
display citizens' rights in offices	15(23)	19(23)	15(15)	13(28)	12(25)
better appeal/complaints procedures	10(16)	15(24)	8(9)	5(13)	11(18)
stricter controls/penalties for officials	6(14)	10(23)	8(16)	2(8)	3(10)
fewer official forms/documents	9 (9)	12(12)	8(10)	8(8)	6(7)
higher salaries for officials	26 (7)	34(10)	29(14)	6(0)	33(5)
better training for officials	9 (6)	13(12)	4(5)	4(2)	13(6)

Notes: 'Don't know', 'mixed/depends' etc. answers were recorded if given spontaneously, but never prompted; they have been excluded from the calculation of percentages.

Figures in brackets are based on the replies by officials.

Entries in this table are sorted by rates of resistance amongst street-level officials.

On average, across the four countries, a mandatory 'code of conduct' and 'whistle-blowing' tied for third place. A mandatory 'code of conduct' for officials was opposed by over one-fifth of the public in every country except Ukraine. 'Whistle-blowing' was opposed by more than one-quarter of the public in both the Czech and Slovak Republics, though much less elsewhere. Other surveys have also revealed wide-

spread public scepticism with respect to these reforms, even though
Western experts view this public scepticism as misplaced.[101]

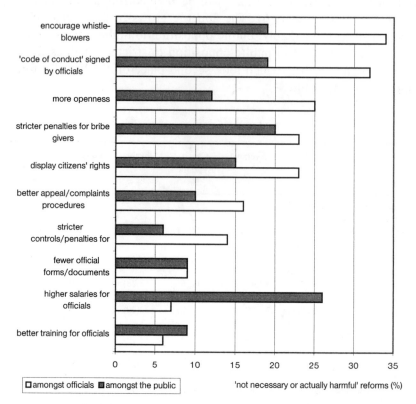

Fig. 9.4. Resistance to reform amongst street-level officials
(reforms displayed by degree of resistance amongst street-level
officials)

Resistance amongst street-level officials: There was little difference
between the public and officials on their level of opposition to six of the
ten reforms. But few officials opposed higher salaries for themselves.
Conversely, and less obviously, officials were about 14 per cent more
antagonistic than the public towards a mandatory 'code of conduct', towards encouragement of 'whistle-blowers', and towards requirements
for 'more openness'. Surprisingly, these proposals irritated officials
more, and in some cases much more, than the prospect of 'stricter controls and penalties'. Officials, for example, were over twice as opposed
to mandatory 'codes of conduct' or encouraging 'whistle-blowers' as
they were to 'stricter controls and penalties for officials'.

Perhaps officials felt more comfortable with traditional hierarchical 'controls' than with the new and unfamiliar disciplines of openness and citizen empowerment imported from Western bureaucracies. That may be part of the explanation. But Czech officials, surely not the least Western, were the most antagonistic towards these three reforms: 36 per cent of Czech officials opposed requirements for 'more openness', 45 per cent opposed a mandatory 'code of conduct', and a massive 51 per cent opposed the encouragement of 'whistle-blowers'. We know that Czech officials were uniquely self-satisfied and complacent about their relationship with their clients. Complacency may be another part of the explanation. But multivariate analysis of our data shows that this complacency cannot explain away all of the Czech antagonism to whistle-blowing. That must derive from other causes. Moreover, the Czech and Slovak publics were also especially opposed to 'whistle-blowing', even though bureaucratic 'whistle-blowers' are no threat to the public. Perhaps that opposition reflected the bitter experience of 'informing' under an externally imposed communist regime. The Czechoslovak public had voted communist in large numbers immediately after their liberation from Nazi occupation in the 1940s. But their enthusiasm for the Soviet-backed regime was short lived and after the suppression of the 1968 Prague Spring, the communist regime in Czechoslovakia was viewed as a new foreign domination—to a degree that even the regimes in Bulgaria and Ukraine were not.

What is naturally interpreted in Britain or America as 'going public' may still have the smell of traitorous collusion with an occupying regime in Central Europe.

ALTERNATIVE WAYS OF ENCOURAGING OFFICIALS

Expert opinion points to a variety of ways to encourage officials other than increasing their salaries. Going beyond our ten-item menu, we asked respondents to compare higher salaries with alternative incentives for officials. We asked: 'In your view, which of these would do most to encourage officials to treat citizens with more fairness, politeness and consideration—higher salaries, more pleasant offices, less pressure of work, or more respect from the public?'

Just over half the public opted for 'higher salaries', followed, a long way behind, by 'less pressure of work' and 'more respect from the public'. Very few chose 'more pleasant offices' as the most effective incentive for officials, despite some comments in focus-group discussions about short-tempered officials in overcrowded offices. The views of officials themselves were very similar. (Table 9.9)

Table 9.9. Four ways to encourage officials

	Average	Czech Republic	Slovakia	Bulgaria	Ukraine
	%	%	%	%	%
Which would do most to encourage officials to treat citizens with more fairness, politeness and consideration?					
higher salaries	51(55)	36(46)	45(39)	72(72)	53(63)
less pressure of work	25(26)	37(28)	31(40)	14(15)	17(21)
more respect from the public	19(17)	23(22)	18(19)	12(13)	24(14)
pleasanter offices	5 (2)	5(5)	6(3)	2(0)	6(1)

Notes: 'Don't know', 'mixed/depends' etc. answers were recorded if given spontaneously, but never prompted; they have been excluded from the calculation of percentages.

Figures in brackets are based on the replies by officials.

Cross-national variations were considerable, however. Overwhelming majorities opted for 'higher salaries' in Bulgaria, along with smaller majorities in Ukraine. But there was no majority for higher salaries in either the Czech or the Slovak Republic. Indeed, 'less pressure of work' was the top choice of the Czech public and of Slovak officials, even if by a statistically insignificant margin of only 1 per cent in each case. In very sharp contrast, however, pressure of work was not a contender in Bulgaria or Ukraine.

According to expert opinion, a better example at the top is another important way to encourage junior officials. We asked: 'Which comes closer to your view? To stop officials taking money or presents from ordinary people, would it be more effective for those at the top: (i) to impose stricter controls on their subordinates; or (ii) to set a better example by refusing to take bribes themselves?' A large majority of the public (61 per cent), and an even larger majority of officials (74 per cent), opted for 'a better example at the top'. Cross-nationally there was a particular emphasis on the need for a better example at the top in Slovakia and Ukraine.

Yet another way to encourage street-level officials might be to target bribe givers as much as bribe takers. On average, 47 per cent of street-level officials (but only 36 per cent of the public) opted to punish bribe-giving clients as severely as bribe-taking officials.

Taking public demands for a better example at the top along with public indulgence towards bribe-giving clients, it is clear that the public was unsympathetic to top officials but sympathetic to clients. In comparison to the public, however, junior officials were somewhat less sympathetic to both. When it came to reform, street-level officials reacted relatively aggressively against both their superiors and their clients. To a modest but significant degree they responded as if they consciously felt that they were indeed 'caught between state and citizen'. (Table 9.10)

Table 9.10. A better example at the top? Stricter penalties for clients?

	Average	Czech Republic	Slovakia	Bulgaria	Ukraine
	%	%	%	%	%
set a better example at the top	61(74)	52(67)	72(80)	50(69)	68(80)
punish bribe givers as severely as bribe takers	36(47)	47(50)	42(53)	36(52)	20(32)

Notes: 'Don't know', 'mixed/depends' etc. answers were recorded if given spontaneously, but never prompted; they have been excluded from the calculation of percentages.

Figures in brackets are based on the replies by officials.

DOWNSIZING THE STATE

Realistically, 'higher salaries' must be funded and post-communist publics seem even less willing to pay taxes than West Europeans. They had little confidence in the competence or honesty of their governments and administrations. In such circumstances, payments 'at the point of use' then appear to correspond to identifiable benefits. Unlike taxes, such payments do not just disappear without trace into a 'black hole' of mismanagement and corruption.

We asked about two proposals for raising officials' salaries while minimising the need for higher taxes: 'less bureaucracy' and 'user charges'. Both might be described as Thatcherite solutions, based on 'downsizing the state'. In principle at least, both may reduce the service provided by the state to its citizens. They may have benefits but they are not cost-free options for clients. We asked whether the combination of higher salaries for officials with one or other of these ways of meeting the cost would lead, on balance, to a better or worse deal for citizens. We took care to make the costs as well as the benefits explicit in our question wording.

To gauge support for the '*less bureaucracy*' option we asked: 'Suppose the government raised the salaries but reduced the number of officials. Would officials then treat citizens:

(i) better because their salary was higher; or
(ii) worse because they would be under more pressure?'

On average, an unusually large number (19 per cent) spontaneously offered a 'mixed/depends' answer of some kind. But by a margin of around 16 per cent both the public and street-level bureaucrats thought the combination of better pay but fewer officials would benefit clients. It won strong support in Bulgaria and Ukraine where large reductions in the number of administrative jobs had, in fact, recently been announced.[102] But opinion was evenly divided in the Czech Republic, and actually hostile in Slovakia.

To gauge support for the '*user charges*' option we asked: 'Suppose the government raised the salaries of doctors and nurses, but set official charges for hospital treatment. For patients, would that be:

(i) better, because doctors and nurses would not try to get extra money from patients; or
(ii) worse, because patients would have to pay official charges?'

There was less evidence of mixed or indecisive views on this option, and opinion was considerably less favourable. By a margin of 22 per cent the public felt this combination would make things worse for patients. (Table 9.11, Fig. 9.5)

Table 9.11. Downsizing the state

	Average	Czech Republic	Slovakia	Bulgaria	Ukraine
		% 'better' – % 'worse'			
	%	%	%	%	%
higher salaries + fewer officials	+13(+19)	+4(+5)	–12(–23)	+44(+45)	+17(+52)
higher salaries + user charges in health care	–22 (–4)	–42(–26)	–51(–44)	0(+33)	+8(+21)

Notes: Because of the unusually high number of unprompted 'mixed/depends' answers to these questions (17 per cent on 'fewer officials' and 12 per cent on 'user charges') they have been included in the calculation. Entries show the difference between the numbers saying 'better' and 'worse' as a percentage of all those giving 'better', 'worse', or 'mixed/depends' answers. 'Don't know' answers have been excluded from the calculation of percentages as usual.

Figures in brackets are based on the replies by officials.

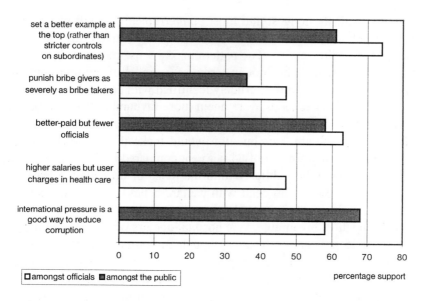

Fig. 9.5. Hard choices for reform

Cross-national differences were striking. Opinion was overwhelmingly hostile in the Czech and Slovak Republics. Although Czechs[103] and Slovaks[104] already had a compulsory insurance-based system of health-care charging they regarded it as a bureaucratic variant on a tax-based system rather than as a system of privately paid medicine on the American model. Once again, public opinion was markedly more favourable in Bulgaria and Ukraine. The Bulgarian public was evenly divided and the Ukrainian public was in favour of user charges, if only by a small margin. Bulgarians and Ukrainians were perhaps all too familiar with the need to pay real user charges for health care (without the benefit of insurance), whether these charges were legal or not. For Bulgarians and Ukrainians, officially decreed user charges might reduce the uncertainty and racketeering that citizens faced when seeking health care. Slovaks also paid unofficial charges to doctors, but they did not feel so confident that official user charges would help to solve the problem, perhaps because they felt that their health-care system was already funded by their insurance payments and that their doctors were not underpaid.

The cross-national pattern of opinion sheds an interesting sidelight on the impact of a historical/cultural tradition versus the impact of contemporary circumstances, however. Ironically, it was precisely in those countries with the longest and most uninterruptedly socialistic regimes that the public had least faith in the concept of a 'free-at-the-point-of-use' public health service. The pattern makes sense in terms of contemporary circumstances but not in terms of a model of cultural continuity—at least not if culture is crudely identified with dominant regimes.

Street-level bureaucrats were again more favourable than the public to financing better pay for health-care staff by means of user charges. Officials also felt this combination would make things worse for patients, but by a margin of only 4 per cent compared to the margin of 22 per cent amongst the public. Within the ranks of officials the least favourable were those who dealt with welfare benefit claimants. Such officials were no more favourable than the public to this reform. Conversely, the most favourable were hospital doctors who supported it by a margin of 15 per cent on balance, though an unusually large number of doctors had mixed views (23 per cent). Perhaps doctors knew more about the problem of extortion within the health services. Or perhaps doctors just thought they would gain most from officially decreed health-care charges and this warped their judgement about the true interests of their patients.

TRAINING AND GUIDANCE

Better technical training came third on the public's list of the 'most effective' reforms and second on the officials' list. By contrast, ethical training, at least as represented by our question about 'a mandatory code of conduct', came low down on both lists. We explored attitudes towards training and guidance in more detail when we interviewed officials, asking about their experience of six types of training, their priorities for more training, and their attitudes towards international training programmes.

Officials reported that they had actually received the least training in customer relations, in ethics, and, most especially, in 'what to do with offers of money or presents'. They had received the most training in the use of equipment and the application of relevant laws.

However, officials' own top priorities for additional training were in exactly those areas where they had already received the most. (Table 9.12) Their top priorities were for more training in laws and equipment (69 per cent). Their lowest priorities were for more training in ethics or what to do with offers of money or presents (8 per cent). About a fifth opted for more training in customer relations or the rights of citizens. Paradoxically, Czech officials, who were so opposed to a mandatory code of conduct, encouragement of whistle-blowers, or more openness to the press, nonetheless put more emphasis than officials in other countries on customer relations and the rights of citizens, and less on technical training. It was almost as if they viewed the rights of their clients as their own professional concern, not something that required pressure from outside.

Table 9.12. Training—experience, priorities and attitude to international assistance

	have had 'little or no' training in this area	top priority is for more training in this area	international assistance would be 'very useful' for training in this area
	%	%	%
Topic area for training:			
laws and regulations	12	41	28
use of equipment	12	28	44
legal rights of citizens	14	14	27
good relations with citizens	20	8	29
ethics	21	6	29
what to do with gifts of money, presents etc.	42	2	21

Notes: 'Don't know', 'mixed/depends' etc. answers were recorded if given spontaneously, but never prompted; they have been excluded from the calculation of percentages.

Based on the replies by officials. Detailed questions about training were not put to the public.

Listed by priority areas for further training.

Officials felt that training by a Western or international organisation would be most useful in the area of equipment. But they thought international training would be significantly less useful in all other areas including laws, regulations and the rights of citizens. They put the usefulness of international training in 'what to do with offers of money or presents' at the very bottom of the list in every country. In Ukraine, for example, 44 per cent thought international training would be 'very useful' if it applied to the use of equipment, but only 16 per cent if it applied to offers of gifts from clients. If they were going to be lectured at by foreigners, they much preferred lectures on computing rather than on bribery.

Perhaps, of course, the notion of 'training' in what to do with offers of money or presents is absurdly over-complex. It is not a technically difficult problem, after all. Guidelines might suffice. So we asked officials specifically whether there were 'any guidelines about taking presents in your work' and whether such guidelines 'would be useful'. On average, 83 per cent of officials said there were no such guidelines in their workplace. But on average, 64 per cent also said that such guidelines would not be useful.

Indeed, guidelines of any sort were unpopular with street-level officials. Twice as many (41 per cent) complained that they were subject to 'too many' instructions and guidelines as complained about insufficient guidance (23 per cent). Twice as many wanted more freedom and discretion to make their own decisions (60 per cent) as wanted more detailed guidelines (29 per cent).

REFORM ITSELF AS THE PROBLEM?

Experts have criticised communist legislation for a lack of clarity, for confusion and contradictions that irritated clients and provided opportunities for corrupt officials. They have also criticised post-communist legislation for adding to the confusion rather than eliminating it.

Street-level officials agreed that reform was part of the problem. Fully 61 per cent said that the laws, regulations and instructions 'that they themselves had to follow in their own job' were actually 'clear and consistent', and only 26 per cent said that these laws were 'unclear and contradictory'. At the same time, two-thirds complained that there had been 'too many changes to the laws in recent years'. Although only a quarter said these changes had been simply 'bad', another half said they had been 'good in their aims but bad in their design', which left only the remaining quarter who fully supported recent changes in the law.

Although their criticisms may have partly echoed those expressed by public administration experts (with regard to recent changes), there was a conservative tone to the responses of street-level officials that did not reflect the experts' criticism of communist law as well as it did their criticism of recent changes.

PUBLIC SUPPORT FOR INTERNATIONAL PRESSURE

Finally, we asked directly about the value of international pressure as an aid to reform. Some observers view outside pressure as an unacceptable attempt to impose Western values or, less dramatically, as unacceptable interference in the internal affairs of sovereign states. This 'cultural argument—that corruption is an accepted practice among developing countries—is one of the strongest barriers to rooting out the phenomenon' according to Peter Eigen of Transparency International.[105] Until very recently it was used as an excuse for Western commercial companies to finance the corruption of state officials in other parts of the world, often with the complicity of Western governments, which made the cost of the bribes 'tax deductible'.[106]

Carolyn Hotchkiss quotes a Thai deputy minister of the interior as calling upon his staff to accept any money offered to them on the grounds that 'this is part of traditional Thai culture'.[107] (The Thai minister did not permit his staff to 'ask for bribes or circulate price lists' but he justified their acceptance of bribes by their 'low level of pay' as well as their 'culture'.[108]) But Hotchkiss also quotes the contrary view of a Nigerian head of state: 'In the African concept of appreciation and hospitality, the gift is usually a token. It is not demanded...It is usually done in the open, never in secret. Where it is excessive, it becomes an embarrassment and it is returned.' Indeed, there are reasons to be sceptical about such concepts as 'Asian or African or East European values', whatever the practice in parts of those territories. Evidence from around the world—in Asia, Africa and Latin America—suggests that the public who are forced to give bribes to corrupt officials do not support the idea that corruption is a valuable part of their unique local culture.[109] In Rose-Ackerman's judgement, 'corruption can be routine and commonplace without being viewed as acceptable by the population that bears its costs'.[110]

Ivan Krastev suggests a less cultural or value-based reason for resistance to international pressure—namely, self-interest. 'Local businesses are much better positioned in the corruption market because they are plugged into existing networks...a corrupted business environment is much more favourable to local businesses than a transparent market. This patriotic side of corruption is one of the major reasons for...the tacit unwillingness of post-communist governments to crack down seriously on corrupt practices.'[111] There is certainly a strata within post-communist countries that benefits from a corrupt environment. That is recognised by the public. A large majority in every country in our survey thought that the chief beneficiaries of the transition had been, and would continue to be, either 'politicians and officials' or 'the mafia'. (See Chapter 2) But the public themselves felt excluded from the benefits of a corrupt transition. They could hardly be expected to support it.

Indeed they resented it. They were very clear that the interests of politicians and mafia business were not the interests of the people. The overwhelming vote in the April 2000 referendum to restrict the immunity of
Ukrainian MPs confirms our survey evidence.

Moreover, globalisation has eroded the concept of state sovereignty.
Membership of international organisations involves trading sovereignty
against other goals, and the countries of post-communist Europe in particular are keen to stress that they share a common European heritage.
They want to 'rejoin Europe' after the Cold War. Even if 'Asian values',
or 'African values' or 'Latin American values' justified corruption—
which in reality the evidence suggests they do not—post-communist
Europe cannot and does not claim the excuse of different values from
those in other parts of Europe. Post-communist Europe cannot simultaneously seek membership of international organisations and object to
international interference.

Table 9.13. Support for international pressure to combat corruption

	Average	Czech Republic	Slovakia	Bulgaria	Ukraine
	%	%	%	%	%
If an international organisa-tion refused to provide aid or investment for (your coun-try) unless the government took strong action against corruption, that would be...					
a good way to reduce cor-ruption	58(52)	57(45)	51(42)	69(61)	56(58)
unacceptable interference	28(36)	28(44)	36(49)	20(25)	27(28)
depends	14(12)	15(12)	13 (9)	11(14)	17(14)
good – unacceptable	+30(+16)	+29(+1)	+15(–7)	+49(+36)	+29(+30)

Notes: 'Don't know', 'mixed/depends' etc. answers were recorded if given spontaneously, but
never prompted; they have been excluded from the calculation of percentages.

Figures in brackets are based on the replies by officials.

The phrase ('your country') was replaced by the specific name of the country in which the interview took place.

By the late 1990s, international aid donors were increasingly focusing on corruption as a key 'obstacle to the encouragement of good government',[112] and good governance was itself defined to include 'low
levels of corruption and nepotism'.[113] 'Conditionality' was the new
fashion for membership of international organisations, and the 'condi-

tions' included action to reduce public-sector corruption. 'In too many cases', however, it was recognised that 'governments were the problem' and 'anti-corruption campaigns then degenerated into political rhetoric designed more to appease foreign donors and international financial institutions than to address the major issues'.[114]

So it was no longer a purely hypothetical question when we asked: 'Which comes closer to your view? If an international organisation refused to provide aid or investment for (our country) unless our government took strong action against corruption, would that be: (i) unacceptable interference in (our country's) internal affairs; or (ii) a good way to reduce corruption in (our country)?' Both the public and street-level officials gave majority support to the use of international pressure on their own country to reduce corruption. (Table 9.13)

The margin of support over opposition ran at 30 per cent amongst the public and at 16 per cent amongst street-level bureaucrats. Support was weakest amongst Czech and Slovak officials but it was particularly strong amongst street-level officials in Bulgaria and Ukraine. No doubt they would have reacted more adversely if international pressure were applied for other, less popular purposes. No doubt state sovereignty might still have its uses in the public imagination. But the defence of corrupt officials was not one of them.

WHY DO PEOPLE WITHIN THE SAME COUNTRY HAVE DIFFERENT VIEWS ABOUT REFORM?

Within any one country, public opinion about bureaucracy is likely to be founded on a specific and commonly shared experience of conditions in that particular country. Where officials are more corrupt, we might expect that public attitudes to reform would be different, even if the people themselves are no different from those elsewhere. There can be no doubt that the same team of assessors travelling from Ukraine to Bulgaria, Slovakia and the Czech Republic, would discover very different problems and might therefore propose very different solutions in different countries.

Conversely, everyone within a single country lives under the same political and bureaucratic system. So if opinions merely reflected the object of those opinions—in this case the bureaucratic system and its norms of behaviour—then all citizens in one country would take the same view of reform. Of course, we did not find unanimity anywhere. Random differences between individuals within a country are to be expected even if opinions are primarily determined by reactions to the same bureaucratic system. But if opinions are primarily determined by reactions to the same bureaucratic system they should not be *systematic* within-country differences.

Yet systematic within-country differences are possible. Within one country, different categories of people may view the same bureaucracy somewhat differently because they have different information about it, different aspirations for it, or different experience of it. When it comes to proposals for reform, the costs of different reforms (in higher taxes, for example) and the way in which these costs are likely to be distributed may be more in the interests of some categories of citizens than others.

THE WEAK IMPACT OF SOCIAL CHARACTERISTICS

Correlations between our menu of reform proposals or the detailed supplementary questions about reform on the one hand, and standard social background variables such as age, sex, education and size of settlement (from capital cities down to villages and rural areas) were almost uniformly weak. The explanation of differences in attitudes to reform within countries should not therefore be sought in terms of these broad, general-purpose sociological classifications. Instead, it should be sought more in terms of individuals' different perceptions, experience and perspectives on the bureaucracy itself.

THE IMPACT OF UNFAIR TREATMENT IN BUREAUCRATIC ENCOUNTERS

Within countries, personal experience of unfair treatment by officials shifted the public's priorities for reform. The greatest impact was on the priorities given to 'tighter control' and 'administrative efficiency'. (Table 9.14) Those who had frequently experienced unfair treatment were on average 7 per cent more likely to prioritise tighter controls and penalties and 7 per cent less likely to prioritise administrative efficiency reforms.

Table 9.14. The impact of unfair treatment on reform priorities

	Composite 4-country data-set	Average	Czech Republic	Slovakia	Bulgaria	Ukraine
	% amongst those who 'rarely or never' received fair treatment *minus* % amongst those who 'usually' received fair treatment					
	%	%	%	%	%	%
Single most effective reform:						
tighter control	+16 (–2)	+7(–4)	+11	+1	+7	+10
encourage officials	–4(+14)	–3(+6)	–1	+3	–9	–6
administrative efficiency	–15(–15)	–7(–6)	–17	–4	+2	–7
empower citizens	+3 (+2)	+3(+2)	+5	+1	+2	+2
openness and transparency	0 (0)	0(+2)	+2	0	–3	+1

Note: Ten-point menu compressed into five categories—as described in the text. Figures in brackets are based on the replies by officials.

THE SUPER-ADDITIVITY MODEL

There was some evidence of a super-additivity effect cross-nationally. In a composite four-country data set, the impact of ill-treatment appears more than twice as strong as the average of within-country impacts. This super-additivity effect is best illustrated in Figures 9.6a and 9.6b. Figure 9.6a shows the levels of priority given to 'stricter control' and Figure 9.6b the levels of priority given to 'administrative efficiency' reforms.

For simplicity, these figures are restricted to the two extreme cases of Ukraine and the Czech Republic. Within both countries, unfair treatment increases the priority given to 'stricter control' and decreases the priority given to 'administrative efficiency'. But, in addition, all citizens in the Czech Republic—whatever their personal treatment by officials— are more likely than Ukrainians to prioritise 'administrative efficiency' and less likely to prioritise 'stricter control'. What creates the super-additivity effect is that Czechs were treated fairly by officials far more often than Ukrainians. So in any analysis of the composite data set formed by merging the Czech and Ukraine surveys, the reform priorities of those who usually received fair treatment reflected the priorities of the many well-treated Czechs much more than the priorities of the relatively few well-treated Ukrainians. Conversely, the reform priorities of those who seldom received fair treatment reflected the priorities of the many badly treated Ukrainians much more than the priorities of the

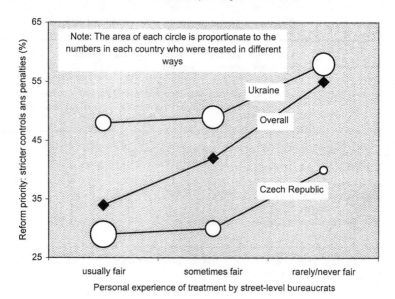

Fig. 9.6a. The impact of unfair treatment on the priority given to 'stricter control'

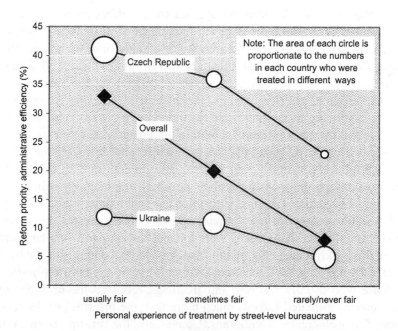

Fig. 9.6b. The impact of unfair treatment on the priority given to 'administrative efficiency'

relatively few badly treated Czechs. (In Fig. 9.6a and Fig. 9.6b the numbers of Czechs and Ukrainians who were treated well or badly are indicated by the size of the circles.)

Thus the trend line indicating the impact of unfair treatment in the composite data set not only reflects the trends within countries but also moves from close to the Czech line on the left of the figure to a position close to the Ukrainian line on the right of the figure. That makes the line based on the composite data set about twice as steep as the trend line within either country.

Such super-additivities are never mere technicalities or statistical quirks. Powerful super-additivities indicate some kind of social, psychological or political interaction processes at work. Either individuals are directly sensitive (through observation) to the problems faced by other citizens in their locality or they absorb (perhaps through conversation) the attitudes of other local citizens which in turn are affected by the problems faced by these other citizens.[115] In this way individuals develop attitudes that reflect not just their own problems but the *typical problems* faced by their fellow-citizens.

In this present case, it seems that where unfair treatment is the norm, even those individuals who have received fair treatment adopt reform priorities that to some extent reflect a reaction against unfair treatment. Conversely, where unfair treatment is the exception, even those individuals who have had the misfortune to suffer unfair treatment still have reform priorities that reflect, to some degree, the general experience of fair treatment.

THE IMPACT OF DECLINING LIVING STANDARDS

Personal experience of adverse economic trends during a mismanaged transition might be expected to make the public reluctant to 'encourage officials', even street-level officials, by means of higher salaries. In fact, however, the greatest impact of declining living standards on public attitudes to reform was to increase the priority they put on 'stricter controls and penalties'. (Table 9.15) Amongst the public, personal experience of declining living standards increased the priority put on 'stricter controls' by 11 per cent. Amongst officials, by contrast, personal experience of declining living standards decreased the priority they put on 'stricter controls' (and increased the priority they put on increased salaries for officials).

Table 9.15. Impact of declining living standards on reform priorities

	Composite 4-country data–set	Average	Czech Republic	Slovakia	Bulgaria	Ukraine
	% amongst those whose living standards had got 'much worse' *minus* % amongst those whose living standards had got 'better'					
	%	%	%	%	%	%
Single most effective reform:						
tighter control	+20 (–1)	+11(–6)	+17	+4	+12	+11
encourage officials	–5(+22)	–6(+6)	–4	–1	–14	–4
administrative efficiency	–17(–21)	–6(–5)	–13	–5	–3	–4
empower citizens	+1 (–1)	0(+1)	+2	+2	+2	–8
openness and transparency	+1 (+1)	+1(+4)	–2	+1	+2	+5

Note: Ten-point menu compressed into five categories—as described in the text. Figures in brackets are based on the replies by officials.

Once again there is evidence of super-additivity effects since Ukrainians had suffered the worst decline in living standards and Ukrainians also tended to support 'stricter controls' more than others. So within a four-country merged data set the apparent impact of declining living standards would be to increase the public's prioritisation of 'stricter controls' and officials' prioritisation of higher salaries by over 20 per cent.

THE IMPACT OF PERSPECTIVES ON CORRUPTION

Perspectives on corruption might be expected to influence attitudes towards reform in a number of different ways. Perceptions that officials were motivated by greed or that they were more corrupt than officials in other countries might increase the priority put on 'stricter controls and penalties'. But on the other hand, the public's own willingness to give or take bribes should rationally reduce support for controls and penalties.

In fact, perceptions that officials were more corrupt than local businessmen or than officials in other East European countries increased the priority the public put on 'stricter controls and penalties' by an average of around 12 per cent. But perceptions that bribery was motivated by 'greed' rather than 'poor pay' had even more impact on attitudes to reform. It increased the priority the public put on 'tighter control' by an average of 22 per cent and decreased the priority given to increasing salaries by 30 per cent. (Amongst officials themselves the impact of such perceptions was similar, though somewhat smaller.) There was clearly a strong moral dimension to reform priorities. (Table 9.16)

Table 9.16. The impact of perceptions of the cause of bribery on reform priorities

	Average	Czech Republic	Slovakia	Bulgaria	Ukraine
	% amongst those who attribute bribe taking to 'greedy officials' *minus* % amongst those who attribute bribe taking to 'poor pay'				
	%	%	%	%	%
Single most effective reform:					
tighter control	+22(+12)	+24	+21	+23	+18
encourage officials	−30(−21)	−39	−33	−25	−21
administrative efficiency	+3 (+3)	+7	+11	−3	−4
empower citizens	+4 (+8)	+6	+2	+2	+5
openness and transparency	+1 (−2)	+2	−1	+3	+2

Note: Ten-point menu compressed into five categories—as described in the text. Figures in brackets are based on the replies by officials.

An unwillingness to give or take bribes also correlated with public attitudes towards stricter penalties for clients. Compared to those who would pay a bribe if asked, those who would refuse to pay were 15 per cent more likely to say that bribe givers should be punished as severely as bribe takers. The public's unwillingness to take bribes had less impact (only 12 per cent). So reform attitudes amongst the public were more dependent upon their unwillingness 'to give' than 'to take'.

By contrast, reform attitudes amongst street-level officials were more dependent upon their unwillingness 'to take' (17 per cent) than 'to give' (11 per cent).

THE IMPACT OF GENERAL POLITICAL ORIENTATIONS

General political orientations might also be an important factor in determining attitudes to some specific reforms.

Using support for 'a strong leader with a free hand' as a general indicator of *authoritarian tendencies* there was no significant correlation between authoritarian tendencies and reform priorities for 'controls and penalties'.

But *socialist values* had a significant impact on attitudes to user charges in health care. Socialist values, as indicated by support for state control of health care, large-scale industry or farming, did not in fact correlate with opposition to raising the salaries of officials as such. But they did correlate with public opposition to raising health-service salaries by means of imposing user charges. Socialists were only 4 per cent less likely to prioritise better salaries for officials, but 23 per cent less likely to support raising health-service salaries by imposing user charges. Amongst officials themselves, socialist values had a similar but smaller effect (16 per cent).

We used voting preferences for a nationalist-oriented party as an indicator of *nationalist values*. In addition to specific questions about voting choice, which inevitably varied in content from country to country, we also asked a more general and internationally applicable question about voting orientations: 'If there were a parliamentary election held this week, what kind of party would you most prefer to vote for—a communist party; a socialist party; the party most strongly committed to the market economy; a (country name) nationalist party; a party representing minority nationalities within (country name); [in Ukraine only] a party representing ethnic Russians within Ukraine; a Green party; another kind of party; or none?' In this question '(country)' was replaced by the specific name of the country where the interview took place. The option of an 'ethnic Russian' party was offered explicitly in Ukraine because of the ambiguous status of Russians in Ukraine.

Those who preferred a 'country' or 'state' nationalist party (e.g. Slovak nationalist in Slovakia, Bulgarian nationalist in Bulgaria) were around 15 per cent more resistant to international pressure than those with no party preference. Conversely, those who preferred an 'ethnic minority' party of any kind were 13 per cent less resistant to international pressure than those with no party preference—and thus 28 per cent less resistant to international pressure than 'state' nationalists. (Table 9.17)

On average, communist, socialist and market-oriented voters did not differ much from those who had no party preference in terms of their resistance to international pressure. But their stance varied from country to country. In the winter of 1997–98, socialist- or communist-oriented voters were:

- more opposed to international pressure than market-oriented voters in Slovakia and Bulgaria;
- very similar to market-oriented voters in Ukraine; but
- less opposed to international pressure than market-oriented voters in the Czech Republic.

Table 9.17. The impact of nationalism on resistance to international pressure

| | International pressure is unacceptable interference | | | | |
| | Average | Czech Republic | Slovakia | Bulgaria | Ukraine |
	%	%	%	%	%
Views expressed by those who would prefer to vote for...					
a (country) nationalist party	45(55)	na	57	40	39
a communist or socialist party	34(45)	24	39	37	36
no party preference	31(39)	38	39	17	30
the party most committed to the market economy	29(38)	36	27	18	33
a party representing minority nationalities	18(na)	na	29	18	8

Notes: '(country)' was replaced by the specific name of the country in which the interview took place, i.e. 'Czech nationalist' in the Czech Republic etc.

'Don't know', 'mixed/depends' etc. answers were recorded if given spontaneously, but never prompted; they have been excluded from the calculation of percentages.

Based on the augmented samples of the public including the extra interviews in ethnic minority areas in order to have sufficient respondents with preferences for ethnic minority parties. na = less than 20 respondents.

Figures in brackets are based on the combined sample of officials (not, in this table, the average of within-country samples which were too small for party breakdowns).

That probably reflected the particular and transient links between various ideologically oriented voters and their governments. International pressure to cut corruption had been applied to Klaus's market-oriented regime in the Czech Republic, to Mečiar's regime in Slovakia, which combined communist and 'state' nationalist tendencies, and to the recently defeated socialist regime in Bulgaria.

DIAGNOSIS AND PRESCRIPTION

One general explanation for variations in reform priorities is that prescriptions for reform reflected perceptions of the illness.

The public attributed bribery mainly to the greed of officials, while officials attributed it mainly to their poor pay. The varying pattern of their attitudes to reform reflects that diagnosis. 'Stricter controls and penalties for officials' was the public's top priority; 'higher salaries' was the top priority amongst street-level officials.

Cross-nationally, the relationship between diagnosis and prescription is clearest if we contrast public opinion in the Czech Republic with that in Ukraine. The Czech public complained of bureaucratic inefficiency and emphasised administrative-efficiency reforms such as fewer official forms and more technical training for officials. Czechs were 31 per cent more likely than Ukrainians to complain about the increasing number of bureaucratic forms and certificates since the fall of communism, and consequently 20 per cent more likely to describe 'fewer official forms and documents' as a 'very effective reform' (and six times as likely as Ukrainians to choose it as the 'single most effective' reform).

By contrast, the public in Ukraine had stronger criticisms to make about their officials. They had widespread experience of giving, or 'having to give', bribes—though, by their own account, they are far more willing to give and far more tempted to take bribes than people in the other countries we investigated. That made the public in Ukraine peculiarly indulgent to bribe givers but peculiarly antagonistic towards bribe takers.

The Bulgarian public attributed bribery mainly to the inadequate salaries of their officials. Consequently, Bulgarian priorities for reform put a unique emphasis on higher salaries and gave less emphasis to administrative efficiency reforms than in Slovakia or the Czech Republic and also less emphasis to stricter penalties than in Ukraine.

Cross-nationally, a simple relationship between diagnosis and prescription is least evident in the case of Slovakia. Some elements of Slovak experience differed sharply from Czech experience but reform priorities were surprisingly similar. The Slovak emphasis on administrative reforms fits well with our finding that very few Czechs or Slovaks complained that corrupt officials caused their most frequent or most annoying problems with the bureaucracy. The similarity between Czech and Slovak attitudes to reform fits well with the fact that very few in either country reported that officials had 'asked directly' for a gift. But it does not fit so well with the fact that far more in Slovakia had felt that an official 'expected something', and rather more felt that officials had caused 'unnecessary problems' in order to get a gift. However it is significant that both Czechs and Slovaks attributed bribery mainly to importunate clients rather than to the greedy or poorly paid officials. Slovaks themselves admitted to a much greater willingness to pay a bribe 'if asked'. Moreover, although Slovaks were somewhat more likely than Czechs to perceive that their officials were corrupt, they were far less likely to do so than Bulgarians or Ukrainians. So although the relationship is more complex in Slovakia than in the Czech Republic, some connection between diagnosis and prescription is visible.

Nonetheless, there may be an additional tendency for Slovak views on reform to reflect a subconscious feeling that their problems are 'really' not much worse than those in the Czech Republic and susceptible to similar solutions—even though their actual experience and behaviour is not so similar. It would be an exaggeration, but with an element of truth in it, to say that Slovaks 'thought like Czechs and behaved like Ukrainians'.

ANALYTIC PERSPECTIVES: FOCUSING REFORMS ON SITUATIONS RATHER THAN PARTICIPANTS

We have argued that it is useful to test experts' proposals for reform against the opinions of the public and street-level bureaucrats. Reforms that 'go with the grain' of public opinion are likely to be easier to implement and likely to be more effective. Reforms that 'go against the grain' of public opinion or provoke deep resentment amongst street-level bureaucrats are likely to be less easy to implement and less effective in practice as large numbers of citizens or street-level bureaucrats try to circumvent them.

But proposals for reform should also be tested against some of the analytic findings that have emerged from our study, findings that do not correspond to simple and overt questions of public support.

In bribery 'it takes two to tango'. If either official or client refuses to join in, the dance is over. But our own analytic findings highlight the corruptibility of both citizens and officials in the face of extortion or temptation. Not every citizen who was 'asked directly' by an official for a gift actually gave one, and not every official who was offered a gift by a client actually accepted it. Nonetheless, our analysis reveals the powerful impact of requests and offers. Direct requests increased the rate of clients' giving money or an expensive present by 28 per cent, and their rate of giving small presents by 37 per cent. On the other side, we found that frequent offers from clients increased the rate of officials' accepting money or an expensive present by 22 per cent, and their rate of accepting small presents by 41 per cent. Requests and offers were only part of the story, but a very significant one.

Moreover, we found high rates of accepting large gifts amongst hospital doctors (but not amongst nurses), amongst traffic police (but not amongst other police), and amongst customs officials (but not amongst passport officials). That seemed to reflect the bargaining power and opportunities of certain specific occupations.

The implication for reform is that specific bargaining relationships encourage clients to make explicit offers and encourage officials to make explicit requests, and both offers and requests have a powerful impact—an impact that is over and above the moral stance or economic circumstances of the individuals involved. Umit Berkman lists the nature and setting of 'the corrupt act' as one of the 'major factors' in his 'conceptual framework' for 'bureaucracy and bribery'[116] and our analysis confirms his insight. However upright and however poor they may be, citizens find it difficult to resist extortion; and however upright and however well-paid they may be, officials find it difficult to resist temptation.

This implies a need to give special attention to situations as distinct from the participants. It is not so much a matter of devising new reforms, radically different from the ones we have already discussed, as *focusing those reforms on situations* where they would have the most effect. These are situations in which the client has an unusual amount at stake, and where the interaction between client and official is unusually private or monopolistic and where, in consequence, the client is particularly at the mercy of the official.

That leads us to put more weight than either the public or street-level officials themselves on opening up the interactions between officials and their clients. Rather than prioritising stricter controls and penalties (as do the public) or higher salaries (as do officials)—which might reduce tendencies towards extortion and temptation generally—our emergent analytic findings point to the importance of reducing the situations in which those tendencies are likely to be translated into action.

That means providing clients with alternative access points and better appeal procedures. It means more clearly and publicly set out rights for clients on the one hand, and more clearly and publicly set out user charges, tariffs or 'price lists' on the other. It also implies a more public setting for client–official interactions. All of these are designed to *stiffen clients' resistance* to extortion and to *reduce their incentive* to offer gifts. In that sense, all 'go with the grain' of public opinion. Large numbers of the public (and street-level officials) describe such measures as 'very effective' and few describe them as 'unnecessary or harmful'. But few pick them as their top priority because they underestimate the impact of situation or circumstance on action, and overestimate the impact of personal background and values. We are all corruptible.

It is undoubtedly difficult to open up activities that typically take place in closed settings. In the American context, Lipsky lamented the fact that interaction between office bureaucrats and clients usually took place in private offices under norms of confidentiality. Teaching was done in classrooms that principals and supervisors did not normally enter without giving warning. Only a suspect, or a partner who would usually shield them from criticism, normally observed police officers.[117] Judges were amongst the few officials in Lipsky's study that tended to operate in public.

But although Lipsky was concerned about competence and fairness, he did not identify corruption as a major concern. Where corruption is a problem, the problem of openness is even greater. There are incentives to hide the specifically corrupt part of the transaction (the giving and receiving of bribes) even though the rest of the interaction takes place in a more public setting. That is especially true where a bribe has been given only to secure fair treatment for the client (as was so often the case in post-communist Europe) and the treatment itself can therefore be given quite openly.

Let us take the three occupations highlighted by our analysis of the confessions made by street-level bureaucrats: hospital doctors, traffic police and customs officials. Our focus-group discussions revealed the extent to which patients gave money or expensive gifts to doctors out of fear rather than gratitude, and to traffic police or customs officials out of impotence rather than gratitude. More openness, more awareness of rights, and better appeals and complaints procedures would all help clients deal with such officials. More top-down control, for example through professional monitoring of doctors' performance (now a well-publicised issue in the British National Health Service under the title of 'clinical governance'), would also help.

Of course, that would help in other less vital situations also. But the need for reform is particularly acute in such situations. Wherever the client can 'come back another day', 'try another official' or 'wait for an appeal to be considered' they are in a relatively strong position. When they cannot, they are at the mercy of the official and it is on these situations that reform (of any kind) should be focused.

If customs officials and traffic police cannot be reformed their numbers can be reduced or they can be abolished. That option is hardly available in the case of hospital doctors, but it is a serious possibility for customs officials and traffic police. A recent CEPS (Centre for European Policy Studies) *Shadow Green Paper* on the enlargement of the European Union into Eastern Europe urges 'a clean break from the present use of customs posts as instruments of state corruption' by creating a 'zero-tariff free trade zone' extending into Eastern Europe.[118] George

Soros has taken the view that a Customs Union should be the foundation of a Stability Pact for South-Eastern Europe because 'first of all it will eliminate corruption and the interference in trade which Customs produce'.[119]

It is worth asking whether traffic police in Central and Eastern Europe serve any useful purpose. Or rather, whether their usefulness actually exceeds the trouble they cause. Far fewer traffic police and rather more speed cameras might produce more revenue for the state as well as both tighter and fairer control of traffic.

No one would suggest that hospital doctors be abolished or even that numbers be reduced. But if they cannot be reformed they might at least be regularised. If health-service users have to pay, then what they pay can be formalised so that the patients who pay most are those that get the most expensive treatment or those who have the greatest ability to pay, rather than those who are treated by the most grasping and unscrupulous doctors. 'If there were some price lists showing how much everything costs then I would go to a doctor and receive a receipt. Having a receipt I could demand something. But the way we pay now...you do not know to whom you give the money and for what.'(Sh 6) Once users have paid an official charge they may be considerably more reluctant to pay an unofficial one (though we recognise that this may not always be so). Privatisation and user charges may be repulsive to those with socialist ideals but they may still be better than the corrupt alternative—a 'second-best' rather than a 'third-best'. They can be so constructed as to mitigate their worst features. It is significant that we found public support for user charges to be greatest in the poorest countries and the ones with the longest socialist traditions.

Our analytic conclusions about whether the public were victims of extortion or agents of corruption are also important for any consideration of reform proposals. The findings suggest that people who give bribes to officials in the Czech Republic and, to a lesser extent, in Slovakia, are not victims but accomplices or worse. Reforms in those countries might therefore aim as much at bribe givers as bribe takers. In principle, it may be more difficult to reform the people than to reform the administration, but the task is easier in countries where the public explicitly blame bribe givers more often than bribe takers. Indeed, when the public were asked explicitly we found that the numbers who thought bribe givers should be punished as severely as bribe takers ranged from a mere 20 per cent in Ukraine up to 42 per cent in Slovakia and 47 per cent in the Czech Republic. Moreover, in the Czech Republic the task would be made easier by the relatively low incidence of bribery in day-to-day dealings with street-level bureaucrats. So the target in the Czech Republic would not be the people as a whole, but a deviant minority. It would be made easier in both the Czech and Slovak Republics by the greater possibility we found in these countries of making bribe givers feel 'ashamed' of their conduct.

In Bulgaria, and more especially in Ukraine, however, the public were less inclined to place the burden of guilt on clients. In their own view, the people of Ukraine were the passive and guiltless victims of rapacious officials. In consequence, reforms targeted at bribe givers in Bulgaria and more especially in Ukraine might only make people feel that they were the 'victims twice over', victims of the street-level bureaucrats who extorted bribes from them and then victims of other officials who punished them for their submission to extortion.

Anti-corruption campaigns that focus on propaganda rather than structural reform have a poor record of success.[120] But insofar as anti-corruption campaigns do use publicity and propaganda in an attempt to change public attitudes, our analytic findings suggest that it would be a waste of time to focus on persuading the public to condemn the use of contacts, presents and bribes as a means of influencing officials. In principle, they already condemn such practices in every country. The problem is that many citizens, especially in Ukraine, submit so readily to extortion. Ukrainians were uniquely submissive. They experienced extortion twice as frequently as in the Czech Republic and, when they did experience it, extortion was three times as effective as in the Czech Republic. The public needs to be convinced, not that bribery is *wrong* (which they recognise already), but that bribery is *unnecessary* and that extortion *can be resisted* successfully.

So anti-corruption campaigns should avoid conveying the message that corruption is an overwhelming problem (which merely encourages submission to extortion) and focus instead on the possibilities of resistance—on ways of achieving citizens' legal objectives without submission to extortion. That means focusing on the success of argument, persistence and appeal strategies rather than on the immorality of contacts, presents and bribes.

In more structural terms it means changing procedures to make it easier to 'come back another day', to 'try another official' or to 'wait for an appeal to be considered' rather than trying to shock and scandalise the public. That can be done, for example, by providing multiple access points, alternative officials, citizens' advice bureaux and ombudsmen to

ensure speedy consideration of appeals. It means reform strategies that
focus more on empowerment than on moralising.

COULD 'GLORIOUS SUMMER' FOLLOW THE 'WINTER OF DISCONTENT'?

We began this chapter by quoting the first line of Shakespeare's Richard
III: 'Now is the winter of our discontent.' It is a popular English-
language description for a time of political troubles. It was applied, for
example, to the widespread industrial unrest in the winter of 1978–79
that led to the defeat of the British Labour government and the subsequent election of the 'Iron Lady', Margaret Thatcher.

But it is a misleading quotation, only half a sentence. The full sentence reads: 'Now is the winter of our discontent made glorious summer
by this sun of York.' In fact, Shakespeare's 'now' refers to the 'glorious
summer', not to the 'winter of discontent', and it underlines the distinction between a permanent culture or climate and a transient season.

It is easy to be pessimistic about bureaucratic behaviour in post-
communist Europe. In true mafia style, the future Richard III felt that he
could prosper better in a 'winter of discontent' than in a 'glorious summer' of contentment. Reform is not in everyone's interest. Even if reform is possible, it is unlikely to be achieved without a struggle. Even if
an immutable culture and the 'dead hand of history' do not make reform
impossible, powerful present-day interests may do so.

Against the background of the economic and moral chaos in the early
stages of the transition, Verheijen and Dimitrova concluded that there
may be few fast-working remedies on offer. 'The problem of changing
state institutions simultaneously with redefining statehood and implementing austere economic restructuring programmes based on strict financial discipline may be simply *too much to solve.*'[121]

But the public do not agree. Although few think that ordinary citizens will ever prove to be the main beneficiaries of the transition, the
overwhelming majority of the public think it would at least be possible
to cut corruption amongst street-level bureaucrats and improve the relationship between citizens and officials. Only a minority of the public in
post-communist Europe believe that current levels of corruption are 'a
permanent part of their culture'. A large majority believe in the possibility of reform, though they criticise their governments for not making
'a strong and sincere effort' to achieve it. They do believe that a

'glorious summer' of fair treatment by street-level bureaucrats is possible, even if they know that it is uncertain and fear that it is unlikely.

But who might fulfil the role of Shakespeare's 'sun of York'? The public is rightly sceptical about long-term office holders. The public emphasises the importance of a better example at the top, and street-level officials put even more emphasis on that than do the public. But that remedy is difficult to achieve. Can those who have set a bad example at the top ever be expected to set a good one? As Lord Acton famously remarked (with regard to papal domination within his beloved church) 'power tends to corrupt'.[122] A lengthening tenure of power is more likely to increase corruption at the top than to reduce it. A 'reformed tsar' is an unlikely saviour.

Democratic elections provide one possibility for renewal—but not if they simply re-elect incumbents or their anointed heirs as they have done, so far, in Russia. An electorally victorious opposition, untainted by power and swept into office on an anti-corruption platform, might provide an opportunity for reform. But not if that platform is merely a cynical electoral strategy, and not if the former opposition has already been compromised by accepting a share of the spoils even when in opposition—under some kind of formal or informal '*proporz*' system on the classic Austrian model.[123]

The alternative is pressure—the pressure of internal public opinion implying a threat either of future electoral defeats or simply of 'ungovernability'; the pressure of international business unwilling to invest in unusually corrupt locations; and the pressure of international political organisations with their own notions of 'good governance'.

The impact of electoral pressure can easily be overestimated. It depends upon whether citizens are willing to vote against corrupt politicians. That, in turn, depends upon whether voters feel that they have any alternative. Overall, we found that 70 per cent of the public claimed that corruption would influence their votes at least to some extent, and 35 per cent said that it would influence their votes 'a great deal'. Yet the issue of corruption seemed to have least influence over votes in Ukraine where public criticisms of politicians and bureaucrats were most severe. Relatively unstructured politics and pervasive high-level corruption can prevent the issue of corruption having a real impact on electoral politics. It may encourage abstention in elections. It can affect votes in a referendum such as the recent Ukrainian referendum on restricting the immunity of parliamentary deputies. But it cannot form the basis of electoral choice until there are trusted and visibly non-corrupt political options available. Without such options, the major component of internal pressure must be the threat of ungovernability rather than the threat of electoral defeat. By definition, corruption always degrades democracy, but democracy does not necessarily erode corruption.

The weakness of internal electoral pressure increases the significance of external pressure. Governments enjoy less sovereignty than they did. Moreover, our findings show that the public would not back their own governments if they did claim full sovereignty. None of the four publics that we surveyed dismissed international pressure on their government to cut corruption as 'unacceptable interference' in their country's internal affairs. They might resent or resist external pressure if it were applied for other purposes but they welcome external pressure, rather than resent it, when it is applied to cut corruption. Only the nationalist party supporters within Slovakia seemed particularly sensitive to the indignity of international pressure when applied to cut corruption.

We can usefully compare our four countries with Russia. If Russia had been one of the countries in our study its public opinion would probably have looked quite similar to that which we found in Ukraine. (Indeed, one reason for excluding Russia from this study was that our previous study of democratic values found so much similarity between Russian and Ukrainian public opinion.) In particular, public support for reform would no doubt have been strong.

But what are the chances of it happening? Russia is too big and its government is too proud to respond positively to external pressure, its electoral politics are relatively unstructured, and there is a dearth of trusted and visibly non-corrupt opposition politicians. Most important of all, Russia has no track record of an opposition victory at 'peak' level (i.e. presidential level in a presidential republic). That leaves only the possibility of a 'reformed tsar', the product (and possibly the prisoner) of the existing corrupt establishment.

By contrast, however, none of the countries in our survey is big enough to ignore external pressure. All of them have a track record of opposition victories in 'peak' elections during the post-communist period (parliamentary in Bulgaria and in the Czech and Slovak Republics, presidential in Ukraine). The Kostov government in Bulgaria and perhaps the new Dzurinda government in Slovakia come close to the prescription of a 'victorious opposition, untainted by power and swept into office on an anti-corruption platform'—however tainted by power they may later become. There is a realistic prospect of reform in these countries. Ukraine remains a more difficult case, but the referendum on reducing parliamentary deputies' immunity might be interpreted as a step in a similar direction. The 1998 opposition victory in the Czech Republic merely led to 'a kind of parliamentary coalition, albeit unusual and covert', but despite a Czech taste for malicious gossip, fuelled by clear evidence of high-level corruption, corruption amongst street-level officials was not a major problem for Czech citizens.

Despite Verheijen and Dimitrova's well-founded pessimism, the prospects for the reform of relations between street-level officials and their clients do not look quite so bleak in Slovakia, Bulgaria, and even Ukraine, when viewed against the contrast with Russia. In the Czech Republic the main task (at street level) is the more tractable problem of inefficiency rather than corruption. For these parts of post-communist Europe at least, current expert pessimism about the prospects for reform may be exaggerated. For these countries the summer may come, even if it is not quite 'glorious', and the sun may at least begin to thaw out the relations between citizens and street-level officials.

NOTES

1 Richard, Duke of Gloucester (afterwards Richard III) in Shakespeare's *Richard III* Act I, Scene 1, line 1.
2 Almond and Verba, *The Civic Culture*.
3 Katz, Gutek, Kahn and Barton, *Bureaucratic Encounters*.
4 Lipsky, *Street-Level Bureaucracy*.
5 Heidenheimer, *Political Corruption*; Heidenheimer, Johnston and LeVine, *Political Corruption: A Handbook*.
6 World Bank, *World Development Report 1997*, 102.
7 Langseth and Dubrow, *Ukraine National Integrity Systems*, 2.
8 Butler, Adonis and Travers, *Failure in British Government*.
9 de Speville, *Hong Kong: Policy Initiatives Against Corruption*.
10 Rose-Ackerman, *Corruption and Government*, 159.
11 Berkman, 'Bureaucracy and Bribery', 1359–60.
12 Smeltz and Sweeney, *On the Take*, 10.
13 *RFE/RL Newsline* 3, no. 171, part 1 (2 September 1999).
14 Ukrainian Radio (8 January 1997), quoted in *OMRI Daily Digest* 6, part 2 (9 January 1997).
15 Pylyp Orlyk Institute for Democracy, *Information Bulletin* (5 June 1998), quoted in *Corruption Watch* 1, no. 8 (24 June 1998).
16 *OMRI Daily Digest* 33, part 2 (17 February 1997).
17 *Corruption Watch* 1, no. 5 (13 May 1998).
18 Baker, 'Corruption among State Officials in Eastern Europe'. See also: Council of Europe, *Links between Corruption and Organised Crime*; Council of Europe, *Octo-*

pus Project: The Fight Against Corruption and Organised Crime in States in Transition.

19 *Corruption Watch* 1, no. 7 (10 June 1998).

20 *RFE/RL Newsline* 2, no. 108, part 2 (8 June 1998), quoting an interview with *Reuters* (5 June 1998).

21 'Czech PM Forced from Office by Campaign Funding Scandal', *Scotsman* (1 December 1997): 9.

22 *RFE/RL Newsline* 2, no. 97, part 2 (22 May 1998).

23 *Clean Future* (Coalition 2000's newsletter) 2 (Spring 1999) accessible via *www.online.bg/coalition2000.*

24 'Filchev Imitates Clean Hands', *Kapital* (22 May 1999), quoted in Coalition 2000's *Weekly Review of Bulgarian Press Coverage of Corruption* (22–28 May 1999).

25 *Kremenchuk Information Bulletin* no. 32 (7 August 1998), quoted in *Corruption Watch* 1, no. 12 (19 August 1998).

26 *Uriadovyi Kurrier* (18 February 1997), quoted in *Corruption Watch* 1, no. 13 (2 September 1998).

27 Goble, 'The corruption of power'.

28 Kuzio, *Ukraine under Kuchma*, 49.

29 *Gorod* (11 February 1999), quoted in *Corruption Watch* 2, no. 4(25) (17 Febrary 1999).

30 Verheijen and Dimitrova, 'Corruption and Unethical Behaviour', 234.

31 Crampton, 'The Bulgarian Elections', 562–3.

32 Marada, 'The 1998 Czech Elections', 56.

33 Pope, 'Elements of a Successful Anti-corruption Programme'; World Bank, *World Development Report 1997*, Chapter 6: 'Restraining Arbitrary State Action and Corruption', especially at 104–108.

34 Verebélyi, 'Hungary Proposes Strategic Plan to Reform the Public Administration', 3.

35 SIGMA/OECD, *Bureaucratic Barriers to Entry*, 15.

36 Tanzi, 'Corruption around the World', 574.

37 Hopkinson and Freibert, 'Law Drafting in Central and Eastern Europe', 11.

38 Rose-Ackerman, *Corruption and Government*, 6.

39 Anechiarico and Jacobs, *The Pursuit of Absolute Integrity*, 193.

40 Rose-Ackerman, *Corruption and Government*, 52–59.

41 Rose-Ackerman, *Corruption and Government*, 68.

42 Rose-Ackerman, *Corruption and Government*, 53; Hepkema and Booysen, 'Bribery of Public Officials'.

43 Krawchenko, *Administrative Reform in Ukraine*, 17–18.

44 Van Rijckeghem and Weder, 'Corruption and the Rate of Temptation', 31.

45 Van Rijckeghem and Weder, 'Corruption and the Rate of Temptation', 41.

46 Besley and McLaren, 'Taxes and Bribery', 119–41.

47 Rose-Ackerman, *Corruption and Government*, 74.

48 SIGMA/OECD, *Bureaucratic Barriers to Entry*, 14.

49 Verheijen and Dimitrova, 'Corruption and Unethical Behaviour', 240.

50 Popov, 'Law Drafting in Bulgaria', 6.

51 Verebélyi, 'Hungary Proposes Strategic Plan to Reform the Public Administration' 3.

52 Kandeva, 'Corruption in Transitional Public Service', 204.

53 Kandeva, 'Corruption in Transitional Public Service', 205.
54 Rose-Ackerman, *Corruption and Government*, 82.
55 UNDP, *Corruption and Good Governance*, 71–2.
56 Krawchenko, *Administrative Reform in Ukraine*, 8–12.
57 Kandeva, 'Corruption in Transitional Public Service', 204.
58 SIGMA/OECD, *Bureaucratic Barriers to Entry*, 8.
59 Mauro, 'Corruption and Growth', 685.
60 O'Toole, 'The Concept of Public Duty', 91.
61 Gole, *The Role of Civil Society in Containing Corruption*, 7.
62 SIGMA/OECD, *Bureaucratic Barriers to Entry*; Verheijen and Dimitrova, 'Corruption and Unethical Behaviour'.
63 SIGMA/OECD, *Bureaucratic Barriers to Entry*, 17.
64 SIGMA/OECD, *Bureaucratic Barriers to Entry*, 16.
65 Verheijen and Dimitrova, 'Corruption and Unethical Behaviour', 236.
66 SIGMA/OECD, *Bureaucratic Barriers to Entry*, 18.
67 *OMRI Report* (26 March 1997).
68 SIGMA/OECD, *Public Management Profiles*, 42, 61 and 225.
69 *CSD Monitor* issue 5 (Sofia: Centre for the Study of Democracy, 1999): 18.
70 Varese, 'Pervasive Corruption'.
71 Johnston, 'Fighting Systematic Corruption', 85–86, 87 and 91.
72 Illner, 'Workshop on the Decentralisation of Governance'.
73 Rose-Ackerman, *Corruption and Government*, 162.
74 Verheijen and Dimitrova, 'Corruption and Unethical Behaviour', 243.
75 Gole, *The Role of Civil Society in Containing Corruption*, 7–14.
76 Coalition 2000, *Clean Future (Newsletter)*.
77 Ukraine National Coalition for Integrity, *Newsletter*.
78 *Corruption Watch* 2, no.19(31) (12 May 1999).
79 OECD, *Ethics in the Public Service*, 6; see also: OECD, *Public Sector Corruption*.
80 Huang and Wu, 'More Order Without More Law', 393; Klitgaard, *Controlling Corruption*.
81 Kudrycha, *The Ethical Codes of Polish Public Officials*, 20.
82 Kandeva, 'Corruption in Transitional Public Service', 205.
83 Verheijen and Dimitrova, 'Corruption and Unethical Behaviour', 241.
84 Pope and Mohn, *The Fight Against Corruption*, Chapter 4: 'The Islands of Integrity Concept and the TI Integrity Pact', 55–8.
85 Illner, 'Workshop on the Decentralisation of Governance', 11.
86 Rose-Ackerman, *Corruption and Government*, 49.
87 Verheijen and Dimitrova, 'Corruption and Unethical Behaviour', 243.
88 Rose-Ackerman, *Corruption and Government*, 171.
89 Rose-Ackerman, *Corruption and Government*, 171.
90 de Speville, *Hong Kong: Policy Initiatives Against Corruption*, 29.
91 Rose-Ackerman, *Corruption and Government*, 39.
92 Kaufmann, 'The Missing Pillar of a Growth Strategy for Ukraine'.
93 SIGMA/OECD, *Bureaucratic Barriers to Entry*, 14.
94 *RFE/RL Newsline* 3, no. 182, part 2 (17 September 1999).
95 Rose-Ackerman, *Corruption and Government*, 47.

96 Rose-Ackerman, *Corruption and Government*, 151; UNDP, *Corruption and Good Governance*, 62.

97 OECD, *Public Sector Corruption*, 21.

98 OECD, *Public Sector Corruption*, 22.

99 Verheijen and Dimitrova, 'Corruption and Unethical Behaviour'; Kandeva, 'Corruption in Transitional Public Service'.

100 Eigen, 'Combating Corruption Around the World', 162.

101 Johnson and Kraft, 'Bureaucratic Whistleblowing', 869.

102 *OMRI Report* (4 April 1997); *OMRI Report* (7 April 1997).

103 Illner, 'The Changing Quality of Life', 148.

104 Lawson and Nemec, 'Central European Health Reform', 244; Lawson and Nemec, 'Health Care Reform'; Maly, 'Current Problems and a Possible Future'.

105 Eigen, 'Combating Corruption Around the World', 160.

106 Klich, 'Bribery in Economies in Transition'.

107 Hotchkiss, 'The Sleeping Dog Stirs', 111.

108 Transparency International, *Newsletter* (March 1997).

109 Ayittey, *Africa Betrayed*, quoted in Rose-Ackerman, *Corruption and Government*, 177; Cooksey, 'Address to the Rotary Club of Dar es Salaam'; Geddes, *Politician's Dilemma*; Pasuk and Sungsidh, *Corruption and Democracy in Thailand*.

110 Rose-Ackerman, *Corruption and Government*, 177.

111 Krastev, 'Dancing with Anticorruption', 57.

112 Doig, 'Good Government and Sustainable Anti-corruption Strategies', 151.

113 British Council, *Development Priorities: Good Government*.

114 Williams, *Political Corruption in Africa*, 125.

115 Miller, 'Social Class and Party Choice in England'; MacAllister, Johnston, Pattie, Tunstall, Dorling and Rossiter, 'Class Dealignment and the Neighbourhood Effect'.

116 Berkman, 'Bureaucracy and Bribery', 1347.

117 Lipsky, *Street-Level Bureaucracy*, 169.

118 CEPS, *A System for Post-War South-East Europe*, 7.

119 *Kapital* weekly (18–24 September 1999), quoted in *Weekly Review of Bulgarian Press Coverage of Corruption* (18–24 September 1999).

120 White, *Russia Goes Dry*.

121 Verheijen and Dimitrova, 'Corruption and Unethical Behaviour', 233.

122 Trevor-Roper, 'Introduction', 11–13.

123 Lehmbruch, *Proporzdemokratie ('Proportional democracy')*.

BIBLIOGRAPHY

With few exceptions, citations of articles in the press or on electronic newsletters are not listed individually in this bibliography. The newsletters (mainly electronic) regularly cited in the notes include:

Corruption Watch, Kyiv, accessible via kam@political.kiev.ua.

RFE/RL Newsline (and *OMRI Daily Digest*), accessible via www.rferl.org/newsline/search/

USIA Opinion Analysis (Washington: United States Information Agency)

Weekly Review of Bulgarian Press Coverage of Corruption, Sofia, accessible via www.online.bg/coalition2000.

Ades, Alberto and Rafael Di Tella. 'The New Economics of Corruption.' *Political Studies* 45, no. 3 (1997): 496–515.

Almond, Gabriel A. and Sidney Verba. *The Civic Culture: Political Attitudes and Democracy in Five Nations*. Princeton, N.J.: Princeton University Press, 1963. (Reprinted, London: Sage, 1989.)

Anechiarico, Frank and James B. Jacobs. *The Pursuit of Absolute Integrity: How Corruption Control Makes Government Ineffective*. Chicago: University of Chicago Press, 1996.

Ayittey, George B. N. *Africa Betrayed*. New York: St Martin's Press, 1992.

Ayres, Ian. 'Judicial Corruption: Extortion and Bribery.' *Denver University Law Review* 74 (1997): 1231–53.

Bac, Mehmet. 'The Scope, Timing and Type of Corruption.' *International Review of Law and Economics* 18, no. 1 (1998): 101–120.

Bacova, Viera, Maria Homisinova and Marc-Philippe Cooper. 'Questions Connected with the Reform of Public Administration in Slovakia in Regard to the Nationally Mixed Areas.' (In Slovak, but English summary at 53–54 of English section.) *Sociologia* 26, no. 5–6 (1994): 438–446.

Baker, Joel. 'Corruption among State Officials in Eastern Europe.' *RFE/RL Newsline* 52, part 2 (13 June 1997).

Baldersheim, Harald, Michal Illner, Audun Offerdal, Lawrence Rose and Pawel Swianiewicz, eds. *Local Democracy and the Processes of Transformation in East-Central Europe*. Boulder, Col: Westview, 1996.

Barany, Zoltan. 'Ethnic Mobilisation and the State: the Roma in Eastern Europe.' *Ethnic and Racial Studies* 21, no. 2 (1998): 308–27.

Barany, Zoltan. 'Orphans of Transition: Gypsies in Eastern Europe.' *Journal of Democracy* 9, no. 3 (1998): 142–56.

Bell, Daniel. 'After Ideology, Corruption—the Old War.' *The New Republic* 209, no. 8–9 (August 23/30 1993): 18–22.

Benacek, Vladimir and Alena Zemplinerova. 'Problems and Environment of Small Businesses in the Czech Republic.' *Small Business Economics* no. 7 (1995): 437–50.

Bennett, Robert J., ed. *Local Government in the New Europe*. London: Belhaven, 1993.

Berkman, Umit. 'Bureaucracy and Bribery: a Conceptual Framework.' *International Journal of Public Administration* 15, no. 6 (1992): 1345–68.

Besley, Timothy and John McLaren. 'Taxes and Bribery: the Role of Wage Incentives.' *Economic Journal* 103, no. 416 (1993): 119–41.

Biryukov, Nikolai and Victor Sergeyev. *Russia's Road to Democracy: Parliament, Communism and Traditional Culture*. Aldershot, England: Edward Elgar, 1993.

Biryukov, Nikolai and Victor Sergeyev. 'The Idea of Democracy in the West and in the East.' In David Beetham, ed., *Defining and Measuring Democracy*. London: Sage, 1994.

Bold, Alan, ed. *The Penguin Book of Socialist Verse*. London: Penguin, 1980.

Bonanno, Alessandro, Andrei Kuznetsov, Simon Geletta and Mary Hendrickson. 'To Farm or Not to Farm: Rural Dilemma in Russia and Ukraine.' *Rural Sociology* 58, no. 3 (1993): 404–23.

Boukhalov, Oleksandr and Sergei Ivannikov. 'Ukrainian Local Politics after Independence.' *The Annals of the American Academy of Political and Social Science* 540 (July 1995): 126–36.

British Council. *Development Priorities: Good Government*. London: British Council, 1993.

Butler, David, Andrew Adonis and Tony Travers. *Failure in British Government: the Politics of the Poll Tax*. Oxford: Oxford University Press, 1994.

Campbell, Adrian. 'Regional and Local Government in Ukraine.' In Coulson, *Local Government in Eastern Europe*, 115–127.

Centre for the Study of Democracy. *CSD Monitor* no. 5. Sofia: Centre for the Study of Democracy, 1999.

CEPS. *A System for Post-War South-East Europe*. Working Document no. 131. Brussels: Centre for European Policy Studies, 1999 (4th revision 3 May 1999). Accessible via *www.ceps.be*.

Churilov, Nikolay and Tatyana Koshechkina. 'Public Attitudes in Ukraine.' In Richard Smoke, ed., *Perceptions of Security: Public Opinion and Expert Assessments in Europe's New Democracies*. Manchester, England: Manchester University Press, 1996, 189–208.

Coalition 2000. *Clean Future*. (Coalition 2000's newsletter) no.2 (Spring 1999) accessible via *www.online.bg/coalition2000*.

Cooksey, Brian. 'Address to the Rotary Club of Dar es Salaam, October 9, 1996.' *Transparency International, National Chapter Newsletter* no.11 (11 November 1996).

Coulson, Andrew, ed. *Local Government in Eastern Europe: Establishing Democracy at the Grassroots*. London: Edward Elgar, 1995.

Coulson, Andrew. 'From Democratic Centralism to Local Democracy.' In Coulson, *Local Government in Eastern Europe*, 1–22.

Coulter, Philip B. 'There is a Madness in the Method: Redefining Citizen Contacting of Government Officials.' *Urban Affairs Quarterly* 28, no. 2 (1992): 297–316.

Council of Europe. *Structure and Operation of Local and Regional Democracy in Bulgaria, Slovakia, and the Czech Republic*. Strasbourg: Council of Europe, 1993.

Council of Europe. *Links between Corruption and Organised Crime*. Report presented by the minister of justice of the Czech Republic at the 21st Conference of European ministers of justice, Prague, 10–11 June 1997. Strasbourg: Council of Europe, 1997.

Council of Europe. *Octopus Project: The Fight against Corruption and Organised Crime in States in Transition*. Multilateral conference on the joint project between the Commission of the European Communities and the Council of Europe, Sofia, 12–14 December 1996. Strasbourg: Council of Europe, 1997.

Crampton, Richard. 'The Bulgarian Elections of 19 April 1997.' *Electoral Studies* 16, no. 4 (1997): 560–563.

Danglova, Olga. 'Rural Community in the Process of Socio-Economic Changes.' *Collegium Antropologium* 19, no. 1 (1995): 129–44.

Danova, Savelina. 'Roma Calls for Inclusion Are Heard in Bulgaria.' *Open Society News*. New York: Open Society Institute/Soros Foundations Network, Summer 1999: 17–19.

Davey, Kenneth. 'The Czech and Slovak Republics.' In Coulson, *Local Government in Eastern Europe*, 41–56.

deLeon, Peter. *Thinking about Political Corruption*. Armonk, N.Y.: M. E. Sharpe, 1993.

Della Porta, Donatella and Alberto Vannucci. 'The Perverse Effects of Political Corruption.' *Political Studies* 45, no. 3 (1997): 516–38.

de Speville, Bertrand. *Hong Kong: Policy Initiatives Against Corruption*. Paris: OECD, 1997.

DiFranceisco, Wayne and Zvi Gitelman. 'Soviet Political Culture and Covert Participation in Policy Implementation.' *American Political Science Review* 78, no. 3 (1984): 603–21.

Doig, Alan. 'Good Government and Sustainable Anti-corruption Strategies: a Role for Independent Anti-corruption Agencies?' *Public Administration and Development* 15, no. 2 (1996): 151–66.

EBRD. *Ten Years of Transition: Transition Report 1999*. London: European Bank for Reconstruction and Development, 1999.

Eigen, Peter. 'Combating Corruption around the World.' *Journal of Democracy* 7, no. 1 (1996): 158–68.

Elander, Ingemar. 'Between Centralism and Localism: on the Development of Local Self-government in Postsocialist Europe.' *Environment and Planning C: Government and Policy* 15 (1997): 143–59.

Elander, Ingemar and Mattias Gustafsson. 'The Re-emergence of Local Self-Government in Central Europe.' *European Journal of Political Research* 23 (1993): 295–322.

Eminov, Ali. *Turkish and Other Muslim Minorities of Bulgaria*. London: Hurst, 1997.

Ensor, Tim and Larisa Savelyeva. 'Informal Payments for Health Care in the Former Soviet Union: Some Evidence from Kazakhstan.' *Health Policy and Planning* 13, no. 1 (1998): 41–49.

Faltan, Lubomir and Richard A. Dodder. 'Privatising the Housing Sector: the Case of Slovakia.' *Public Administration and Development* 15, no. 4 (1995): 391–96.

Fisher, Sharon. 'Backtracking on the Road to Democratic Reform.' In *Building Democracy: the OMRI Annual Survey 1995*. London: M. E. Sharpe, 1996, 25–35.

Fisher, Sharon. 'Slovakia Heads towards International Isolation.' *Forging Ahead, Falling Behind: The OMRI Annual Survey 1996*. London: M. E. Sharpe, 1997, 22–27.

Friedgut, Theodore H. and Jeffrey W. Hahn, eds. *Local Power and Post-Soviet Politics*. Armonk, N.Y.: M. E. Sharpe, 1994.

Gabzdilova, Sonia. 'Quality and Structure of Education of the Slovak Population in Relation to Ethnic Differentiation.' (In Slovak, but English summary at 65–66 of English section.) *Sociologia* 26, no. 5–6 (1994): 473–78.

Ganev, Venelin I. 'Bulgaria's Symphony of Hope.' *Journal of Democracy* 8, no. 4 (1997): 125–39.

Geddes, Barbara. *Politician's Dilemma: Building State Capacity in Latin America*. Berkeley: University of California Press, 1994.

Giddens, Anthony. *The Third Way: The Renewal of Social Democracy*. Cambridge, England: Polity Press, 1998.

Gillard, Michael and Martin Tomkinson. *Nothing to Declare: the Political Corruptions of John Poulson*. London: John Calder, 1980.

Gilman, Stuart C. and Carol W. Lewis. 'Public Service Ethics: A Global Dialogue.' *Public Administration Review* 56, no. 6 (1996): 517–24.

Girling, John. *Corruption, Capitalism, and Democracy*. London: Routledge, 1997.

Goble, Paul. 'The Corruption of Power.' *RFE/RL Newsline* 2, no. 133, part 1 (14 July 1998).

Goldman, Marshall I. *Environmental Pollution in the Soviet Union: The Spoils of Progress*. Cambridge, Mass.: MIT Press, 1972.

Gole, Juliet S. *The Role of Civil Society in Containing Corruption at the Municipal Level*. Discussion Papers no. 10, Local Government and Public Service Reform Initiative. Budapest: CEU/OSI Publications, 1999.

Gole, Juliet S. 'Public Opinion Polls as an Anti-corruption Technique.' *LGI Newsletter* 1, no. 1 (Budapest: Local Government and Public Service Reform Initiative of the Open Society Institute, 1999): 1–2.

Golovakha, Evgenii, Natalia Panina and Nikolai Churilov. 'Russians in Ukraine.' In Vladimir Shlapentokh, Munir Sendich and Emil Payin, eds. *The New Russian Diaspora: Russian Minorities in the Former Soviet Republics*. Armonk, N.Y.: M. E. Sharpe, 1994, 59–71.

Grime, Keith and Vic Duke. 'A Czech on Privatisation.' *Regional Studies* 27, no. 8 (1993): 751–57.

Grødeland, Åse B., Tatyana Y. Koshechkina and William L. Miller. '"In Theory Correct, but in Practice...": Public Attitudes to Really Existing Democracy in Ukraine, Bulgaria, Slovakia and the Czech Republic.' *Journal of Communist Studies and Transition Politics* 14, no. 3 (1998): 1–23.

Grødeland, Åse B., Tatyana Y. Koshechkina and William L. Miller. '"Foolish to Give and Yet More Foolish Not to Take": In-depth Interviews with Post-communist Citizens on their Everyday Use of Bribes and Contacts.' *Europe-Asia Studies* 50, no. 4 (1998): 649–675. Reprinted in Robert Williams, ed., *The Politics of Corruption*. London: Edward Elgar, 2000.

Hague, Judy, Aidan Rose, and Marko Bojcun. 'Rebuilding Ukraine's Hollow State: Developing a Democratic Public Service in Ukraine.' *Public Administration and Development* 15 (1995): 417–33.

Harris, Chauncy D. 'New European Countries and their Minorities.' *Geographical Review* 83, no. 3 (1993): 301–20.

Harrop, Martin and William L. Miller. *Elections and Voters: a Comparative Introduction*. London: Macmillan, 1987.

Heady, Ferrel. 'Bureaucracies.' In Mary Hawkesworth and Maurice Kogan, eds., *Routledge Encyclopedia of Government and Politics*. London: Routledge, 1992.

Heidenheimer, Arnold J., ed. *Political Corruption*. New Brunswick. N.J.: Transaction Books, 1970.

Heidenheimer, Arnold J. 'Perspectives on the Perception of Corruption.' In Heidenheimer, Johnston and LeVine, *Political Corruption: A Handbook*.

Heidenheimer, Arnold J., Michael Johnston and Victor T. LeVine, eds. *Political Corruption: A Handbook*. New Brunswick. N.J.: Transaction Books, 1989.

Hepkema, Sietze and Willem Booysen. 'Bribery of Public Officials: An IBA Survey.' *International Business Lawyer* 25, no. 9 (1997): 415–6 and 422.

Holmes, Leslie. *The End of Communist Power: Anti-Corruption Campaigns and Legitimation Crisis*. Cambridge, England: Polity Press, 1993.

Holmes, Leslie. 'Corruption and the Crisis of the Post-communist State.' *Crime, Law and Social Change* 27 (1997): 275–97.

Holmes, Stephen. 'Citizen and Law after Communism.' *East European Constitutional Review* 7, no. 1 (1998): 70.

Hopkinson, Belinda and Anke Freibert. 'Law Drafting in Central and Eastern Europe.' *SIGMA Public Management Forum* 3, no. 1 (published by SIGMA/OECD 1997).

Hotchkiss, Carolyn. 'The Sleeping Dog Stirs: New Signs of Life in Efforts to End Corruption in International Business.' *Journal of Public Policy and Marketing* 17, no. 1 (1998): 108–15.

Huang, Peter H. and Ho-Mou Wu. 'More Order Without More Law: a Theory of Social Norms and Organisational Cultures.' *Journal of Law, Economics and Organisation* 10, no. 2 (1994): 390–406.

Huntington, Samuel P. 'Modernization and Corruption.' In Heidenheimer, *Political Corruption*, 492–500.

Huntington, Samuel P. 'The Clash of Civilisations.' *Foreign Affairs* 72, no. 3 (1993): 22–49.

Huntington, Samuel P. 'The West v the Rest.' *The Guardian* (23 November 1996): 23.

Huntington, Samuel P. 'Democracy for the Long Haul.' *Journal of Democracy* 7, no.2 (1996): 3–13.

Illner, Michal. 'Workshop on the Decentralisation of Governance in Central and Eastern Europe and the CIS.' *NISPAcee News* 4, no. 4 (December 1997): 10–11.

Illner, Michal. 'The Changing Quality of Life in a Post-communist Country: The Case of the Czech Republic.' *Social Indicators Research* 43 (1998): 141–70.

Illner, Michal. 'Local Democratisation in the Czech Republic after 1989.' In Dietrich Rueschemeyer, Marilyn Rueschemeyer and Bjorn Wittrock, eds., *Participation and Democracy : East and West*. Armonk, N.Y.: M. E. Sharpe, 1998, 51–82.

Illner, Michal. 'Territorial Decentralisation: An Obstacle to Democratic Reform in Central and Eastern Europe?' In Jonathan D. Kimball, ed., *The Transfer of Power:*

Decentralisation in Central and Eastern Europe. Budapest: Local Government and Public Service Reform Initiative, 1999, 7–29.

Jackson, Michael and Rodney Smith. 'Inside Moves and Outside Views: an Australian Case Study of Elite and Public Perceptions of Political Corruption.' *Governance: An International Journal of Policy and Administration* 9, no. 1 (1996): 23–42.

Jahoda, Marie, Paul F. Lazarsfeld and Hans Zeisel. *Marienthal: The Sociography of an Unemployed Community.* London: Tavistock, 1972. Originally published in 1993 as *Die Arbeitslosen von Marienthal* (The Unemployed of Marienthal).

Jepson, David, Valerie McDonnell and Belin Mollov. 'Local Government in Bulgaria.' In Coulson, *Local Government in Eastern Europe,* 102–14.

Johnson, Roberta Ann and Michael E. Kraft. 'Bureaucratic Whistleblowing and Policy Change.' *Western Political Quarterly* 43 (1990): 849–74.

Johnston, Michael. 'Public Officials, Private Interests, and Sustainable Democracy.' In Kimberly Ann Elliot, ed., *Corruption and the Global Economy.* Washington, D.C.: Institute for International Economics, 1997, 61–81.

Johnston, Michael. 'Fighting Systematic Corruption: Social Foundations for Institutional Reform.' *European Journal of Development Research* 10, no. 1 (Special Issue 1998): 85–104. This special issue was also published as Mark Robinson, ed., *Corruption and Development.* London: Frank Cass, 1998.

Kandeva, Emilia. 'Corruption in Transitional Public Service: A Bulgarian Experience.' In Jak Jabes, ed., *Professionalisation of Public Servants in Central and Eastern Europe.* Bratislava: NISPAcee/SIGMA, 1997, 192–206.

Katsenelinboigen, Aron. 'Corruption in the USSR: Some Methodological Notes.' In Michael Clarke, ed., *Corruption: Causes, Consequences and Control.* London: Pinter, 1983, 220–238.

Katz, Daniel, Barbara A. Gutek, Robert L. Kahn and Eugenia Barton. *Bureaucratic Encounters: A Pilot Study in the Evaluation of Government Services.* Ann Arbor: University of Michigan Press, 1975.

Kaufmann, Daniel. 'The Missing Pillar of a Growth Strategy for Ukraine: Institutional and Policy Reforms for Private Sector Development.' In Peter K. Cornelius and Patrick Lenain, eds., *Ukraine: Accelerating the Transition to Market.* Washington, D.C.: International Monetary Fund, 1997.

Kaufmann, Daniel and Paul Siegelbaum. 'Privatisation and Corruption in Transition Economies.' *Journal of International Affairs* 50, no. 2 (1996): 419–58.

Kettle, Steve. 'Of Money and Morality (in the Czech Republic).' *Transition* (15th March 1995): 36–9.

Khakhulina, L. A. and M. Tuchek. *Zhilishchnye usloviia v byvshikh sots-stranakh: rezul'taty sravnitel'nogo issledovaniia.* (Living Conditions in Former Soviet Countries: Results of a Survey.) Issue no. 5 (Moscow: VTsIOM, 1995).

Klich, Agnieszka. 'Bribery in Economies in Transition: The Foreign Corrupt Practices Act.' *Stanford Journal of International Law* 32, no. 1 (1996): 121–47.

Klitgaard, Robert. *Controlling Corruption.* Berkeley: University of California Press, 1988.

Kovács, Petra. *A Comparative Typology of Ethnic Relations in Central and Eastern Europe.* Discussion Papers no. 5, Local Government and Public Service Reform Initiative. Budapest: CEU/OSI Publications, 1998.

Krastev, Ivan. 'Party Structure and Party Perspectives in Bulgaria.' *Journal of Communist Studies and Transition Politics* 13, no. 1 (1997): 91–106.

Krastev, Ivan. 'Dancing with Anticorruption.' *East European Constitutional Review* 7, no. 3 (1998): 56–58.

Krawchenko, Bohdan. *Administrative Reform in Ukraine: Setting the Agenda*. Discussion Papers no. 3, Local Government and Public Service Reform Initiative. Budapest: CEU/OSI Publications, 1997.

Kudrycha, Barbara. *The Ethical Codes of Polish Public Officials*. Discussion Papers no. 8, Local Government and Public Service Reform Initiative. Budapest: CEU/OSI Publications, 1999.

Kutuev, Pavlo. 'Public Service Ethos in Ukraine.' In Jak Jabes, ed., *Professionalisation of Public Servants in Central and Eastern Europe*. Bratislava: NISPAcee/SIGMA, 1997, 93–99.

Kutuev, Pavlo and Volodymyr Svintsitsky. *Institutions of the Executive Power in Ukraine: Current Situation and Prospects for Democratisation*. Kyiv: Centre for Comparative Politics, 1995.

Kuzio, Taras and Andrew Wilson. *Ukraine: Perestroika to Independence*. London: Macmillan, 1994.

Kuzio, Taras. *Ukraine under Kuchma*. London: Macmillan, 1997.

Lampert, Nicholas. *Whistleblowing in the Soviet Union: Complaints and Abuses under State Socialism*. London: Macmillan, 1985.

Lancaster, Thomas D. and Gabriella R. Montinola. 'Towards a Methodology for the Comparative Study of Political Corruption.' *Crime, Law and Social Change* 27, no.3–4 double issue (1997): 185–206.

Langseth, Peter and Geoff Dubrow, eds. *Ukraine National Integrity Systems: Awareness Raising and Planning Workshops I and II* . Kyiv: Ukraine Ministry of Justice in association with the World Bank, 23 May and 24 June 1997.

Lawson, Colin and Juraj Nemec. 'Central European Health Reform: The Case of Slovakia 1990–97.' *Journal of European Social Policy* 8, no. 3 (1998): 237–52.

Lawson, Colin and Juraj Nemec. 'Health Care Reform: The Case of the Slovak Republic.' In Jak Jabes, ed., *Public Administration and Social Policies in Central and Eastern Europe*. Bratislava: NISPAcee/SIGMA, 1999, 183–193.

Ledeneva, Alena V. *An Economy of Favours: Informal Exchanges and Networking in Russia*. Cambridge, England: Cambridge University Press, 1998.

Leff, Nathaniel. 'Economic Development through Bureaucratic Corruption.' *American Behavioral Scientist* 8 (1964): 8–14.

Lehmbruch, Gerhard. *Proporzdemokratie: Politisches System und politische Kultur in der Schweiz und in Österreich ('Proportional Democracy': Political Systems and Political Culture in Switzerland and in Austria)*. Tübingen: Mohr, 1967.

Levine, Jeffrey. 'Excuse Me...I've No Machinery, No Money and No Market: How Do I Farm?' *Demokratizatsiya: The Journal of Post-Soviet Democratisation* 3, no. 1 (Winter 1995): 98–102.

Levitas, Ruth. 'Fiddling while Britain Burns: the Measurement of Unemployment.' In Ruth Levitas and Will Guy, eds., *Interpreting Official Statistics*. London: Routledge, 1996, 45–65.

Lindbeck, Assar. *Swedish Lessons for Post-Socialist Countries*. Stockholm: University of Stockholm Institute for International Economic Studies, 1998.

Linz, Juan J. *The Breakdown of Democratic Regimes: Crisis, Breakdown, and Reequilibration.* Baltimore, Md.: Johns Hopkins University Press, 1978.

Linz, Juan J. and Alfred Stepan. *Problems of Democratic Transition and Consolidation.* Baltimore, Md.: Johns Hopkins University Press, 1996.

Lipsky, Michael. *Street-Level Bureaucracy: Dilemmas of the Individual in Public Services.* New York: Russell Sage Foundation, 1980.

Los Angeles Times-Mirror. *The Pulse of Europe: A Survey of Political and Social Values and Attitudes.* Los Angeles: Times-Mirror, 1991.

Lotspeich, Richard. 'Crime in the Transition Economies.' *Europe-Asia Studies* 47, no.4 (1995): 555–589.

Lui, Terry T. and Terry L. Cooper. 'Values in Flux: Administrative Ethics and the Hong Kong Public Servant.' *Administration and Society* 29, no. 3 (1997): 301–324.

Magocsi, Paul Robert, ed. *A New Slavic Language is Born: The Rusyn Literary Language of Slovakia.* New York: Columbia University Press, 1996.

Mallon, Ray, William Bratton, Charles Pollard, John Orr, William Griffiths and Norman Dennis, eds., *Zero Tolerance: Policing a Free Society.* London: Institute of Economic Affairs, 1998.

Maly, Ivan. 'Current Problems and a Possible Future of Czech Health Care Reform.' In Jak Jabes, ed., *Public Administration and Social Policies in Central and Eastern Europe.* Bratislava: NISPAcee/SIGMA, 1999, 194–200.

Marada, Radim. 'The 1998 Czech Elections.' *East European Constitutional Review* 7, no. 4 (1998): 51–58.

Matute, Helena. 'Learning and Conditioning.' In Michael Eysenck, ed., *Psychology: An Integrated Approach.* London: Longman; New York: Addison Wesley, 1998, 68–99.

Mauro, Paolo. 'Corruption and Growth.' *Quarterly Journal of Economics* 110, no. 3 (1995): 681–712.

McAllister, Ian. 'Keeping Them Honest: Public and Elite Perceptions of Ethical Conduct among Australian Legislators.' *Political Studies* 48, no. 1 (2000): 22–37.

McAllister, Ian, Ron J. Johnston, Charles J. Pattie, Helena Tunstall, Danny F. Dorling and David J. Rossiter. 'Class Dealignment and the Neighbourhood Effect: Miller Revisited.' *British Journal of Political Science* 30, no.3 (2000, forthcoming).

Meny, Yves. *La Corruption de la République (The Corruption of the Republic).* Paris: Fayard, 1992.

Miller, William L., ed. *Alternatives to Freedom: Arguments and Opinions.* London: Longman, 1995.

Miller, William L. 'Social Class and Party Choice in England: A New Analysis.' *British Journal of Political Science* 8, no. 3 (1978): 257–84. Reprinted in David T. Denver and Gordon Hands, eds., *Issues and Controversies in British Electoral Behaviour.* London: Harvester Wheatsheaf, 1992.

Miller, William L. 'Quantitative Methods.' In David Marsh and Gerry Stoker, eds., *Theory and Methods in Political Science.* London: Macmillan, 1995, 154–72.

Miller, William L., Annis May Timpson and Michael Lessnoff. *Political Culture in Contemporary Britain: People and Politicians, Principles and Practice.* Oxford: Oxford University Press, 1996.

Miller, William L., Stephen White and Paul Heywood. *Values and Political Change in Post-Communist Europe.* London: Macmillan, 1998.

Miller, William L., Malcolm Dickson and Gerry Stoker. *Models of Local Governance: Political Theory and Public Opinion in Britain.* London: Macmillan, 2000.

Mitev, Petar-Emil. 'The Party Manifestos for the Bulgarian 1994 Elections.' *Journal of Communist Studies and Transition Politics* 13, no.1 (1997): 64–90.

MRG International. *Minorities in Central and Eastern Europe.* London: Minority Rights Group, 1993.

Neuburger, Mary. 'Bulgaro-Turkish Encounters and the Re-imaging of the Bulgarian Nation.' *East European Quarterly* 31, no. 1 (1997): 1–20.

Noonan, John T. *Bribes: The Intellectual History of a Moral Idea.* Berkeley: University of California Press, 1987.

Norris, Pippa, ed. *Critical Citizens: Global Support for Democratic Governance.* Oxford: Oxford University Press, 1999.

OECD. *Ethics in the Public Service: Current Issues and Practice.* Public Management Occasional Papers no.14. Paris: OECD, 1996.

OECD. *Council Decision: Improving Ethical Conduct in the Public Service.* Paris: OECD, 23 April 1998—accessible via www.oecd.org/puma/gvrnance/ethics.

OECD. *Public Sector Corruption: An International Survey of Prevention Measures.* Paris: OECD, 1999.

Osborne, Stephen P. and Anikó Kaposvári. *Non-governmental Organisations, Local Government and the Development of Social Services: Managing Social Needs in Post-Communist Hungary.* Discussion Papers no.4, Local Government and Public Service Reform Initiative. Budapest: CEU/OSI Publications Office, 1998.

O'Toole, Barry J. 'The Concept of Public Duty.' In Peter Barberis, ed., *The Civil Service in an Era of Change.* Aldershot, England: Dartmouth, 1997, 82–94.

Paddock, Richard. 'Greasy Palms are Rampant in Russia.' *Los Angeles Times* (20 October 1999).

Pasuk, Phongpaicht and Piriyarangsan Sungsidh. *Corruption and Democracy in Thailand.* Bangkok: Chulalongkorn University, 1994.

Pope, Jeremy. 'Elements of a Successful Anti-corruption Programme.' In Langseth and Dubrow, *Ukraine National Integrity Systems.*

Pope, Jeremy and Carel Mohn. *The Fight Against Corruption: Is the Tide Now Turning?* Transparency International Report 1997. Berlin: Transparency International, 1997.

Popov, Chavdar. 'Law Drafting in Bulgaria: The Need for Professionally Trained Public Servants.' *SIGMA Public Management Forum* 3, no. 1 (published by SIGMA/OECD 1997).

Potucek, Martin. 'Current Social Policy Developments in the Czech and Slovak Republics.' *Journal of European Social Policy* 3, no. 3 (1993): 209–26.

Radaev, Vadim. *Corruption and Violence in Russian Businesses in the late 1990s.* Jesus College, Cambridge: Cambridge International Symposium on Economic Crime, 13–19 September 1998. Revised version published in Alena V. Ledeneva and Marina Kurkchiyan, eds., *Economic Crime in Russia.* Amsterdam: Kluwer, 2000, 63–82.

Rafferty, Kevin. *City on the Rocks: Hong Kong's Uncertain Future.* London: Penguin, 1991.

Reed, John. 'The Great Growth Race.' *Central European Economic Review* (9–11 December 1995).

Reed, Quentin. 'Transition, Dysfunctionality and Change in the Czech and Slovak Republics.' *Crime, Law and Social Change* 22 (1995): 323–337.

Reid, Anna. *Borderland: A Journey Through the History of Ukraine.* London: Weidenfeld and Nicholson, 1997.

Ridley, Fred F. 'Civil Service and Democracy: Questions in Reforming the Civil Service in Eastern and Central Europe.' *Public Administration and Development* 15, no. 1 (1995): 11–20.

Rose, Richard and Christian Haerpfer. *New Democracies Barometer* 5. Glasgow, Scotland: Strathclyde University Centre for the Study of Public Policy, 1998.

Rose, Richard, William Mishler and Christian Haerpfer. *Democracy and its Alternatives: Understanding Post-Communist Societies.* Cambridge, England: Polity Press, 1998.

Rose-Ackerman, Susan. *Corruption and Government: Causes, Consequences and Reform.* Cambridge, England: Cambridge University Press, 1999.

Sajó, András. 'Corruption, Clientalism and the Future of the Constitutional State in Eastern Europe.' *East European Constitutional Review* 7, no. 2 (Winter 1998): 37–46.

Schleifer, Andrei and Robert W. Vishny. 'Corruption.' *Quarterly Journal of Economics* 108 (1993) 599–617.

Schlozman, Kay Lehman and Sidney Verba. *Insult to Injury: Unemployment, Class, and Political Response.* Cambridge, England: Cambridge University Press, 1979.

Schmitter, Philippe C. 'Dangers and Dilemmas of Democracy.' In Larry Diamond and Marc F. Plattner, *The Global Resurgence of Democracy.* Second edition. Baltimore, Md.: Johns Hopkins University Press, 1996, 76–93.

Scott, James C. *Comparative Political Corruption.* Englewood Cliffs, N.J.: Prentice-Hall, 1972.

Service, Robert. 'Russia's Putrefying Corpse.' *The Guardian* (25 October 1997): 23.

Shafik, Nemat. 'Making a Market: Mass Privatisation in the Czech and Slovak Republics.' *World Development* 23, no. 7 (1995): 1143–56.

Shelley, Louise I. 'Organised Crime and Corruption in Ukraine: Impediments to the Development of a Free Market Economy.' *Demokratizatsiya: The Journal of Post-Soviet Democratization* 6, no. 4 (1998): 648–663.

Shelley, Louise and Anna Repetskaya. 'Corruption Research among Convicted Government and Law Enforcement Officials.' *Organised Crime Watch* 1, no. 3 (Washington: Transnational Crime and Corruption Center at American University, 1999) accessible via www.american.edu/transcrime.

Shlapentokh, Vladimir. *The Public and Private Life of the Soviet People.* Oxford: Oxford University Press, 1989.

SIGMA/OECD. *Bureaucratic Barriers to Entry: Foreign Investment in Central and Eastern Europe.* Report GD (94) 124. Paris: OECD, 1994.

SIGMA/OECD. *Public Management Profiles: SIGMA Countries, Revised Edition.* Report GD (95) 121. Paris: OECD, 1995.

Šiklova, Jiřina. 'Lustration or the Czech Way of Screening.' *East European Constitutional Review* 5, no. 1 (1996): 57–62.

Šiklova, Jiřina and Marta Miklusakova. 'Denying Citizenship to the Czech Roma.' *East European Constitutional Review* 7, no. 2 (1998): 58–64.

Simis, Konstantin M. *USSR: Secrets of a Corrupt Society.* London: Dent; New York: Simon and Shuster, 1982.

Smeltz, Dina S. and Anna E. Sweeney. *On the Take: Central and East European Attitudes towards Corruption.* Washington, D.C.: USIA, October 1999.

Snavely, Keith and Lena Chakarova. 'Confronting Ethnic Issues: the Role of Nonprofit Organisations in Bulgaria.' *East European Quarterly* 31, no. 3 (1997): 311–327.

Sogomonov, A. and A. Tolstykh. 'O nashikh zabotakh.' (Our Most Pressing Problems.) *Kommunist* no. 9 (1989): 75.

Soulsby, Anna and Ed Clark. 'Privatisation and the Restructuring of Enterprise, Social and Welfare Assets in the Czech Republic.' *Industrial Relations Journal* 26, no. 2 (1995): 97–109.

Steel, Brent S., Sally Davenport and Rebecca L. Warner. 'Are Civil Servants Really Public Servants? A study of Bureaucratic Attitudes in the USA, Brazil and Korea.' *International Journal of Public Administration* 16, no. 3 (1993): 409–442.

Stewart, Debra W., Norman Sprinthall and Renata Siemienska. 'Ethical Reasoning in a Time of Revolution: a Study of Local Officials in Poland.' *Public Administration Review* 57, no. 5 (1997): 445–453.

Swain, Nigel. 'Agricultural Restitution and Co-operative Transformation in the Czech Republic, Hungary and Slovakia.' *Europe-Asia Studies* 51, no. 7 (1999): 1199–1219.

Szymanderski, Jacek. 'Moral Order and Corruption in Transition to the Market: Popular Beliefs and their Underpinnings.' *Communist Economies and Economic Transformation* 7, no. 2 (1995): 249–257.

Tanzi, Vito. 'Corruption Around the World: Causes, Consequences, Scope and Cures.' *IMF Staff Papers* 45, no. 4 (Washington, D.C.: International Monetary Fund, 1998): 559–94.

Teleki, Ilona. 'Loss and Lack of Recognition: Identifying Fears in the Slovak-Hungarian Relationship.' *Slovo* 10, no. 1/2 (1998): 199–218.

Tomova, Ilona. 'Gypsy-Bashing: Palpable Frustration, If Not Outright Contempt.' *The Insider* 1 (1992): 20–21.

Toynbee, Arnold. *A Study of History: Revised and Abridged Edition.* Oxford: Oxford University Press, 1972.

Transparency International. *Transparency International Newsletter* (March 1997) at www.transparency.de.

Transparency International. *Corruption Perception Index 1999.* Berlin: Transparency International, 1999, also accessible via www.transparency.de.

Traynor, Ian. 'Czech Gypsies Fear Ghetto Wall.' *The Guardian* (20 June 1998): 16.

Trevor-Roper, Hugh. 'Introduction.' In Hugh Trevor-Roper, ed., *Lord Acton: Lectures on Modern History.* London: Collins, 1960, 7–15. (Lord Acton's lectures themselves were originally published in London by Macmillan, 1906.)

Turner, Bengt, József Hegedűs and Iván Tosics. *The Reform of Housing in Eastern Europe and the Soviet Union.* London: Routledge, 1992.

Ukraine National Coalition for Integrity, *Newsletter*, accessible via the UNCI website www.nobribes.org/unci.

UNDP. *Corruption and Good Governance.* Discussion Paper no. 3. New York: United Nations Development Programme, 1997.

USIA. *The People Have Spoken: Global Views of Democracy I.* Washington, D.C.: United States Information Agency, January 1997.

USIA. *The People Have Spoken: Global Views of Democracy II.* Washington, D.C.: United States Information Agency, September 1999.

Van Rijckeghem, Caroline and Beatrice Weder. 'Corruption and the Rate of Temptation: Do Low Wages in the Civil Service Cause Corruption?' *IMF Working Paper* 97/93 (Washington, D.C.: International Monetary Fund, 1997).

Varese, Federico. 'Pervasive Corruption.' In Alena Ledeneva and Marina Kurkchiyan, eds., *Economic Crime in Russia.* London: Kluwer Law International, 2000, 99–111.

Verba, Sidney, Norman H. Nie and Jae-on Kim. *Participation and Political Equality: A Seven-Nation Comparison.* Cambridge, England: Cambridge University Press, 1978.

Verebélyi, Imre. 'Hungary Proposes Strategic Plan to Reform the Public Administration.' *SIGMA Public Management Forum* 2, no. 5 (published by SIGMA/OECD 1996).

Verheijen, Tony. 'The Relevance of Western Public Management Reforms for Central and Eastern European Countries.' *SIGMA Public Management Forum* 2 no. 4 (published by SIGMA/OECD 1996): 8–9.

Verheijen, Tony and Antoaneta Dimitrova. 'Private Interests and Public Administration: the Central and East European Experience.' *International Review of Administrative Sciences* 62, no. 2 (1996): 197–218.

Verheijen, Tony and Antoaneta Dimitrova. 'Corruption and Unethical Behaviour of Civil and Public Servants: Causes and Possible Solutions.' In Jak Jabes, ed., *Professionalisation of Public Servants in Central and Eastern Europe.* Bratislava: NISPAcee/SIGMA, 1997, 219–43.

Weber, Max. *The Theory of Social and Economic Organization.* London: Free Press, 1947.

Weitzman, Eben. *Computer Programs for Qualitative Data Analysis.* London: Sage, 1995.

White, Stephen L. *Russia Goes Dry: Alcohol, State, and Society.* Cambridge, England: Cambridge University Press, 1996.

Williams, Robert. *Political Corruption in Africa.* Aldershot, England: Gower, 1987.

Wilson, Andrew. *Ukrainian Nationalism in the 1990s: A Minority Faith.* Cambridge, England: Cambridge University Press, 1997.

Wing Lo, T. *Corruption and Politics in Hong Kong and China.* Buckingham, England: Open University Press, 1993.

World Bank. *World Development Report 1997.* New York: Oxford University Press, 1997.

Yerkes, R. M. and J. D. Dodson. 'The Relation of Strength of Stimulus to Rapidity of Habit Formation.' *Journal of Comparative and Neurological Psychology* 18 (1908): 459–82, quoted in Edmund Rolls, 'Motivation.' In Michael Eysenck, ed., *Psychology: An Integrated Approach.* London: Longman; New York: Addison Wesley, 1998, 503–31.

Zelizer, Viviana A. *The Social Meaning of Money.* New York: Basic Books, 1994.

INDEX